Forensic Science Reform

Forensic Science Reform
Protecting the Innocent

Edited by

Wendy J. Koen
Child Refuge, Inc.,
Formerly of the California Innocence Project,
Menifee, CA, USA

C. Michael Bowers
Clinical Associate Professor,
Ostrow School of Dentistry,
University of Southern California,
Los Angeles, CA, USA;
Deputy Medical Examiner,
Ventura County, CA, USA

ELSEVIER

AMSTERDAM • BOSTON • HEIDELBERG • LONDON
NEW YORK • OXFORD • PARIS • SAN DIEGO
SAN FRANCISCO • SINGAPORE • SYDNEY • TOKYO

Academic Press is an imprint of Elsevier

Academic Press is an imprint of Elsevier
125 London Wall, London EC2Y 5AS, United Kingdom
525 B Street, Suite 1800, San Diego, CA 92101-4495, United States
50 Hampshire Street, 5th Floor, Cambridge, MA 02139, United States
The Boulevard, Langford Lane, Kidlington, Oxford OX5 1GB, United Kingdom

Notices
Knowledge and best practice in this field are constantly changing. As new research and
experience broaden our understanding, changes in research methods, professional practices,
or medical treatment may become necessary.

Practitioners and researchers must always rely on their own experience and knowledge
in evaluating and using any information, methods, compounds, or experiments described
herein. In using such information or methods they should be mindful of their own safety and
the safety of others, including parties for whom they have a professional responsibility.

To the fullest extent of the law, neither the Publisher nor the authors, contributors, or editors,
assume any liability for any injury and/or damage to persons or property as a matter of
products liability, negligence or otherwise, or from any use or operation of any methods,
products, instructions, or ideas contained in the material herein.

Library of Congress Cataloging-in-Publication Data
A catalog record for this book is available from the Library of Congress

British Library Cataloguing-in-Publication Data
A catalogue record for this book is available from the British Library

ISBN: 978-0-12-802719-6

For information on all Academic Press publications
visit our website at https://www.elsevier.com/

Working together
to grow libraries in
developing countries

ELSEVIER   Book Aid
            International

www.elsevier.com • www.bookaid.org

Publisher: Sara Tenney
Acquisition Editor: Elizabeth Brown
Editorial Project Manager: Joslyn Chaiprasert-Paguio
Production Project Manager: Lisa Jones
Designer: Maria Ines Cruz

Typeset by TNQ Books and Journals

*To my dad, William C. Keith, who taught me to love words
and the stories they weave.*
–Wendy J. Koen

*To Cynthia, who continues to support me through the challenges of
life with smiles and encouragement.*
–C. Michael Bowers

Contents

CHAPTER 9   Bloodstain Pattern Analysis 271

Case Study: David Camm 272

Wendy J. Koen

Bloodstain Pattern Analysis 279

Barie Goetz

CHAPTER 10   Crime Scene Reconstruction............................ 299

Faulty Crime Scene Reconstruction: Glenn Ford 300

Wendy J. Koen

Crime Scene Reconstruction............................ 307

Barie Goetz

List of Contributors

C. Michael Bowers
University of Southern California, Los Angeles, CA, United States

Kathleen L. Bright-Birnbaum
Desert Forensics, Tucson, AZ, United States

Sarah L. Cooper
Birmingham City University, Birmingham, United Kingdom

Rachel Dioso-Villa
Griffith University, Mt Gravatt, QLD, Australia

Simon Ford
Lexigen Science and Law Consultants, San Francisco, CA, United States

Barie Goetz
Sangre de Cristo Forensic Services, Parker, PA, United States; Pennsylvania State University, Sharon, PA, United States

Christopher Halkides
The University of North Carolina at Wilmington, Wilmington, NC, United States

Max M. Houck
Forensic & Intelligence Services, LLC, St. Petersburg, FL, United States

Wendy J. Koen
Child Refuge, Inc., Menifee, CA, United States

Dan E. Krane
Wright State University, Dayton, OH, United States

Ray Krone
Co-founder, Witness to Innocence, Philadelphia, PA, United States

John J. Lentini
Scientific Fire Analysis, Islamorada, FL, United States

Kimberly Lott
Lott Law, PLLC, Durham, NC, United States; NCAST (North Carolina Attorneys for Science and Technology), Durham, NC, United States

Waney Squier
Oxford University John Radcliffe Hospital, Oxford, United Kingdom

Foreword

Since the late 1980s, DNA analysis has helped identify the guilty and exonerate the innocent. To date, over 300 innocent prisoners have been freed as a result; in almost half of those cases, the true perpetrator was identified. When used properly, validated scientific disciplines are a force for good; when used improperly, or when pseudoscience is admitted into the courtroom, lives are destroyed. Of the first 300 postconviction DNA exonerations, unsound forensic science, or improper claims about legitimate disciplines, were a significant contributors in about half of the cases.

In fact, unvalidated forensic science is the second greatest contributor to wrongful convictions. But while DNA exonerations provide a window into the effect of unvalidated forensic science and its contribution to wrongful convictions, they only offer a truncated glimpse. Only 5–10% of all criminal cases involve biological evidence that can be subjected to DNA testing. In the other 90–95% of crimes, DNA doesn't exist, or, in older cases, it has been lost or degraded. The result? There are countless criminal convictions that are based to one degree or another on discredited forensic disciplines. We have no way to test the legitimacy of these convictions, though, because there is no DNA to test.

In my particular line of business, what makes matters worse is that courts, both trial and appellate, are irredeemably hidebound, it seems, to believe anything other than that the statistics previously cited either didn't happen at all, or, if they did, would never happen in the specific courtroom in question. Simply put, what that means is this: the likelihood of a court granting an innocently convicted prisoner relief from a wrongful conviction, or a trial court holding a robust hearing where it is determined that a spurious forensic discipline is inadmissible, is distressingly small. How did the exonerees mentioned above gain their freedom, then? Not by raising a claim of innocence based on faulty forensic science. Doing so is close to fruitless. In fact, the US Supreme Court has denied 30 petitions for certiorari filed by *actually innocent* exonerees. In one case, Larry Youngblood's, the Court denied relief for Youngblood's claim that law enforcement had failed to properly preserve biological evidence that could, if tested, have proven his claim of innocence.

Youngblood had been charged and convicted for the abduction and rape of a 10-year-old boy from a carnival grounds in Pima County, Arizona. The young male victim was taken to a hospital where semen samples and his clothing were collected as evidence. Based on the victim's description of the assailant as a man with one disfigured eye, Youngblood was charged with the crime. Youngblood maintained his innocence, but no forensic testing was conducted on the evidence because the police had improperly stored the evidence and allowed it to degrade. Youngblood was convicted and sentenced to a lengthy prison term.

Not only did the decision affect Youngblood, it offered no incentive for law enforcement to adopt procedures to ensure preservation of critically important evidence, to preserve, that is, the very material that is the lifeblood of forensic science. Fortunately for Youngblood, in 2000, at the request if his attorneys, new DNA technology permitted the testing of the damaged evidence. The results exonerated Youngblood, and he was released. Early the following year, the DNA profile that had been generated was found to match the DNA profile of another individual, who, blind in one eye, was then serving time in Texas on unrelated charges. In 2002, he was convicted of the offense and sentenced to 24 years in prison.

So why the continuing intractability? Among the problems is that trial judges cannot contemplate that disciplines that they or their colleagues may have been admitting for years, even decades, are rife with problems. The very idea would shake the foundations of their professional work. For appellate judges, the problem is even worse. Many have never actually practiced criminal law, or, if they have, many are former prosecutors and are no more skeptical as jurists than they were when they were champions of law and order. They are also hindered by procedural strictures that, even if they were so inclined, frequently prevent them from getting at the crux of the problem in the first place.

Were I to prescribe a solution, I might just say "context." These judges and prosecutors, and for that matter, ill-informed defense counsel, need something more than another continuing legal education course or even news story, brief and not terribly substantive, about yet another exoneration. People need to understand how these cases occur, from start to finish. What happened? How did they get investigated? What was the attraction that led law enforcement to engage a certain forensic discipline? Was it a novel technique that held promise? Or was it a time-tested technique that was virtually unquestioned? And who were the purported experts: an independent scientist or someone who came of age professionally in the service of law enforcement?

This text provides that context. In chapter after chapter, each devoted to a separate forensic discipline, the authors (all of whom are experts in the particular discipline that they're discussing) treat not only the nuances of the forensic practice, but also the history of the case itself. Take the chapter on Composition Bullet Led Analysis (CBLA), for example. Readers will discover early in the chapter that CBLA tests "the minute amount of trace elements in the metal making up the bullet to see if different bullets have the same or different amounts of these trace elements." After a National Academy of Sciences review of the CBLA in 2002, the discipline was found to be without any scientific basis and that, in any event, FBI examiners had overstated the data and their conclusions from it. But what this chapter and the others do well is to layer in the cascading series of developments that resulted from the erroneous reliance on the unsound discipline. The defendant in the case had no criminal record to suggest that he would have committed the type of offense, a child abduction and homicide; his unkempt condition was the result of his penchant to "dumpster dive" for cheap food that he would distribute to the needy; soil on the bottom of his shoes did not match the soil from the victim's shoes. But these facts were eclipsed by the misplaced in CBLA. Nevertheless, the defendant was convicted and later executed by the state of Texas in 1999.

Whether this defendant, James Otto Earhart, was guilty or innocent, we will likely never know. What we do know for sure is that CBLA is not a basis to secure that conviction, much less a sentence of death. For readers and practitioners, be they forensic scientists, lawyers, or anyone interested in criminal justice, that is as much context as you will need.

Tucker Carrington
Assistant Professor
Director, George C. Cochran Innocence Project
University of Mississippi School of Law, Oxford, MS, United States

Preface

"Forensic," meaning scientific tests or techniques used in connection with the detection of crime, is a generic term which has reached its zenith (as in 32 million Google links) of public interest, social media coverage, literature of both science and law, and courtroom verdicts. "Science" suggests images of laboratory research and novel approaches achieved to solve challenges to our human existence. "Reform" may be more easily understood as "change."

"Protecting the Innocent" has "wrongful convictions" as a synonym, and turns our idea of the protection of the innocent on its ear as it has become clear that our systems of justice actually vilifies, incarcerates, and sometimes kills those who are actually innocent. Although the punishment of the innocent is done with the best of intentions, those pure intentions are of little relief to the innocent left wasting for decades or who have met their end.

We wrote and edited this book to establish a stronger link between public knowledge, forensic science, police science, and the legal systems that use forensic disciplines and hire their practitioners. Using the voices of actual practitioners and the stories of actual victims of justice systems' flawed or misused science, this book explores 11 major disciplines of forensic evidence, enlightening the reader about the history of development, current uses, and trends. We also take a novel approach by shining the light of legally determined wrongful convictions back onto each of those disciplines. The results show that there is an inter-relationship between "change" occurring within certain forensic and police sciences being spurred by the steady flow of wrongful convictions discovered and made public in the United States and abroad.

We hope the reader will find this book's forensic discourse, its separation of mere forensic opinion from actual scientific fact and the resulting discussion of the intersection of forensic evidence and protecting the innocent a meaningful experience.

C. Michael Bowers & Wendy J. Koen

Acknowledgments

It was only with the dedication and assistance of the following groups and individuals that this volume could be assembled. This book was made possible by a community of justice seekers who forged a pathway by alerting the world of the plight of the wrongfully convicted and working tirelessly to see justice done. This community consists of students and lawyers at innocence projects around the globe, upstanding forensic specialists who speak the truth, sometimes to their detriment, and families and laypersons who have supported the movement to reform the forensic sciences and improve our justice systems.

Thank you, not only for your input, but also for fighting for justice daily. You have rescued the wrongfully convicted from the hell of incarceration and given hope to scores of innocent inmates and their families. You have endured the heartache of lost cases and witnessed the devastation caused by those losses. You have also shared in the sheer joy caused by your clients' victories, and these victories have increased your tenacity and resolve. The world is better for your unfailing dedication.

Arizona Justice Project

Association in Defense of the Wrongfully Convicted

C. Michael Bowers

California Innocence Project

Chris Halkides, University of North Carolina at Wilmington

Equal Justice Initiative

Injustice Anywhere

Ray Krone

Sarah Chu at the Innocence Project, NY

The Marshall Project

Tom Zupancic, Applied Biomolecular Technologies, Inc.

Compositional Bullet Lead Analysis

1

CHAPTER OUTLINE

Forensic Science Reform. http://dx.doi.org/10.1016/B978-0-12-802719-6.00001-7
2017 Published by Elsevier Inc.

Case Study: James Otto Earhart

Wendy J. Koen

Child Refuge, Inc., Menifee, CA, United States

The dead cannot cry out for justice; it is the duty of the living to do so for them.

Lois McMaster Bujold

On the afternoon of May 12, 1987, a grimy, morbidly obese, junk dealer named James Otto Earhart was seen talking to 9-year-old Kandy Kirtland in front of her house (*Earhart v. State*, 1991). Earhart was socially awkward. He was not above telling a lie or two if it helped him make a few dollars off of a junk transaction. The 400 pounds of weight he carried fit awkwardly on his 5′9″ frame. He was not pretty. His clothes were filthy, and he needed a shower and a shave. Earhart drank a case and a half of beer every day and was never a picture of sobriety or health. His psychiatrist described him as psychotic and "not dealing with a full deck" (*Earhart v. State*, 1994, p. 762). He inspired disgust in the eyes of the good, God-fearing people of Bryan, Texas. He was easy to spot and impossible to forget.

When 9-year-old Kandy Kirtland went missing the same day she had a conversation with 43-year-old Earhart, neighbors who saw Earhart and Kandy talking were quick to inform the police. After all, based on his appearance alone, Earhart could not be more accurately cast as a depraved miscreant. Housewives who had called Earhart when they needed old appliances hauled away suddenly remembered him as threatening. Memories of innocent conversations they had with Earhart about their children suddenly turned nightmarish and tinged with peril. Everyone wanted to help, and people started to remember sighting Earhart's car, a light-colored Chevrolet, around Kandy's home.

When Earhart read the local paper and found out the little girl he had been talking to had disappeared and that police were looking for a man of his unique size and description driving a light-colored Chevrolet, he instinctively knew that he was in trouble. He was aware of how things looked. So, he fled. He traded the car he had been driving for a maroon Oldsmobile and drove to a campsite at a national forest just over an hour away. He would later tell the police why he fled:

> *Well I heard about [Kandy's disappearance] in the paper the next morning and I, I, just, uh, I knew that, you know, they were going to blame me because, I knew they would probably blame me, so I, uh, panicked. I got in the car and left…I just went, you know, took some of my clothes. I don't, uh, shouldn't have done it, you know, but I did. I just panicked.*

Earhart v. State (1991, p. 615)

On May 26, 1987, Kandy Kirtland's decomposing body was found buried in trash and debris a couple of miles from her home in Bryan, Texas. Her arms were bound behind her back with an electrical cord, and she had been shot once in the head. She was wearing the same turquoise shorts, white shirt, white tennis shoes, and jewelry she wore when she disappeared 2 weeks earlier.

The same day Kandy's body was found, Earhart was found living in his newly acquired maroon Oldsmobile at a campsite at Sam Houston National Forest (*Earhart v. State*, 1991, p. 614). Among Earhart's belongings, police found a shirt with a small amount of blood on it. Although the blood was type O and Earhart and 45% of the rest of the population have type O blood, an expert testified that the blood was not Earhart's because it contained a different enzyme (*Id.*). Kandy's blood was also type O, and Kandy could not be excluded as the source of the blood. Earhart was arrested, and police seized a 0.22 caliber revolver he had in his car. The weapon had a small amount of blood on the barrel; it was too small of an amount to be typed (*Earhart v. State*, 1991).

There were other reasons to believe Earhart had something to do with Kandy's disappearance and murder. At one point in his interrogation, Earhart explained why he came to be at Kandy's house on the day of her disappearance and the interaction he had with the girl:

> *Well I went over to look at a compressor [Kandy's father was selling] on Monday, and then I came back on Tuesday and she got off the bus there, and I was sitting there. I was fixing to take off and she came up to me and wanted to know if I would give her a ride up to the end of the road there, and so I, I did. She went in the house and, and she came back, and I, I pulled in the driveway and she got in the car and so I took her up and let her off at the end of Gabbard Road and 2818. And that's all I know about it….After I let her out of the car, she crossed Gabbard Road, to that side, and I left her standing there on the corner … she told me that her, uh, girlfriend was going to pick her up, her girlfriend and her mother, her girlfriend's mother is what she told me….All I asked her was where she was going, whether, she said she was going over to her friend's house and, uh, I asked her what time her mother was going to be in before I could look at the compressor and she said later on that evening.*

Earhart v. State (1991, p. 614)

Since his own words placed him with Kandy, he became the perfect suspect for her disappearance and her murder.

Bryan Police officer Jerry Stover testified that he searched Earhart's home and recovered three 0.22 caliber bullets from Earhart's bedroom (*Earhart v. State*, 1991). FBI Agent John Riley ran compositional bullet lead analysis (CBLA) on the bullets found in Earhart's bedroom, the bullets in the handgun found in his car, and the bullet from the victim's body. CBLA tests the minute amount of trace elements in the metal making up the bullet to see if different bullets have the same or different amounts of these trace elements. After CBLA, all of these bullets were classified as "analytically indistinguishable." This feat of science conclusively tied the junk man to the murder of the little girl. It would seal his fate.

At trial, Agent Riley explained to the jury that bullets that are "analytically indistinguishable" are "typically found within the same box of ammunition" (*Earhart v. State*, 1991, p. 615). He testified, "from my 21 years' experience of doing bullet lead analysis and doing research on boxes of ammunition down through the years I can determine if bullets came from the same box of ammunition" (Giannelli, 2010, p. 310, quoting Testimony of John Riley, *State v. Earhart*, No. 4064, Dist. Ct. Lee County, 21st Judicial Dist., Texas, Transcript at 5248–49). He later clarified his statement, saying that "analytically indistinguishable bullets which do not come from the same box most likely would have been manufactured at the same place on or about the same day; that is, in the same batch" (*Id.*). He testified that based on all 0.22 caliber bullets made in one year, the probability that two 0.22 caliber bullets came from the same batch is approximately 0.000025%, "give or take a zero" (*Id.*). On cross-examination, he acknowledged the numbers which he relied upon to reach the 0.000025% statistic did not consider that there are several different types of 0.22 caliber bullets made each year (0.22 long and 0.22 long rifle, etc.) (*Id.*).

Although Earhart's defense counsel effectively cross-examined Riley, no authoritative expert at the time of trial was questioning the reliability of the FBI's CBLA evidence. It was held as infallible, solid, precise, scientific evidence that linked Earhart to Kandy's murder. The testimony of the FBI agent was revered. Regardless of the weakness of the case against Earhart, this testimony tied him unquestionably to Kandy's brutal murder. As we will see later, this evidence has proven meaningless. However, given that the spot of blood on the gun and that the bullets found in Earhart's possession were "analytically indistinguishable" from the bullet that killed Kandy, it is easy to see why the jury convicted Earhart. Given the brutality and senselessness of the crime and the innocence and age of the victim, it is also easy to understand why Earhart was sentenced to death.

But there were some pieces to the puzzle that did not quite fit. For one thing, in spite of Earhart's appearance, which would instantly typecast him as the villain in a grade B horror movie, Earhart was not an evil person. He had no criminal record. Although he was 43 years old and often spent time with family and friends who had children, he was seen as kind and gentle and he had no history of harming children in any way (*Earhart v. State*, 1994, p. 762). People who knew him trusted him with their children.

One reason he was grimy was that two or three times a day, he would go into the dumpsters behind grocery stores and collect expired produce, canned goods, and baked goods that were still edible. Once he gathered the food, he took it to his mother and then distributed groceries to the elderly in his neighborhood (*Earhart v. State*, 1994, p. 762). He also lived with and cared for his mother, regularly bringing her food and taking her to church. People who knew him best testified that in spite of his appearance and social awkwardness, he was gentle and kind.

Other forensic evidence failed to inculpate Earhart. FBI agent Ronald Rawalt testified for the defense. Rawalt ran extensive soil analyses from the crime scene and compared it to soil recovered from Earhart's shoes, boots, the 0.22 caliber gun, and both of the cars Earhart drove. While Kandy's shoes contained two types of soil found at the crime scene, sandy and silty, Earhart's shoes contained soil and sand that did not match. Earhart's boots and shoes that were recovered from the trunk of his Oldsmobile failed to match the crime scene. The soil on the gun, soil found inside the Chevrolet, and dirt on the tires did not originate from the crime scene.

A woman who was shopping at a Bryan shopping mall on May 14, 1987, 2 days after Kandy disappeared, testified that she saw a girl matching Kandy's description and wearing a white shirt, turquoise shorts, ankle socks and tennis shoes, the clothing Kandy was wearing when she disappeared and when her body was found. Because the woman had heard of Kandy's disappearance, she immediately called the police. In addition, a clerk at a Bryan toy store testified that on May 14, 1987, around 11:00 a.m., she saw a girl matching Kandy's description in the toy store. The girl was dressed in turquoise shorts, a white shirt, and white tennis shoes. The clerk testified that a woman who looked like Kandy's mother, Janice Dell, was in the store "pulling" the girl around. When the clerk saw Kandy's picture in the newspaper that same day, she called the police.

These sightings become all the more relevant because of other evidence gathered by police. On the day Kandy disappeared, she was planning to run away from her home. She lived with her father, her stepmother, and her stepbrother. She intended to sneak away and return to her birth mother, Janice Dell (*Earhart v. State*, 1991). She told a friend at school that day that she had her chance. Her brother and stepmother were going to a medical appointment after school. Kandy would be arriving home alone and would have the perfect opportunity to sneak away.

There was much discord at home. Kandy's stepmother was physically abusive to Kandy. There was conflict between her father and her stepmother that centered around how Kandy was treated by her stepmother. Kandy's mother and stepmother were in constant turmoil and had a heated confrontation days before Kandy disappeared (*Earhart v. State*, 1991). Until Earhart became the focus of the case, there were many avenues of investigation open to the police that lead away from Earhart.

Another discordant piece was motive. Although the police theorized Earhart abducted Kandy so that he could fulfill some twisted sexual desire, there was not even a hint of evidence that a sexual assault took place. He was often with friends and family who had children (*Earhart v. State*, 1994, p. 762). He had no history of child molestation and there was nothing except brash speculation that showed he had any unhealthy interest in children. There was not one reason for Earhart to harm Kandy. None.

COMPOSITIONAL BULLET LEAD ANALYSIS CHALLENGE

During habeas proceedings in 1998, Earhart's counsel argued that Earhart received ineffective assistance of counsel because his trial counsel did not request funds for and did not look for an expert to counter the state's evidence that the bullets found in Earhart's possession came from the same box or batch as the bullet that killed Kandy (*Earhart v. Johnson*, 1998). The court held that "[g] iven the significant role the bullet evidence played in the prosecution's case ... Earhart could have made a sufficient threshold showing that he was entitled to a defense expert under Texas law." (*Earhart v. Johnson*, 1998). However, the court concluded that "Earhart was not entitled to relief on these grounds because, in this habeas proceeding, he still had failed to show or even allege that an expert could be found whose testimony would have altered the outcome of the state court trial." (*Earhart v. Johnson*, 1998). Indeed, even by the time of Earhart's habeas proceedings, it was difficult to find an expert to contradict the CBLA evidence presented by the FBI (Piller and Mejia, 2003). Although the evidence that convicted Earhart was becoming suspect, because there were no experts available to challenge CBLA at the time of Earhart's trial, his petition for a new trial failed.

Of course, today, experts know more. As will be fully explored in the chapter below, testimony such as that given by Agent Riley was terribly overstated, and its application to the case was not based on scientific principles. Although the FBI used the technique for over 30 years, CBLA evidence is no longer allowed in American courts because it is not reliable (Giannelli, 2010). There were likely many gun owners in the Bryan, Texas area that held 0.22 caliber ammunition of the same composition as the bullet that killed Kandy. Riley's estimate of a 0.00025% likelihood of finding a bullet of that composition was incorrect and not based on reality. The only physical evidence that directly connected Earhart to Kandy's horrible death was simply meaningless.

SUFFICIENCY OF THE EVIDENCE

Earhart also challenged his conviction based on a claim that the state had not presented sufficient evidence to establish his guilt. If this same challenge was lodged today when we know that the CBLA evidence as presented against Earhart is meaningless, Earhart may very well meet the standard. In order to show that there was insufficient evidence to convict, Earhart would need to show that there was a reasonable hypothesis other than his guilt (*Earhart v. State*, 1991). Specifically, the standard is, "if there is a reasonable hypothesis other than the guilt of the accused, then it cannot be said that guilt has been established beyond a reasonable doubt" (*Earhart v. State*, 1991). Without the CBLA evidence directly linking Earhart's gun to Kandy's murder, the only evidence that remains is that a grubby junk man had the audacity to stop and talk to a little girl. The traces of blood on shirts found in Earhart's car has little weight; nearly half of the population could have left that blood. The fact that Earhart owned a 0.22 meant little. Many Texans in the 1980s owned 0.22s.

Nine-year-old Kandy was running away from home. She was willing to get into the car of a stranger. She was vulnerable to anyone with evil intent that could have happened upon her as she fled her home. It is a reasonable hypothesis that someone other than Earhart, someone who had a motive to abduct a little girl, crossed paths with Kandy.

Is it reasonably *possible* that Earhart killed Kandy? Absolutely. Is it also reasonably *possible* that someone other than Earhart committed the murder? Absolutely. And there lies the problem.

James Otto Earhart was executed by lethal injection on August 11, 1999, in Huntsville, Texas (Cothron, 2009; Office of the Attorney General New Release Archive, 1999). He is not alive to challenge his conviction that was based on junk science. There is no one who can advocate for Earhart or who can be his voice. Although we may never be certain, there is much doubt about the guilt of James Earhart (Cothron, 2009; Porter, 2010; Northwestern University). It should not sit easy with us that false evidence was instrumental in a capital conviction that ended a man's life. It should also not sit easy with us that had the blood evidence been preserved, it may have been able to put to rest questions about Earhart's factual guilt or innocence. If Earhart was still alive, his case would be back in court because of what we now know about the frailty of CBLA evidence. Was justice done for Kandy? We will never be certain. One thing is certain: although we may never know the truth about the death of Kandy Kirtland, Earhart should never have been convicted and executed based on CBLA evidence.

REFERENCES

Cothron, G.R., 2009. Killing Innocents. Available at SSRN 1906718.

Earhart v. Johnson, 132 F.3d 1062 (5th Cir. 1998).

Earhart v. State, 823 S.W.2d 607 (Tex. Crim. App. 1991).

Earhart v. State, 877 S.W.2d 759 (Tex. Crim. App. 1994).

Giannelli, P.C., 2010. Comparative bullet lead analysis: a retrospective. Criminal Law Bulletin 47, 306.

Northwestern University School of Law. Executing the Innocent. Available at: http://web.archive.org/web/20100627053204/http://www.law.northwestern.edu/wrongfulconvictions/issues/deathpenalty/Executinginnocent/.

Office of the Attorney General New Release Archive, August 10, 1999. Media Advisory of Tuesday. Available at: https://www.texasattorneygeneral.gov/newspubs/newsarchive/1999/19990810earhartadvsy.htm.

Piller, C., Mejia, R., 2003. Science Casts Doubt on FBI's Bullet Evidence. Available at: http://cironline.org/reports/science-casts-doubt-fbis-bullet-evidence-1860.

Porter, C., 2010. The Conviction of the Innocent: How the Law Can Let Us Down. Random House. ISBN: 9781864714364. Available at: http://www.randomhouse.com.au/books/chester-porter/conviction-of-the-innocent-9781864714364.aspx#sthash.1WiJ6sl8.dpuf.

Exquisite Measurements, Erroneous Inferences: Compositional Bullet Lead Analysis

Max M. Houck

Forensic & Intelligence Services, LLC, St. Petersburg, FL, United States

INTRODUCTION

Many crimes, especially homicides, involve firearms. When fired bullets are recovered from a victim or scene, they can be compared visually with fired bullets from a suspected firearm to determine if the questioned bullets could have been fired from that weapon. Many times, however, bullets are damaged or fragmented from hitting hard objects, ruining the physical information on the surface of the bullet and precluding a visual comparison. Additionally, the firearm used is not always available for test fires in that the firearm in question may not be recovered.

In the 1970s, the idea of comparing the constituent elements of a bullet was explored (Lukens and Guinn, 1971). Elements are substances that are made of the same types of atoms. Elemental analysis identifies which elements are present and quantifies them, typically in weight percentage. When different elements are combined and held together by chemical bonds, they form chemical compounds. For example, sodium and chlorine are elements, but can be combined to form the chemical sodium chloride (salt).

The assassination of President Kennedy in 1963 spurred the concept when the investigation into his death tried to determine the number of bullets used based on analysis of the fragments recovered (Randich et al., 2002; Randich and Grant, 2006; Spiegelman et al., 2007). Because bullets are made in batches, like most manufactured goods, it was thought that the variation of elemental content *within* a batch would be less than the variation *between* batches, allowing for an association to be made at some level of manufacture.

Comparative bullet lead analysis or CBLA offered a scientific forensic potential in otherwise hopeless firearms cases. With the best instrumentation at the time, only three elements could be analyzed simultaneously. Even at that early stage, the researchers noted limitations on the method because of the high degree of compositional uniformity from at least one manufacturer, leading them to conclude that matching concentrations of three elements does not mean that two bullets came from the same lot or pour (Lukens and Guinn, 1971). Complicating matters, the terms "lot" and "pour" are not well defined in the industry.

Newer methods, which allowed for up to seven elements to be analyzed, were applied to CBLA in the 1990s. These methods provided precise measurements of the amount of elements down to a few parts per million. The exact minimum detection limit (MDL) for an element depends on the instrumentation used and what other elements are present. Elements can influence the detection and quantitation of each other, thus changing the MDL for a particular element in different compounds. The elements of interest in CBLA are antimony, arsenic, bismuth, cadmium, copper, silver, and tin.

CBLA was a method used in the US solely by the FBI Laboratory to compare the content of bullet lead and make an attribution of source to some level of manufacture or distribution (production unit or box of bullets). Over 2500 cases were analyzed for CBLA by the FBI since the 1980s, and those results played a significant role in many of them, including death penalty cases. A joint investigation by CBS News' *60 Minutes* and *The Washington Post* prompted the FBI to review CBLA cases, many of which have problems in testimony or results (Solomon, 2007).

In 2002, based upon mounting criticism of the technique and testimony about it, the FBI asked the National Academy of Sciences to conduct an independent review of CBLA. The 2004 report found that the assumptions and the model for interpreting bullet composition results was flawed and without a scientific basis, that testimony by FBI examiners was overstated, and that the evidence as presented in reports and testimony was misleading to juries. In 2005, the FBI discontinued the method, citing that neither scientists nor bullet manufacturers could explain the significance of a "match" (Committee on Scientific Assessment of Bullet Lead Elemental Composition Comparison and National Research Council, 2004).

The leap made from exquisite measurement to erroneous interpretation is a common one in science. Simply because something can be precisely detected does not mean it can be meaningfully interpreted; this is a lesson the vaunted "gold standard," DNA evidence, is learning currently (Dror and Hampikian, 2011; Cale, 2015). Science and technology have progressed, but the philosophical assumptions upon which forensic science routinely interprets evidence need to be updated as well for the sake of justice (Crispino and Houck, 2013).

THE FBI'S ORIGINAL PREMISES

Based on the previous work done in CBLA, the FBI developed a protocol for conducting these examinations in criminal cases based on a set of premises. The first is that a few small samples taken from the bullets are compositionally representative of the source from which they originated. The second assumption was that the molten source of the lead from which the bullets came was homogeneous. And, finally, the assumption was made that each molten source of lead was unique in its composition (Tobin and Duerfeldt, 2002). The FBI's hypothesis that supported the use of CBLA was that the elemental concentrations of the lead in a batch of bullets is unique, and therefore, bullets that come from the same batch of lead should have the same concentrations of elements (Spiegelman and Kafadar, 2006). The second and third assumptions will be dealt with in detail next, while the first assumption will be addressed here.

Assumption One: *A Few Small Samples Taken From the Bullets Are Compositionally Representative of the Source From Which They Originated*

Sampling is a basic concept in statistics, but one that has insufficient attention paid to it because its complex and demanding nature. If data are collected inappropriately, any analysis or interpretation from them is in danger of being misguided or inaccurate. The presumption of sampling is that the population of interest is too large or difficult to count or measure each member, so a subset of that population is collected to be representative of or a proxy for that population. Samples can be chosen in a wide variety of ways, but can be condensed into three basic categories: probability (each member of the population has an equal chance of being chosen), judgment (only the blue members are selected, for example), or bulk (a portion of a larger amount that is not made up of separate units).

FBI examiners would take three samples of 60 mg each from a bullet. The analytical methods that were used are destructive of the sample, so analyzing the entire bullet would be scientifically and legally inappropriate. The weight of a bullet varies by caliber (size of the bullet measured in tenths of an inch or in millimeters), from about 2.5 g (2500 mg) for a 0.22 bullet to almost 10 g (100,000 mg) for a 0.38. The location the sample was taken from on the bullet would vary with the size and shape of the deformed bullet. Therefore, the resulting 180 mg of sampled bullet lead would comprise between about 0.0006–7% of a whole bullet, potentially more from deformed fragments. Between 85 and 118 million pounds of lead (3,855,600,000 to 53,524,800,000 g) are used to make about 9 billion bullets each year (NRC, 2009). To assume representativeness of such small samples from such a large population is untenable (Randich et al., 2002; Tobin and Duerfeldt, 2002; Spiegelman and Kafadar, 2006):

> *The composition of a very small metal sample derived from a large casting is not likely to be a representative sample of the overall or average casting composition because of the metallurgical phenomena that occurred during the casting process.*
> **Tobin and Duerfeldt (2002, p. 27)**

This is well known to metallurgists and material scientists, who understand the chemistry and components involved in manufacturing, but perhaps not as well understood by analytical chemists, who are concerned with specimens and instrumentation. Nilsen explains it well:

> *Because the sophistication and automation of today's instruments tend to minimize the need for subjective measurement and observation, an unskilled person can be trained within six weeks to be an effective, accurate, and productive analyst. This person may know little chemistry, but can work productively as an "analytical chemist," performing analyses and turning in correct results as long as nothing goes wrong. When something does go wrong, analyst who do not really understand chemistry cannot recognize problems effectively. Even when things go right…an analyst with an understanding of the chemistry will produce better quality data, work more effectively, and be able to improve his or her science."*
> **Nilsen (1996, p. 10)**

Assumptions Two and Three: *The Molten Source of the Lead From Which the Bullets Came Was Homogeneous and Each Molten Source of Lead Was Unique in Its Composition*
To address the second and third assumptions, the manufacture and distribution of bullets as a product need to be explained and in some depth. Luckily, it's interesting.

WHAT IS A SUPPLY CHAIN?

Finished products like shoes, cars, and bullets represent a finalized item, which is encoded with the details of its manufacturing history; these details are imbedded in its composition, component parts, design, and intended end use. Working backwards from the finished product to tease out the manufacturing history can be variously successful. Details may be clear and closely narrow down a manufacturing source, while others may be traceable but obscured or unintelligible at a "forensic level" of relevant distinction. To narrow down or identify the originating source of a product, a first principles approach is necessary, first going forward through the manufacturing process to learn what forensically useful traits are retained in the finished product, as well as which ones are analytically useful. Sadly, many forensic sciences do not do this, simply analyzing as-found items of evidence with perhaps an inadequate understanding of what they contain or how they are produced.

The information encoded in a finished product is reflective of the network of raw materials and intermediate processes that resulted in it; this network is called a supply chain. Technically, a supply chain is the system of organizations, people, suppliers, intermediate processors, activities, and resources involved in moving a product or service from supplier to customer. Supply chains may also be internal to a company, such as a finishing or polishing process, but unless the company produces everything they need for manufacturing their product, an external network of suppliers must exist.

Cumulatively, the exchanges throughout a supply chain will be between companies sharing varied relationships, each seeking maximum profits based on those things they can control. Ironically, each company may have little or no knowledge of or interest in the companies up- or downstream in the supply chain; they receive a good or service that meets their specifications and may not be interested in the "why" or "how" of its production (Shapiro, 2007). This complicates the forensic scientist's job in trying to source any one item of evidence; the relevant and required documentation may not exist with the producer. Contingent and incidental characteristics can accumulate in a product. As long as they do not affect the customer's specifications, they can be ignored. Forensic science exploits these incidental traits, but does not always understand them (Houck and Siegel, 2015). Supply chains, even for the simplest of products, can become a complex process of machinery, human activity, and quality control.

BILLETS TO BULLETS[1]

The bullet manufacturing process is complicated and variation can occur at a variety of steps along the way (Fig. 1.1). Specifications for bullet performance vary, but are not exacting; a bullet needs to survive the firing process, fly straight, hit its target, and have impact. They are created in mass and designed to be expendable. Bullets, therefore, are made from scrap lead, typically old automotive batteries. So-called secondary refiners smelt the scrap lead into molten sources or lots of up to 250,000 pounds each. The lead is refined to meet the bullet manufacturers' specifications for elemental content. Trace elements, such as copper, bismuth, silver, and cadmium, must be below specified levels (around 0.1% or less), while others must be above certain levels, like antimony, because they help harden the lead to make a more effective bullet.

MELTING AND SPECIFICATIONS

The lead arrives at the bullet manufacturers as either ingots (also called pigs) or billets. Ingots and billets are about the same size, but a premium is charged for billets

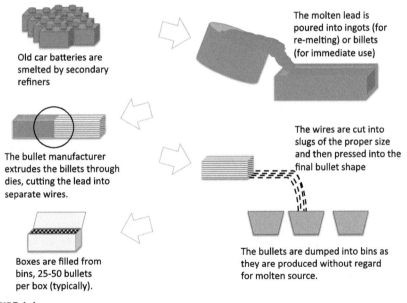

Old car batteries are smelted by secondary refiners

The molten lead is poured into ingots (for re-melting) or billets (for immediate use)

The bullet manufacturer extrudes the billets through dies, cutting the lead into separate wires.

The wires are cut into slugs of the proper size and then pressed into the final bullet shape

Boxes are filled from bins, 25-50 bullets per box (typically).

The bullets are dumped into bins as they are produced without regard for molten source.

FIGURE 1.1

The Bullet Manufacturing Process.

---

[1] For readability purposes, the material in this section is taken generally from NRC, 2009; Finkelstein and Levin, 2005; Goho, 2004; Imwinkelried and Tobin, 2003; Randich et al., 2002; Tobin and Duerfeldt, 2002. Citations are included where appropriate.

because they are "ready-made" for the bullet manufacturing process. Ingots must be remelted before they can be used; billets do not. This is a significant point: remelting an ingot can change the composition of the material. During melting, the molten lead is "stirred" by convective forces and all of the bullets made from one melt would tend to have the same elemental composition. Some smelters add lead to replenish the lot while pouring (to "top it off"), and this can change the composition of billets during an extended pour. As the billet solidifies, minor components (solutes) will move to its center (called segregation), increasing inhomogeneity. It has been known in the forensic science community for some time that "the variability [of the elemental mix] within a production run … has not been addressed in a comprehensive study" (Peele et al., 1991).

Despite having specifications for the materials they receive, bullet manufacturers do not analyze the composition of the lead they use. When they contract with refiners, bullet manufacturers do not specify an exact amount of each element, but rather permit variation in a prescribed range. Secondary refiners are thus contracted to produce uniform molten lots; inhomogeneous billets or ingots are acceptable. Commercial norms and scientific reality make such variations accepted and expected. Therefore, the secondary refiners are the only ones who have comprehensive data about what goes into bullet lead. When battery manufacturers make car batteries, they have to follow fairly tight specifications because their products have tight requirements for electrical conductivity and corrosion. Only a small portion of the lead smelted by secondary refiners goes to bullet manufacturers; however, the main use of the lead from old automotive batteries is to make new ones (the lead already meets that product's specifications). Therefore, the secondary refiners do as little as possible to accommodate bullet manufacturers because they are such small customers.

During the pour process, additional lead from other ingots may be added into the melt to keep a continuous stream of production. Elemental concentrations can vary during a pour because of the added materials; for example, researchers found one example where the amount of tin decreased by 60% over 30 min (Koons and Grant, 2002). One billet can produce 12,000 to 60,000 0.22 caliber bullets; a large pour can yield up to 35 million bullets.

There are a few important outcomes to note from the foregoing. First, since battery manufacturers follow strict compositional requirements for their primary customers and also must satisfy specifications for bullet manufacturers, the range of freedom they have to vary the elemental content of their product is narrowed on two counts. This means that in any given year, the probability increases that manufacturers will produce lead melts that are analytically indistinguishable. Moreover, this is true for *all* bullet manufacturers because of the basic physical needs for their end products. Second, remember that some bullet manufacturers prefer to use billets (even at higher cost) than ingots. Billets do not require remelting, thus increasing the chance of analytically indistinguishable bullets from different molten sources. Finally, smelting, as an industry, has changed little and is, by its nature, conservative. As Tobin and Duerfeldt point out, "[b]ullet manufacturers have used so many molten sources over the years that there is good reason to believe that there are frequent coincidental 'repeats' and 'overlaps' among the huge supply of bullets available to consumers" (2002). Randich et al. studied secondary lead manufacturers' lead production data over two periods (1987–1988 and 1998–2000), analyzing samples taken from the beginning, middle, and end of 100-ton molten source pours. One refiner's data showed variations in antimony by almost 12%, copper by 142%, tin by 1871%, and arsenic by 31% from the beginning to the end of the pour. They confirmed that multiple indistinguishable shipments of lead alloys from secondary lead refiners are provided to the bullet manufacturers "reasonably often" each year (Randich et al., 2002). This translates into bullets with indistinguishable compositions being found in many boxes produced in the same or closely related production runs. When the FBI's own CBLA database was reviewed, a number of analytically indistinguishable samples from unrelated cases were discovered (Imwinkelreid and Tobin, 2003). Despite this empirical knowledge, the FBI continued using CBLA in many cases until 2005.

EXTRUSION AND WIRES

Bullet manufacture varies by the company that makes them, but follows the same basic pattern. The lead alloy is forced through dies that cut the metal into wires, much like pushing pasta dough through a cutter to make spaghetti. The wires are cut into slugs sized for the caliber of intended bullet. The slugs are then pressed into the appropriate shape desired for the bullets. The finished bullets are dumped into bins without regard to which melt they came from. The bullets are then taken from the bins and boxed, another potential source of source mixture. Lead from many different sources can be intermingled at many points in the manufacturing process. Therefore, a box of ammunition is likely to contain bullets from multiple volumes of lead (NRC, 2009; Goho, 2004). Bullet manufacturers are reluctant to share their data, claiming it is proprietary. Batch uniqueness, a fundamental assumption by the FBI, has yet to be supported. Thus, a "batch" could contain thousands or millions of bullets; a bullet from one box (typically 25–50 bullets) could match bullets from hundreds or thousands of other boxes.

SALES AND DISTRIBUTION

Manufacturing is only part of the supply chain; the products still have to get to the customer. Manufacturers sell their bullets to wholesalers who then sell them to retail venues like sporting goods stores or larger stores like Wal-Mart. Because bullets are not made to order and are sold in bulk, clustering occurs in the distribution and sales of bullets. A large retailer, like Wal-Mart, may receive many of the bullets from a particular molten source simply because of the size of the order placed. Those bullets may be shipped to a limited geographical area. The number of potential customers will vary by population size, density, store location, and rate of bullet purchase. For example, if bullets from a single melt are bought by a distributor in a small town or to a sales venue in a local neighborhood, every firearm owner in the region may own bullets from that melt. Clustering and local or regional economics makes it more likely that bullets from the same area may be analytically indistinguishable, leading to false positive associations. Even the putative pioneer of CBLA, Dr. Vincent Guinn, knew that sales and distribution would affect the relative frequency of composition-ally indistinguishable bullets:

> [Y]ou only look into these things in cases, in a criminal case. That's the only time you get around to wondering about the composition of these [bullets]. If you just went around and visited farmhouses in the area and saw them [bullets] and gathered up a lot of them, you'd probably find a lot of those were from some of this same material... (Huffington v. Nuth, 140 F.3d 572 (4th Cir. 1988), as cited in Tobin and Duerfeldt, 2002).

Researchers found very high degrees of geographic concentration of bullet packing codes (Cole et al., 2005). For example, one Wal-Mart in Virginia yielded potentially hundreds of customers who had purchased bullets with the same packing code from the manufacturer, demonstrating they had been made at about the same time. In another sales outlet in Alaska, it was calculated that the chances ranged from 87% to 100% of the bullets would have the same packing codes and, therefore, would be suspects in a hypothetical investigation.

Consider the following scenario. If most of the bullets (Brand X, 0.22, for example) for sale for a given region came from the same pour, the forensic or probative value of any "match" would need to be adjusted for that fact. In a more extreme case, if *all* of the Brand X 0.22 bullets in that same region were derived from the same pour, then a "match" between a questioned bullet and a known bullet from the suspect would have little meaning, if any. Remember that the same pour or lot may be used to manufacture bullets of different calibers. Consequently, bullets of other calibers can be analytically indistinguishable and could be found in the same region. If everybody's bullets are the same, then none of them have value and could have come—literally—from anyone.

THE EASY PART: ANALYSIS

None of the reports or research on CBLA questions the methodology of analysis, whether it is the older neutron activation analysis (NAA) or the newer inductively-coupled plasma optical emission spectrometry (ICP-OES). The FBI would take three samples from each bullet or fragment and dissolve them in acid; the sample in solution was placed into the instrument. In ICP-OES, the sample goes into a plasma[2], which generates a temperature on the order of 10,000°C (18,032°F). The heat excites the elements in the sample, causing them to emit light at wavelengths specific to each one. The wavelengths are plotted on a graph, and the elements are quantified based on the strength of their signals (Keto, 1999).

---

[2] A plasma is one of the four types of matter, the other three being solid, liquid, and gas. A plasma is highly charged and energetic; a neon sign is an example of a plasma.

The FBI would then take the mean of the three measurements and the standard deviation for each element[3]. The concentrations in each fragment depend on the element involved. Statistical tests were used to compare the elements in each questioned fragment with the elements in each of the known bullets (Leonard, 2015). If any of the questioned and known bullets were determined to be "analytically indistinguishable" for all of the elements, the conclusion would be drawn that the questioned and known samples could have come from the same "source":

> *When a crime-scene bullet contains the same analytical elemental concentrations (i.e., match in composition) as the bullets from known cartridges, a single source for these bullets cannot be excluded…those lead specimens that share the same composition are generally packaged within the same box of cartridges, or in boxes of cartridges of the same caliber and type at the same manufacturing plant, on or about the same date.*
>
> **Peters (2002)**

The phrase "analytically indistinguishable" is a point of conceptual conflict: what does it mean? If two things (samples) have all of the same characteristics, what does that tell you about the universe of things from which they came (population) (Cole, 2009)? CBLA might be more meaningful if only a thousand bullets had the same elemental composition rather than several million bullets (Gianelli, 2010). And, again, what does "source" mean? A lot, a pour, a billet, a box?

The identification of elements is dependent on what other elements are present, however. Early research using NAA was limited to the analysis of only three elements at a time, which the researchers recognized as not being sufficient for concluding the bullets came from the same source (Lukens and Guinn, 1971; Schlesinger et al., 1970). With the advent of ICP-OES, seven elements could be analyzed simultaneously; however, practical constraints limited even this advance. Although on the list of elements to be analyzed, cadmium is either absent or in exceedingly low amounts (one or two parts per million). Tin is not always found. Bismuth and silver are present only in very restricted ranges. These constraints may force the chemist to only work with three elements, the same ones determined to be of insufficient value in the original NAA research (Imwinkelried and Tobin, 2003).

"MATCHING" AND CHAINING

The statistics involved in the FBI's methods and in the unraveling of the problems with them are detailed and intricate. This chapter has avoided a more in-depth discussion of the particulars in favor of elucidating the problems with the foundational assumptions; those interested parties with a background in statistics and math should read Appendix K by Kafadar and Spielgeman in the NAS report (NRC, 2009).

---

[3] The mean is the sum of a group of numbers divided by the number of entries; the standard deviation is a measure that shows the variation or dispersion of numbers around the mean.

The FBI used three statistical approaches to determine whether two bullets "matched." The first, the "2-SD Overlap" ("SD" for standard deviation"), compared the absolute value of the difference between the average composition for each element from the questioned bullet to those in the known bullet[4]; if the difference was less than twice the sum of the standard deviation for each element from the bullets, then the bullets matched. The second approach, the "Range Overlap," is similar to the 2-SD except that the intervals defined by the minimum and maximum values (the range, statistically) for each of the seven elements are used. The Range Overlap approach tended to generate fewer false positives (Finkelstein and Levin, 2005). Finally, the third approach was "Chaining." With Chaining, compositionally similar groups of bullets are created from a reference population of bullets[5]. Making the assumption that each bullet in the population is unique, a single bullet is selected and compared to each of the other bullets in the population using the 2-SD approach. If the first bullet is determined to match another bullet, their compositional groups are collapsed into a new, single group. This process is repeated for the entire population, with the membership of the groups increasing while the number of groups decreases. Taking compositional data from a questioned bullet and a known bullet, these are compared to the compositional groups created. If the questioned bullet is found to match the same compositional group as the known bullet, then the questioned and known bullets are said to match. The FBI left unspecified some aspects of the method, like what to do with a compositional group with one member or what happens if the bullets of interest match more than one compositional group. Nevertheless, it is important to note that the bullets are being compared and matched to *groups* and not each other. Therefore, if Bullet A matches Bullet B, and Bullet B matches Bullet C, Bullet A *may not match* Bullet C (NRC, 2009). Fig. 1.2 from the National Academies of Science (NAS) report demonstrates this situation. Bullet #1044 (picked randomly, the data for which is represented by the first line in each vertical grouping of lines) matches 12 other bullets in the dataset, and each of those matches 12 other bullets. As the NAS reported (NRC, 2009, p. 202):

> *Over 71,000 bullets have been chemically analyzed by the FBI during the last 15 years; thousands more will be analyzed, and millions more produced that will not be analyzed. In addition, thousands of statistical clustering algorithms have been proposed to identify groups in data with largely unknown success. For reasons outlined above, chaining, as one such algorithm, is unlikely to serve the desired purposes of identifying matching bullets with any degree of confidence or reliability.*

---

[4] That is, if $|ave(Q) - ave(K)| < 2\,((sd(Q) + sd(K))$.

[5] "Such a population should be collected through simple random sampling from the appropriate subpopulation of bullets relevant to a particular case, which to date has not been carried out, perhaps because an 'appropriate' subpopulation would be very difficult to define, acquire, and test." (NRC, 2009; p. 32).

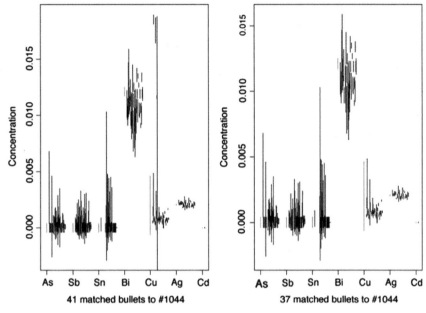

FIGURE 1.2

Illustration of chaining. The 2-SD interval for bullet 1044 (the first line of each data set) followed by the 2-SD interval for each of the 41 bullets whose intervals overlap with that of 1044 (NRC, 2009; p. 34). Note that while the ranges "overlap," the amount and variance of the overlap is extreme.

The proposition to be tested ought to have been "the mean values are not equal" (connoting innocence) rather than "the mean values are equal" (suggesting guilt) (Spiegelman and Kafadar, 2006).

A deeper and perhaps more fundamental issue may be that the presence and quantity of the elements in a bullet lead sample are not independent. The elements are present because of design requirements for the lead's original purpose, automotive batteries, which will not work if the elemental compositions are outside of specifications. The bullet manufacturers need certain elements within certain ranges as well; otherwise, the bullets will not function properly (too hard or too soft to be processed or fired). The presence of antimony is intentional as a hardening agent. Independence in statistics means the probability of one event does not affect the probability of another event. However, with CBLA, the dataset being mined necessarily is dependent on each of the elements in combination. This means that the testing conducted on the seven elements was not independent and, therefore, statistically suspect at best and misleading at worst.

PROBLEMS WITH TESTIMONY-COMPOUNDED PROBLEMS WITH INTERPRETATION

Issues with the statistics aside, the FBI examiners gave inconsistent and misleading testimony on CBLA. For example, one FBI expert testified in *State v. Earhart* (No. 4064, Dist. Ct. Lee County, 21st Judicial Dist., Texas) that bullets that are analytically indistinguishable are found within the same box of ammunition, and while bullets that have the same composition can also be found in other boxes of ammunition, it is most likely those boxes would have been manufactured at the same place on or about the same date. However, another testified that,

> *We have never testified, to my knowledge, that that bullet came from that box. We'd never say that. All we are testifying is that that bullet, or that victim fragment or something, the bullet, either came from that box or the* many *boxes that were produced at the same time.*
>
> **Commonwealth v. Wilcox, KY**

Some experts testified that the evidence bullets were "analytically indistinguishable" (the vagueness of that phrase having been already mentioned), while in others, their testimony ranged far and wide (Giannelli, 2010):

- the bullets could have come from the same "source" or "batch";
- the bullets came from the same source;
- they could have come from the same box;
- the bullets came from the same box of ammunition;
- they could have come from the same box or a box manufactured on the same day;
- were consistent with having come from the same box of ammunition;
- probably came from the same box; and
- must have come from the same box or from another box that would have been made by the same company on the same day.

With boxes containing 25 to 50 bullets, saying the questioned bullet came from the same box as that owned by the suspect is extremely strong evidence.

Some went too far. For example, in *United States v. Davis*, the expert testified that the "bullets must have been manufactured at the same Remington factory, must have come from the same batch of lead, must have been packaged on or about the same day, and could have come from the same box." In *State v. Washington*, the FBI expert testified that the elemental profile of bullets in a melt was "unique."

The nadir of CBLA testimony is that of Kathy Lundy in *Commonwealth v. Ragland*. Lundy testified at a pretrial admissibility hearing that the questioned bullet fragment from the victim's body was analytically indistinguishable from known bullets found in the home of the defendant's parents. However, Lundy testified that the company that made the bullets, Winchester Company, bought its bullet lead in ingot form prior to 1996, remelting for bullet production. On cross-examination in trial, Lundy admitted that she knew prior to the pretrial hearing that the company actually bought its lead in billet form in 1994. As discussed, billets have less variability than ingots, and Winchester could have made millions more bullets with similar elemental profiles. After trial, Lundy admitted to the FBI that she had lied on the stand, later pleading guilty to perjury (Giannelli, 2010).

The worst example identified to date was in *State v. Earhart*, the capital murder case addressed in the case study. The FBI expert testified that based on 21 years of experience and research, bullets could be sourced to the same box of ammunition. Earhart was executed prior to the NAS report being published (Giannelli, 2010). The FBI's own research showed that a single box of ammunition could contain as many as 14 distinct compositional groups (Goho, 2004).

Extensive experience without ground truths or base rates is no substitute for solid scientific research. Although the FBI testified with seemingly impressive credentials and reams of chemical data, the truth was more a matter of faith and unproven assumptions than science (Fig. 1.3).

Bullet-Lead Analysis: No Longer A Smoking Gun

Testing the chemical composition of bullets was thought to be a way to match bullets to their source, allowing the FBI to link bullets to suspects, much as it uses blood type to link evidence to an individual. Accepted as evidence for 30 years in criminal cases, bullet-lead analysis led to many convictions. However, scientific studies starting in 2001 have shown that FBI courtroom testimony about bullet lead is flawed:

Background: How bullets are made

Lead alloy is melted from leftover car batteries. The liquid is poured into a mold. All bullets poured from the same batch of molten lead are considered to be from the same "lot." Studies estimate that as many as 35 million bullets can come from a single source.

Two assumptions were made about this process, leading to the theory that a single bullet's characteristics would be representative of all other bullets in the lot:

ASSUMPTION 1: The molten source has a uniform composition throughout.

ASSUMPTION 2: No two molten sources have the same composition.

The Old Theory: Matching Bullet Composition Equals Shared Source

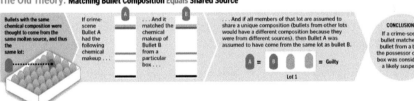

Current Science: Matching Bullet Composition Does Not Necessarily Prove Shared Source

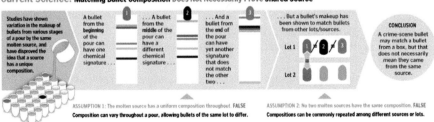

ASSUMPTION 1: The molten source has a uniform composition throughout. FALSE
Composition can vary throughout a pour, allowing bullets of the same lot to differ.

ASSUMPTION 2: No two molten sources have the same composition. FALSE
Compositions can be commonly repeated among different sources or lots.

FIGURE 1.3

An Outline of the CBLA Issues.

WHERE DOES THIS LEAVE BULLET LEAD ANALYSIS?

The FBI stopped conducting CBLA in September of 2005, noting that its decision was significantly influenced by the fact that neither scientists nor bullet manufacturers are able to definitively attest to the significance of an association made between bullets in the course of a bullet lead examination. No comprehensive review of the 2500 cases worked by the FBI has been conducted or at least published. According to the FBI, only 20% of the cases involving CBLA had those results submitted at trial (FBI, 2005). This, of course, ignores one of the realities of the criminal justice system, that plea agreements are offered—and accepted—based on the evidence as one believes it will be presented at trial. There is no way to calculate how many reports resulted in individuals choosing to take a plea agreement for lesser time rather than risk more serious consequences having gone to trial and lost.

SUMMARY

Forensic science, like many sciences, is a combination of categorization and comparison. And, like many sciences, these methods are at least documented, if not validated. The real difference with forensic science is the jump it makes to interpreting uncertain materials for the purposes of investigations and the courtroom. The inferences forensic scientists draw on samples whose production provenance is unknown or unknowable relies heavily on the scientist and the organizational environment they work in. CBLA was conducted by only one laboratory, one with an unprecedented and unrepeated reputation, and presented the results as solid scientific fact. This apparent certainty was probably compounded by the amount of actual science involved in the analysis of the bullet lead samples, adding to the impression that the conclusions were based on well-characterized and verifiable data. As Tobin and Duerfeldt (2002) note,

> *the very exactitude of those measurements can be beguiling. It can distract the judge and trier of fact and mislead them into thinking that the precision of the measurements in the earlier analytic stages somehow guarantees the validity of the ultimate inference drawn in the later, evaluative stage. There is no such guarantee.*

The faults in CBLA are numerous and complex (Kadafar and Mazza, 2015). There is the lack of baseline data from the manufacturers, a lack of understanding or acknowledgment of the sources of variation in bullet lead content, the organizational environment of the FBI to assume mastery of a topic in the face of contradictory empirical evidence and its reluctance to admit its mistakes, and the wobbly and unverified statistical approaches used; the list could go on and on. Moreover, the unwillingness of the FBI to share data, results, and methods with the scientific community resulted in decades of bad science that harmed and even killed the innocent.

For the 2500 cases that are in a review limbo (perhaps purgatory), there may be little comprehensive hope. Individual cases may be addressed, but a broad-based approach, like that taken with hair examinations, cannot be expected anytime soon. Going forward then, the diligent attorney must understand that doing science is about two things: documentation and reproducibility. If the data do not exist, if the samples are lost, if the bench notes are gone, its rumor and anecdote, it is not science. If the results cannot be—or are not—shared, if only one person in the world can do it, then it is not science. Even advanced instrumentation that can measure infinitesimal amounts can be used to make bogus interpretations and false conclusions. "The harsh reality is that even after making an exquisite measurement, a trace evidence analyst may draw an erroneous inference" (Tobin and Duerfeldt, 2002, p. 34). Making the same mistake for years and calling it experience is the bugbear of forensic science: too little data, not enough validation, merely the ipse dixit of someone who has done it for a long time. CBLA stands as a wonderful example of the horrible science that can affect the criminal justice system.

REFERENCES

Cale, C., 2015. Forensic DNA evidence is not infallible. Nature 526, 611.

Cole, S.A., 2009. Forensics without uniqueness, conclusions without individualization: the new epistemology of forensic identification. Law, Probability and Risk 8 (3), 233–255.

Cole, S.A., Tobin, W.A., Boggess, L.N., Stern, H.S., 2005. A retail sampling approach to assess impact of geographic concentrations on probative value of comparative bullet lead analysis. Law, Probability and Risk 4 (4), 199–216.

Committee on Scientific Assessment of Bullet Lead Elemental Composition Comparison, National Research Council, 2004. Forensic Analysis: Weighing Bullet Lead Evidence. National Academy of Sciences, Washington, DC.

Crispino, F., Houck, M.M., 2013. Basic principles of forensic science. In: Siegel, J., Sauko, P. (Eds.), Encyclopedia of Forensic Sciences, second ed. Elsevier, Amsterdam.

Dror, I.E., Hampikian, G., 2011. Subjectivity and bias in forensic DNA mixture interpretation. Science and Justice 51 (4), 204–208.

Federal Bureau of Investigation, 2005. FBI Laboratory Announces Discontinuation of Bullet Lead Examinations. Press release, September 01. Online at: https://www.fbi.gov/news/pressrel/press-releases/fbi-laboratory-announces-discontinuation-of-bullet-lead-examinations.

Finkelstein, M.O., Levin, B., 2005. Compositional analysis of bullet lead as forensic evidence. JL and Pol'y 13, 119.

Giannelli, P.C., 2010. Comparative bullet lead analysis: a retrospective. Criminal Law Bulletin 47, 306.

Goho, A., March 27, 2004. Forensics under fire: chemical matching of bullets comes under fire. Science News 165 (13), 202.

Houck, M., Siegel, J., 2015. Fundamentals of Forensic Science, third ed. Academic Press, Elsevier.

Imwinkelried, E.J., Tobin, W.A., 2003. Comparative bullet lead analysis evidence: valid inference or ipse dixit? Oklahoma City University Law Review 28 (1).

Kadafar, K., Mazza, A., February 24, 2015. Using faulty forensic science, courts fail the innocent. Live Science. Online at: http://www.livescience.com/49929-faulty-forensic-science-failing-united-states-court-system.html.

Keto, R., 1999. Analysis and comparison of bullet leads by inductively-coupled plasma mass spectrometry. Journal of Forensic Sciences 44 (5), 1020–1026.

Koons, R.D., Grant, D.M., 2002. Compositional variation in bullet lead manufacture. Journal of Forensic Sciences 47 (5), 950–958.

Lukens, H.R., Guinn, V.P., 1971. Comparison of bullet lead specimens by nondestructive neutron activation analysis. Journal of Forensic Sciences 16 (3), 301–308.

Leonard, B., October 5, 2015. The right to competent, not perfect, counsel. Courthouse News Service. http://www.courthousenews.com/2015/10/05/the-right-to-competent-not-perfect-counsel.htm.

National Research Council (NRC), 2009. Strengthening Forensic Science: A Path Forward. National Academies Press, Washington, DC.

Nilsen, C., 1996. Managing the Analytical Laboratory: Plain and Simple. CRC Press, Boca Raton, FL.

Peele, E.R., Havekost, D.G., Halberstam, R.C., Koons, R.D., Peters, C.A., Riley, J.P., 1991. Comparison of bullets using the elemental composition of the lead component. In: Proceedings of the International Symposium on the Forensic Aspects of Trace Evidence, 57, p. 68.

Peters, C.A., 2002. The basis for compositional bullet lead comparisons. Forensic Science Communications 4 (3).

Randich, E., Duerfeldt, W., McLendon, W., Tobin, W., 2002. A metallurgical review of the interpretation of bullet lead compositional analysis. Forensic Science International 127 (3), 174–191.

Randich, E., Grant, P.M., 2006. Proper assessment of the JFK assassination bullet lead evidence from metallurgical and statistical perspectives. Journal of Forensic Sciences 51 (4), 717–728.

Schlesinger, H.L., Guinn, V.P., Hackleman, R.P., 1970. Forensic Neutron Activation Analysis of Bullet-Lead Specimens. Gulf General Atomic, Incorporated. U.S. Atomic Energy Commission Report GA-10141.

Shapiro, J., 2007. Modeling the Supply Chain. Thompson Higher Education, Belmont, CA.

Solomon, J., November 18, 2007. FBI's forensic test full of holes. The Washington Post.

Spiegelman, C.H., Kafadar, K., 2006. Data integrity and the scientific method: the case of bullet lead data as forensic evidence. Chance 19 (2), 17–25.

Spiegelman, C., Tobin, W.A., James, W.D., Sheather, S.J., Wexler, S., Roundhill, D.M., 2007. Chemical and forensic analysis of JFK assassination bullet lots: is a second shooter possible? Annals of Applied Statistics 1 (2), 287–301.

Tobin, W.A., Duerfeldt, W., 2002. How probative is comparative bullet lead analysis? Criminal Justice 17 (3), 26–34.

Microscopic Hair Comparison

Forensic Science Reform. http://dx.doi.org/10.1016/B978-0-12-802719-6.00002-9
2017 Published by Elsevier Inc.

Case Studies: Colin Campbell Ross and James Driskell

Wendy J. Koen

Child Refuge, Inc., Menifee, CA, United States

Dear ones do not fret too much for me. The day's coming when my innocence will be proved.

Colin Campbell Ross, before he was hanged for a crime he did not commit.

The greatest challenge faced by forensic hair examiners is to be able to leave the witness box with a feeling of assurance that members of a jury, or a judge acting alone, have the same appreciation as the examiner does of the proper level of significance to be given to the hair evidence (Crocker, 1991). Meeting this challenge will help ensure that hair microscopy does not lead to wrongful convictions, unless, of course, the examiners themselves overvalue the significance of the evidence. Although hair microscopy is forensically useful in varied situations and is especially useful when it excludes a party, when used incorrectly or when results are exaggerated or communicated poorly to juries, or when examiners themselves do not understand the very real possibility of a coincidental "match," forensic hair microscopy can result in injustice. Two cases, decades and a world apart, are illustrative of such injustice.

COLIN CAMPBELL ROSS

Perjured informant testimony and exaggerated microscopic hair comparison testimony led to the conviction and execution of 28-year-old Colin Campbell Ross for the rape and murder of a 12-year-old girl, Alma Tirtschke (Lack and Morgan, 2005;

Brennan, 1922, pp. 45). In his book, *Gun Alley Tragedy* (Brennan, 1922), then junior defense counsel T.C. Brennan dissected the trial of Ross that took place in 1922 in Melbourne, Australia. Ross was arrested 2 weeks after Alma's naked body was found in Gun Alley (McQueen, 2004). Based on paid informants' testimony, investigators theorized that young Alma was at Ross's wine bar for 3 h on the day of her murder and that Ross raped and killed her. The prosecution supported their theory with physical evidence, long golden hairs they recovered from some blankets that belonged to Ross and were found folded on a sofa in the vestibule of Ross's home (Brennan, 1922, p. 8, 46).

The government chemist analyzed Alma's hair and the hairs recovered from the blanket and testified that these hairs came "from the scalp of one and the same person" (Cowan, 2008; Brennan, 1922). The chemist noted that the hairs recovered from the blanket were a lighter golden color and Alma had deep red hair. He explained the discrepancy in color by telling the jury that the hair found on the blanket must have come from the front of Alma's head and was lighter because of exposure to the sun. The known sample of Alma's hair came from behind her ear and would therefore appear much darker (Brennan, 1922, p. 47). When he examined the hairs from the blanket and the known sample under a microscope, he concluded the hairs were very similar because they were all relatively course, and the shafts of the hairs were identical (*Id.*). Although the hairs from the blanket were finer in diameter than the known sample, the chemist concluded that although it was possible the hairs from the blanket came from someone other than Alma, it was not probable (Brennan, 1922, p. 48).

Ross was swept up in a moral panic and faced execution. The shocking and senseless rape and murder of a little girl demanded justice. Before he was hanged, he told his family, "…dear ones do not fret too much for me. The day's coming when my innocence will be proved" (Morgan, p. 256). After the trial was over and Ross had paid the ultimate price, it was noted that during the trial "public opinion was inflamed as it has not been inflamed within the memory of a generation" (Brennan, 1922, from the preface). As is generally the case when the law runs afoul of justice, the human impulse to find and destroy the monster in our midst led investigators to use whatever means possible to secure a conviction.

It would not be until over eight decades later that the truth would be discovered and Ross's innocence would finally be announced (Kaladelfos, 2010). In 2008, the Victorian government issued Ross a posthumous pardon based upon evidence gathered by former librarian and researcher Kevin Morgan (Kaladelfos, 2010). During Kevin Morgan's exhaustive review of all of the evidence, he found the three golden hairs that had tied Ross to Alma's murder. Mitochondrial DNA (mtDNA) testing on the three hairs was conducted and proved, finally and conclusively, that Ross was innocent; the hairs did not belong to Alma (Kaladelfos, 2010).

Ross's tragic story leaves us with two valuable lessons, the first of which every forensic expert and attorney involved in a case with hair evidence should know: microscopic hair evidence should never be used to identify a source; it is simply not scientifically prudent to rest an identification on such evidence because hair is not unique and the analysis of hair is subjective and thus, open to bias. Secondly, the value of hair microscopy is increased by the added analysis of mtDNA. If Ross lived in a time when mtDNA analysis was possible, his story might not have ended so tragically. The case of James Driskell has several similarities to Ross, and both illustrate the importance of informing the jury of the potential that hairs that "match" microscopically do not necessarily come from the same source.

JAMES DRISKELL

James Driskell did not live in the early part of the 1900s. By the 1990s and the time of Driskell's trial, courts worldwide had learned from past blunders like the wrongful execution of Colin Ross. Still, with evidence strangely similar to that used to convict Colin Ross, Canadian James Driskell was convicted of murdering his friend, Perry Harder, based in part on expert testimony that underplayed the possibility of a coincidental "match" between the questioned hairs and the victim's hair sample (Manitoba, 2007).

In 1989, Driskell and Harder were arrested and jointly charged in connection with a "chop shop" operation they ran (Manitoba, 2007, p. 6). Harder admitted to police that he and Driskell stole vehicles, disassembled them, and then sold them for parts. Before trial, both men indicated to their counsel they would enter into a plea deal offered by the prosecutor. They would plead guilty to some of the charges against them and would each serve 2 to 3 years in prison (Manitoba, 2007, p. 8). However, on June 21, 1990, the day calendared for the pleas to be entered, Harder did not appear. A warrant was issued for Harder's arrest (*Id.*).

Over 3 months later, Harder's badly decomposed body was discovered in a shallow grave near some railroad tracks (*Id.*). Harder had been shot twice in the chest. Investigators theorized that Driskell killed Harder to avoid serving a prison sentence, and investigators began building a thin case against Driskell. In October of 1990, based on information offered by two informants who said that Driskell confessed to killing Harder, Driskell was arrested and charged with murder (Manitoba, 2007, p. 13).

At the time of arrest, the police stopped Driskell and his friend Donald Bannerman, who were driving in Bannerman's van (Manitoba, 2007, p. 146). The van belonged to Driskell at the time of Harder's disappearance; Driskell sold it to Bannerman in August of 1990. The police seized the van because they believed Driskell might have used it to transport Harder's body. Thirty-four hairs were collected from the van and sent to the Royal Canadian Mounted Police forensic laboratory for microscopic comparison (Manitoba, 2007, p. 147). Hair and fiber examiner Tod Christianson compared the 34 hairs—the questioned hairs—microscopically against a representative array of 26 hairs—the known hairs—that were recovered from Harder's gravesite. Harder's body had been disturbed by animals, and the clump of hair was found very near the body. Christianson determined that three of the questioned hairs from the van were microscopically consistent with the known hairs. For each of the three questioned hairs, he found a specific single known hair with similar characteristics. Thus, Christianson testified that the three hairs from the van were consistent with having come from Harder. At trial, Christianson explained to the jury:

> *And the point about this type of analysis is that it's not a positive identification, all right, because the only way you could do that is to look at all the hairs from all the person's head that exist, and that's an impossibility. But, I can tell you, based on my experience, that the chances of just accidentally picking up a hair and having it match to a known sample are very small. So if the hair [from the van] is consistent, that means it either came from the same person as that known sample [i.e., Harder] or from somebody else who has hair exactly like that.*

> **Manitoba (2007, p. 150)**

The hair examiner's testimony at Driskell's trial is typical of how hair microscopy evidence is generally presented in Canada and the US (Manitoba, p. 165; Geddes, 2015; Fabricant and Carrington, 2015). Christianson testified according to recommended standards and went to great lengths to explain to the court how he had compared the known and questioned hairs and concluded that they were similar with each other, and these similarities made it likely that the hairs in the van came from Harder (Manitoba, p. 50).

However, he may not have explained adequately why he concluded the similarities between the known hairs and the questioned hairs could not have been a simple coincidence. He certainly did not explain the state of the science to the jury, which was that anything known about the probability of a coincidental match had not been scientifically verified. He preferred to explain the probability of a coincidental match by using terms like "remote," "very small," or "not very high" (Manitoba, p. 151). Obviously, these terms are subjective; they are resorted to because of a complete absence of data, and they are left open to uninformed interpretations by jurors.

In addition, the expert did not give the jury all the evidence they needed to know in order to judge the probability of a coincidental match occurring from the hair analysis. A coincidental match would occur if the hairs collected from the van were similar to Harder's but did not actually come from Harder. The jury needed to understand that the more questioned hairs one examines in a case, the greater the chances are of finding coincidental matches (Manitoba, p. 167). Investigators recovered more than three hairs from the van; the expert did not simply find and examine three hairs and conclude that they all matched Harder's hair. The expert identified these 3 hairs by examining 34 unknown hairs recovered from the van. So, the question the jury should have considered was the probability that at least 3 of the 34 hairs would coincidentally match the known sample. The probability increases as the number of questioned hairs examined increases.

POOL OF UNKNOWN SIZE

Harder's case illustrates one of the most persistent and harmful problems with hair microscopy: the pool of possibilities is of an unknown size. The questions that needed to be answered are: how many people have hair similar to Harder? How many people with hair similar to Harder may have been in the van over the years? Given these unanswered questions, simply finding hair similar to Harding's in the carpet of a van used by innumerable people over a span of years means next to nothing. But the attorney made certain that the expert fashioned and framed his testimony in a way that made this weak evidence the smoking gun.

Because the jury members were not told and had no idea how many questioned hairs the expert analyzed, they were not able to address this question (Manitoba, p. 167). Also, because Christianson did not include the number of unknown hairs collected from the van in his report (Manitoba, p. 160), the defense attorney was not afforded the correct information needed to adequately challenge the "match" as coincidental. In this way, the expert's report and testimony was incomplete, and the value of the hair microscopy evidence was overplayed, which led the jury to conclude that it was highly likely the three hairs recovered from the van came from Harder.

Further, when Christianson testified to clarify what he meant when he said that a questioned hair was "consistent with" the known sample, he mistakenly explained to the jury that this meant that the questioned hair had "all of the features that the known samples had, within biological variation." This was not true. The three questioned hairs that were found to be consistent with the known hair did not have *all* of the features of *every* known hair Christianson examined. Instead, Christianson should have testified that each of the three questioned hairs had the same combinations of characteristics as one of the known hairs within normal biological variation (Manitoba, p. 154). In the end, based on the overvalued hair microscopy evidence and the testimony of two informants, Driskell was convicted of murdering Harder, and he was sentenced to life in prison with a possibility of parole after 25 years.

Driskell maintained his innocence and appealed his conviction, but in 1992, the Manitoba Court of Appeal denied his appeal. Nine years after Driskell's conviction, in the summer of 2000, the Assistant Deputy Minister of Manitoba asked Crown prosecutor Dale Schille to review the Driskell file because of media interest in the case and allegations that the informants were less than truthful about their compensation for testifying (Manitoba, p. 96). The inquiry discovered that one witness was granted immunity in an arson case, threatened to recant his testimony against Driskell if he faced charges in the arson case, and was given at least $80,000 (Manitoba, 2007, pp. 20, 45, 69, 99; Lett, 2005). Both informants were given cash rewards from Crime Stoppers (Manitoba, p. 108), witness protection, and relocation services (*Id*. p. 21). At the time of trial, the crown had denied that any favorable consideration was granted other than witness protection and did not disclose to defense counsel requested information about compensation or incentives to testify (Manitoba, 2007, p. 45).

Although both informants were given generous consideration for the information they shared with officers and for their testimony, neither the defense nor the court were informed of this consideration. In fact, when defense counsel questioned one of the informants at trial about compensation for his testimony, the informant told the jury that he had lost money and was financially disadvantaged by his cooperation with investigators. The jury was seriously misled as to the informant's considerable motivation to testify against Driskell (Manitoba, 2007, p. 102).

After questions arose about the informant's motivation to testify and their probable perjury, it became clear that the foundation upon which Driskell's conviction was built was crumbling. Driskell continued to proclaim his innocence and fight for vindication. In time, Driskell discovered the Association in Defense of the Wrongfully Convicted (AIDWYC). AIDWYC is a Canadian nonprofit organization whose goal is to identify, advocate for, and work to exonerate those who have been wrongfully convicted. AIDWYC conducted a thorough investigation of Driskell's case.

In 2002, arguing that the microscopic hair evidence on which Driskell's conviction was built was not as reliable as results that could be obtained using newer technology, AIDWYC persuaded Manitoba Justice to perform mtDNA testing on the three hairs that had linked Driskell to Harder's murder. Unlike microscopic hair examination alone, mtDNA testing can identify the contributor of the unknown hair with a greater degree of scientific certainty (Saks and Koehler, 2005). The hairs from Driskell's case were sent to the UK for mtDNA testing by the Forensic Science Service (FSS) (Manitoba, 2007, p. 155). The FSS found that there were several differences between Harder's known hair and the three hairs taken from the van that were determined to be consistent with Harder's hair at trial. The mtDNA proved that the three hairs did not come from Harder. Further, the three hairs did not even match each other; they came from three different individuals (Manitoba, 2007, p. 155). This finding revealed that the "match" was indeed coincidental and proved that the only physical link between Driskell and the murder of Perry Harder was nonexistent.

Although the hair comparison techniques used to analyze the three hairs from the van did not result in error—the three hairs were, after all, microscopically similar to the known samples, and the victim could not be excluded as the source of those three hairs by microscopic comparison analysis—the real possibility that these hairs coincidentally "matched" the victim's hair should have been explained to the jury in a meaningful way. Because the expert himself believed the probability of a coincidental match was "remote" (Manitoba, p. 151), no one really could explain with any kind of authority what the chances of a coincidental match were. The statistics simply do not exist. With a dearth of statistics, the jury was left with the impression that the three hairs came from the victim.

After the hair microscopy result used to convict Driskell were refined and rectified by mtDNA testing, Driskell filed an application for ministerial review of his conviction as allowed under Section 696.1 of the Canadian Criminal Code (AIDWYC, 2005). In Canada, "[a]nyone convicted of an offence under a federal law or regulation may submit an application for ministerial review" (Minister of Justice, 2011). While the application was being reviewed, Driskell was released on bail. He was finally free after spending 13 years in prison (AIDWYC, 2005).

Based on the mtDNA findings, Driskell's conviction was quashed by the Minister of Justice on March 3, 2005. The Crown decided that there was not enough evidence to pursue another trial, and the proceedings against Driskell were stayed, ending Driskell's nightmare (AIDWYC, 2005). The province of Manitoba and the Queen's Bench do not now dispute that Driskell was incarcerated for over 13 years for a crime he did not commit and for which he should never have been convicted (Manitoba, 2007, p. 1).

Others, including Colin Ross, are not so lucky (Dalton, 2008; Lack and Morgan, 2005; Brennan, 1922, pp. 45.). Although the Ross case closely mirrors the evidence in Driskell, the outcomes were very different, due in large part to Canada's refusal to implement the death penalty as well as the advent of mtDNA testing. The truth came much too late for Ross. Driskell, too, would have every right to argue that the truth came 13 years too late for him, although he is at least able to taste freedom again. Other innocent prisoners remain incarcerated, some waiting for the day the hair evidence used to build the case against them can be reviewed and retested by more discerning means, and others are waiting in vain and paying their penalties in full.

The FBI has long been aware of problems with hair microscopy evidence. In 1996, the Justice Department studied the nation's first 28 DNA exonerations and found 20% of the cases involved hair comparison (Hsu, 2012). That same year (1996), the FBI Laboratory stopped declaring matches in hair cases on visual comparison alone and began requiring DNA testing as well. It would be several years before the FBI would take a look at the thousands of cases that were affected by overstated hair analysis.

In 2012, a strange coalition made up of the FBI, the Innocence Project (IP), and the National Association of Criminal Defense Lawyers (NACDL) began a review of thousands of microscopic hair comparisons performed by FBI examiners (Kaye, 2015). This unlikely coalition was formed after three men, convicted by microscopic hair analysis, were exonerated by DNA testing in 2010 and 2011 (Geddes, 2015). This cluster of hair evidence–related exonerations, coupled with the National Academy of Science report's finding that hair microscopy was lacking in any statistical or scientific foundation, opened the door for scrutiny. In the three cases that led to the review, the prosecution relied primarily on expert testimony from FBI hair examiners to prove the defendants were guilty. It was undeniable that the experts had presented scientifically invalid testimony. Based on these exonerations, the IP approached the FBI and asked that hair cases be scrutinized. After the IP convinced the FBI that there was indeed a problem with how their agents were testifying, the FBI agreed to review all cases where FBI analysts had declared microscopic hair matches. However, the FBI agreed only to look at the expert testimony and would not agree to an investigation into the validity or value of the science underlying the testimony (Neufeld, 2016). What their review revealed is that the same problems that led to injustice for both Ross and Driskell were typical of cases involving the FBI's handling of microscopic hair examination.

As of 2015, they have reviewed transcripts from approximately 500 out of as many as 4000 convictions that involved hair analysis (Geddes, 2015). Of the first 500 cases they reviewed, the FBI provided expert witness testimony concerning hair analysis in 268 cases (Geddes, 2015). In 2015, Geddes reported that 96% of the 268 cases were built on errors or scientifically invalid testimony proffered by FBI agents (Geddes, 2015). This does not mean everyone convicted by flawed or overstated expert testimony was actually innocent, but it does mean that false and compelling scientific evidence contributed to their convictions. For some of these convicts, there is now hope that they will be vindicated. For some of these convicts, there is no path to remedy the injustice that has been done because, of the 33 convicts who received death sentences based on flawed hair evidence, we have executed nine, and five died on death row (Geddes, 2015).

The review found that overclaiming worked to turn evidence that known and unknown hairs were similar into evidence that, for all practical purposes, identified a party. At least this magical transformation took place in the minds of the jurors. Everyone agrees that, to some degree, something has gone very wrong with the FBI's handling of cases involving hair examination. Some, like Kaye, have called out the media for overreacting and dabbling in some overclaiming of its own. Others are eager to end the forensic use of microscopic hair examination forever. Whatever your stance, Kaye has offered a common sense reaction to the problems caused by overreaching:

> *To promote more complete understanding of the nature and extent of overclaiming, the review process should be made more transparent and the materials it produces should be readily available for researchers and the public to study.[1] New state or local evidence reviews should be designed accordingly. Finally, in all areas of forensic science, clear standards for presenting identification evidence without overclaiming should be devised, and training and monitoring programs should be implemented to ensure that laboratory personnel and prosecutors adhere to them.*

Attorneys toiling in the trenches are well aware of how they can use the opinions offered by experts to build or destroy a case. When opinions are rendered by experts then re-rendered by the lawyer in the strongest possible terms and laid at the juror's feet before deliberations commence, a simple and rather ambiguous finding that hairs are similar or that they "match" can seal a conviction. Until clear standards for presenting evidence are devised, identification language will creep into testimony. Because hair analysis is not able to identify a party, any statement that leads the jury to believe it can is an overstatement, and innocent defendants will be convicted.

REFERENCES

AIDWYC, 2005. Jim Driskell. The AIDWYC Journal 5 (Spring 2005), 4. Available as of 05/21/15 at: http://www.aidwyc.org/cases/historical/james-driskell/.

Brennan, T.C., 1922. Gun Alley Tragedy: Record of the Trial of Colin Campbell Ross: Including a Critical Examination of the Crown Case with a Summary of the New Evidence, third ed. Gordon & Gotch, Melbourne. Available as of 05/30/2015 at: http://nla.gov.au/nla. aus-vn4585796.

Cowan, J., 2008. Pardon Not Enough, Murdered Girl's Relative Says. Australian Broadcasting Corporation News. 2008-05-27, available as of 05/30/2015 at: http://www.abc.net.au/ news/2008-05-27/pardon-not-enough-murdered-girls-relative-says/2450334.

Crocker, E.J., 1991. Trace evidence. In: Chayko, G.M., Gulliver, E.D., MacDougall, D.V. (Eds.), Forensic Evidence in Canada. Canada Law Book, Aurora, Ontario, Canada, pp. 259–299.

---

[1] This information is already available because they are part of the public record.

Dalton, S., 2008. The old Melbourne city Watch House: fast-forward to the past. Agora 43 (4), 60.

Fabricant, M.C., Carrington, W.T., 2015. The Shifted Paradigm: Forensic Sciences's Overdue Evolution from Magic to Law. Available at SSRN 2572480.

Geddes, L., 2015. Hanging by a thread. New Scientist 226 (3019), 27.

Hsu, S.S., 2012. Convicted Defendants Left Uninformed of Forensic Flaws Found by Justice Dept. Washington Post, available as of 5/9/2016 at: https://www.washingtonpost.com/local/crime/convicted-defendants-left-uninformed-of-forensic-flaws-found-by-justice-dept/2012/04/16/gIQAWTcgMT_story.html.

Kaladelfos, A., 2010. Murder in Gun Alley: girls, grime and gumshoe history. Journal of Australian Studies 34 (4), 471–484.

Kaye, D.H., 2015. Ultracrepidarianism in forensic science: the hair evidence debacle. Washington & Lee Law Review Online 72.

Lett, D., February 13, 2005. Driskell witness lied about payments: defense lawyer didn't know of $83,000 compensation package. Winnipeg Free Press. Available at Injustice Busters: "James Driskell (6)" http://injusticebusters.org/05/Driskell_James.shtml.

Lack, J., Morgan, K., 2005. Ross, Colin Campbell Eadie (1892–1922). Australian Dictionary of Biography. National Centre of Biography, Supplementary Volume, Australian National University. Retrieved 2008-05-27.

Manitoba. Commission of Inquiry into Certain Aspects of the Trial and Conviction of James Driskell, & LeSage, P., 2007. Report of the Commission of Inquiry into Certain Aspects of the Trial and Conviction of James Driskell.

McQueen, H., 2004. Social Sketches of Australia. Univ. of Queensland Press.

Minister of Justice, 2011. Annual Report. Available as of 5/26/15 at:http://www.justice.gc.ca/eng/rp-pr/cj-jp/ccr-rc/rep11-rap11/p2.html.

Neufeld, P., 2016. Telephone Conversation.

Saks, M.J., Koehler, J.J., 2005. The coming paradigm shift in forensic identification science. Science 309 (5736), 892–895.

Is Microscopic Hair Comparison a Legitimate Science?

Max M. Houck

Forensic & Intelligence Services, LLC, St. Petersburg, FL, United States

WHAT IS THE PROBLEM WITH FORENSIC HAIR EVIDENCE?

Santae Tribble, Kirk L. Odom, and Donald Gates are now free because DNA analysis refuted the results offered by FBI hair examiners that crime scene hairs could have come from them (Hsu, 2014). Thousands of other inmates, including some on death row, await review in what is now the US government's largest postconviction review of forensic evidence, being conducted by the Department of Justice (DOJ).

The validity of forensic microscopic hair examinations has been questioned for some time and, to date, only one study addresses that question.

SANTAE TRIBBLE

Tribble was linked to the homicides of two men by informants. Tribble was tried for both killings, one resulting in acquittal due to a lack of evidence, the other (in 1980) resulting in a conviction and a sentence of 20 years to life. In that trial, an FBI hair examiner testified that a hair from a ski mask "matched in all microscopic characteristics" to the known hairs of Tribble. While there is nothing implicitly wrong with that statement, the prosecutor misstated the result in closing remarks by saying that there was "one chance in 10 million" that the hair belonged to anyone else. In 2012, Tribble's attorneys secured mitochondrial DNA testing of the 13 hairs from the ski mask, none of which matched Tribble, and one, in fact, wasn't even a human hair.

The DOJ's review of FBI hair examinations has looked at one end of the issue, testimony, rather than a holistic review of the methods applied (Kaye, 2015). The DOJ found that all but two examiners testified beyond the limits of science, such as testifying that the hairs "matched" to a "high degree of probability," when there is no basis for such a probability, or even worse, testifying that the hairs came from a specific individual. Those that testified are now faced with the knowledge that some of their conclusions as to the source of the hairs were wrong. The question then remains: if conducted properly, are microscopic hair examinations a legitimate form of science that should be admitted into court? What can be determined from a hair examination? Can hairs identify individuals? What are the limits, and how are they explained to jurors? What was it about the testimony that was so bad? And what should be done about hair examinations in the future?

The reexamination of forensic hair microscopy can be considered a sentinel event for other traditional forensic sciences: how should the criminal justice system address weaknesses in past forensic testimony and methods without damning methods that were considered acceptable at the time and may still serve as useful forensic tools? For example, the traditional ABO system of blood typing[2] used by medicine and clinics for years was also used in forensic laboratories to include or exclude a blood stain into one of the three types, A, B, or O.[3] If a blood stain analysis confirms that a crime scene stain and a suspect have the same blood type (B, for example), it follows that the crime scene blood could have been left by the suspect. If later DNA testing excludes him, does that mean the blood typing was wrong? Technically, no: Because the person's blood type is, in fact, B, the answer is correct as far as it goes. Blood types cover only certain percentages of the population, and the suspected individual is in that group. But the blood typing is wrong as to the *source* of the blood; it did not come from the suspect.

---

[2] The ABO system of categorizing blood is one of many possible systems. Serology, the identification and analysis of body fluids, was used several in forensic tests until DNA usurped their usefulness.

[3] The Rhesus System, or Rh Factor, which tests for the presence of an inherited protein on the surface of red blood cells (positive means the protein is present), was not used by forensic laboratories because of the difficulty in typing the protein and the advent of DNA technologies.

KIRK L. ODOM

Odom was a suspect in a 1981 rape and robbery on Capitol Hill; he came under suspicion because a patrol officer thought he resembled a composite drawing. The victim identified Odom as her attacker in a lineup. During the ensuing trial, an FBI Special Agent testified that a hair from the victim's nightgown was "indistinguishable" from Odom's known sample. The Special Agent then went on to say that he had found hairs to be indistinguishable only "8 or 10 times in the past 10 years, while performing thousands of analyses," thus implying a frequency or rate of occurrence. Odom was convicted on September 9, 1981, and sent to prison. Decades later, in 2009, DNA testing of semen from a crime scene pillowcase and robe, as well as mitochondrial DNA testing of the hair, all excluded Odom. The results were linked to a convicted sex offender. A comparison of photographs contemporary to the crime showed that Odom did not look like the perpetrator. Odom was exonerated and freed in 2012.

This leads to the concept of *resolution*, or the amount of detail that can be deciphered by a given forensic method. Some methods (like DNA) are more specific than others (like blood typing), and even methods within a category are more specific than other similar methods. Nuclear DNA is more specific than mtDNA, for example. To say blood typing was wrong demonstrates a lack of understanding of science and the resolution of scientific methods and a misinterpretation of "error" (Christensen et al., 2014).

This same logic applies to other forensic examinations, including hair microscopy. If a crime scene (or questioned) hair exhibits the same characteristics as hairs from a suitable known sample of hairs from an individual, then the hair appears to be associated with possibly originating from that person. If DNA (either nuclear or mitochondrial) analysis later determines that the individual is excluded as the source of the questioned hair, that does not mean the hair did not visually have the same kind and range of characteristics as the known sample. The conclusion drawn by the microscopic examination of the hair could have been valid, but it had a lower resolution than the DNA analysis.

The DNA analysis relies on the genotype, the genetic profile, of the individual, whereas the microscopy relies on the phenotype, the expression of the genetic profile and its potential. Genotypes are constant (mutations notwithstanding), while phenotypes can vary according to the genotypes' interaction with the environment.

DONALD GATES

Gates was implicated by a police informant in the rape and murder of a Georgetown University student in 1981. Gates had been arrested for failing to appear in court on an unrelated case and provided a hair sample during processing. The informant said that Gates talked him into robbing the student, and then Gates killed her when she resisted. The informant was paid for his information by the police. At trial, an FBI Special Agent testified that he had matched the hairs from the victim's body to Gates' known hairs and that he could remember only two times out of 10,000 cases when he could not distinguish hairs from two different people. Gates was convicted in 1982 and sentences to 20 years to life in prison. In 2007, DNA testing eliminated Gates as the perpetrator.

More details on these and other cases of wrongful conviction can be found at www.innocenceproject.org.

Claiming that hairs are "junk science" and demanding their removal from the forensic landscape ignores their potential to eliminate from consideration or exclude suspects, or even vindicate the wrongfully convicted. When defense attorneys seek to have a hair case reviewed, they would do well to find a knowledgeable hair examiner to review the physical evidence before sending it for DNA analysis, which results in destroying the hair or a portion of it, rather than simply denying that the hair may have some relevance. Hairs have been shown to be useful in investigations, prosecutions, and exonerations. Therefore, it is important to discuss what is the resolution of hair examinations and how that specificity should be communicated to courts and juries.

WHERE DOES HAIR EXAMINATION COME FROM?

In the 17th and 18th centuries, hair was a readymade specimen for scientists like Robert Hooke (1635–1703), Antonie van Leeuwenhoek (1632–1723), and Henry Baker (1698–1774), eager to use a startling new instrument: the microscope (Bisbing, 2002). Renaissance interest in nature and organisms, so-called descriptive biology, meant that the microscope was a natural tool to expand the observations of plants, animals, and their structural components. With this realization and exploration of the depth of the natural world came the desire to categorize living things in a sensible framework, that is, taxonomy (Mayr, 1982).

Early medical and forensic investigations used microscopic observations of hair intermittently, setting the stage for hairs, both human and nonhuman, to be routinely used as evidence (Balthazard and Lambert, 1910; Glaister, 1931; Hoffman, 1898; Marx, 1906). Anthropologists studied human hair in the 20th century as a means to understanding and describing human variation (Garn, 1951; Trotter, 1922, 1930; Trotter and Dawson, 1934). Forensic scientists continued to apply microscopy to the identification and association of hair and used it as evidence (Gamble and Kirk, 1940; Kirk, 1941; Kirk et al., 1941; Kirk and DeForest, 1973).

The establishment of the FBI Laboratory in 1932 and the Law Enforcement Assistance Administration (now the National Institute of Justice) support of nonfederal forensic laboratories in the 1970 and 1980s pushed the boundaries of available science in criminal investigations. The FBI's emphasis on research and training, by establishing the Forensic Science Research and Training Center at Quantico, Virginia, led to a broader use of hair microscopy at state and local laboratories.

In 1977, the FBI published what became the definitive "text" on forensic hair microscopy, *Microscopy of Hairs: A Practical Guide and Manual*, written by Special Agent John Hicks (1977). This booklet was the first summary publication on the topic and helped establish forensic hair microscopy as an applied method in the discipline. Sensationalized cases, like the Atlanta Child Murders, the Goldman–Simpson murders, the murder of Laci Peterson, and others, brought additional attention, both good and bad, to forensic hair microscopy.

Hairs are studied by many sciences, including biology, zoology, anthropology, archeology, chemistry, cosmetic chemistry, pathology, and forensic science (Montagna and Ellis, 1958; Montagna and Dobson, 1969; Montagna and Parakkal, 1974; Paus and Cotsarelis, 1999). The analyses in other disciplines are microscopic or biochemical in nature, although other types of examination can be performed (testing a new cosmetic hair dye, for example) (Benner et al., 2003; Midler and Karleskind, 1978; Parakkal et al., 1963). These all relate to the general nature of hairs and their characteristics or their responses to treatments (class characteristics). Forensic scientists are the only ones, however, that routinely are concerned with *source attribution*, which attempts to determine whether a hair came from a specific individual.

WHAT IS SOURCE ATTRIBUTION?

Forensic science works at two levels of information: class and source attribution (often called individual). All things are considered to be unique; no two objects are identical (Bell and Borely, 1999). They can, however, be grouped according to criteria that help distinguish sets of items from one another. The class level of information is the examination of the chemical and physical properties of an object and categorizing it as a member of a group. Once its group membership is established, it has been identified.

IDENTIFICATION

Confusingly, forensic sciences use the word "identification" to mean more than one process. In one sense, it means the classification of objects into groups, as described in the text. In another sense, "identifications" mean the sourcing of something to one and only one source, typically an individual through biometric methods (DNA, fingerprints, dental X-rays). This dual meaning has developed over time as "terms of art" and, while unavoidable, can be misleading if the distinction is not understood.

All the characteristics used to identify an object refine that object's membership in one or more groups. Performing an analysis on a white powder and concluding it is cocaine, determining that a small, colored chip is automotive paint, and examining debris from a crime scene and deciding it contains hairs from a dog are all examples of identification. This description places the hairs into a group of objects with similar characteristics, called a class (Houck, 2012). As the object and methods allow, the process of identification of evidence can be increasingly specific, and the object may be classified into groups with successively fewer members. A class has a movable definition. For a particular case, it may not be required to classify the objects beyond dog hairs because something else is sought, like human hairs.

Stating that two objects are members of the same class suggests they could have come from a common source, the same dog, for example. But what is meant by "common source" depends on a variety of things, like what the object is made of, how it was made, the specificity of the criteria used to classify the object, among many others. The object itself may limit the specificity: it may not be possible to further classify the dog hairs beyond being "dog hairs" because the breed of that dog cannot be determined through microscopic hair traits, that dog's hairs are less specific (mixed breed, perhaps), or the hairs may be damaged, and information useful to further specification is gone.

In forensic science, if an object can be grouped into a class with only one member, it is said to have been *individualized*. *Individualized* is used synonymously with the word *identified* (discussed in Sidebar Identification). An individualized object has been associated with one, and only one, source. To that extent, individualization is a logical theoretical extension of classification.

The concept of individualization rests on two assumptions. The first is that all things are unique in space and time, and the second is that the properties by which a thing is classified are constant over time. These two assumptions come with baggage, however. First, the assumption of uniqueness of space is acceptable but not scientifically provable (Cole, 2009). Thus, any claim that a questioned object has one and only one source is untenable. The population size of all members of any one class (hairs, fingerprints, bullets) is too large to account for. Thus, regardless of how similar a questioned hair is to a sample of known hairs, you cannot scientifically prove that the questioned hair has the same source as the known hairs. You have not looked at all the sources of hair.

Second, the assumption of consistency over time is a matter of degree, not kind. Nothing in the universe is immutable, and entropy always wins (Lindsay, 1959). Some objects are more stable than others, even in biology (Yoon and Jain, 2015), but ultimately will degrade to the point where the discriminating criteria are no longer useful. Without definitive assignment of an object to one and only one source, forensic science should be relegated to making interpretive statements based on statistical methods. As Schum (1994, p. 2) clearly explains,

> *Such evidence, if it existed, would make necessary a particular hypothesis or possible conclusion being entertained. In lieu of such perfection we often make use of masses of inconclusive evidence having additional properties: The evidence is incomplete on matters relevant to our conclusions, and it comes to us from sources (including our own observations) that are, for various reasons, not completely credible. Thus, inferences from such evidence can only be probabilistic in nature.*

Schum's point is that if scientists were absolutely certain of their samples or the accuracy of their methods, statistics would not be needed. Forensic science deals with the ultimate uncertainties in the real world of criminal activities with varying physical objects. The gap between the controlled laboratory and the real world is central to forensic science's fundamentals: uncertainty is everywhere. Even in DNA analysis, where each person's genetic material—except for identical twins—is known to be unique, statistics are used. Statistics are, in fact, what give forensic DNA analysis its power.

WHAT ARE HAIRS AND HOW DO THEY "FUNCTION"?

Hairs are a specific biological structure found only on the skin of mammals; other animals may have structures that appear to be or are even called hairs, like the "hairs" on a tarantula, but they are not true hairs. Hairs grow from the skin (epidermis) in a structure called the follicle that is a cylindrical tube with a wider pit at the base (Fig. 2.1). Hairs grow from the bottom of the follicle upward towards the skin. At the base of the follicle (the papilla), the hair is still very soft; as the hair grows up the follicle, it slowly begins to harden and dry out. Hair is made of keratin, a tough, protein-based material from which nails, horns, and scales are also made; the hardening process is called keratinization. Hair is one of the most durable materials produced by nature. This is one reason hairs can be good forensic evidence: they persist and are stable for long periods of time.

Hairs go through three phases of growth. In the actively growing phase, called anagen, the follicle continually produces new cells in a hair as it grows up from the bottom of the follicle. Specialized cells in the follicle produce small, colored granules, called melanin, that give hairs their color; these cells are called melanocytes. The active growth phase lasts for a length of time depending on a person's genetics and the kind of hair in question. The follicles of head hairs, the longest hairs on a human, can stay in the anagen phase for many years. After a period of time, the hair transitions into a

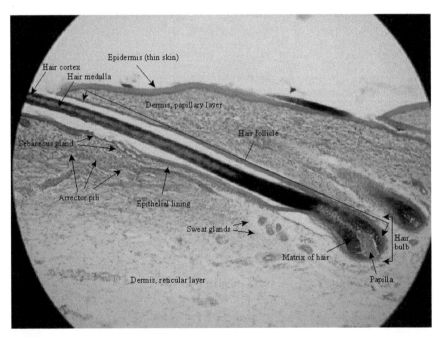

FIGURE 2.1

Cross-section of the skin, a hair follicle, and a hair.

resting phase, called the catagen phase. In the catagen phase, the follicle shuts down production of hair cells, the cells begin to shrink, and the root condenses into a bulb-shaped structure called a root bulb. The catagen phase lasts only a few weeks. Finally, the hair moves into the telogen phase, which is the resting phase for the follicle. Cell production has ceased completely, the root has condensed into a bulb, and the hair is held in place by a mechanical connection at the base of the root and follicle. When this mechanical connection is broken through combing, brushing, or other activity, the hair is shed. This signals the follicle to return to the anagen phase, and the cycle begins again. It is said that humans, on average, lose about 100 scalp hairs a day, providing an adequate and constant source of potential evidence for transfer and collection.

WHAT DO HAIRS LOOK LIKE UNDER A MICROSCOPE?

A hair is complicated with many intricately organized structures, only some of which are visible under the microscope. A single hair has a root, a shaft, and a tip. The root is that portion that formerly was in the follicle. The shaft is the main portion of the hair, and the tip is the furthermost point of the hair.

The three main internal structures in a hair are the cuticle, the cortex, and the medulla. The cuticle is a series of overlapping layers of scales that act as a protective covering. Animal hairs have patterns of scales that vary by species, and these patterns are a useful diagnostic tool for identifying animal hairs. Humans have only one scale pattern, called imbricate. Despite historical attempts to use scales as an individualizing tool for human hairs (for example, see Kirk, 1940), they are not generally useful in forensic examinations. The next structure is the cortex that makes up the bulk of the hair. The cortex consists of needle-shaped cells that contain or constrain other structures. Pigment granules are found in the cortex, dispersed variably throughout it. The granules vary in size, shape, and distribution, which are useful in forensic comparisons. Other structures, like cortical fusi (small air bubbles trapped in the cortex) or ovoid bodies (large collections of pigment), may appear irregularly in the cortex. Hair micro-anatomy provides a rich source of visual information for classification and comparison.

Hairs, whether human or from an animal, are often associated with criminal activity. The determination of the potential source of a hair is often of interest to the investigators and the principal reason for a microscopical examination and possible comparison. The process of hair examination is a process of forensic classification (Hicks, 1977):

- Is the object a hair?
- If it is, is it human or animal?
  - If it is an animal hair, what kind of animal did it come from (order, genus, species)?
  - If it is a human hair, the hair is examined for the following information:
    - body area of origin (head, pubic, etc.)
    - estimation of ancestry (race)

- evaluation of root for growth phase and presence of tissue
- evaluation for damage, disease, and treatment; and
- assessment of the hair's suitability for microscopic comparison.

Forensic hair examination and comparison is a biological discipline grounded in microscopy, biology, anatomy, histology, and anthropology.

HOW CAN YOU TELL IF A HAIR IS HUMAN OR NOT?

It is relatively easy to determine whether a hair is from a human or another animal by a simple microscopic examination. Determining what kind of animal hair it is, however, may be more difficult. Animal hairs have several macroscopic characteristics that distinguish them from those of humans (Moore, 1988). For example, some animal hairs are color-banded, showing abrupt color transitions along the shaft of the hair, including the tip. As a simple identification of human or animal, this is a highly reliable class categorization.

CAN YOU DETERMINE WHERE ON A BODY THE HAIR ORIGINATED?

From this point on, human hairs are the topic of discussion. Unlike other animals, humans exhibit a wide variety of hair forms on their bodies; animals have only three types: fur, guard, and whiskers. The characteristics of various human hairs may allow for an estimation of body area origin. The typical body areas that can be determined are head (or scalp), pubic, and facial. Other body areas, like the chest, armpits, and eyelashes, may have distinctive features, but only head and pubic hairs are considered suitable for microscopic comparison. Hairs from other parts of the body do not have sufficient information for comparisons; they tend to be highly variable in the expression of their traits.

Nevertheless, classifying a hair as only a body hair may have important consequences for a case. For example, in one reported case, an adult pubic-area hair was found on a preadolescent victim. A girl of that age could not have biologically produced a pubic-area hair. Because the hair was not truly a pubic hair, it was not suitable for microscopic comparison. DNA from the hair had the same mitochondrial sequence as the suspect; this, in addition to overwhelming trace evidence associating the suspect with the crime, led to a guilty plea [see Ryland and Houck (2000) for more information]. Thus, the value of a hair examination can have many facets.

CAN A PERSON'S RACE BE DETERMINED BY HAIRS?

The general morphology and color of a hair may give an indication of a person's ancestry, but it is only an estimate. Humans exhibit more variation between individuals in hair morphology than any other primate, and this variation tends to correlate with a person's ancestry. For simplicity and accuracy, three main ancestral groups are used: Europeans, Africans, and Asians. In older anthropological and forensic literature, these groups were called Caucasoids, Negroids, and Mongoloids. These terms are archaic and should not be used. The groups are broad and inclusive on purpose (the traits ascribed to "European" include some Hispanics and peoples of the Middle East, for instance), and the geographic terms are as accurate, but less potentially offensive.

Importantly, the estimated ancestry based on hair characteristics may not correlate with how a person identifies racially. In fact, many physical anthropologists have all but given up on the idea of race as a biological reality, instead calling it a social construct, and most deal in populations (Caspari, 2003). Ancestry may be estimated by an examiner, but extreme caution is advised; other dominant traits, like color, may help to exclude hairs without needing to assess race.

WHAT CAN THE GROWTH PHASE OF A HAIR DETERMINE?

As noted previously, hairs go through three phases of growth: active, transitional, and resting. While the growth phase may seem unimportant, there are some characteristics that may be of additional use, like the presence of tissue on the root or shaft of the hair. Forcibly removed hairs may take some of the follicle tissue with them when they are pulled, in a violent struggle, for example. This tissue may be sufficient for nuclear DNA analysis; without tissue on the root, the hair may be relegated to mtDNA analysis. In addition to any physical or microscopic information available from the hair, it is important to note what, if any, DNA testing can be conducted on the hair.

WHAT ABOUT DISEASED, DAMAGED, OR TREATED HAIRS?

Hair is subject to disease, damage, and treatments, all of which are "recorded" in the hair. A handful of diseases manifest themselves in hair, some genetic, some acquired. For example, pili annulati is an inherited condition where the hairs appear to be ringed or banded (Fig. 2.2). Hairs can be damaged by a variety of situations, and they have diagnostic results. The tips of hairs can provide good information about how the hair has been treated. For example, burned hairs present a specific image, as do hairs cut by scissors, razors, or glass (Fig. 2.3). Scissor-cut hair has a straight border, whereas razor-cut hair is angled; even razor cuts vary by blade design. Burned hair is blackened and may appear bubbled or expanded.

Hair is a cultural signal, and humans do many different things to their hair—cutting, dyeing, braiding, shaving—to send messages about status and identity. Artificial treatments like bleaching and dyeing chemically alter the hair and its appearance. Bleaching the hair oxidizes the pigmentation and removes its color. At this point, a new color

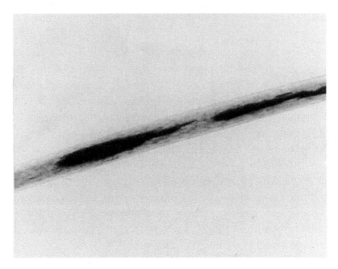

FIGURE 2.2

Pili annulati is a rare genetic condition where the hairs appear to be ringed or banded.

FBI.

(A) **(B)** **(C)**

(D)

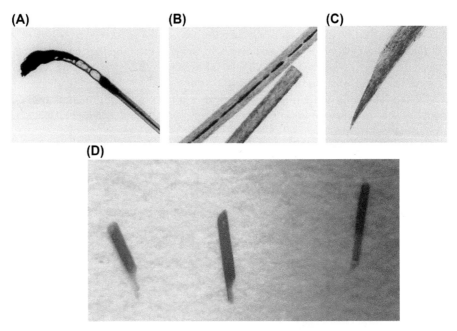

FIGURE 2.3

Hairs can "record" the damage done to them. (A) A hair that has been singed or burned. (B) A hair cut with scissors, which pinch the hair and cleanly break it. (C) A hair cut with a razor. (D) Beard hairs cut with double-edge safety razor (top edge) and multiblade razor (bottom edge); the safety razor made one straight cut, while the multiblade can be seen to cut into the hair, pull it, and then subsequent blades cut the rest.

(A–C) FBI and (D) Reddit user heisenbrau (downloaded October 1, 2015).

may be added to the hair in a process very similar to dyeing wool fibers (both are hair). The point where the treatment was applied becomes visible as an abrupt color change, and this becomes more obvious as the hair grows.

Other characteristics, like lice, fungus, or postmortem root banding (see Koch et al., 2013) may also be present on hairs, and these facts should be noted. Because not all hair has the same history or conditions, examining and describing microscopic conditions of hairs can be an excellent method for sorting hairs and potentially excluding individuals. The identification of postmortem root banding, a kind of microscopic decomposition, assisted in the exoneration of three men in New York, for example (Levy, 2015).

Descriptive examinations of hairs are useful, as far as they can go. If human hairs are sought and cat hairs or textile fibers are found, then the examination is complete. If blond head hairs are of interest and brown pubic hairs are discovered, nothing more is needed. If the suspect had dyed red hair and the hairs from the scene are dyed red, then the suspect is not excluded (as far as the hairs go). Most forensic examinations are stronger in exclusion than inclusion because of the categorical nature of a hierarchical decision tree (Houck, 2012). But what is to be done if all the categorical traits align between a questioned sample from the crime scene and a known sample of hairs? A comparison between the two samples is the next step.

WHAT IS INVOLVED IN A HAIR COMPARISON BY MICROSCOPY?

Much like in the examination process, forensic hair examiners concentrate on microscopic features for comparison. For human hairs, these characteristics can be described in a variety of ways, such as in Fig. 2.4. Any list created is not definitive or exhaustive; no set of standard criteria exists. A comparison is conducted between samples collected from the crime scene or evidence therefrom and a known sample of hairs from an individual of interest. The samples from the scene, victim, or suspect are of a known provenance (where or what from the hairs were collected) but of an unknown or questioned source; hence, these hairs are often called questioned samples or hairs. Samples of hairs from a known source are called known or exemplar hairs. Comparisons must be between like kinds of hairs (scalp to scalp, pubic to pubic, etc.); otherwise, one of the class characteristics will not be the same.

A questioned sample may consist of one or more hairs. A known sample should consist of 50 or more hairs from the area in question and should encompass the variation of the area. For example, hairs at the temples may be graying, dyed hair may be streaked, or lengths may vary. The known sample must be representative of the body area in question. Too often, insufficient known samples are collected, and this hampers the forensic examination. Hair samples should be as contemporaneous as possible, as hair characteristics may vary over time (remember, the phenotype can vary, the genotype cannot).

Root	Scale length	Cortex cells
abundant fusi	short	Pigment size
telogen	medium	shape
anagen	long	density
decomp	Scale overlap	distribution
stretched	slight	patchy
follicular tag	medium	streaky
Tip	large	chaining
cut	Cuticle thickness	Pigment gapping
broken	thin	shallow
split	medium	medium
pointed	thick	deep
rounded	fluctuation	short
Width	Medulla	medium
coarse	absent	long
fine	translucent	Cosmetic
variation along shaft	fragmented	
variation w/in sample	transparent	bleached
Cuticle	discontinuous	dyed
clarity	opaque	time since treatment
color	continuous	Special
damage	cell shape	cracked
Scale protrusion	thick	ovoids
slight	thin	double medulla
medium	medium	diseases
large		Damage vermin

FIGURE 2.4

A range of macro- and microscopic characteristics to describe hairs in a forensic examination. This list is not exhaustive or definitive; the viewing of microscopic traits involves the subjective evaluation of objective criteria.

In a comparison, the known hairs should be examined first. Each hair in the selected sample is examined one at a time, and the sample is thoroughly described with regard to all of the observable characteristics. The variation shown along each hair shaft is noted for each characteristic, and the process is repeated for each hair examined. A description of hair from each individual that expresses the range of traits observed for each characteristic and any significant special features or uncommon traits is recorded. The description is for the sample collectively. The questioned hairs are likewise scrutinized and characterized, but individually.

Finally, the selected hairs from the known are compared with each questioned hair of interest using a comparison microscope. A comparison microscope joins two transmitted light microscopes to provide a split view, right and left. The side-by-side analysis will either support or reject the apparent similarities between known and questioned hair. All characteristics of both the known and unknown specimens must be considered. A single significant difference between the two is a stronger indication of separate sources and could lead to an inconclusive result. Several repeated, fundamental dissimilarities between the known and questioned hairs establish that two specimens are not from a single individual. A positive association rests therefore not only on a combination of corresponding traits, but also on a consistent lack of any dissimilarities between the questioned and known hairs.

Three conclusions can be drawn from a hair comparison. First, the questioned hair exhibits the same microscopic characteristics as the known sample and could have originated from the same source. Second, the questioned hair exhibits different microscopic characteristics as the known sample and is excluded from originating from that source. And, finally, the questioned hair exhibits similarities to and differences from the known sample, and no conclusion can be drawn about the association between the two samples.

When a questioned hair is positively associated with a known source, two logical possibilities exist: either the hair actually originated from the same source as the known hair or it is a coincidental association, that is, while the hairs appear the same, they are from different sources. Since it is possible for two different individuals to have hairs that are microscopically indistinguishable, it has been known that coincidental matches can occur in forensic hair comparisons for some time. Therefore, hairs are not a form of positive identification and never should be relied upon as such (Gaudette and Keeping, 1974; Gaudette, 1976, 1999; Mann, 1990; Wickenheiser and Hepworth, 1990; Bisbing, 2002; Houck and Budowle, 2002).

HOW ACCURATE ARE HAIR EXAMINATIONS?

The goal of forensic hair examinations is the microscopic comparison of a questioned hair or hairs from a crime scene to a known hair sample using a comparison microscope. Research has been conducted to evaluate the resolution of and limits to hair comparisons (Gaudette and Keeping, 1974; Gaudette, 1976, 1999; Mann, 1990; Wickenheiser and Hepworth, 1990; Bisbing, 2002; Houck and Budowle, 2002). To date, no universal approach for estimating or calculating significance has been produced; for microscopy, probably none will be (Gaudette, 1978, 1982; Houck, 1999). Hairs are a complicated biological material, and the expression of hair characteristics across the population is variable. Being 3-D makes quantifying the traits that much more difficult. And now that DNA analysis is more accessible, a statistical approach based on microscopic examination is hardly justified.

Nonetheless, the clinical studies to date are illustrative of the validity of a properly conducted microscopical hair examination (Table 2.1). The use of statistics

Table 2.1 Results of Houck and Budowle (2002)

		Mitochondrial Results			
		Association	**Inconclusive**	**Exclusion**	**Insufficient**
Microscopic results	Association	69	1	9	1
	Inconclusive	15	1	20	1
	Exclusion	0	1	17	1
	Insufficient	13	0	18	3

in evaluating the significance of forensic hair comparisons has been the subject of extensive debate (Gaudette, 1976, 1999, 1985; Gaudette and Keeping, 1974). The appearance of a particular hair characteristic is usually not constant along successive portions of a single hair from root to tip. In some hairs, only slight changes are seen; in others, great changes occur. The variation in any one characteristic for any single hair depends on genetic factors and external factors, such as growth phase, hair length, health, environment, and grooming habits. In addition, hair characteristics may change with age and fashion. Therefore, databases upon which population statistics can be generated, as is done in DNA analysis, is not practical.

But how should we interpret the results of a forensic hair comparison? This process is not as simple as might be imagined. Wording of microscopic hair examination results usually takes the following forms:

- A hair sample from the crime scene and another taken from (the defendant) were "similar" and "consistent."
- The pubic hairs from the crime and (the defendant's) pubic hairs exhibited "similar microscopic characteristics."
- The hairs from the crime scene were "similar" to (the defendant's).
- Hairs from the crime scene exhibited "the same microscopic characteristics" as (the defendant's) hair.

A fundamental misunderstanding about what can and cannot be said with hair evidence lies at the heart of this issue; none of the preceding statements are beyond the realm of what is considered reasonable testimony. But how specific are these statements, and what notions do they convey to laypersons?

The advent of forensic mtDNA in the mid-1990s heralded a new era of biological analysis in forensic science. This was especially true for hairs because it offered a way to add information to microscopic hair examinations; in 1996, the FBI instituted a policy that all positive microscopic associations of hairs were to be checked by DNA analysis. MtDNA sequencing added another test for assessing the significance of attributing a hair to an individual. Neither the microscopic nor molecular analysis alone, or together, provides positive identification. The two methods complement each other and maximize the information provided. For example, mtDNA typing can often distinguish between hairs from different sources, although they have similar, or insufficient, microscopic hair characteristics; the microscope can tell you the sample is a hair and not a synthetic wig fiber that contains no DNA. MtDNA typing has proved to be a valuable forensic tool (Melton, 2005).

In the only study of its kind to date, the results of microscopic and mitochondrial examinations of human hairs submitted to the FBI Laboratory for analysis were reviewed (Houck and Budowle, 2002). Of 170 hair examinations, 80 hairs were suitable for microscopic associations. Only nine of the hairs associated by microscopy were excluded by mtDNA. Sixty-six hairs that were either unsuitable for microscopic examinations or yielded inconclusive microscopic associations were analyzed with mtDNA; six of these hairs did not provide enough mtDNA, and another three yielded inconclusive results. This study demonstrates the strength of combining the two techniques.

Despite its critics, hair is a potentially important type of physical evidence, and the combination of microscopical and mtDNA examinations has made it far more powerful and reliable than ever before. Aristotle said, "[i]t is the mark of an educated man to look for precision in each class of things just so far as the nature of the subject admits," and, thus, to look for—or claim—more precision in microscopic hair comparisons than is in the nature of hairs is foolish.[4] What does a positive association of known and questioned hair samples mean? It means that the questioned hair(s) could have come from the same source as the known hairs; that is all. If that does not sound terribly convincing, that is because it is not, at least as far as that wording goes. The lack of statistical backing for assessing the strength of a hair conclusion limits the specificity of the statements that can be made; language does not have the same level of precision for minute differences as does statistics. The examiner is stuck with an imprecise tool to describe a nuanced result. The Houck and Budowle study was clear that its results did not establish an error rate; the sample was ad hoc (casework involving hairs to date) and, although large by forensic standards, insufficient from which to draw larger conclusions. How, then, to approach assessing the strength and reliability of hair examinations?

Sensitivity and specificity are performance measures of binary classification tests (true/false, correct/wrong, present/absent) used in medicine and other statistical applications, like epidemiology. The following terms are used:

- **sensitivity**: true positive rate
- **specificity**: true negative rate
- **precision** (positive predictive value, or PPV): proportion of true positives against all positive results
- **negative predictive value** (NPV): proportion of true negatives against all negative results
- **accuracy**: proportion of true results

As an example of sensitivity and specificity of hair examinations, the results from the Houck and Budowle study are shown below. The insufficient results were excluded from the following analyses. The difference between the associations and exclusions concluded by mtDNA that microscopic comparison called inconclusive was less than 3% of the sample size; therefore, the inconclusive results were excluded from this example. Removing insufficient and inconclusive results, microscopic hair comparisons (as judged against mitochondrial results) perform as follows (Table 2.2):

The value of microscopic hair comparisons in exclusion (NPV = 1.0) is higher than in associations (PPV, or precision = 0.88), as has been noted anecdotally in the literature. Microscopic hair comparisons are a highly sensitive (1.0), but only

---

[4] Numerous critics and journalists have tried to say that hair microscopy was touted as a means of personal identification. Nowhere in the peer-reviewed literature and in no publicly available statement from a credible authority that the author is aware of has this claim been made with supportable data. To say that hairs have been widely called a means of positive personal identification by any individual or agency is fiction.

Table 2.2 Sensitivity and Selectivity Calculations

		Mitochondrial Results		
Microscopic result		Positive association	Negative association	
	Positive association	69 true positives	9 false positives	0.88 precision
	Negative association	0 false negatives	17 true negatives	1.00 negative predictive value
		1.00 sensitivity	0.65 specificity	0.91 accuracy

From Houck, M.M., Budowle, B., 2002. Correlation of microscopic and mitochondrial DNA analysis of hairs. Journal of Forensic Sciences 45 (5), 1–4.

moderately specific test (0.65). An accuracy of 0.91 and a precision of 0.88 would argue in favor of the method, all things being equal. The numbers from the Houck and Budowle study are based on the results of FBI hair examiners and are specific to their levels of education, training, and experience.

The exonerations of Tribble, Odom, and Gates in Washington, D.C. would argue that something is amiss in the case-specific application of the method. Thus, microscopic hair examinations have utility in forensic investigations, largely through description and exclusions, but positive associations of any significant evidence should be the province of DNA analysis.

TESTIMONY

With the foregoing discussion about the accuracy of microscopic hair examinations, it is important that forensic hair examiners be cautious about how they testify. The wording used to describe the significance of a positive association provides a scale, even if implicit, to the court (Houck, 1999). The examiner is left in a quandary: how to describe the relative strength of an association without using statistics? What words can convey the strength of the results without resorting to quasi- or semiquantitative terminology? Only stating that two hairs were compared and corresponded in all observed characteristics without rendering an opinion as to what that correspondence means abrogates the examiner's role as expert: they are present for the purpose of and explicitly allowed (under Federal Rules of Evidence 702) to provide their opinion. Questions like, "How certain are you of your results?" and "Are your results accurate to a reasonable degree of scientific certainty?" do not help clarify the outcome for the court.

To that end, statistics regarding a positive hair comparison must not be presented to the court. They may, however, be discussed with regard to the forensic literature, clinical attempts to assess the specificity and sensitivity of microscopic hair examinations, or other aspects of the studies as they pertain to basic forensic research. Because of the structure of the published research, the statistics used in the published forensic literature are not applicable to any one case. Neither are estimates based on casework experience; by its nature, casework has no accurate, verifiable answers like research does. Sufficient examples exist, regrettably, to act as cautionary object lessons (Connors et al., 1996; Scheck et al., 2000).

DEPARTMENT OF JUSTICE HAIR TESTIMONY REVIEW

The DOJ is reviewing over 20,000 cases from the FBI Laboratory involving hair microscopy. Of those, only about 1600 involve positive associations between a questioned hair and an individual. The DOJ, with the FBI Laboratory, cooperated with the IP and the NACDL on this review. While including case files (presumably), the testimony of the individual examiners was the focal point of the review. Three types of errors in testimony were looked for:

- Type I, where an examiner said or implied that the questioned hair could be associated with an individual to the exclusion of all others;
- Type II, where an examiner assigned to the association a statistical weight or probability or "provided a likelihood that the questioned hair originated from a particular source...that could lead the jury to believe that valid statistical weight can be assigned" (Reimer, 2013); and
- Type III, when an examiner cites the number of cases worked or hairs examined as a basis to bolster the conclusion.

In April of 2015, the FBI issued a statement acknowledging that FBI examiners' testimony in at least 90% of 268 trial transcripts contained erroneous statements (FBI, 2015). The media was breathless in its reinterpretation of these results: hairs were discredited, "fairytale...evidence" (Allocca, 2015), and misstated that the FBI was "wrong in 96% of cases" (Slobidian, 2015). The FBI has recommended that states whose forensic agencies conduct hair examinations initiate their own case reviews; Texas and Massachusetts have already begun. Case closed on hairs?

Not quite. In an excellent exposition on this issue, Kaye questions the 90% figure:

On the basis of some of the scientific literature on hair comparisons, the public descriptions of the hair review project that have emerged, and some of the confessions of scientific error that the FBI has issued, it reaches three conclusions: (1) associating two hairs by their physical features can be at least slightly probative of whether they originated from the same source; (2) the hair review project does not bear on the validity of these associations or the quality of the examinations; rather, it is supposed to flag cases in which examiners have overstated the power of a match to identify the source of the trace evidence; (3) some questionable determinations have been issued, the 90% figure may not be a valid and reliable measure of overclaiming

Kaye (2015, p. 247)

Did examiners overstate their results? Yes, sadly. Are hair examiners hampered by a lack of precision in language to communicate their results? Yes, frustratingly. Any microscopic hair examinations must be followed up with DNA analysis; the qualitative assessment of hairs by microscopy, while accurate to a measureable degree as discussed previously, is still subject to potentially significant examiner bias. Testimony becomes less problematic because the DNA cross-checks the microscopic exam, and a number of some sort can be assigned to the likelihood of identification. Hairs as evidence have some probative value; only one study to date looks at anything like accuracy, and not everyone may agree with the "rules" set forth in the DOJ hair review (as outlined by the NACDL and created by the FBI). Until cooler heads like Kaye's prevail, the future for forensic hair examinations is murky, at best.

WHAT COMES NEXT FOR HAIRS?

When coupled with DNA analysis, hair microscopy has strong value in excluding individuals from being the source of a questioned hair. Microscopy and DNA analysis can provide important information to an investigation because they both analyze different characteristics. The question left hanging is to what extent microscopic examinations should be conducted prior to DNA analysis. "[I]t may well be the case that there will be little if any reduction in the level of microscopic examination as it will be both necessary and desirable to eliminate as many questioned hairs as possible and concentrate mtDNA analysis on only key hairs" (Robertson, 1999, p. 127). The data in the Houck and Budowle study support the usefulness of both methods and for different reasons (phenotypic and genotypic).

For those who may doubt the need for a microscopic examination of hairs, consider the following scenario. Hairs recovered from a bandana reportedly left at the crime scene were analyzed for their mtDNA and found to contain the same mtDNA type as the defendant, and the frequency was reported to be 1 in 5000. Based on the microscopic descriptions of the hairs from two separate laboratories, the questioned hairs were described as light to reddish-brown, but the defendant had short-cropped black hair, similar to African Americans. The investigators request that the hairs be examined microscopically and compared directly with the defendant's known sample. The defendant's hair is short and black; the questioned hairs are longer, straighter, and finer than the known hairs; moreover, they are bleached. A clear line of demarcation between the grown-out root and the bleached shaft is readily observable when under the microscope. The defendant never had bleached hair. The questioned hair could not have been the defendant's; it could, perhaps, have come from a maternal relative, as mitochondrial sequences are inherited through the mother's lineage. Thus, while the mtDNA results could have led to a conviction, hair microscopy provided vital information that excluded the defendant. This cautionary tale is based on a real case, one that initially involved no hair microscopy at all.

Throwing out the scientific baby with the testimonial bathwater helps no one. What would help would be targeted research to assist in the assessment of the resolution of hair microscopy and better practices by examiners conveying hair comparison results to juries. The more evidence that is ignored, the worse the criminal justice system becomes for victim and defendant alike.

REFERENCES

Alloca, S., July 7, 2015. In the public eye: FBI's fairytale hair evidence and the real-life consequences. Forensic Magazine. Online at: www.forensicmag.com/videos/2015/07/public-eye-fbis-fairytale-hairevidence-and-real-lifeconsequences?et_cid=4663527&et_rid=454869145&location=top.

Balthazard, V., Lambert, M., 1910. Le poil de l' homme et desanimaux. G. Steinheil, Paris, France.

Ball, P., Borley, N.R., 1999. The Self-made Tapestry: Pattern Formation in Nature, vol. 198. Oxford University Press, Oxford.

Benner, B.A., Goodpaster, J.V., DeGrasse, J.A., Tully, L.A., Levin, B.C., 2003. Characterization of surface organic components of human hair by on-line supercritical fluid extraction-gas chromatography/mass spectrometry: a feasibility study and comparison with human identification using mitochondrial DNA sequences. Journal of Forensic Sciences 48, 1.

Bisbing, R., 2002. Forensic hair comparisons. In: Saferstein, R. (Ed.), Forensic Science Handbook, vol. 1. second ed. Prentice-Hall, Englewood Cliffs, NJ.

Caspari, R., 2003. From types to populations: a century of race, physical anthropology, and the American Anthropological Association. American Anthropologist 105 (1), 65–76.

Christensen, A., Crowder, C.M., Ousley, S.D., Houck, M.M., 2014. Error and its meaning in forensic science. Journal of Forensic Sciences 59 (1), 123–126.

Cole, S.A., 2009. Forensics without uniqueness, conclusions without individualization: the new epistemology of forensic identification. Law, Probability and Risk 8 (3), 233–255.

Connors, E.F., McEwen, T., Lundregan, T., Miller, N., 1996. Convicted by Juries, Exonerated by Science—Case Studies in the Use of DNA Evidence to Establish Innocence after Trial. US Government Printing Office, Washington, DC.

Federal Bureau of Investigation, April 20, 2015. FBI Testimony on Microscopic Hair Analysis Contained Errors in at Least 90 Percent of Cases in Ongoing Review. Press Release. Online at: www.fbi.gov/news/pressrel/pressreleases/fbi-testimony-on-microscopic-hair-analysis-contained-errors-in-at-least-90-percent-of-cases-in-ongoing-review.

Gamble, L.H., Kirk, P., 1940. Human hair studies II: scale counts. Journal of Criminal Law, Criminology, and Police Science 31, 627.

Garn, S.M., 1951. Types and distribution of the hair in man. Annals of the New York Academy of Sciences 53, 498.

Gaudette, B., 1976. Probabilities and human pubic hair comparisons. Journal of Forensic Sciences 21, 514–517.

Gaudette, B., 1978. Some further thoughts on probabilities and human hair comparisons. Journal of Forensic Sciences 23, 758–763.

Gaudette, B., Keeping, E.S., 1974. An attempt at determining probabilities in human scalp hair comparison. Journal of Forensic Sciences 19, 599–606.

Gaudette, B., 1982. A supplementary discussion of probabilities and human hair comparisons. Journal of Forensic Sciences 27, 279–289.

Gaudette, B., 1985. Strong negative conclusions: a rare event. Canadian Society of Forensic Science Journal 18, 32.

Gaudette, B., 1999. Evidial value of hair examination. In: Robertson, J. (Ed.), Forensic Examination of Hair. Taylor and Francis, London, UK.

Glaister, J., 1931. A Study of Hairs and Wools (Belonging to the Mammalian Group of Animals, Including a Special Study of Human Hair, Considered from a Medico-legal Aspect). Egyptian University Library, Giza, Egypt.

Hicks, J.W., 1977. Microscopy of Hairs—a Practical Guide and Manual. Federal Bureau of Investigation, Washington, DC.

Hoffman, V., 1898. Lehrbuch der perichtlichen medizin. Vienna, Austria.

Houck, M.M., Budowle, B., 2002. Correlation of microscopic and mitochondrial DNA analysis of hairs. Journal of Forensic Sciences 45 (5), 1–4.

Houck, M.M., October 1999. Statistics and trace evidence: the tyranny of numbers. Forensic Science Communications. 1 (3). www.fbi.gov.

Houck, M., 2012. Classification. In: Siegel, J.A., Saukko, P.J. (Eds.), Encyclopedia of Forensic Sciences. Academic Press.

Hsu, S., July 29, 2014. Federal review stalled after finding forensic errors by FBI unit spanned two decades. The Washington Post.

Kaye, D., 2015. Ultracrepidarianism in forensic science: the hair evidence debacle. Washington & Lee Law Review Online. 72, 227. http://scholarlycommons.law.wlu.edu/wlulr-online/vol72/iss2/1.

Kirk, P., DeForest, P.R., 1973. Forensic individualization of hair. Criminologist 8, 35.

Kirk, P.L., 1940. Human hair studies. 1. General considerations of hair individualization and its forensic importance. Journal of Criminal Law, and Criminology (1931–1951) 486–496.

Kirk, P., 1941. Human hair studies I. General considerations of hair individualization and its forensic importance. Journal of Criminal Law, Criminology, and Police Science 31, 486.

Kirk, P., Greenwell, M.D., Wilmer, A., 1941. Human hair studies III. Refractive index of crown hair. Journal of Criminal Law, Criminology, and Police Science 31, 746.

Koch, S.L., Michaud, A.L., Mikell, C.E., 2013. Taphonomy of hair—a study of postmortem root banding. Journal of Forensic Sciences 58 (s1), S52–S59.

Levy, A., April 13, 2015. The price of a life. The New Yorker. www.newyorker.com/magazine/2015/04/13/the-price-of-a-life.

Lindsay, R.B., 1959. Entropy consumption and values in physical science. American Scientist 376–385.

Mann, M., 1990. Hair transfers in sexual assault: a six year case study. Journal of Forensic Sciences 35, 951.

Marx, H., 1906. Ein beitrag zur identitatsfrage bei der forensicschen haaruntersuchung. Archive fur Kriminologie 23, 75.

Mayr, E., 1982. The Growth of Biological Thought: Diversity, Evolution, and Inheritance. Harvard University Press.

Melton, T., et al., 2005. Forensic mitochondrial DNA analysis of 691 casework hairs. Journal of Forensic Sciences 50, 1–8.

Midler, O., Karleskind, A., 1978. Hair dyes acting by oxidation. Their identification and estimation by high-performance liquid chromatography. Parums Cosmetics Aromestics 23, 77.

Montagna, W., Dobson, R.I., 1969. Advances in Biology of Skin. Hair Growth, vol. IX. Pergammon Press, New York, NY.

Montagna, W., Ellis, R.A., 1958. The Biology of Hair Growth. Academic Press, New York, NY.

Montagna, W., Parakkal, P.F., 1974. The Structure and Function of Skin. Academic Press, New York, NY.

Moore, J.E., 1988. A key for the identification of animal hairs. Journal of the Forensic Science Society 28 (5), 335–339.

Parakkal, P.F., Montagna, W., Motoltsy, A.G., 1963. An electron microscopic study of the structure and formation of red pigment granules in hair follicles. Journal of Investigative Dermatology 41, 275.

Paus, R., Cotsarelis, G., 1999. The biology of hair follicles. New England Journal of Medicine 341, 491.

Reiner, N., July 2013. The hair microscopy review project: an historic breakthrough for law enforcement and a daunting challenge for the defense bar. Champion. Online at: www.nacdl.org/Champion.aspx?id=29488.

Robertson, J. (Ed.), 1999. Forensic and microscopic examination of human hairs. In: Forensic Examination of Hair. Taylor and Francis, Philadelphia.

Ryland, S., Houck, M.M., 2001. Only circumstantial evidence. In: Houck, M.M. (Ed.), Mute Witnesses. Elsevier. pp. 117–138.

Saks, M.J., Koehler, J.J., 2005. The coming paradigm shift in forensic identification science. Science 309 (5736), 892–895.

Scheck, B., Neufeld, P., Dwyer, J., 2000. Actual Innocence: Five Days to Execution and Other Dispatches from the Wrongly Convicted. Doubleday, New York, NY.

Schum, D.A., 1994. The Evidential Foundations of Probabilistic Reasoning. Northwestern University Press.

Slobodzian, J., 2015. Hair Analysis a Discredited Tool: FBI Review Shows it Was Wrong in 96 Pct. of Cases. Philadelphia Inquirer, p. A1. May 12.

Trotter, M., Dawson, H.L., 1934. The hair of French Canadians. American Journal of Physical Anthropology 18, 443.

Trotter, M., 1922. A Study of Facial Hair in White and Negro Males, 9. Washington University Studies, p. 273.

Trotter, M., 1930. The form, size, and color of head hair in American whites. American Journal of Physical Anthropology 14, 433.

Wickenheiser, R.A., Hepworth, D.G., 1990. Further evaluation of probabilities in human scalp hair comparisons. Journal of Forensic Sciences 35, 1323.

Yoon, S., Jain, A., 2015. Longitudinal study of fingerprint recognition. Proceedings of the National Academy of Sciences. early publication, online at: http://www.pnas.org/content/early/2015/06/23/1410272112.full.pdf?sid=d0e6fe16-8ca6-4d79-8f14-abcc2b5f9189.

Arson

3

CHAPTER OUTLINE

Forensic Science Reform. http://dx.doi.org/10.1016/B978-0-12-802719-6.00003-0

Case Study: Cameron Todd Willingham

Rachel Dioso-Villa

Griffith University, Mt Gravatt, QLD, Australia

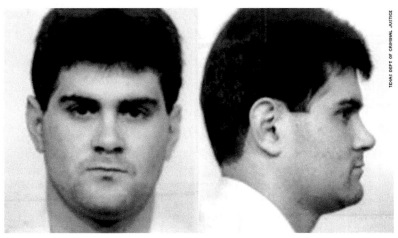

Cameron Todd Willingham

Slow and painful has been man's progress from magic to law…Sometimes, with the benefit of insight gained over time, we learn that what was once regarded as truth is myth, and what was once accepted as science is superstition.

Han Tak Lee v. Franklin Tennis (2014)

INTRODUCTION

Cameron Todd Willingham was executed for the arson deaths of his three infant daughters. Many believe his execution should never have taken place, and as fire science advances, it is becoming clearer that Texas executed an innocent man. Willingham's case is one of the most scrutinized arson investigation cases in the US due to the serious questions raised regarding the validity of the methodology employed in the investigation and the potential that the fire was a tragic accident, and Willingham was executed for a crime that never was (Grann, 2009; Innocence Project, 2006). The fire and arson investigation evidence played a key role in Willingham's conviction and has subsequently been the subject of independent investigations by journalists (Grann, 2009; Mills and Possley, 2004), the Innocence Project (2006), and the Texas Forensic Science Commission (2011). Conclusions from these parties concurred that the claims made by the Deputy Fire Marshal and Assistant Fire Chief and relied upon by the jury were unsupported by the evidence and that their testimonies overstepped the purview of their expertise. Though Willingham was not officially exonerated by a court of law, in 2012, former Justice Charlie Baird, who led an inquiry into the state's activity in the case regarding recanted testimony by a jailhouse informant, concluded that Willingham was wrongly executed (McLaughlin, 2012; Baird, unpublished opinion).

Willingham's case exemplifies the use of outdated methods in arson investigation and how conclusions based on these methods can form the foundation of a wrongful conviction. It highlights the dangers of confirmation bias, the consequences of investigators drawing conclusions that are unsupported by evidence and research, and the lack of general scrutiny paid by defense counsel, the prosecution, judges, and appellate justices. More research is needed to improve the empirical basis of the methodologies used in fire and arson investigation, and greater resources and effort should be afforded educational programs for legal practitioners who encounter this evidence in court.

THE FIRE

On December 23, 1991, in Corsicana, Texas, police and firefighters arrived onsite to put out a fire that had engulfed a one-story house. The resident of the house, Cameron Todd Willingham, was home caring for his 2-year-old daughter, Amber, and 1-year-old twin girls, Karmon and Kameron. His wife was Christmas shopping. Willingham told police that he was asleep when the fire started, and he was awoken by thick smoke in the room. He exited the house to look for help, instructed his neighbor to dial 911, and reentered the home to look for his daughters. He was unable to find the girls, and firefighters restrained him from reentering the house due to the intensity of the fire. Willingham's eldest daughter was found in the master bedroom, and the twins were found in the children's room, having suffered severe burns. Medical examiners later concluded the children died from smoke inhalation and that Willingham had suffered minor burns on his feet and had evidence of smoke in his lungs.

THE FIRE INVESTIGATION

The Assistant Fire Chief of Corsicana, Douglas Fogg, arrived first on site and conducted the initial investigation. He had over 20 years of experience as a firefighter and was a certified fire investigator (Grann, 2009). Deputy Fire Marshal Manuel Vasquez from the State Fire Marshal's Office joined the investigation a few days later. Vasquez had investigated over 1200 fires and was highly experienced in arson investigation (Grann, 2009). Vasquez and Fogg examined all rooms in the house and its perimeter and collected samples for gas chromatography and mass spectrometry (GC–MS) testing for traces of accelerants. Their investigation included several avenues of inquiry that were not restricted to the examination of the fire site. They interviewed Willingham and his wife on several occasions as well as eyewitnesses to the fire and Willingham's friends and neighbors. They accessed medical reports from the hospital that treated Willingham for injuries sustained in the fire and the coroner's reports of the death of the three children. They also worked closely with the Houston Police, who shared with them Willingham's criminal record of truancy, driving under the influence, shoplifting, and a past history of domestic abuse.

During their site investigations, they noted burn patterns throughout the house and looked for natural explanations of how, why, and where the fire might have started, including claims of faulty electrical wiring. Between them, they identified over 20 burn patterns that they believed were evidence that the fire was intentionally set. They also collected over a dozen samples throughout the premises to test for the presence of accelerants through GC–MS. The results came back negative for all of the samples, with the exception of one sample on the front porch where the family kept the home barbecue and its gas tank. The investigators concluded that the fire was intentionally set; it was arson.

THE TRIAL

Cameron Todd Willingham was charged with three counts of murder and was eligible for the death penalty. The state offered him a life sentence if he pled guilty; however, Willingham refused the offer. The trial took place over 2 days, and the prosecution's case included eyewitness testimony about the events on the day of the fire and Willingham's behavior during and after the fire, a positive chemical test of the sample retrieved from the porch outside the house, the testimony of a jailhouse informant who testified that Willingham confessed to having set the fire to intentionally kill his children, and the expert testimony of fire investigators, Fogg and Vasquez.

Two months after the fire that killed Willingham's daughters, the US National Fire Protection Association (NFPA) published a guide for fire investigators (NFPA 921) that, if followed, would have debunked the evidence against Willingham (Mills and Possley, 2004). Fogg and Vasquez did not rely on the NFPA 921 (Mills and Possley, 2004). They identified several indicators that they believed were the results of arson, including irregular patterns on the floors that they believed were puddle configurations or pour patterns caused by the use of accelerants. These pour patterns were found under the children's beds and in doorways, strengthening the State's contention that Willingham intended to block escape routes and kill his children. They testified that multiple V patterns on the walls caused by smoke and low burn patterns on the bedroom walls indicated multiple ignition sites that would not be present in an accidental fire. They also testified that charred wood on the base of a screen door, alligatoring of floor boards, melted bed springs, and spider web patterns on glass windows, known as "crazed" glass, indicated the fire burned hotter than would a naturally occurring fire (Hurst, 2004). All of these characteristics were said to be proof that the fire that killed Willingham's three children was intentionally set. After 90 min of deliberation, the jury found Willingham guilty on all counts, and the judge sentenced him to death.

POSTCONVICTION

Willingham appealed his conviction nine times before the Texas State Court of Appeals on different issues; however, none challenged the validity of the expert testimony by the fire investigators at trial (Dioso-Villa, 2013). He filed a habeas corpus petition that the US District Court denied. It too did not take issue with the contested fire investigation; this may be blamed on the relative complexities inherent when scientific expert evidence is challenged postconviction (Wolf, 2008). In a final step, Willingham sought clemency from the Governor of Texas and requested a 90-day stay of execution to investigate the potentially erroneous fire and arson investigation evidence in the case. To accompany the petition, his lawyer filed a report written by fire and explosives expert, Gerald Hurst, who had the opportunity to review the evidence in the case and identified errors in Fogg and Vasquez's testimonies and conclusions that the fire was intentionally set (Hurst, 2004). Hurst reviewed each of Fogg and Vasquez's identified indicators of arson and contested their explanations, concluding that the patterns the investigators identified are often present in naturally occurring fires. Hurst also stressed that the presence of an accelerant could only be established by chromatographic analysis in a laboratory; recall that the only area that tested positive for an accelerant was the front porch where the family kept their barbeque. Thus, the prosecutor's theory that there were multiple areas of origin marked by pour patterns proving Willingham used an accelerant was patently false. Regardless of compelling evidence that the fire was not arson, Governor Rick Perry and the Texas Board of Pardons and Paroles ultimately declined the petition for a stay of execution, and Willingham was executed by lethal injection as scheduled after having served 12 years in prison.

FIRE AND ARSON INVESTIGATION

This case highlights key issues that arise when fire and arson investigation testimony is admitted into court as expert evidence. As a reconstruction science that includes interpretive analysis, it is unlike comparative analysis (such as fingerprint examination or tool mark comparisons) or empirical analysis (such as chemical analysis, drug identification, forensic DNA testing, or gunshot residue or explosive residue analysis), and distinct from strict observations (such as eyewitness accounts) (Porter, 2011). Unlike its forensic counterparts, fire investigators must determine whether a crime has taken place at all. There are challenges to this, considering that training may vary across jurisdictions and by investigator, as may the resources and tools available to the investigator, independent of which tools he or she may decide to use during the course of each investigation (Dioso-Villa, 2013; May, 2011; Plummer and Syed, 2012).

TRAINING: EXPERIENCE-BASED EXPERTISE

According to Willingham's trial transcripts, Douglas Fogg, the Assistant Fire Chief for the Corsicana Fire Department, had been a part of the fire department for 22 years; little else is revealed or discussed regarding his qualifications and expertise, though he was admitted as an expert witness and permitted to give evidence at trial. Deputy

State Fire Marshall Manuel Vasquez testified as having been a certified peace officer for 15 years through his previous work in the armed forces, and a certified fire investigator for 15 years. He was a member of Texas Law Enforcement Intelligence Association and the North Texas Fire Investigators Association. He testified that he had investigated between 1200 and 1500 fires as a certified fire investigator and that "with the exception of a few, most all of them" were arsons (Statement of Facts, 1992, p. 228). At the time of the trial, he had testified as an expert witness in over 25 trials, and in all cases, with the exception of a few civil cases, he testified on behalf of the prosecution.

As the variations in the two fire investigators' training and experience in Willingham's case demonstrates, there is no current requirement that fire investigators have specific certifications in order to testify as an expert witness, nor is there any formal training or specialized courses that a person must take before conducting fire investigations (Dioso-Villa, 2013; Lentini, 2006). Given the consideration of varied training, experience, and resources, two fire investigators may arrive at different conclusions about the cause(s) or origin(s) of the same fire, or they may arrive at the same conclusions using very different investigative techniques.

TOOLKIT: OUTDATED ARSON INDICATORS AND THIRD-PARTY EVIDENCE

As discussed in depth below, fire investigators have repeatedly relied upon heuristics passed down from mentor to apprentice to determine whether a fire was intentionally or accidentally set. Some of these heuristics include what became known among fire investigators as arson indicators and remained undisputed until the 1980s (Lentini, 2006). Vasquez, Fogg, and the fire investigation community in general believed that arson fires produced burn patterns distinguishable from naturally set fires based on the widely accepted premise that fires that used an accelerant burned hotter and faster than a natural burning fire. In the Willingham case, Fogg and Vasquez identified over 20 arson indicators, such as melted metal (since metal melts at such a high temperature not reached in a natural fire), alligatoring (alligator patterns on wooden floor boards produced by an accelerant), and crazed glass (spider web patterns on windows believed to have been produced by extreme temperatures in a room) (Innocence Project, 2006). Although by the time of Willingham's trial in the early 1990s, new evidence suggested that natural fires that occurred in small, enclosed spaces could produce artifacts consistent with arson indicators if the room reached flashover (Dioso-Villa, 2013; Lentini et al., 1993; May, 2011; Plummer and Syed, 2012), Fogg and Vasquez were not aware that what they observed in the aftermath of the Willingham fire was the natural consequence of flashover. In Willingham's small house, flashover occurred when a hot gas layer built up to the ceiling with no chance of escaping causing the combustible material in the room to ignite at the same time, thus causing artifacts, Fogg and Vasquez interpreted, as indicators of arson.

The Innocence Project, investigative journalists, the courts, a special investigative task force, and the media have questioned Willingham's conviction and execution, given the weight that the jury must have attributed to the fire investigators' expert testimony that relied so heavily on "arson indicators." In addition to arson indicators that lack scientific rigor, fire investigators have a host of other tools available to them to assist with determining the origin and cause of fires. In Willingham's case, Fogg and Vasquez accessed medical records and coroners' reports, interviewed eyewitnesses and character witnesses, interviewed the suspect, read fire reports, conducted site inspections, collected samples for GC–MS testing, and had access to Willingham's criminal record. These reports and the collection of investigative facts are part of how a fire investigator may reach his or her conclusion about the cause and origin of the fire.

Unfortunately, as the National Academy of Sciences' report on the evaluation of the forensic sciences points out, fire and arson investigation, like other forensic disciplines, lacks the necessary empirical rigor to make the claims that fire investigators make in court. In addition, they recommend that their training, reporting, and testimony should attempt to be standardized to address these limitations.

> By contrast [to the analysis of explosions], much more research is needed on the natural variability of burn patterns and damage characteristics and how they are affected by the presence of various accelerants. Despite the paucity of research, some arson investigators continue to make determinations about whether or not a particular fire was set. However, according to testimony presented to the committee, many of the rules of thumb that are typically assumed to indicate that an accelerant was used (e.g., "alligatoring" of wood, specific char patterns) have been shown not to be true. Experiments should be designed to put arson investigations on a more solid scientific footing.
>
> **(National Research Council (2009, pp. 5–34 to 5–35)**

THE IMPACT OF EXTRA-LEGAL FACTORS

The key features of fire investigation can pose problems for judges and jurors as they interpret the testimony and evidence. Fire investigators reach conclusions that are based on physical evidence found at the fire site and may also incorporate investigative facts about the crime or defendant in reaching a determination of arson. In Willingham's case, Vasquez testified that his conclusion was based in part on external factors independent of the physical evidence, including his experience, training, and interviews with witnesses and the defendant. This holistic view is not uncommon in the forensic sciences, given the argument that forensic examiners may benefit from knowing case facts in order to select the analyses required and to conduct the analyses accurately (Thompson, 2011). In the case of fire investigation, this raises the question of whether the fire investigator has any reason at all to investigate such issues as the defendant's character or criminal history. That is, is this information required in order to make a scientific determination about how a fire started? If a holistic approach is desired, then it should be restricted to only evidence that touches directly on the physical aspects of fire science. Any further inquiry by fire investigators into the character of the defendant is so far removed from the fire investigator's role that it runs the increased risk and likelihood of bias and the misinterpretation of the physical evidence.

CONFIRMATION BIAS

Confirmation bias can occur when an analyst knowingly or unknowingly seeks or interprets information in a way that supports their beliefs, hypotheses, and expectations (Nickerson, 1998). For example, investigative facts, such as knowing that the suspect confessed or that the suspect has a criminal record of similar offenses, may affect how an analyst interprets findings (Dror et al., 2006). In Willingham's case, we can draw inferences that suggest confirmation bias led to his conviction. From Vasquez's testimony at trial, he appeared to see Willingham as a physically abusive husband who had reacted to the deaths of his children in unexpected ways. These impressions about Willingham's character, informed by eyewitness statements and criminal record, certainly could have influenced the way in which Vasquez interpreted the physical evidence in his investigations. The likelihood of bias increases when analyses are made and conclusions are drawn based on "art" and not on empirical analysis. Thus, it is telling that Vasquez believes, "the fire tells a story" and he is just the fire's "interpreter," and Fogg believes, "the fire talks to you…[t]he structure talks to you…[y]ou call that years of experience" (Mills and Possley, 2004).

THE ULTIMATE ISSUE

When forensic examiners testify at trial, there is a danger that they may make claims that extend beyond the science, methodology, or their expertise, or they may exaggerate the value of the evidence (National Research Council, 2009). This is especially dangerous for fire investigators since their task is to determine the cause and origin of the fire, which can broach the ultimate issue of the case: whether there was a crime at all and whether the defendant intended to commit the crime.

In Willingham's case, Vasquez testified that he believed that the fire was intentionally set. He also testified that he believed, based on the investigation and his experience, that Willingham started the fire with the intent to kill his three infants (Dioso-Villa, 2013; Grann, 2009). In general, there are no scientific methods that can support such specific claims of a person's intent. However, in cases where arson is suspected, it is natural that fire investigators may think that they have found absolute proof of intent to kill, such as here, where the expert testified a specific pattern proves the defendant poured an accelerant under his child's bed as well as in doorways in order to block the child's means of escape. Endowing any expert with the faculty to prove both that a crime was committed and that the suspect intended the death of the victim is inherently dangerous, and the enormity of this faculty should require that experts be vetted to a much greater extent.

CONCLUSION

Willingham was convicted and sentenced to death in 1992. He had nine unsuccessful appeals, an unsuccessful habeas corpus petition, his clemency petition was rejected, and he served 12 years in prison before being executed in 2004. Since then, the practice of relying on arson indicators as a method of fire investigation has been contested and challenged within the fire investigation community and in the general media. The Innocence Project submitted a petition that the Texas Forensic Science Commission reinvestigate the case because the investigators relied on outdated and disproven arson indicators in their investigations. Although the case fell out of the Commission's jurisdiction, likely due to political considerations, the Commission nonetheless issued a report that stated that the methods used in the investigation were flawed (Texas Forensic Science Commission, 2011). Willingham's conviction and execution have illustrated the dangers of admitting unsound arson evidence into court and the blind reliance on experts who do not have a science-based foundation for their beliefs. To address these concerns requires considerable attention to the training and vetting of experts and greater understanding of the science of fire and arson by legal practitioners involved in fire-related litigation.

REFERENCES

Baird, C. Cameron Todd Willingham (unpublished opinion). Available at: http://camerontoddwillingham.com/.

Dioso-Villa, R., 2013. Scientific and legal developments in fire and arson investigation expertise in *State of Texas v. Cameron Todd Willingham*. Minnesota Journal of Law, Science and Technology 14 (2), 817–848.

Dror, I.E., Charlton, D., Peron, A.E., 2006. Contextual information renders experts vulnerable to making erroneous identifications. Forensic Science International 156, 74–78.

Grann, D., September 7, 2009. Trial by fire: did Texas execute an innocent man? The New Yorker.

Hurst, G., 2004. Affidavit by Gerald Hurst - Report on Cameron Todd Willingham, p. 3 Navarro County, Texas: 366th Judicial District.

Innocence Project, A.R.C., 2006. A Report on the Peer Review of the Expert Testimony in the Cases of *State of Texas v. Cameron Todd Willingham* and *State of Texas v. Ernest Ray Willis*. Innocence Project, New York.

Lentini, J., Smith, D.M., Henderson, R.W., 1993. Unconventional wisdom: the lessons of Oakland. The Fire and Arson Investigator 43 (4), 1–4.

Lentini, J., 2006. Scientific Protocols for Fire Investigation. Taylor and Francis, Boca Raton.

May, T.R., 2011. Fire pattern analysis, junk science, old wives tales and *Ipse Dixit*: emerging forensic 3D imaging technologies to the rescue? Richmond Journal of Law and Technology 16 (4), 1–50.

McLaughlin, M., 2012. Cameron Todd Willingham Exoneration was Written but Never Filed by Texas Judge. (Huffington Post).

Mills, S., Possley, M., December 9, 2004. Man Executed on Disproved Forensics: Fire that Killed his Three Children Could Have Been Accidental. Chicago Tribune.

National Fire Protection Association, 2008. NFPA 921: Guide for Explosion and Fire Investigations. Jones & Bartlett Learning, Quincy, MA.

National Research Council, 2009. In: Press, N.A. (Ed.), Strengthening Forensic Science in the United States. National Academy of Sciences, Washington, D.C, p. 254.

Nickerson, R.S., 1998. Confirmation bias: a ubiquitous phenomenon in many guises. Review of General Psychology 2 (2), 175–220.

Plummer, C., Syed, I., August 2012. 'Shifted science' and post-conviction relief. Stanford Journal of Civil Rights and Liberties VIII (2).

Porter, G., 2011. A new theoretical framework regarding the application and reliability of photographic evidence. International Journal of Evidence and Proof 15, 26–61.

Statement of Facts vol. XII at 228, Texas v. Willingham, no. 24–467 (Tex. Dist. Ct. August 18, 1992).

Texas Forensic Science Commission, 2011. Report of the Texas Forensic Science Commission Willingham/Willis Investigation. Texas Forensic Science Commission, Huntsville, Texas, pp. 1–52.

Thompson, W.C., 2011. What role should investigative facts play in the evaluation of scientific evidence? Australian Journal of Forensic Sciences 43 (2), 123–134.

Wolf, M.P., 2008. Habeas relief from bad science: does federal habeas corpus provide relief for prisoners possibly convicted on misunderstood fire science. Minnesota Journal of Law, Science & Technology 10, 213.

Confronting Inaccuracy in Fire Cause Determinations

John J. Lentini

Scientific Fire Analysis, Islamorada, FL, United States

With a few exceptions, forensic science disciplines lag behind many other sciences. This is largely because the underpinnings of the forensic sciences do not lie in academia or industry, but were developed as a response to a need for information by the justice system.

As with any historical science, it is difficult (maybe impossible) to accurately measure the rate of error of many forensic science methodologies, and among the forensic disciplines, fire investigation probably presents one of the more difficult challenges. In the absence of a video of the actual fire in progress, it is difficult to determine whether a fire investigator's conclusions are accurate or wide of the mark. It is possible, however, to state with some confidence that while the situation is improving, there are still many errors that occur.

Fire investigation is different from many sciences, and even from many forensic sciences, by virtue of the fact that its practitioners largely lack any formal scientific education. Yet every day, we ask them to make sophisticated decisions about chemistry, heat transfer, fluid dynamics, and electricity. Fire investigators are generally drawn from the ranks of the police and fire services. Training historically has been done "on the job" with an experienced mentor passing on his belief system to new recruits. Thus, fire investigation suffers from two major challenges to its reliability: unqualified practitioners and invalid methodology.

LACK OF QUALIFICATIONS

In Europe, there is much variation in the quality of fire cause investigations and practitioner standards (Tedim et al., 2015). In England, in 2007, they created a regulatory entity to set and maintain standards for forensic scientists, and appointed a Forensic Regulator. Fire scene investigators are accredited and must conform to standards set forth in International Standards Organization Section 17020. In Norway and the Netherlands, neutral experts are appointed by the court (Stridbeck et al., 2013; Brants, 2011). In Canada, fire scene investigation training is not standardized. Some provincial Offices of the Fire Marshal have adopted NFPA standards (Wright and Singer, 2014). Marshals regulate training of fire investigators who may qualify as expert witnesses (Id.; Office of the Fire Marshal and Fire Departments). In 1994, the Supreme Court of Canada established that the admission of expert testimony depends on its relevance and necessity in assisting the trier of fact, the absence of any exclusionary rule, and a properly qualified expert (R. v Mohan, 1994). The "qualified expert" must have "acquired special or peculiar knowledge through study or experience in respect of the matters on which he or she undertakes to testify" (R. v Mohan, 1994).

Federal Rule 702 and most state rules regarding experts begin with the phrase, "an expert who is qualified…" Until 2010, however, who is qualified was a decision left up to the individual and almost always ratified by the judge if the individual had previously been qualified as an expert witness. This is changing due to the changes in the *Standard for Professional Qualifications for Fire Investigator*, known as NFPA 1033.

NFPA 1033 sets forth an objective list of subjects that the investigator is required to know at a level beyond high school. The document reads as follows:

1.3.7* The investigator shall have and maintain at a minimum an up-to-date basic knowledge of the following topics beyond the high school level:

1. fire science
2. fire chemistry
3. thermodynamics
4. thermometry
5. fire dynamics
6. explosion dynamics
7. computer fire modeling
8. fire investigation
9. fire analysis
10. fire investigation methodology
11. fire investigation technology
12. hazardous materials

13. failure analysis and analytical tools
14. fire protection systems
15. evidence documentation, collection, and preservation
16. electricity and electrical systems (NFPA 1033, 2014)

This list of required knowledge provides the courts with guidance on who is qualified and who is not. While challenges to experts have typically been challenges to methodology, it is now becoming common for fire investigators to be required to endure a "quiz," testing their knowledge of the subjects listed above. At the very least, someone who holds himself out as an expert should be able to define the subjects.

NFPA 921, *Guide for Fire and Explosion Investigations*, described as follows, defines **Fire science**, the first item on the list, as "the body of knowledge concerning the study of fire and related subjects (such as combustion, flame, products of combustion, heat release, heat transfer, fire and explosion chemistry, fire and explosion dynamics, thermodynamics, kinetics, fluid mechanics, fire safety) and their interaction with people, structures, and the environment" (NFPA 921, 2014).

Fire is a rapid oxidation process, an exothermic (energy releasing) chemical reaction involving the generation of heat and light in various quantities. Heat and light are forms of energy, and it can be argued that a fire investigator who does not know the basic units of energy is really not qualified to render expert opinions the behavior of fire. The very basic knowledge in the following paragraphs is something that a fire expert should know in his or her bones, but sadly, many purported experts do not possess this knowledge (*see the deposition excerpts in the sidebar*).

Energy. Energy is a property of matter that is manifest as an ability to perform work, either by moving over a distance or by transferring heat. Energy can be changed in form (e.g., from chemical to mechanical energy) or transferred to other matter, but it can neither be created nor destroyed. Energy is measured in joules (J) or calories (cal) or British Thermal Units (Btu). A joule is the heat produced when 1 A is passed through a resistance of 1 Ω for 1 s, or it is the work required to move over a distance of 1 m against a force of 1 N. A calorie is the amount of energy required to raise the temperature of 1 g of water by 1°C (from 14°C to 15°C); a calorie is equal to 4.184 J. A Btu is the quantity of heat required to raise the temperature of one pound of water 1°F at a pressure of 1 atm and a temperature of 60°F; a British thermal unit is equal to 1055 J, and 252.15 calories.

Power. Power is a property of a process such as fire that describes energy released *per unit time*. The same amount of energy is required to carry a load up a flight of stairs whether the person carrying it walks or runs, but more power is needed for running because the work is done in a shorter amount of time. Raising the temperature of a volume of water requires the same amount of energy whether the temperature increase takes place in 10 s or in 10 min. Raising the temperature more rapidly requires more power because the energy is transferred more rapidly. Power is measured in joules per second (J/s) or watts (W).

Heat flux. Heat flux is a property of a process such as fire that describes the amount of power *per unit area*. A kilowatt spread over one square meter is approximately equal to the radiant heat flux outdoors on a sunny day. If that same kilowatt is concentrated

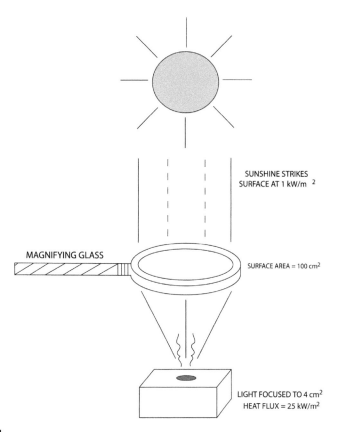

MAGNIFYING GLASS

SUNSHINE STRIKES
SURFACE AT 1 kW/m^2

SURFACE AREA = 100 cm^2

LIGHT FOCUSED TO 4 cm^2
HEAT FLUX = 25 kW/m^2

FIGURE 3.1

Using a magnifying glass to concentrate the radiant heat flux from the sun.

by a factor of 25 using a magnifying glass, there will be sufficient energy transferred to that area to cause ignition of combustibles (See Fig. 3.1).

Heat flux is measured in kW/m^2 or W/cm^2. There are 10,000 square centimeters in a square meter. The value for the smaller area is important in evaluating the *competence* of a proposed ignition source. The critical radiant heat flux necessary to cause ignition is 25–$30 kW/m^2$, which might seem like a lot of power, but most fires start small, and it only takes 2.5–$3 W$ to ignite a combustible fuel if the energy is concentrated in an area smaller than a square centimeter.

Fire chemistry covers many subjects, but one would have to think that knowing the formula for the combustion of hydrogen, the simplest of all combustion reactions, would be something even a novice fire investigator would learn $(2H_2 + O_2 \rightarrow 2H_2O)$. The simplest of all *hydrocarbon* combustion reactions is the combustion of methane, the main ingredient of natural gas $(CH_4 + 2O_2 \rightarrow CO_2 + 2H_2O)$. One volume of natural gas requires two volumes of oxygen (10 volumes of air) for complete combustion.

What follows are examples of testimony of fire investigation "experts" who could arguably be prevented from testifying because of their failure to know the basics about how fire behaves.

This expert is from testimony given by an electrical engineer (PE) who investigates fires (April 12, 2012).

Q. How is radiant heat flux measured?

A. Oh, I can't remember the actual units but I could look it up. I just don't remember what the actual units are because it's not a common…

Q. Do you know what the generally accepted value of radiant heat flux that will result in a flashover is?

A. No.

Q. If you were outside like today on a cloudless day at noon, what is the radiant heat flux that a square meter of the earth's surface is receiving from the sun?

A. I don't know.

Many of the other subjects listed in NFPA 1033 are duplicative, but it is not unreasonable to expect a fire investigator who proposes the "elimination of all accidental causes" to have sufficient knowledge of electrical systems to wire a house and to know enough about fire protection systems to understand whether they did or did not function properly.

This testimony was offered by a certified fire investigator (CFI) with over 30 years of experience. He was working with the previous investigator. He "determined" there were seven areas of origin, all of which were contiguous, in a warehouse fire that burned for at least 6 h.

Q. What is radiant heat flux?

A. That is a measurement of the heat being radiating such as the sun is radiant heat.

Q. And how is it measured?

A. The sun is measured in temperatures, in degrees, both Fahrenheit and Celsius.

Q. Is there a generally accepted value of radiant heat flux that will result in a flashover?

A. Yes.

Q. Do you know what that is?

A. What, flashover?

Q. What the value is?

A. No.

Q. Do you know what the chemical symbol for hydrogen is?

A. No, but I know where to look it up.

Q. What about a chemical formula for hydrogen gas, do you know what that symbol is?

A. No.

Q. Or the chemical symbol for oxygen?

A. I know where to look them all up.

Q. And likewise, do you know what the chemical symbol for oxygen gas is?

A. No, but I know where to look them up.

Q. What is the chemical reaction for the combustion of hydrogen?

A. I don't recall.

"Knowing where to look it up" is not what the writers of NFPA 1033 had in mind when they prescribed a knowledge of fire chemistry, but that is the fallback answer of many investigators.

> This expert was the investigator (CFI) in a contested cooking fire case (October 24, 2013).
>
> Q. What are the basic units of energy?
> A. Basic units of energy. Power, and I forgot what the other one was right now.· But I can look that up for you also.
> Q. What are the basic units of power?
> A. Basic units of power?·I would have to look that up for you also.
>
> Q. Well, what is a watt?·Define it.
> A. Define a watt.·I'd have to look it up for you.

Challenges to experts' qualifications will often take place well before a court is asked to rule on them, and, in fact, when one party's expert is unable to answer simple questions about fire and energy, the result is frequently that the case settles because counsel does not feel comfortable with the expert anymore. The sidebar contains actual excerpts from transcripts of certified fire investigators with many years of experience and shows that being certified is not the same as being qualified. Challenges based on a lack of qualifications are becoming more common. The author once witnessed a successful challenge of a proposed expert who was unable to describe the combustion of hydrogen. Without being asked, the Judge interrupted the proceedings and stated, "I'm sorry. If you don't know H_2O, you will not be rendering opinion testimony in my courtroom."

> This testimony was given by a second investigator (CFI) who replaced the "expert" above (December 29, 2014).
>
> Q. What are the basic units of energy?
> A. Kilowatts, watts, horsepower, joules. I could go on.
> Q. All of those are basic units of energy?
> A. Yes.
> Q. What are the basic units of power?
> A. Those are your forces. I'd have to look that up for you.
> Q. What is a "watt"?
> A. Watt is a measurement of energy.
> Q. What is it, though?
> A. It's like a kilowatt. If I produce – it's named after Mr. Watt. Hang on. If you want me to tell you, I have to look it up for you, the exact definition.

What is the solution to the problem of underqualified or completely unqualified individuals holding themselves out as expert fire investigators? Unfortunately, short-term solutions are not available. The likelihood that an investigator, who has managed to obtain certification and make a comfortable living investigating fires for 30 years despite the lack of basic knowledge, will decide to learn some science is low. Investigators such as this can be discredited one case at a time, and eventually, that will reduce their workload as clients decide to hire someone who knows the basics. This is not going to change the overall picture, at least not quickly. As the great scientist Max Planck stated, "science advances one funeral at a time." To put it more kindly and apply it to the situation at hand, fire investigation advances one retirement at a time.

A certified fire and explosion investigator (CFEI), who claims a "magma [sic] cum laude" degree in fire science, opined that a propane-fired weed burner was used to set a fatal fire. The defendant was charged with capital murder on this basis (November 11, 2010).

Q. Do you know how many BTUs are present in a typical cubic foot of propane?
A. Not at this time.
Q. Do you know what the chemical formula for propane is?
A. I'm unsure at this time.
Q. Can you write down the chemical equation that describes the burning of propane in air?
A. I'm unsure.
Q. How many volumes of oxygen are required to burn a volume of propane?
A. Unsure.
Q. Can you explain the difference between heat and temperature?
A. My opinion? Not "921" or any…
Q. Yeah, your opinion.
A. Heat is the production of light and temperature from a product, and temperature is the natural measurement of that heat that's produced.
Q. Okay. What's the basic unit of energy called?
A. I'm unsure at this time.
Q. You ever heard of a joule?
A. I have.
Q. What is it?
A. It's a measurement of energy or that's how – it has to do with electricity as well.
Q. What are the basic units of power called?
A. AC and DC.
Q. I'm sorry?
A. AC and DC.
Q. Have you ever heard of a watt?
A. Yes, sir.
Q. Would that be the correct answer?
A. More than likely.
Q. What is a watt?
A. I mean I'm unsure. If you want me to look at a manual and give you these answers…
Q. Do you know what a watt is?
A. No, sir.
Q. Okay. How is the size of a fire measured?
A. I'm unsure at this time.
Q. Okay. What is radiant heat flux?
A. I'm unsure at this time.

(The prosecutor moved for dismissal when she saw how her "star" witness was going to perform at trial.)

The long-term solution is to improve the quality of the applicant pool. This can only be accomplished by requiring a scientific background (as opposed to a fire extinguishing background or in addition to a fire extinguishing background) and paying individuals commensurate with that requirement. Faced with the prospect of a $40,000 annual salary as a fire investigator or a $100,000 annual salary as a fire protection engineer, most college graduates will opt for the latter. Until we as a society decide that fire investigation is a profession that requires a basic curriculum and that should command a decent salary, the problem of unqualified fire investigators will persist.

INVALID METHODOLOGY

Federal Rule 702 and most state rules devote more ink to methodology than to qualifications. The rule reads as follows:

A witness who is qualified as an expert by knowledge, skill, experience, training, or education may testify in the form of an opinion or otherwise if:

1. the expert's scientific, technical, or other specialized knowledge will help the trier of fact to understand the evidence or to determine a fact in issue;
2. the testimony is based on sufficient facts or data;
3. the testimony is the product of reliable principles and methods; and
4. the expert has reliably applied the principles and methods to the facts of the case.

While all four subparagraphs provide avenues for challenge, it is the failure to meet the requirement that "the testimony is the product of reliable principles and methods" that is likely to result in inaccurate determinations of origin and cause.

The "methodological" failures in fire investigation do not often happen because of acts or omissions, but because of a failure to properly *interpret* postfire artifacts. While NFPA 921 does prescribe many desirable actions that should be accomplished by a fire investigator (methods), it is the interpretation of postfire artifacts, based on scientific research (principles), that is the most important part of the document. Most fire investigation errors can be attributed to failing to follow NFPA 921's extensive guidance on interpretation.

The first systematic study of potential problems with fire investigation methodology happened in 1977 when a team from the Aerospace Corporation, working for the US Department of Justice, conducted a survey of fire investigators and asked them what "indicators" they used to help them investigate fires and determine arson (Boudreau et al., 1977).

The indicators listed in the Justice Department report, all of which involved interpretation, included the following postfire artifacts:

Crazing of glass. Formation of irregular cracks in glass believed to be caused by rapid, intense heating, and thus an indicator of the use of a liquid accelerant (see Fig. 3.2).

Depth of char. The depth of burning of wood was used to estimate the duration of burning. It was widely believed that wood burned at a fixed rate. The deepest char must have been burning the longest.

Line of demarcation. On floors or rugs, a "puddle-shaped" line of demarcation was believed to indicate a liquid fire accelerant. In the cross-section of wood, a sharp, distinct line of demarcation indicates a rapid, intense fire (see Fig. 3.3).

Sagged furniture springs. Because of the heat required for furniture springs to collapse from their own weight (1150°F) and because of the insulating effect of the upholstery, sagged springs are believed to be possible only in either a fire originating inside the cushions (as from a cigarette rolling between the cushions) or an external fire intensified by a fire accelerant.

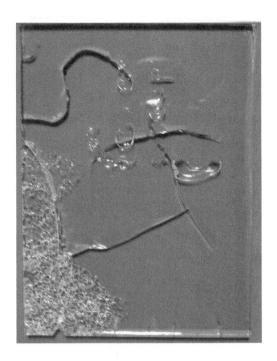

FIGURE 3.2

Crazed glass. Crazing only occurs in those areas to which water was applied. The author was able to write his initials using a wet cotton swab. Despite numerous textbooks that state the opposite, it is impossible to cause glass to craze by rapid heating. Crazed glass can only be caused by rapid cooling.

FIGURE 3.3

Sharp, continuous, irregular lines of demarcation between burned and unburned areas. The irregular patterns were caused by alternating exposure and protection of the underlying floor by the shrinking carpeting.

Spalling. This response by concrete to heating causes the surface of the concrete to chip or even explode violently. Brown stains around the spall were said to indicate the use of a fire accelerant (see Fig. 3.4).

In addition to those "indicators," there were several other widely publicized and accepted means used to analyze a fire, including those listed here.

Fire load: Knowing the energy content (as opposed to the energy release rate) of the fuels in a structure was believed to allow an investigator to calculate the damage that a "normal" fire should produce in a given time frame. Some investigators referred to a "standard time temperature curve."

Low burning and holes in the floor: Because heat rises, it was widely believed that burning on the floor, particularly under furniture, indicated an origin on the floor.

V-pattern angle: A V-pattern is caused by the interaction of a conical fire plume with a vertical surface, such as a wall. The angle of a V-pattern was believed to indicate the speed of the fire, with a wide V indicating a slow burning fire and a narrow V indicating a rapidly burning, and therefore accelerated fire.

Time and temperature: By estimating the speed of a fire or establishing the temperature achieved by a fire, it was believed that an investigator could determine whether it was accelerated or advanced at a "normal" rate.

All of these "indicators" are correctly categorized as "junk science." What is amazing is that so much junk science has permeated fire investigation over the decades. The introduction and persistence of invalid indicators (all of which, by the way, were supposed to suggest an intentional fire) in fire investigation are an unfortunate part of the history of the discipline and a subject that many fire investigators do not like to think about. Some would like to keep these dirty little secrets locked away in a closet in the hope that people will gradually forget about them and they will not be a problem anymore. It is this failure to address a serious problem in

FIGURE 3.4

Concrete spalling on the ceiling of a parking garage under construction that caught fire.

the training and education of fire investigators that causes the myths to persist. The unfortunate consequence is that innocent lives are destroyed by well-meaning but ignorant investigators.

Just as in the study of Greek or Roman mythology, no single reason explains how or why a fire investigation myth develops. Certainly, no reason exists to believe that any investigator deliberately set out to promulgate something that he knew to be untrue. It is likely that most myths came about as a result of unwarranted generalizations. For example, an investigator might observe that in a garage fire, a pattern of spalling surrounds the remains of a gasoline container and makes an association of gasoline with spalling. The next time he sees spalled concrete, he infers that gasoline must have been involved.

Some myths arise because of intuitively obvious "deductions." The notion that gasoline burns hotter than wood is appealing; as anyone who has ever started a wood fire knows, it is much easier to start it with liquid fuel, and certainly after a short time, a fire started with, for example, gasoline, is throwing off much more heat per unit time (kilowatts) than the fire burning wood only. Therefore, the flame temperature must be higher, right? Wrong! But even Paul Kirk, arguably one of the finest forensic scientists of his time, bought into this notion. In the first edition of his book *Fire Investigation* (1969), he described the utility of examining melted metals:

> *Whenever any residues of molten metal are present at the fire scene, they will reliably establish a minimum temperature for the point of their fusion in the fire. The investigator may use this fact to advantage in many instances, because of the differences in effective temperature between simple wood fires and those in which extraneous fuel, such as accelerant is present.*

Kirk (1969)

To this day, investigators sometimes infer the presence of accelerants when they observe a melted aluminum threshold.

The authors of the 1977 study correctly pointed out that there was no scientific underpinning for **any** of these indicators and suggested that a series of experiments be conducted and a "handbook" for fire investigators be published. Unfortunately, the handbook was published in 1980 **without the experimental data!** Even more unfortunately, the *Handbook* was published by the US National Bureau of Standards (NBS, now known as NIST for National Institute of Standards and Technology), one of the most highly respected scientific and engineering bodies in the world (Brannigan et al., 1980). The indicators were often quoted in textbooks and thus became firmly embedded in the culture of fire investigation.

One by one, investigators and experimenters tested whether these indicators were, in fact, valid, and one by one, they were proven not to be (Lentini, 2012a,b). A large problem existed in the training methodology of the fire investigation profession. Well-meaning professional groups would conduct weekend seminars in which a structure or two was intentionally set on fire and then quickly put out. Fire investigators could then "learn how to recognize arson." The difficulty with this type of test fire was that it did not mimic real-world fires, which often burn for tens of minutes as fully involved fires. Throughout the 1980s, such exercises reinforced the belief that one could tell what a "flammable liquid pour pattern" looked like by visual observation alone.

Here, the investigator (CFI, CFEI) is testifying in a civil arson case based on a "pour pattern" at an alleged second area of origin (April 25, 2013).

Q. So the difference between heat and temperature.
A. Heat would be the, what is produced by something, and temperature would be what the air is, or what the surroundings are.
Q. What are the basic units of energy?
A. Like I guess I don't understand your question.
Q. I don't know how to make it any clearer.
A. Are you asking me like how energy's measured, like with British thermal units, things like that, or are you asking how heat's transferred?
Q. No, I'm asking you what are, how, what are the basic units of energy called? How are they identified?
A. Like kinetic energy, energy, things like that, is that what you're referring to?
Q. No. I don't…
A. I don't know how to answer your question.
Q. Okay. That's fair.
A. All right.
Q. What are the basic units of power?
A. I don't know how to answer your question again, I'm sorry, I don't understand what you're asking.
Q. What is a watt, W-A-T-T?
A. It's an output of electricity, or I think it can be applied to heat and things like that, but commonly referred to in electricity.
Q. How is the size of a fire measured?
A. In a number of ways. The heat output, if you're asking that, like how hot it got, or how many BTUs it produced, or if you're asking like the area that it covered or how much damage it did.
Q. What's radiant heat flux?
A. The … I know what radiant heat is. I don't know the specific definition of radiant heat flex.
THE REPORTER: Flux or flex?
ATTORNEY: Flux, F-L-U-X.

THE WITNESS: Flux, okay.
Q. What is the generally accepted value of radiant heat flux that will result in flashover?
A. I don't know (continued).

It was only after a few highly publicized "arson" cases were examined closely that it became clear that fully involved fires could create patterns of damage that looked remarkably like patterns created by flammable liquids, even when no flammable liquids were present (Lentini, 1992). A study conducted in Oakland, California, after the devastating fires that began on October 19, 1991, revealed that many previously identified "indicators of arson" could be routinely found in structures that burned in fires known to be accidental (Lentini et al., 1992).

Laboratory experimentation demonstrated that the temperature of a normal well-ventilated wood fire was the same or even higher than the temperature of a well-ventilated fire involving liquid hydrocarbons. The liquid hydrocarbon fire has a higher heat release rate (kW) than the wood fire, but the flame temperature (°F or °C) is no different. The proposition that glass would craze in response to rapid heating was disproved. As most chemists have learned, glass will only craze when it is heated and then rapidly cooled.

(Continued) The following excerpt was then offered into evidence as Exhibit 3: It is the position of the International Association of Arson Investigators (IAAI) that NFPA Document 921 is widely recognized as an authoritative guide for the fire investigation profession. In addition, NFPA 921 is an important reference manual, and it sets forth guidance and methodology regarding the determination of the origin and cause of fires. This Association uses NFPA 921, along with other documents, including NFPA 1033, as a foundation for its training and certification programs. The statement reaffirms the IAAI's long-standing recognition of the importance of NFPA 921 to the knowledge and methodology of fire investigation.

"Authoritative" means the guide is an accepted source of information and is known to be accurate and reliable. By its own terms, the document is not a "standard" and is subject to revision and updating on a periodic basis to allow it to remain current with the expanding scientific and technical knowledge in the fire investigation field.

Q. It's the IAAI position statement regarding NFPA 921 and 1033. Why don't you just take a minute and read it.
   ATTORNEY: Objection. Objection to the relevancy or what the point is of what the IAAI's position is in this particular case.
Q. Go ahead.
A. Okay, I've read it.
Q. Do you agree with that?
A. No, I don't.
Q. What part don't you agree with?
A. The authoritative part.
Q. You don't believe 921 is authoritative?
A. No, I don't.
Q. When you investigated this case, did you strictly adhere to NFPA 921?
A. Yes.
Q. All right. And the reason you strictly adhered to NFPA 921 is because it's reliable?
A. It's reliable, yes (continued).

Despite the debunking of many fire investigation myths during the 1990s, some authors failed to get the message, and there are textbooks still in print that unwitting criminal justice professionals may encounter that ensure the myths live on for the next generation of law enforcement officers. For example, the *Encyclopedia of Security Management* (2007) (Fay, 2007), and *Criminal Investigation*, 10th Edition (2013) (Orthmann and Hess, 2013) both repeated the six original fire investigation myths from the NBS *Fire Investigation Handbook*. The dated nature of the (mis) information presented in these two texts has been pointed out to the authors, but the damage done by the publications over the years is unknown.

(Continued)
Q. Would you agree that combustion of hydrogen in the presence of air to form water is the simplest of all chemical combustion reactions?
A. It … I don't know if … if that's true or not.
Q. Do you know the chemical symbol for hydrogen?
A. I believe it's just H.
Q. What about hydrogen gas?
A. I believe it's still just H.
Q. What's the chemical symbol for oxygen?
A. O.
Q. What's the chemical formula for oxygen gas?
    ATTORNEY: Objection. I do not know how this is possibly relevant, and this is exactly what I was objecting on before.
A. O_2.
Q. What's the concentration of oxygen in air?
    ATTORNEY: Objection.
A. What's the concentration of it?
Q. Yeah.
A. Like the air we breathe? 92%. I don't know if that's right or not but it's in that area.

As a result of the shifting of the science, many cases of alleged arson were revisited, and a few convictions were overturned, but the primary beneficiaries of the new knowledge were people who had been accused but not yet convicted, and those who would have been accused by the last generation of investigators. As time went by, the percentage of fires declared to have been intentionally set dropped as fire investigators became aware that their determinations were likely to be seriously challenged (Mann, 2009). The debunking of the fire investigation myths took place largely in a document prepared by the Technical Committee on Fire Investigations within the NFPA, based in Quincy, Massachusetts. NFPA 921, *Guide for Fire and Explosion Investigations*, was first published in 1992, and subsequent editions are published on a 3-year cycle. The document is constantly being updated (NFPA 921, 2014). The eighth edition was published in 2014, and the ninth (2017) edition is being prepared as of the date of this publication.

When NFPA 921 was first published, the vast majority of fire investigators in the US emphatically rejected its guidance because it was so at odds with what they had "learned." Eventually, however, the fire investigation discipline embraced a more scientific approach to fires, and many of the "old-school" fire investigators retired. The resistance was understandable. To admit to sending an innocent person to prison or causing a family to lose their life's savings is to admit to an unspeakable error. Denial is the easier route.

The first serious challenge to the "old school" of fire investigators came in 1996 in *Michigan Millers Mutual Insurance Company v. Janelle R. Benfield* in which a fire investigator who failed to properly document his observations was excluded from testifying. In the appeal of that exclusion, the IAAI filed an *amicus curiae* brief in which they contended that fire investigators should not be held to a strict reliability inquiry because fire investigation was "less scientific" than the kind of scientific testing addressed in the *Daubert* decision of 1993 (Burke). Eventually though, there were enough court rulings, including the unanimous Supreme Court decision in *Kumho Tire v. Carmichael*, to persuade the majority of fire investigators that it was necessary to accept the scientific method recommended by NFPA 921.

It is difficult to state exactly when NFPA 921 became "generally accepted by the relevant scientific community," but 2000 was an important turning point. That year, the US Department of Justice released a research report entitled *Fire And Arson Scene Evidence: A Guide For Public Safety Personnel* (Fig. 3.5), which identified NFPA 921 as a "benchmark for the training and expertise of everyone who purports to be an expert in the origin and cause determination of fires." That same year, the IAAI for the first time endorsed the adoption of the new edition of NFPA 921.

FIGURE 3.5

Cover of the US Department of Justice publication (2000) that embraced the use of NFPA 921.

THE QUESTIONABLE VALIDITY OF FIRE ORIGIN DETERMINATION

The situation today is dramatically improved from 30 years ago, but the fire investigation profession is still struggling to understand the complexities of fire behavior. Recent developments have made abundantly clear that as with many disciplines, "the more one learns, the less one knows." This point was brought home in 2005 and 2007 when agents of the US Bureau of Alcohol, Tobacco, Firearms and Explosives (ATF), which investigates many of the high-profile fires in the US today, conducted studies that reflected rather poorly on the reliability of fire investigators' determinations of where a fire started. It is axiomatic that unless one finds the correct origin (defined as the *place* where fuel, oxygen, and an ignition source come together), one is likely to come up with an incorrect cause determination. In the 2005 study, two test fires were set in single-room structures and allowed to burn for 2 min after flashover.

Here, an investigator (CFI) was testifying in a civil arson case. His arson determination was based solely on the appearance of a "pour pattern" in a fully involved room (November 10, 2010).

Q. What is your estimate of the heat release rate of the individual fuel packages in the room?
A. I don't know.
Q. Did you ever come to that … did you ever have an opinion as to that?
A. No.
Q. What is your estimate of the number of kilowatts or megawatts that the fire would have needed to bring the room to a flashover?
A. I don't know.
Q. Did the room have a flashover?
A. I don't know.

Q. [Quoting NFPA 921-08 at 6.3.7.8.] Do you agree that irregular patterns such as those that appeared on the floor of the [subject] residence can be created by fires that do not involve ignitable liquid, and I'm going to refer to that definition of irregular patterns?
A. No.

Q. Based on your experience, do you believe you know a flammable liquid pour pattern when you see one?
A. Yes (continued).

Flashover is a transition point in a structure fire's development where a "fire in a room" becomes a "room on fire." This happens when a hot gas layer develops at the ceiling. The fire serves as a "pump" to increase the volume and temperature of that hot gas layer until it begins to radiate its heat in all directions, including downward. When the temperature approaches 1200°F, every exposed combustible surface in the room ignites more or less simultaneously. The diagrams in Fig. 3.6 below illustrate this progression.

Fifty-three investigators were shown the two rooms and asked to write down the quadrant in which they believe the fire originated. Relying on their interpretation of the fire patterns and their belief that the lowest and deepest char indicated the origin, 50 of the 53 selected the wrong quadrant. In the second room, the results were the same. Only 3 of 53 correctly identified the quadrant of origin. Fig. 3.7 shows the fire pattern that most investigators thought indicated the origin. Fig. 3.8 shows the fire pattern above the true origin.

(Continued)

Q. What's your definition of "fire chemistry"?

A. I'm not really sure how I would define that.

Q. Well, what is your understanding of what fire chemistry means?

A. The … I don't know.

Q. Do you agree that combustion of hydrogen in the presence of air to form water is the simplest of all chemical combustion reactions?

A. Can you restate that?

Q. Do you agree that the combustion of hydrogen in the presence of air to form water is the simplest of all chemical combustion reactions?

A. I don't know.

Q. What is the chemical symbol for hydrogen?

   ATTORNEY: Object to the form of the question.

A. I don't know.

Q. Do you agree that the combustion of methane is the simplest of all combustion reactions involving a hydrocarbon?

A. I don't know.

Q. What is the chemical formula for methane?

   ATTORNEY: Object to the form.

A. I don't know.

Q. What's the chemical reaction for the combustion of methane?

   ATTORNEY: Object to the form.

Q. If I gave you a piece of paper, would you be able to write it down?

A. No.

Q. What courses have you taken that would qualify you as postsecondary education in thermodynamics?

A. I don't know.

Q. Do you know what the definition of "thermodynamics" is?

A. No (continued).

In the 2007 study, three test fires were set and allowed to burn for 30 s, 70 s, and 3 min beyond flashover. Again, investigators were asked only to choose the quadrant where they believe the fire originated. For the fire with 30 s of full room involvement, 59 of 70 investigators correctly identified the quadrant of origin. For the fire with 70 s of full room involvement, 44 of 64 investigators who chose to identify a quadrant of origin got it correct. Six investigators admitted that they could not tell. That number rose to 17 investigators for the fire that burned for 3 min beyond flashover when only 13 of the 53 who ventured a guess correctly identified the quadrant of origin. That number is no higher than it would be if the quadrant of origin had been selected at random or if the investigators had depended on two coin

(Continued)

Q. Do you know what the relationship between temperature, volume, and pressure is?

A. No.

Q. Okay. What are the basic units of energy?

A. I believe it's endothermic, exothermic, and I don't recall.

Q. Well, would the basic units of energy be described or referred to as Joules, J-O-U-L-E-S?

A. I don't know.

Q. What are the basic units of power?

ATTORNEY: Object to the form.

A. Amps, watts.

Q. If I refresh your recollection and said "watts" or "kilowatts," would that refresh your recollection?

A. Yes.

Q. What is a "watt"?

A. I don't know.

Q. Is it 1 J per second?

A. I don't know.

Q. What is "radiant heat flux," F-L-U-X?

A. Again, I can refer to 921.

Q. Okay.

A. It discusses radiant heat. I don't see radiant heat flux.

Q. If I walked outside on a cloudless day at noon, what is the radiant heat flux that a square meter of earth's surface is receiving from the sun, would you know?

A. No (continued).

FIGURE 3.6

Sequence of events in the development of a typical compartment fire.

FIGURE 3.7

Large, conspicuous ventilation-produced pattern on the wall opposite the door, incorrectly identified as the origin of the fire by many investigators in the 2005 Las Vegas test. There was no competent ignition source or fuel source at the base of the pattern. The wide base on the pattern may have led some investigators to believe that an ignitable liquid was spread along the wall.

FIGURE 3.8

Roughly V-shaped fire pattern located above the true origin of the Las Vegas test fire.

tosses (Carman, 2009). These results caused significant consternation in the fire investigation community. Origin determination is supposed to be a fire investigator's core competency, but these tests suggested that unless the origin is obvious to an untrained person, the fire investigation profession is not up to the challenge of determining even where the fire began.

What misleads fire investigators in the case of full room involvement is ventilation-generated fire patterns, which are created only after flashover and have no relationship to the origin of the fire. Once flashover occurs, the oxygen concentration in the room drops to near zero, so burning at the origin can practically stop. The room is charged with hot combustible fuel, the products of combustion, which themselves can only burn in the presence of sufficient oxygen. Thus, the most intense burning takes place where that fuel finds an oxygen source.

Interpreting ventilation-generated patterns is not a straightforward exercise. The ventilation that comes in through a door may create a fire with a radiant heat flux of $150 \, \text{kW/m}^2$ on the wall opposite the door. Fig. 3.9 shows the output of a computer model of the 2005 Las Vegas test fire and explains why there was such a large fire on the wall opposite the door. Every fire pattern in a fully involved room needs to be examined to determine whether it can be explained in terms of ventilation, and if it can, the investigator needs to look elsewhere for the origin.

(Continued) Here, the same investigator is testifying on a later civil arson case, opposed by the same law firm. This time the investigator bases his arson determination on a "pour pattern" and two alleged areas of origins with contiguous burning (October 4, 2013).

Q. Do you recall giving a deposition on November the 10th of 2010 in the [previous case]?
A. Yes, I do.
Q. I'll give you a copy of that deposition so that you'll have it. Do you recall being asked on page 74…
   ATTORNEY: A copy for counsel as well.
Q. Do you recall on page 74, you were asked, "Do you agree that the combustion of hydrogen in the presence of air to form water is the simplest of all chemical combustion reactions," and your answer was "I don't know"?
A. Yes.
Q. Were you under oath when you gave that answer?
A. Yes, I was.
Q. And was that in November of 2010?
A. Yes.
Q. And was this investigation that you did in this [case] August and September of that same year prior to that deposition?
A. I believe so.
Q. Is it fair to say that your investigation you conducted in [this case] was in August and September of 2010 and the deposition I've just quoted was in 2 months thereafter, November?
A. Yes.
Q. Do you know what the chemical symbol for hydrogen is?
A. I believe it's H.
Q. Do you know what the chemical formula for hydrogen gas is?
A. No.
Q. Do you know what the chemical reaction for the combustion of hydrogen is?
A. I'm sorry?
Q. Do you know what the chemical reaction for the combustion of hydrogen is as it relates to fire science?
A. No.
Q. Do you know if the combustion of methane is the simplest of all combustion reactions involving a hydrocarbon?
A. I'm not sure (continued).

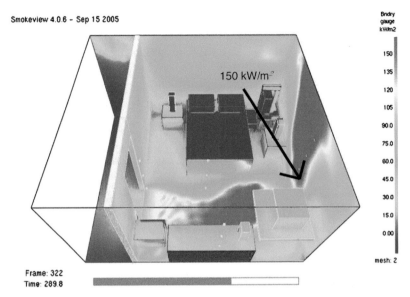

FIGURE 3.9

Output of a fire dynamics simulator computer program used to model the Las Vegas test fire. Because of the influx of oxygen from the doorway, a large, but not terribly meaningful fire pattern developed on the opposite wall.

Adding to the complexity of origin determination is the recently discovered fact that if the origin is elevated above the floor, say on a range top, the development of the hot gas layer might even lead a fire investigator to choose the wrong room of origin. Carman describes an experiment where a fire that started in the kitchen caused the adjacent living room, but not the kitchen, to undergo flashover (Carman, 2011).

Of course, the problem with identifying the wrong point of origin or area of origin is that the ignition source and the first fuel ignited will not be there. Using the discredited methodology called "negative corpus," investigators will state that there were no potential sources of accidental ignition at the "origin," and therefore the fire "must have been" intentional. Investigators might then opine that the first fuel ignited "must have been" a flammable liquid, and the ignition source "must have been" an open flame that whoever poured flammable liquid took with them. There may even be a ventilation induced "irregular pattern" on the floor at the base of the fire pattern determined to have been located just above the "origin." When one considers how fires can be ventilated, keep in mind that usually the hot gases and flames exit the top of the opening, while cool fresh air is drawn in at the bottom. This will result in floor level burning, which, prior to the 1990s, was believed to indicate flammable liquids burning on the floor because as we all know, "heat rises." An incorrect origin determination followed by negative corpus reasoning led to the fire damage shown in Fig. 3.10 being incorrectly characterized as an arson fire.

(Continued)

Q. Do you know what the chemical formula for methane is?

A. No, I don't.

Q. Do you know what the chemical reaction for the combustion of methane is?

A. No.

ATTORNEY: Object to the form.

Q. Do you know how many volumes of air does it take to react to one volume of methane?

A. No, I don't.

ATTORNEY: Object to the form.

Q. In fire science and in fire investigations, is it useful to know the relationship between temperature, volume, and pressure?

A. Yes.

Q. What is that relationship between temperature, volume, and pressure?

A. Well, it produces heat under pressure, so the amount of pressure on substances would be important.

Q. Do you recall being asked whether you knew the relationship between temperature, volume, and pressure on November the 10th, 2010, in the deposition in the [other] matter?

A. Yes.

Q. Do you recall the question "Do you know what the relationship between temperature, volume, and pressure is," and your answer was "No"…

A. Yes.

Q. …page 75?

A. Sorry.

Q. Okay. And were you under oath back in November the 10th of 2010?

A. Yes.

Q. All right, sir. In relationship to fire dynamics and fire investigations, what are the basic units of energy?

A. I believe it's exothermic and endothermic (continued).

FIGURE 3.10

The V-shaped pattern in the upper right was incorrectly identified as the origin of the fire. The pattern was created late in the fire as evidenced by its location on the interior of the second layer of drywall. The pattern was the result of ventilation. Because he was unable to locate any ignition source at the base of the V, the investigator concluded that the fire must have been set.

In a compartment fire, heat rises only until it meets an obstruction such as a ceiling, and then the hot gas layer forms. This causes fire behavior that is unfamiliar to individuals who know only about unconfined fires, such as trash fires and campfires. Such people are easily misled. Once the radiant heat flux from the hot gas layer reaches a value of approximately $20\,kW/m^2$, every exposed combustible surface in the room ignites within a matter of a few seconds. This includes floors and floor coverings. Fire burning on a floor is only "unnatural" if the floor burns prior to flashover.

COMMON MISINTERPRETATIONS OF FIRE ARTIFACTS

The understanding of the phenomenon of flashover has been critical to the improvement of the accuracy of fire investigation, but the profession still has a long way to go. There are still far too many investigators who believe in the fire myths and far too many who believe that they can, based on their years of experience, identify a flammable liquid "*pour pattern*" by visual observation alone. Such individuals are subject to a reliability challenge based on NFPA 921, which has warned against such practices in ever-stronger terms since its first edition. The 2014 edition carries these warnings about "irregular patterns."

(Continued)

Q. What are the basic units of power?

A. Joule.

Q. Do you know how a watt relates to a joule?

A. No. I can reference it in 921. I know it's documented, but…

Q. You can find it in there if you looked?

A. Yes.

Q. Okay. What is radiant heat flux?

A. I believe it's the … I think it's the area that's divided in a compartment, the area of heat.

Q. Okay, sir. If you were to measure … try to measure radiant heat flux, how would you measure it?

A. I don't know.

Q. Do you know what the generally accepted value of radiant heat flux is that will result in a flashover fire?

A. No.

Q. You mentioned you took a 6-h course in computer fire modeling. Do you know what mathematical modeling is used for?

A. Not specifically.

Q. Do you know the difference between a zone model and a field model?

A. No, I'm not familiar with that.

6.3.7.8 **Irregular Patterns**. Irregular, curved, or "pool-shaped" patterns on floors and floor coverings should not be identified as resulting from ignitable liquids on the basis of visual appearance alone. In cases of full room involvement, patterns similar in appearance to ignitable liquid burn patterns can be produced when no ignitable liquid is present.

6.3.7.8.2 Irregular patterns are common in situations of postflashover conditions, long extinguishing times, or building collapse. These patterns may result from the effects of hot gases, flaming and smoldering debris, melted plastics, or ignitable liquids. If the presence of ignitable liquids is suspected, supporting evidence in the form of a laboratory analysis should be sought.

6.3.7.8.5 The term *pour pattern* implies that a liquid has been poured or otherwise distributed and therefore is demonstrative of an intentional act. Because fire patterns resulting from burning ignitable liquids are not visually unique, the use of the term pour pattern and reference to the nature of the pattern should be avoided. The correct term for this fire pattern is an irregularly-shaped fire pattern. The presence of an ignitable liquid should be confirmed by laboratory analysis. The determination of the nature of an irregular pattern should not be made by visual interpretation of the pattern alone.

NFPA 921 contains more warnings about this particular misinterpretation than any others. The reason is that the number of wrongful convictions that have occurred as a result of fire investigators making this misinterpretation is quite large.

One of the first arson convictions overturned as a result of the new knowledge of flashover-generated patterns was that of Ray Girdler in Arizona. Mr. Girdler was convicted based on low-burning, irregular patterns, crazed glass, and a medical examiner's unsupported opinion that the high carboxyhemoglobin (COHb) levels in Girdler's wife and daughter indicated an accelerated fire. After an extraordinary 11-day evidentiary hearing, the trial judge (James Sult, the same judge who had sentenced Girdler to life without parole 8 years earlier) ruled that the artifacts relied upon as evidence of arson were now known to result from accidental as well as intentional fires.

This is the case with most overturned arson convictions. The *corpus delicti*, which the state is supposedly required to prove beyond a reasonable doubt, is later proved to have no scientific basis. The visual (mis)interpretation of irregular patterns is usually a factor. In these cases, it frequently happens that the laboratory analysis has come back with negative results. Laboratory analysis is considerably more objective than fire scene analysis, but laboratory errors have been important factors in several miscarriages.

If fire scene investigators incorrectly characterize an irregular pattern as one caused by an ignitable liquid, then the laboratory incorrectly identifies gasoline in a debris sample, the suspect's goose is cooked unless the lab error is detected by the defense. There is (usually) no good reason for there to be gasoline on the living room carpet, and if the lab finds it, the scene investigator's confidence in his findings will be boosted to the point where it is unshakeable. For this reason, it is imperative that the lab results be examined early in the litigation process. If the gasoline determination is a righteous one, there is little point in contesting the incendiary classification of the fire. Note that the finding of almost any other ignitable liquid residue besides gasoline may have an innocent explanation.

Shoes, for example, are known to contain a variety of hydrocarbon solvents. Floor coatings may contain solvents, such as mineral spirits, that may be detectable for decades (Lentini, 2001). Newsprint may test positive for kerosene, and carbonless forms often test positive for a mixture of compounds commonly found in lamp oil (Lentini et al., 2000). In the absence of a comparison sample, the contribution of the background may never be known, and meaningless findings of a trace amount of an ignitable liquid residue will be presented as "evidence of an accelerant."

It was a false finding of gasoline that led to the wrongful conviction of David Lee Gavitt in Michigan. Fire investigators in 1985 declared the fire that killed his wife and two children was intentionally set in three places using a flammable liquid. A profoundly unqualified chemist used profoundly poor methodology to wrongly conclude that 2 of 17 debris samples were positive for gasoline. The error was not discovered until 2011 when the author was asked to examine the laboratory data. There were numerous other errors in the case, but it took 2 more years and a review by the ATF requested by the prosecutor before Mr. Gavitt was finally released (Plummer and Syed, 2012).

Another wrongful conviction overturned was that of Weldon Wayne Carr in Georgia. He was convicted in 1994, despite the fact that 12 samples collected by the fire investigator tested negative at two different laboratories. Prosecutor Nancy Grace, in her last trial before hiring on at CNN, used the positive alerts of a canine named Blaze to persuade the jury that ignitable liquids were involved in the fire. The Georgia Supreme Court found that using unconfirmed canine alerts was akin to the earliest lie detector tests.

> *The first recorded lie detector test was in ancient India where a suspect was required to enter a darkened room and touch the tail of a donkey. If the donkey brayed when his tail was touched the suspect was declared guilty, otherwise he was released. Modern science has substituted a metal electronic box for the donkey but the results remain just as haphazard and inconclusive.*

Carr vs. State (1997)

The use of unconfirmed canine alerts is an insult to the collective intelligence of courts and juries, but overzealous prosecutors will present this pseudoscience anyways. Analogies to drug dogs and explosive dogs are inapt. If a drug dog or an explosive dog alerts to a suitcase, and no drugs or explosives are found, nobody is even arrested. But in the case of accelerant-detecting canines, the handlers (who are not scientists) believe their dogs are more sensitive than the laboratory and insist that the alerts, which are presumptive tests at best, mean that the fire was intentionally set. The sensitivity argument is bogus. A competent laboratory analyst can detect quantities of ignitable liquid as small as $1/500^{th}$ of a drop (0.1 μL) (Lentini, 2012a,b).

In 1996, the NFPA Technical Committee on Fire Investigations declared, "a fraud is being perpetrated on the judicial system" (NFPA Technical Committee on Fire Investigations, 1996) and stated in NFPA 921 that unconfirmed canine alerts should not be considered validated (NFPA 921-14: 17.5.4.7.1). The misuse of unconfirmed alerts diminished but did not stop entirely. The Canine Accelerant Detection Association, the largest professional association of canine handlers, denounced the continued attempt to introduce unconfirmed alerts in 2012. They stated, "… no Prosecutor, Attorney or ADC Handler should ever testify or encourage testimony that an ignitable liquid is present without confirmation through laboratory analysis" (Officers And Directors of the Canine Accelerant Detection Association, 2012).

Another common cause of wrongful classification of accidental fires as intentional is the fire investigator's perception of "multiple origins." When flashover occurs, all of the available exposed fuel ignites nearly simultaneously. The ignition results in the burning of floors and baseboards, even baseboards and floors remote from the place where the fire started. As a result, a fire that starts in one area of a building could, through flashover, ignite fuel in another area of the building, and those two areas could burn more intensely than the area in between due to differences in the available ventilation. Thus, multiple origins are perceived where none actually exist.

In January 2013, the Defense Research Institute sponsored a seminar entitled *Fire Science and Litigation: Smoke and Mirrors, Using Science to Light the Way* in which the science of origin determination was discussed, including a discussion by Steven Carman, the author of the 2005 Origin Accuracy paper and a highly respected former ATF agent, entitled "The Impact of Ventilation in Fire Investigation." The following is Mr. Carman's advice on the possibility of confusion caused by ventilation.

> *Areas of pre- and post-flashover damage created during the same fire can be far removed from each other and show no apparent connection. The post-flashover damage can be far more severe and appear indicative of longer burning. Investigators unfamiliar with post-flashover burning behavior might conclude that separate fires were set independently of the others. Such analyses can mistakenly lead to incorrect origin determinations and cause classifications.*

There is no question that accidental fires almost always begin in one and only one place. Thus, if there is **reliable** evidence of multiple origins, this is powerful evidence indicating that a fire was set. Unfortunately, many fire investigators believe they can discern multiple origins even after full room involvement and even when all of the damage is contiguous.

NFPA 921 discusses multiple origins and warns about potentially confounding influences that will cause a fire investigator to be misled. The following guidance is provided.

> 24.2.1 **Multiple Fires**. Multiple fires are two or more separate, nonrelated, simultaneously burning fires. The investigator should search to uncover any additional fire sets or points of origin that may exist. In order to conclude that there are multiple fires, the investigator should determine that any "separate" fire was not the natural outgrowth of the initial fire.
>
> 24.2.1.1 Fires in different rooms, fires on different stories with no connecting fire, or separate fires inside and outside a building are examples of multiple fires. A search of the fire building and its surrounding areas should be conducted to determine whether there are multiple fires.
>
> 24.2.1.2 Separate fires that are not caused by multiple deliberate ignitions can result from the following:
>   1. fire spread by conduction, convection, or radiation
>   2. fire spread by flying brands

3. fire spread by direct flame impingement
4. fire spread by falling flaming materials (i.e., drop-down), such as curtains
5. fire spread through shafts, such as pipe chases or air conditioning ducts
6. fire spread within wall or floor cavities within "balloon construction"
7. overloaded electrical wiring
8. utility system failures
9. lightning
10. rupture and launching of aerosol containers

Han Tak Lee was convicted of setting the 1989 fire that killed his daughter at a church retreat in rural Pennsylvania. The "science" used to "prove" that the fire was intentionally set included an assertion that the fire had nine separate points of origin in one fully involved room. The state alleged the use of more than 60 gallons of a diesel fuel/gasoline mixture, despite the fact that no container large enough to accommodate this astonishing volume existed in the small cabin where the fire occurred. Mr. Lee's defense counsel argued that it was the mentally disturbed victim who set the fire, but the District Attorney countered that she was not clever enough to have mixed the fuels together. He argued, erroneously, that three samples that tested positive each contained "the very same thing," despite the fact that the chemist had said no such thing when testifying.

Those offering testimony against Mr. Lee were no more qualified than the investigators described at the beginning of this chapter, who do not know the basic units of energy. One of the investigators stated that fire burned abnormally fast because it exceeded the "standard time–temperature curve." That curve describes how to run a fire resistance test, but has no relationship to how an actual fire behaves. That witness also claimed to have investigated 15,000 fires in a 20-year career (do the math.) Some 10 years after the trial, the state's lead investigator, writing in a letter to the editor, defended his investigation, stating that his methodology had not been discredited until after the trial.

It required 21 years of litigation before the state conceded that all of the so-called indicators of arson were invalid. The state was left with the three samples, having "lost" the original data. When those samples were reanalyzed and compared in 2012, they were clearly not "the very same thing" and were easily distinguishable.

In 2014, Federal Magistrate Judge Martin Carlson wrote a remarkable 45-page report and recommendation stating that Mr. Lee should be freed after serving 25 years of a life sentence. The report began with these words: "Slow and painful has been man's progress from magic to law." He continued, "Sometimes, with the benefit of insight gained over time, we learn that what was once regarded as truth is myth, and what was once accepted as science is superstition. So it is in this case" (Tak Lee, 2014).

CONCLUSION

The Lee case presents a microcosm of all that has changed about fire investigation over the last 40 years. NFPA 921, for its first three editions, described fire investigation as "a complex endeavor involving both art and science." The language was changed in 2001 (and thereafter) to read "a complex endeavor involving skill, technology, knowledge, and science." As science has become dominant, the situation has improved, but there is still a significant cadre of investigators who believe in the myths and who are unable to apply science properly in their investigations because they are not scientists and have no plans to become scientists. Thus, there is still a need for vigilance on the part of those who consume the work product of this profession.

In their analysis of the disastrous Cameron Todd Willingham case, the Texas Forensic Science Commission made a list of 17 recommendations for improving the practice of fire investigation and its use in the justice system. Perhaps the most important of the recommendations called for an increase in judicial scrutiny. The Commission recommended that admissibility hearings (also referred to as Daubert/Kelly hearings) be conducted in all arson cases due to the inherently complex nature of fire science and the continuously evolving nature of fire investigation standards (Report of The Texas, 2011). Such hearings will facilitate the "bifurcation" necessary to prevent conviction of individuals based on character assassination rather than on good science.

In the final analysis, however, the situation is unlikely to improve until the people and organizations that hire fire investigators are able to offer salaries sufficiently high to attract educated scientists.

REFERENCES

Boudreau, J., Kwan, Q., Faragher, W., Denault, G., 1977. Arson and Arson Investigation-Survey and Assessment. Law Enforcement Assistance Administration, United States Department of Justice, Washington, DC.

Brannigan, F., Bright, R., Jason, N., 1980. Fire Investigation Handbook. National Bureau of Standards, U.S. Department of Commerce, Washington, DC.

Brants, C., 2011. Comparing criminal process as part of legal culture. Comparative Criminal Justice and Globalization 49–66.

Burke, P.W. Amicus curiae brief filed on behalf of the International Association of Arson Investigators. In: Michigan Millers Mutual Insurance Company v. Janelle R. Benfield. 140 F.3d 915 (11th Cir. 1998). Available at http://caselaw.findlaw.com/us-11th-circuit/1396573.html.

Carman, S. Improving the understanding of post-flashover fire behavior. In: Fire and Materials, Eleventh International Conference, 26–28 January 2009. Interscience Communications, London. Available at: http://carmanfireinvestigations.com/publications.html.

Carman, S. Fire and Materials. In: Twelfth International Conference, 31 January–2 February 2011. Interscience Communications, London. Available at: http://carmanfireinvestigations.com/publications.html.

Carr vs State, 1997. Ga. Lexis 104.

Fay, J.J., 2007. Investigation: arson. In: Fay, J.J. (Ed.), Encyclopedia of Security Management. Elsevier, Amsterdam, pp. 127–130.

From NFPA 921-14: 17.5.4.7.1. In order for the presence or absence of an ignitible liquid to be scientifically confirmed in a sample, that sample should be analyzed by a laboratory in accordance with 17.5.3. Any canine alert not confirmed by laboratory analysis should not be considered validated.

Kirk, P., 1969. Fire Investigation. John Wiley & Sons, Hoboken, NJ, p. 145.

Lentini, J., Henderson, R., Smith, D., August 1992. Baseline Characteristics of Residential Structures Which Have Burned to Completion: The Oakland Experience, Fire Technology, vol. 28 (3). National Fire Protection Association (NFPA), Quincy, MA.

Lentini, J., Dolan, J., Cherry, C., September 2000. The petroleum-laced background. Journal of Forensic Sciences 45 (5).

Lentini, J., September 1992. The Lime Street Fire: Another Perspective, the Fire and Arson Investigator, vol. 43 (1). International Association of Arson Investigators, (IAAI), Crofton, MD.

Lentini, J., November 2001. Persistence of floor coating solvents. Journal of Forensic Sciences 46 (6).

Lentini, J., 2012a. "The Mythology of Arson Investigation," Chapter 8 in Scientific Protocols for Fire Investigation, second ed. CRC Press, Boca Raton, FL, p. 471.

Lentini, J., 2012b. "Analysis of Ignitable Liquid Residues," Chapter 5 in Scientific Protocols for Fire Investigation, second ed. CRC Press, Boca Raton, FL, p. 167.

Mann, D., November 27, 2009. Fire and Innocence. The Texas Observer, Austin, TX.

Millers Mutual Insurance Company v. Janelle, R. Benfield, 140 F.3d 915, 11th Cir. 1998. Available at: http://caselaw.findlaw.com/us-11th-circuit/1396573.html.

NFPA 1033, 2014. Standard for Professional Qualifications for Fire Investigator. National Fire Protection Association (NFPA), Quincy, MA.

NFPA 921, 2014. Guide for Fire and Explosion Investigation. NFPA, Quincy, MA. at 3.3.71.

NFPA Technical Committee on Fire Investigations, August 9, 1996. Existing Judicial Emergency Requiring Issuance of a Tentative Interim Amendment. NFPA, Quincy, MA.

Officers and Directors of the Canine Accelerant Detection Association, September 2012. Available at: http://cadafiredogs.com/wp-content/uploads/2012/01/CADAS-Position-on-Testifying-to-Negative-Samples.pdf.

Orthmann, C.H., Hess, K.M., 2013. Criminal Investigation, tenth ed. Delmar Cengage Learning, Clifton Park, NY, pp. 492–493.

Plummer, C., Syed, I., 2012. 'Shifted science' and post-conviction relief. Standford Journal of Civil Rights and Civil Liberties 8 (2), 259–297.

Report of the Texas Forensic Science Commission, Willingham/Willis Investigation, April 15, 2011. Available at: http://www.fsc.state.tx.us/documents/FINAL.pdf.

Stridbeck, U., Magnussen, D., Svein, P., 2013. Prevention of Wrongful Convictions: Norwegian Legal Safeguards and the Criminal Cases Review Commission. University of Cincinnati Law Review 80 (4), 15.

Tak Lee, H. Petitioner, vs. Franklin Tennis, Respondent, case 4:08-cv-01972-WJN document 80 filed, June 13, 2014.

Tedim, F., Xanthopoulos, G., Leone, V., 2015. Forest Fires in Europe: Facts and Challenges.

Wright, J.D., Singer, J., 2014. Fire and Explosives. Routledge.

Shaken Baby Syndrome

4

Forensic Science Reform. http://dx.doi.org/10.1016/B978-0-12-802719-6.00004-2

Case Study: Ken Marsh

Wendy J. Koen

Child Refuge, Inc., Menifee, CA, United States

Every generation has its quasi-religious orthodoxies, and if there is one certainty in history it is that many beliefs that were firmly held yesterday will become the object of knowing ridicule tomorrow.

Michael Mansfield

Kenneth Marsh. Photo Courtesy of Heidi Cruise and the California Innocence Project at Californian Western School of Law.

Two-year-old Phillip Buell died from massive head injuries that doctors concluded could only have been inflicted by his mother's boyfriend, Kenneth Marsh. According to medical testimony, Marsh must have violently shaken Phillip and repeatedly slammed Phillip's head against a hard, blunt object, causing injury equal to that of an infant who was in a high-speed vehicle accident, unrestrained at the time of impact.

Marsh told a different story: while he was babysitting his girlfriend's two children in April of 1983, Marsh left the children sitting on the couch in the living room just long enough to get the vacuum cleaner (National Registry of Exonerations, hereafter, "Registry"). When he returned to the living room, he found 2-year-old Phillip Buell unresponsive, lying on the fireplace hearth near the couch (Registry). Remnants of broken glass from a candy dish were found near Phillip's body (*People v. Marsh*, 1985). Marsh immediately called 911, and paramedics rushed Phillip to Hospital (Warter, 2004; California Innocence Project).

The doctors at the hospital quickly concluded that Phillip's injuries were the result of a ferocious attack (Warter, 2004). They did not believe Marsh's version of events, and, because Marsh was alone with the children when Phillip became unresponsive, he was the sole suspect. When Phillip's mother, Brenda Buell Warter, arrived at the hospital, Phillip was still alive, and obviously, no autopsy had been performed. Still, the doctors told Warter that Phillip had been murdered (Warter, 2004).

Although San Diego Police investigators initially believed Marsh's account of Phillip's injuries and that Phillip's death was caused by an accidental fall from the couch to the hearth, because the doctors thought Phillip was murdered, they pushed for Marsh's arrest. Marsh was arrested even before the cause of death had been officially determined and before the autopsy report and death certificate had been issued. In the end, the doctors at the hospital, including the pathologist who conducted the autopsy, determined Phillip died from a violent shaking and slamming force, and concluded the manner of death was shaken baby syndrome (SBS) and abusive head trauma (AHT) (Registry). After urging the district attorney's office to file charges against Marsh, the doctors provided the testimony and photographs needed for Marsh's trial.

As we have seen repeatedly in SBS/AHT cases, the doctors all testified Phillip could not have sustained his injuries from a short fall from the couch to the hearth; it was medically impossible, as his injuries were simply too severe. The opinions of the medical experts unanimously ruled out accidental death and found that the injuries were due to violent shaking and Phillip's head making direct contact with a blunt object accompanied by force equivalent to a high-speed automobile crash or fall from a great height, like a second story window (*People v. Marsh*). By Marsh's own admission, he was the only adult present when Phillip was injured (*People v. Marsh*). Therefore, Marsh was the only one who could have administered the violent blows to Phillip's head with the force described.

Marsh's conviction was obtained based on medical science being embraced by doctors and courtrooms throughout the world (Donohoe, 2003; Le Fanu, 2004; Squier, 2010). Very few medical experts disagreed with SBS/AHT science. If an infant presented with a triad of symptoms: subdural hematomas (collection of blood between the covering of the brain, called the dura, and the surface of the brain), retinal hemorrhages (RHs, bleeding in the retina), and cerebral edema (swelling in the brain), the person with the infant when he or she became ill must have injured the infant by violent shaking (Donohoe, 2003). Suspicion should be heightened when the potential abuser was the boyfriend of the mother of the abused (Showers et al., 1985). Thus, Marsh was the perfect suspect.

However, logical scientific arguments were built upon the shakiest of assumptions. Doctors assumed Phillip's injuries could not have been caused by accidental or natural means because they were simply too severe, and, therefore, they must have been caused by brutal, intentional force. Doctors assumed that if Phillip had the triad of symptoms, his injuries were caused by violent shaking. Doctors assumed that because Phillip's injuries were so severe, the person with Phillip at the time he became unresponsive must be the person who inflicted the brutal injuries. In this way, a medical diagnosis of SBS/AHT built on these assumptions, along with Marsh's admission he was the only adult with Phillip at the time he was injured, was all that was needed to convict Marsh.

The biggest assumption on which Marsh's conviction was built was that only a violent attack could have left Phillip with such injuries. Doctors testified that Phillip's short fall from the couch onto the hearth could not have caused his injuries.

Tragically, guilt was determined with no significant consideration of Phillip's health prior to his tragic death. As in many supposed SBS/AHT cases, Phillip had medical problems before the day of his injury and death (Warter, 2004). Notably, medical records establish that Philip's problems began even before his birth. Phillip's amniotic sac broke 18 hours before delivery, and delivery was complicated. After remaining in the birth canal for an unusual length of time, doctors had to resort to the use of forceps to deliver him. This caused Phillip's head and face to be injured. The traumatic birth broke blood vessels in each of Phillip's eyes. Phillip was diagnosed with jaundice and chlamydia pneumonia. Phillip also had an unusually large soft spot (i.e., fontanel) that had not knitted together as is normally expected (Warter, 2004).

In addition to the symptoms caused by a complicated birth, one significant medical condition that mimics the "classic" symptoms of SBS/AHT (i.e., the triad) and can often lead to a misdiagnosis of child abuse is a bleeding disorder (Warter, 2004). Phillip had a bleeding disorder. In January 1983, Warter took Phillip to the hospital for vomiting, constipation, and a hyperextended stomach. It was discovered that Phillip was losing a significant amount of blood. After several visits with the doctor, Warter again rushed Phillip to a hospital emergency room because he was in shock from blood loss. This occurred 3 weeks before his death.

Many experts now firmly believe that birthing complications, like those experienced by Phillip, can lead to symptoms once considered conclusive evidence of abuse. These birthing complications, when coupled with evidence of a bleeding disorder and a short fall onto a hard surface, substantiate an alternative, innocent explanation for Phillip's injuries and death.

One tragedy in this case is that despite Phillip's medical history of a bleeding disorder and knowledge that Phillip fell from the couch and injured his head in the fall, on the day of Phillip's fall, a doctor gave Phillip an injection of Mannitol before he reached the hospital. This injection increased blood flow to Phillips brain, which, in turn, increased bleeding and swelling, severely worsening Phillip's medical condition and intensifying the purported evidence of abuse.

At Marsh's trial, Phillip's medical history and possible innocent explanations for Phillip's death went largely unexplored, and the doctors' unified testimony was convincing. No expert could be found to refute the doctors' consistent and horrifying testimony. Any jury hearing the evidence against Marsh would consider Marsh to be a cruel monster who intentionally murdered a helpless infant by brutal force, and Marsh was convicted of second-degree murder on November 28, 1983, and sentenced to a term of 15 years to life (*People v. Marsh*; Warter, 2004).

POSTCONVICTION APPEALS

After conviction, Marsh's case went through a number of appeals and habeas proceedings, including a direct appeal to the California Court of Appeal for the Fourth District based on insufficiency of the evidence to convict and the prejudicial admission of photographs of Phillip's body. The conviction was upheld by the Fourth

District. Marsh filed a Petition for Writ of Habeas Corpus in the San Diego Superior Court; it was denied. Nearly 10 years later, in 1995, Marsh's attorney filed a subsequent habeas petition in San Diego Superior Court based on newly discovered evidence, relying on the advances in medical science and the unraveling of some of the SBS/AHT dogma. Again, the court denied his petition for relief.

Throughout all of these proceedings, Phillip's mother, Brenda Buell Warter, was Marsh's firmest supporter. Warter explained that she knew if she had been the one home with Phillip on the day he fell, she would have been the one to be charged and convicted of murder (Warter, 2004). Her faith in Marsh's innocence never wavered (Registry). Warter's efforts led to her partnership with attorney Tracey Emblem and the California Innocence Project. Emblem worked pro bono, investigating the advances in the medical sciences, and drafting a massive habeas petition that refuted all of the evidence the jury relied on to convict Marsh. The California Innocence Project and Emblem filed the petition in 2002.

Before resolution of the habeas, on August 4, 2004, San Diego District Attorney Bonnie Dumanis, in cooperation with Marsh's advocates, agreed Ken Marsh's habeas petition for a new trial should be granted (Warter, 2004). Understanding that the SBS hypothesis had been challenged and found wanting, Dumanis had sent Phillip's medical records and other evidence to an independent pathologist for review. The pathologist analyzed the evidence, took Phillip's medical history into consideration, and found that there was not sufficient evidence to support a finding that Phillip was ever abused or that Phillip was abused by Marsh.

On August 10, 2004, after 21 years of wrongful imprisonment, Ken Marsh's conviction was reversed; he was finally freed. Because there was no evidence that a crime had actually been committed or that Marsh had hurt Phillip, it was not surprising that Marsh was not retried.

LITIGATION-DRIVEN SCIENCE

Marsh was just one victim of the frenzy of SBS convictions worldwide based on the belief that a triad of symptoms proved that an infant was abused by being violently shaken. Regardless of the controversy in the medical community worldwide, sick and injured infants are still deemed to be abused based on the medical diagnosis of SBS or AHT. In France, judicial data suggests there are 2.9 fatalities attributed to SBS for every 100,000 infants (Tursz and Cook, 2014). The number of estimated cases attributed to SBS per 100,000 infants varies from country to country; per 100,000, there are an estimated 14 SBS cases in Switzerland, 40 in Estonia (Lips and Manconi, 2010), 30 in the US, 14 in the UK, and 25 in Scotland (Mann et al., 2015).

In the UK, about 250 of these SBS cases go to court each year (Levin, 2011). The top pediatric neuropathologist in the UK, Dr. Waney Squier, is convinced that about 50% of these convictions are wrongful (Levin, 2011). Dr. Squier is well respected internationally and has been studying infant brain trauma for more than 30 years (Squier, 2008). She believes that evidence other than the triad must be considered when deciding an alleged SBS/AHT case (Squier, 2008). She is not alone in her opinion. At least to some degree, changes are being made in how SBS/AHT cases are handled in the UK. Prosecutor guidelines in the UK now make it clear that charges of homicide, attempted murder, or assault are not justified when based only on the triad of injuries (BBC News, UK, 2011; Crown Prosecution Service).

The Canadian and Australian justice systems are also evolving their methods in SBS/AHT cases (Jenecke, 2014). In Australia, prosecutions can no longer be based solely on the presence of the triad of symptoms (Jenecke, 2014). In Canada, the government invested over eight million dollars into a systematic review of SBS-related convictions in Ontario. The resulting 1000-page report called into question convictions based on the triad. The report concluded that medical science has determined the triad is no longer proof of abuse and that short-distance falls can be fatal to infants (Jenecke, 2014).

However, while research presents compelling evidence that the triad alone is not enough for a conviction (Sperhake and Matschke, 2014) and other countries have abandoned prosecutions based on the triad alone (Jenecke, 2014), in the US, convictions based on a medical diagnosis of child abuse and an admission by the defendant that he or she was the only adult with the infant are still occurring (Jenecke, 2014; *Maze v. Lester;* Miller et al., 2015; Pishko, 2014). American law enforcement authorities estimate that there are about 200 shaken baby convictions a year (Jenecke, 2014). In 50–75% of these SBS trials, the triad of symptoms is the *only* evidence of child abuse offered in evidence (Pishko, 2014; Bazelon, 2011). This still happens in the US, in part because stalwart SBS doctors continue to hold onto and testify according to the old SBS dogma (Tuerkheimer, 2014; Pishko, 2014). Because some still believe that in the majority of cases of SBS, there are no visible signs of outward trauma or other injuries suffered by the infant (Health Research Funding, 2015), it follows that the internal injuries (i.e., the triad) will be the foundation for an SBS diagnosis and conviction. This is particularly disquieting because of the internationally well-recognized fact that the causes of subdural hematomas, RHs, and cerebral edema (i.e., the triad) are varied and not well understood (Findley et al., 2015; Miller et al., 2015; Emerson et al., 2007; Squier, 2011; Christian et al., 2009).

American courts' continued reliance on old SBS dogma can also be blamed on the way the American system of justice relies on stare decisis to the detriment of scientific advancement. Despite rapidly changing views among medical experts in the early 21st century, defense attorneys in the US who launch direct challenges to the admission of SBS testimony by experts who embrace debunked SBS dogma are generally unsuccessful (Jenecke, 2014). In fact, the majority of trial courts, when faced with a challenge to expert SBS evidence, have consistently justified their admission of disputed SBS evidence (Jenecke, 2014; Tuerkheimer, 2014). This is because it has been established by precedent that particular doctors and scientists qualify as expert witnesses, and their beliefs about SBS have been accepted in courts throughout the nation.

Regardless of the country, it is clear that far too many parents and caretakers have found themselves at the mercy of the courts based on a medical diagnosis of child abuse. Yet, the litigation-driven science of SBS/AHT lacks adequate evidence that abuse actually happened.

Researchers have noted that child abuse research presents a unique set of problems (Lantz, 2004; Donohoe, 2003). Obviously, no researcher would shake a living infant in order to see just what damage is done. Research using cadavers is limited (Donohoe, 2003). Although biomechanical studies seeking to replicate injuries are informative, they cannot begin to definitively address all of the questions presented by supposed SBS cases (Donohoe, 2003). This leaves law enforcement in an untenable position. At first blush, when there is an innocent, helpless infant, killed or severely injured by inexplicable forces, something, anything must be done to prevent it from happening again. It seems logical to blame the last person caring for the child. When there is no external manifestation of injury, our nature forces us to determine just how the internal injuries occurred. When SBS was first defined, it gave a framework for prosecution and a way for law enforcement to bring some sense of resolution to incidences that include the injury or death of the most vulnerable victims (Lantz, 2004).

However, we now know that this framework is faulty. Norman Guthkelch, the pediatric neurosurgeon who many accredit as the first to observe and document the triad of symptoms and to link the triad with shaking, has concerns regarding how the triad is used to diagnose child abuse (Bache et al., 2015; Shapiro, 2011). He fears doctors and medical examiners rest their medical findings on the triad alone, when other factors could have contributed to or caused the infant's demise (Shapiro, 2011). Attorneys and courts must not rely on this framework and must demand only verifiable evidence in these cases. The difficulty of research in this area and the appalling nature of unexplainable injuries to children do not justify circular reasoning or conclusions that overstep the data (Donohoe, 2003; Tuerkheimer, 2014; Jenecke, 2014).

PRESUMPTION OF INNOCENCE

There is almost universal acceptance of the concept that individuals are innocent until proven guilty.[1] SBS/AHT litigation defies this foundational pillar of justice (Wrennall et al., 2015). SBS/AHT stands alongside arson as the two types of criminal charges that can be substantiated based only on an admission by the defendant that he or she was at the scene and expert testimony establishing that a crime was committed.

---

[1] See Article 6(2) of the 1950 European Convention on Human Rights, which provides: "Everyone charged with a criminal offence shall be presumed innocent until proved guilty according to law." See also Article 14(2) of the 1966 International Covenant on Civil and Political Rights, which provides: "Everyone charged with a criminal offence shall have the right to be presumed innocent until proved guilty according to law" and Article 8(2) of the 1969 American Convention on Human Rights, which provides: "Every person accused of a criminal offence has the right to be presumed innocent so long as his guilt has not been proven according to law." See https://www.icrc.org/customary-ihl/eng/docs/v2_cha_chapter32_rule100_sectionc for a complete list of instruments that guarantee this right around the globe. American Convention on Human Rights, adopted by the OAS Inter-American Specialized Conference on Human Rights, San José, 22 November 1969, also known as Pact of San José, Article 8(2).

If there is a medical diagnosis of SBS/AHT, the person with the child at the time of the injury is guilty of intentional assault on a child or murder. Intent is proven by the expert's opinion of just how violently the shaking or blunt force trauma must have been. Thus, testimony from a medical professional is all that is needed to convict a child's caretaker of the most horrible of crimes (Wrennall et al., 2015). Now, it is up to the defense to refute the medical diagnosis and prove an innocent explanation for the infant's injuries, effectively shifting the burden of proof.

The shift in burden of proof is only made worse by the oft gruesome and heartbreaking nature of these cases. Medical doctors and the prosecutor are armed with horrific autopsy photos of a baby. This alone will infuse juries and triers of fact with righteous anger and a need for retribution. Marsh's trial was tainted by the admission of gruesome photographs of Phillip's body at autopsy that the prosecution displayed several times larger than life-sized (*People v. Marsh*, 1985). On appeal, the court described the photographs:

> *Over Marsh's objection, seven autopsy photographs in vivid color were blown up and projected onto a screen for the jurors' viewing. The least gruesome shows an interior section of the victim's skull with the residue of heavy blood clots. (Exhibit 22). Another shows an almost full view of the victim's nude body the close-up portion of which is the exterior surface of the exposed brain below which dangles part of the bloody scalp and in the background of which is the child's blood-splattered torso "field dressed" with the ribcages rolled back to expose the bowels. Another pictures the victim's neck and head with half of the scalp drawn down over his face and the other half pealed rearward exposing the right hemisphere of the brain. Another exhibits the left brain hemisphere with massive blood clotting and a portion of the severed skull plate lying immediately behind the head.*
>
> **People v. Marsh (1985, p. 997).**

The court on appeal found that the inflammatory nature of the autopsy photographs was heightened because they were shown in sequence with several other photographs of Phillip while he was still alive (*People v. Marsh*, 1985, p. 999). Not only were the photographs gruesome and heartbreaking, their admission was absolutely unnecessary for any legitimate purpose. On direct appeal, the court decided that because the uncontradicted medical testimony identified the precise location and nature of Phillip's injuries, the heart-wrenching photographs of his body had little, if any, additional probative value, and "[t]hey supplied no more than a blatant appeal to the jury's emotions" (*People v. Marsh*, 1985, p. 997).

However, Marsh's conviction remained intact. Although American precedent dictates that the unnecessary admission of gruesome photographs can deprive a defendant of a fair trial (*People v. Burns*, 1952; *People v. Cavanaugh*, 1955) and require reversal of a judgment, and the court on appeal here concluded that "the jury was not enlightened one additional whit by viewing these seven gory autopsy photographs" (*People v. Marsh*, 1985, p. 998), because of the overwhelming cohesive and damning expert evidence of SBS/AHT and the complete lack of a medical defense explanation for Phillip's injuries, any error caused by the admission of the gut-wrenching photos was deemed harmless.

In addition, scientifically dubious, unfounded concepts that are chilling and damning are used that effectively instill horrific images in the mind of the trier of fact. Here, the jury was told that Phillip's injuries were caused by his head's direct contact with a blunt object accompanied by force equal to a high-speed automobile crash or fall from a great height (*People v. Marsh*, 1985, p. 991). In SBS/AHT trials, you will find explanations of the force inflicted, such as "the accused must have picked up the baby and bashed its head against a hard object, or hit the baby's head with an object such as a ball peen hammer." Sometimes experts will demonstrate just how hard and for what duration the baby must have been shaken by violently shaking a doll for the benefit of the jury. These images are inflammatory and, more significantly, they are not supported by science.

In addition, when an infant's caretaker finds the infant unresponsive, a natural response is to jostle or lightly shake the infant to see if it can be awakened. An admission of this natural and harmless type of "shaking" is often flung before the jury as a confession to a violent cold-blooded attack (see, for example, *Maze v. Lester*; *Cavazos v. Smith*, 2011, p. 5). For example, in *Maze v. Jerry Lester*, the court on appeal denied relief because, by Maze's own admission, he was the only person with the infant when the infant became unresponsive, and, although Maze initially denied that he shook the baby, he ultimately acknowledged that he had "jostled" the baby in an attempt to revive him. Although Maze insisted that he did not shake the baby in a violent manner that would have caused injuries, Maze's disclosure that he jostled the infant was relied upon as an admission (*Maze v. Lester*). Shirley Smith faced the same circumstance. After the death of her grandson, Smith was told by a social worker that he had died from SBS (*Cavazos v. Smith*, p. 5). Smith told the social worker that the baby had not responded to her touch while sleeping, so she had picked him up and given him "a little shake, a jostle" to wake him. Thinking her little shake might have hurt the baby, Smith then said something to the effect of, "Oh, my God. Did I do it? Did I do it? Oh, my God" (*Id.*). This exchange was then used as evidence of her guilt (*Id.*).

Just over a decade ago, the defense could rely only on a few experts worldwide who did not buy wholeheartedly into the SBS/NAT diagnosis (Donohoe, 2003; Le Fanu, 2004; Squier, 2010). Even in 2017, defendants are tried without the benefit of experts that can support their version of events (Hartshorne and Miola, 2010). Often, the defense expert's testimony is outweighed by well-established experts still fully entrenched in SBS/AHT tenets (Tuerkheimer, 2014; Simmons, 2014). This occurs, though the available evidence "arguably suggests that the claim of shaken baby syndrome is more an article of faith than a proposition of science" (*Del Prete V. Thompson*, 2014; as quoted by Wrennall et al., 2015).

In addition, juries tend to find for the party that has a cohesive theory of the case (Tuerkheimer, 2014, p. 49). As happened in Marsh's trial, the prosecution in SBS cases often presents a cohesive story that resonates with the jury. The prosecution's story seems to be rooted in decades of science and typically appears irrefutable. In the end, although the defendant is technically free of the burden to prove an innocent cause of the baby's demise, very often the defendant cannot hope for acquittal without meeting that burden (Tuerkheimer, 2014). Indeed, Marsh was convicted because of what appeared to be irrefutable expert SBS/NAT testimony at trial, and his conviction remained intact upon appeal, regardless of the trial court's grossly erroneous admission of autopsy photos because there was no expert who could stand against SBS/AHT dogma or offer an alternative explanation for Phillip's injuries. The court on appeal held explicitly that only the lack of any viable expert explanation for Phillip's injuries prevented a reversal of Marsh's conviction (*People v. Marsh*, 1985, p. 999).

Given the autopsy photos and the explanations of the force needed to create such injury, it becomes relatively easy to make the defendant appear to be a monster. Past incidents of anger become relevant, and evidence of such incidents is admitted into evidence. If an accused caretaker has a violence-free past and nothing vile can be dug up to be admitted into evidence, then he or she must have simply snapped. Any stressor in the caretaker's life around the time of the infant's demise is evidence that the caretaker was on the verge of exploding in anger. In addition, the opinions of those who know the defendant best and who vouch for their steady character are often ignored (Sweeney, 2005). Juries tend to give more credence to the expert's testimony and readily dismiss evidence of a defendant's good character in light of a cohesive theory of abuse presented by experts.

CONCLUSION

Most people want to protect children; we all should. It is a noble and just calling. What seems to begin as something noble can easily turn into an injustice, not only for those wrongly accused or convicted, like Kenneth Marsh and scores of other parents and caretakers, but also for the very people we want most to protect, the infants. Our history of persecuting caretakers based on charges that they were involved in satanic ritual child abuse illustrates how easily a well-intended witch-hunt can hurt the children we are trying to protect (*K. v. Miazga*, 2003). The Court in *K. v. Miazga* stated that:

> "[T]he real threat to society [are] overzealous child protection responses fueled by politically correct or trendy ideologies of the day that are relied upon as a justification to overrule objectivity, reason, common sense and tested and tried legal traditions. These kinds of responses not only jeopardize the freedom of innocent people, but they indirectly harm, and at times even jeopardize, the safety and welfare of the very children that are the subject of the protection efforts."

Statistics tell us that we are doing a better job at keeping our children safe, with one exception, and that is the destruction of families and trauma caused to children when the state steps in and interprets an infant's illness as child abuse (Riggs and Hobbs, 2014). We should be cognizant that should a baby fall ill and demonstrate the triad of symptoms, the parents or guardians of that infant may instantly be judged a danger to that infant, leading to the removal of that infant and any siblings from the home (Miller, 2015; Luttner, 2014). The parent who is judged to be the abuser may then be prosecuted and removed from society, sometimes for life. This destroys not only the lives of the parents, but it also causes trauma and lifelong struggles for the surviving infant and the infant's siblings. The criminal justice systems worldwide should be appalled by this scenario. After all, the justice system is causing inexplicable harm to children. Courts and attorneys for both the prosecution and the defense should be aware of the unnecessary trauma being created and should work to put an end to this state-sanctioned child abuse.

REFERENCES

Bache, B., Barnes, P., Beech, B., Bellone, F., Bohan, T.L., Bonnell, H.J., Gabaeff, S., et al., 2015. Open Letter on Shaken Baby Syndrome and Courts: A False and Flawed Premise.

Bazelon, E., 2011. Shaken-baby syndrome faces new questions in court. New York Times. Available at: http://www.peterdale.co.uk/wp-content/uploads/2012/02/SBS nytFeb2011. pdf.

BBC News, UK, 2011. Shaken Baby Syndrome Guidance Issued by CPS. Available at: http://www.bbc.co.uk/news/uk-12129860.

California Innocence Project, Read their Stories: Kenneth Marsh. Available at: http://californiainnocenceproject.org/index.php/about-the-project/6-kenneth-marsh.

Cavazos v. Smith (2011). 132 S. Ct. 2, 565 U.S. 1, 181 L. Ed. 2d 311.

Christian, et al., 2009. Abusive Head Trauma in Infants and Children, 123 Pediatrics 1409. Crown Prosecution Service. Available at: http://www.cps.gov.uk/legal/l_to_o/non_accidental_head_injury_cases (which advises prosecutors that "To prove a AHT case you will usually require the Triad of injuries plus supporting evidence").

Del Prete V. Thompson, 2014. 90710 F.Supp.3d 907 (N.D.Ill. 2014, f10, pp. 957–958).

Donohoe, M., 2003. Evidence-based medicine and shaken baby syndrome Part I: literature review, 1966–1998. The American Journal of Forensic Medicine and Pathology 24, 239.

Emerson, M.V., et al., 2007. Ocular autopsy and histopathologic features of child abuse. Ophthalmology 114, 1384–1394.

Findley, K.A., Johnson, D.R., Judson, K.H., Staas, M.L., Redleaf, D.L., Hyman, C.J., July 6, 2015. Shaken Baby Syndrome/Abusive Head Trauma: A Complicated Child Welfare Issue. 37.

Hartshorne, J., Miola, J., 2010. Expert evidence: difficulties and solutions in prosecutions for infant harm. Legal Studies 30 (2), 279–300.

Health Research Funding, 2015. 27 Horrifying Shaken Baby Syndrome Statistics. Available at: http://healthresearchfunding.org/shaken-baby-syndrome-statistics/.

Jenecke, C.A., 2014. Shaken Baby Syndrome, Wrongful Convictions, and the Dangers of Aversion to Changing Science in Criminal Law, vol. 48. University of San Francisco Law Review, p. 147.

K. v. Miazga, 2003. SKQB 559 (CanLII). http://canlii.ca/t/1g4gw.

Lantz, P.E., 2004. The evidence base for shaken baby syndrome: response to Reece et al from 41 physicians and scientists. BMJ 329 (7468), 741–742.

Le Fanu, J., 2004. Confounding the experts: the vindication of parental testimony in shaken baby syndrome. In: Narrative Research in Health and Illness, p. 223 (Chapter 13).

Levin, A., 2011. At Least Half of All Parents Tried over Shaken Baby Syndrome Have Been Wrongly Convicted, Expert Warns. Daily Mail. Available at: http://www.dailymail.co.uk/femail/article-1382290/At-half-parents-tried-shaken-baby-syndrome-wrongly-convicted-expert-warns.html#ixzz3G2d7KDzg.

Lips, U., Fanconi, M., August 2010. Shaken baby syndrome in Switzerland: results of a prospective follow-up study, 2002–2007. European Journal of Pediatrics 169 (8), 1023–1028.

Luttner, S.E., 2014. Shaken Baby Syndrome: Inadequate Logic, Unvalidated Theory, Insufficient Science. Argument 1.

Mann, A.K., Rai, B., Sharif, F., Vavasseur, C., 2015. Assessment of parental awareness of the shaken baby syndrome in Ireland. European Journal of Pediatrics 1–7.

Maze v. Jerry Lester, 2014. No. 11–6141 (6th Cir. 2014).

Miller, D., Barnes, P., Miller, M., 2015. The significance of macrocephaly or enlarging head circumference in infants with the triad: further evidence of mimics of shaken baby syndrome. The American Journal of Forensic Medicine and Pathology 36 (2), 111–120.

National Registry of Exonerations, Browse Cases: Kenneth Marsh. Available at: http://www.law.umich.edu/special/exoneration/Pages/casedetail. aspx?caseid=3407.

People v. Burns, 1952. 109 Cal. App.2d 524, 541 [241 P.2d 308].

People v. Cavanaugh, 1955. 44 Cal.2d 252, 268–269 [282 P.2d 53].

People v. Marsh, 1985. 175 Cal. App. 3d 987-Cal: Court of Appeal, 4th Appellate Dist., 1st Div.

Pishko, J., 2014. How Can Doctors Be Sure a Baby's Been Shaken? The Atlanitc. Available at: http://www.theatlantic.com/health/archive/2014/11/how-can-doctors-be-sure-a-babys-been-shaken/382632/?single_page=true.

Riggs, J.E., Hobbs, G.R., 2014. The relationship between "protection of" and "violence against" infants and young children: the U.S. Experience, 1940–2005. Social Sciences 3, 394–403.

Shapiro, J., 2011. Rethinking Shaken Baby Syndrome, Available on NPR, Postmortem: Death Investigation in America. Available at: http://www.npr.org/2011/06/29/137471992/rethinking-shaken-baby-syndrome.

Showers, J., Apolo, J., Thomas, J., Beavers, S., 1985. Fatal child abuse: a two-decade review. Pediatric Emergency Care 1 (2), 66–70.

Simmons, J., 2014. Ironic simplicity: why shaken baby syndrome misdiagnoses should result in automatic reimbursement for the wrongly accused. Seattle University Law Review 38, 127–161.

Sperhake, J.P., Matschke, J., 2014. "Shaken baby syndrome" and forensic pathology. Forensic Science, Medicine, and Pathology 10 (2), 251–252.

Squier, W., 2008. Shaken baby syndrome: the quest for evidence. Developmental Medicine and Child Neurology 50 (1), 10–14.

Squier, W., 2010. 'Shaken Baby Syndrome'–a Response by Dr Waney Squier. Estimating 70,000 SBS/NAT Convictions in the United States and the United Kingdom Combined, Available at: Family Law Week. News (12/04/2010).

Squier, W., 2011. The 'shaken baby' syndrome: pathology and mechanisms. Acta Neuropathologica 122, 519.

Sweeney, J., 2005. Bucking the system. British Journalism Review 16 (4), 47–53.

Tuerkheimer, D., 2014. Flawed Convictions: Shaken Baby Syndrome and the Inertia of Injustice. Oxford University Press.

Tursz, A., Cook, J.M., 2014. Epidemiological data on shaken baby syndrome in France using judicial sources. Pediatric Radiology 44 (4), 641–646.

Warter, B.B., Summer 2004. Toddler's Accidental Death Ends with Babysitter's Murder Conviction – the Ken Marsh Story. Justice: Denied, Issue 25, Available at: http://justicedenied.org/issue/issue_25/ken_marsh.html.

Wrennall, L., Bache, B., Pragnell, C., et al., 2015. Open Letter on Shaken Baby Syndrome and Courts: A False and Flawed Premise, Argument & Critique. Received Jan. Published Feb http://www.argumentcritique.com/special-edition.html.

Shaken Baby Syndrome and Abusive Head Trauma

Waney Squier

Oxford University John Radcliffe Hospital, Oxford, United Kingdom

INTRODUCTION

There is no doubt that parents and others invested with the responsibility of nurturing and protecting the most precious and vulnerable members of our society, young infants, sometimes abandon that responsibility and inflict dreadful harm on those infants. Child abuse has been documented since the beginning of time in ritual, religious, institutional, and individual acts, including by family members and even parents (Heins, 1984; Caffey, 1972a). This chapter is concerned with only one form of abuse, SBS or AHT, and specifically reviews the history with respect to the role of shaking as a potential mechanism, which has been the focus of contention for almost five decades.

Nothing has influenced the mainstream approach to the recognition and diagnosis of child abuse as much as the introduction of the concept of SBS in the early 1970s. This signified a sea change in thinking about abuse to infants; for the first time, it became widely accepted that inflicted trauma could be inferred from a number of intracranial findings in the absence of any objective evidence of impact or violence, such as fractures and external marks of injury such as bruises.

It is enlightening to review current thinking about abusive infant head trauma in the context of its more general history. This informs how, at various points, our views have changed and how, in the course of such changes, we may have lost sight of previously known facts concerning infant intracranial pathology and anatomy, and how features previously recognized as natural conditions have been mischaracterized as the result of inflicted trauma.

CHILD ABUSE BEFORE SHAKEN BABY SYNDROME

An excellent review of the history of child maltreatment was written by Heins, who documents the history of child abuse from the earliest times (Heins, 1984). In ancient cultures, infanticide was accepted as a way of dealing with unwanted children in the face of scarce resources. Early Roman law gave the father absolute right over life or death of his infant, but the church was responsible for replacing infanticide and ritual killing by symbolic acts such as circumcision and baptism, by which a baby was offered the protection of the family and the church. However, the church was not always benevolent; the Puritans established the death penalty for disobedient children, and flogging was considered to help to rid children of innate depravity. Infanticide and abandonment, particularly for illegitimate children, continued into the 19th century.

Knight (1986) cites an ancient Norse rhyme sung by children in the Shetland Islands: "The child will not be quiet, the child will not be quiet, take it by the leg and hit it against the wall, the child will not be quiet."

The first major treatise on maltreatment of children was written by Tardieu in Paris in 1860. He described 32 cases of abused children up to 17 years of age, with autopsy pathology in 18. Most children showed evidence of neglect, disease, or malnutrition; abuse was evidenced by bruises of multiple ages, burns, or marks of whipping. Aggressors included schoolteachers and employers, but most, Tardieu notes with "painful surprise," were parents. Tardieu specifically refers to the appalling treatment of children by employers in forced labor in England.

The article is of limited relevance to our current concept of nonaccidental injury; only two fractures are recorded, and intracranial pathology was described in only three cases. One, a 2-year-old with bruises on the head and limbs, had a "blood collection covering the brain," a second child had meningeal infection and "contusions of the brain and spinal cord," and a third had "hydrocephaly." We do not have sufficient information to evaluate these cases in any detail.

External evidence of trauma was important in the identification of abuse in these children. Knight (1986) highlights examples in Tardieu's paper, including:

> *The character of the brutalities and the traces which they leave on the bodies of the victims vary to the infinite. However, they offer some common characters which one finds in nearly all the cases and to which it is above all necessary to call to the attention of the medico-legalists...It is common to attribute the contusions on the body to falls which the child suffered in playing or in accidents. The distinction is easy if you pay attention to the frightening multiplicity of the traces of wounds which cover nearly all the body - and the site of the contusions, which do not correspond to the usual pattern of accidents and falls.*

We will see how far current mainstream criteria for the recognition of abuse deviate from this.

For almost 100 years, little more was written on child abuse. Then, the advent of radiology brought a resurgence of interest and a new characterization of abuse on the basis of radiology, which could identify changes in the bones, such as healing fractures, which are not detectable by clinical examination (Knight, 1986).

Three people stand out for their contributions to the development of the current mainstream concept of child abuse. Caffey, a pediatrician and radiologist, was the most prolific. Kempe, a pediatrician, was successful in capturing the attention of the media and the legislature. Guthkelch, a neurosurgeon, looked to science to explain potential mechanisms of AHT. Detailed examination of their publications, and particularly Caffey's, reflects the way in which concepts emerged and how his own views evolved over almost 30 years.

Caffey had originally been puzzled by the finding of fresh and healing fractures in association with subdural hemorrhage (SDH) in infants, and in 1946, described six cases (Caffey, 1946). Caffey described two previously unrecognized signs, which he ascribed to bony injury: fragmentation of the metaphysis (the growth plate at the end of the long bones), and thickening of the surface layer (cortex) and covering membrane of long bones, which were not fractured and otherwise healthy. Several of the infants he described had evidence of generalized conditions; one had hemorrhagic disease of the newborn, a condition resulting from inadequate levels of vitamin K, and one had petechial hemorrhages, which are small skin hemorrhages often seen in bleeding disorders. One was malnourished, and two had purulent infections of the middle ear. RHs were described in two babies. The only alternative diagnosis Caffey considered was vitamin C deficiency (scurvy), but he thought the skeletal findings were inconsistent with this diagnosis and maintained that the fractures were inflicted, despite one occurring while the baby was in the hospital. In none was a traumatic explanation given. Recent review of this paper suggests that scurvy would have explained these cases (Clemetson, 2006), and vitamin D deficiency and other metabolic bone fragility syndromes would today be recognized as important differential diagnoses (Ayoub et al., 2014).

Caffey's (1965) address to the American Pediatric Society concerned the importance of the clinical history in diagnosing abuse (Caffey, 1965). Caffey mentions slapping and beating, but he makes no mention of whiplash as a cause of injury. He did mention trauma from accidental falls: "I saw the radiographs of a child, who reportedly had fallen from the eleventh floor of a New York apartment, whose most serious injury appeared to be a fracture of one fibula. On the other hand, children have developed severe subdural hematomas, often, after falls of only a short distance of only 2 or 3 feet." This explanation is not accepted by the current mainstream view and was specifically rejected by Duhaime (1992).

By 1962 Kempe coined the term "battered child syndrome" in what has been considered a "landmark" article. He had formed a child abuse team and reviewed over 700 children less than 3 years of age who were considered to have inflicted traumatic injuries. The criteria indicating a high level of suspicion of abuse were subdural hematoma, multiple unexplained fractures at different stages of healing, failure to thrive, soft tissue swelling, skin bruising, a discrepancy between the degree and type of injury and the given history, and any child dying suddenly. The babies often also had poor general health, malnutrition, poor skin hygiene, and evidence of neglect. Kempe considered several differential diagnoses for the bony lesions, including scurvy, syphilis, and osteogenesis imperfecta, but did not consider rickets or vitamin D deficiency. He suggested mechanisms of injury, such as the parent pulling on a limb or swinging the body of a young baby, possibly during times of uncontrollable temporary rage. Shaking is mentioned only in one case, a 7.5-month-old infant whose X-ray showed bony lesions ranging from 2 weeks to 4 months in age "who was shaken while being held by the legs 4–6 weeks prior to film."

Kempe was anxious to convince his colleagues of the reality of child abuse because he felt that clinicians have difficulty in believing that parents could have harmed their children. There was a huge mass media response, and 300 scientific articles were published in the following 3 years. Kempe was invited to meet members of the Children's Bureau to study federal action, and a model reporting law was drafted. Within 4 years, 49 American states had enacted reporting statutes (Heins, 1984).

Studies of child abuse until this time were largely observational, supported by case reports rather than research or empirical evidence. Guthkelch in 1971 turned to the recent clinical and biomechanical research of Ommaya to suggest mechanisms of SDH in babies who had no external evidence of direct trauma to the head. Guthkelch described 23 babies, mostly under the age of 18 months, in whom parental assault had been proved or was strongly suspected. Thirteen of these babies had SDH, and five of these had no evidence of direct impact to the head. More babies had bruises; fractures of the long bones were seen in six and skull fractures in eight. Guthkelch only mentions RH in one infant, and noted it as a marker of subdural hematoma: "the combination of a tense bulging fontanelle and bilateral retinal hemorrhages gave rise to a suspicion of subdural hematoma…".

Guthkelch wrote, "[I]t seems clear that the relatively large head and puny neck muscles of the infant must render it particularly vulnerable to whiplash injury" and proposed the hypothesis that whiplash-like movements during shaking ruptured the bridging veins, which drain blood from the surface of the brain into the wide venous channels (sinuses), which coarse through the dura and deliver blood into the veins in the neck and so back to the heart. Guthkelch noted that SDH in these infants was bilateral in 78%, compared with only 50% in adults. He explained this by his proposed mechanism: "The rotation-acceleration strains on the brain would tend to occur fairly symmetrically also, in the antero-posterior direction. This may be the same reason why the infantile subdural hematoma is even more often bilateral." The fact that the hemorrhages in the infants were not only bilateral, but also formed thin films, contrasts with the large and space-occupying bleeds seen in older children and adults (Geddes et al., 2001a,b) and is inconsistent with the ruptured bridging vein hypothesis. The bridging veins are few in number, but large, and each carries some 5 cc of blood per minute (Mortazavi et al., 2013). Rupture of even one would produce large-volume, space-occupying clots rather than the thin-film bleeds typical in SBS.

While this study was quite novel in basing a hypothesis on scientific research, Guthkelch did not consider whether it was appropriate to extrapolate these findings to immature human infants. Much later, in 2002, Ommaya wrote that "[i]t is improbable that the high speed and severity of the single whiplash produced in our animal model could be achieved by a single manual shake or even a short series of manual shaking of an infant in one episode." This has been supported by subsequent biomechanical studies.

A year after his 1971 study, Caffey published two further papers. The first, in February 1972, was based on a lecture to the Society for Pediatric Radiology (Caffey, 1972a). The title was "The Parent-Infant Traumatic Stress Syndrome; (Caffey-Kempe syndrome), (Battered Babe Syndrome)." Caffey was clear that his newly described radiological signs of trauma were "the pristine probe-the key and keystone to the discovery and growth of the PITS [The Parent-Infant Traumatic Stress] syndrome." He described the radiological identification of trauma as the best single test for a causal agent of disease in the entire field of pediatrics, surpassing various serologic and skin tests for infections and even blood cell counts for leukemia. He claimed that his own 1946 publication "marked the dawn of the first advance in the detection and study of the ignored and wholly unsuspected PITS syndrome. It has proved to be the open sesame to a den of traumatic, familial, social, and legal ills of still undetermined proportions."

Caffey drew attention to the significance of fractures in different stages of healing as an indicator of repeated abuse. In contrast to his previous publications, he acknowledged Barlow's suggestion that some bony lesions in young infants may be conditioned by prenatal rickets, but this did not modify his opinion about their cause. He noted the high incidence of "denied trauma" in premature babies and sibling twins, but dismissed the possibility that excessive fragility of the infant bones was responsible. He considered the incidence of abuse to be higher in "provocative," deformed, premature, multiple birth, adopted, foster, and stepchildren. In contrast to earlier studies (Tardieu, Kempe), Caffey now said that abused infants were characteristically not neglected or deprived, but almost always clean, well fed, and well clothed.

It was during this lecture that shaking was first suggested as a mechanism of abuse. The basis for this was a Newsweek article from 1956 describing a nanny who had killed 3 babies and beaten 12 others in her care. Caffey quoted her as saying that she had shaken one of the babies. This is the first time that he appears to invoke shaking: "These deaths and injuries suggest that shaking of the young infants is probably an important cause of serious cerebral and skeletal lesions and of deaths, especially when the shakings are repeated frequently." Even so, Caffey was tentative in the terms he used: "These deaths and injuries <u>suggest</u>" and "shaking... is <u>probably</u> an important cause" (author's underlining). He acknowledged Guthkelch's (1971) studies in suggesting a mechanism and a causal relationship of shaking to SDH.

Caffey went on to indicate that milder "but still vigorous" shaking may be an important cause of mental retardation and cerebral palsies, giving examples of common practices, such as "dangling on the knee," "tossing in the air," "slapping on the back after each feeding," and "burping." All, he felt, capable of inducing dangerous acceleration–deceleration forces leading to "stretchings and compressions" of the intracranial blood vessels and the brain.

In June of 1972 Caffey gave the Tenth Annual Abraham Jacobi Award Address, which was published later that year (Caffey, 1972b) and called "On the Theory and Practice of Shaking Infants." In this lecture, he introduced the term "whiplash-shaking." He said, "[D]uring the last 25 years substantial evidence, both manifest, and circumstantial, has gradually accumulated which suggests that the whiplash shaking and jerking of abused infants are common causes of the skeletal as well as the cerebrovascular lesions; the latter is the most serious acute complication and by far most common cause of early death," citing three of his own publications. This was the second of his papers to indicate that whiplash or shaking could cause fractures and intracranial damage in well-cared-for babies and in the absence of any external signs of trauma.

In this presentation, Caffey reviewed 27 previously published cases of abuse, including those of the infamous Newsweek nanny, most with fractures of long bones, and some with SDH and RH. In several of these, shaking had been proposed as the mechanism. For the first time, he discussed RHs, which he suggested would undoubtedly become a valuable sign in the diagnosis of "subclinical inapparent chronic subdural hemorrhage" and a "productive screening test" for whiplash-induced brain damage. Again, RH is seen as a marker to indicate the presence of SDH, reflecting the contemporaneous neurosurgical view that RHs were "pathognomonic" of SDH, whatever the cause (Till, 1968).

Caffey was now so confident of the whiplash hypothesis that he felt it could occur in the most banal situations. He wrote: "the pathogenicity of ordinary, casual, habitual, customary, repeated shaking of infants is generally unrecognized by physicians and parents." He cited activities such as playing with the baby by tossing him in the air, and questioned the pathogenicity of baby bouncers, infant jumpers, seesaws, swings, bicycles, and motor cars driven rapidly and habitually over rough roads. The air vibrations of radios, television, telephones, and vacuum cleaners come under suspicion as interfering with the rest a baby needs, while "violent forms of endogenous trauma," such as repeated convulsions in tetanus or epilepsy, are suggested as causes of whiplash brain damage. Caffey suggested that the baby can be a danger to himself, as the "rhythmic whiplash habits of the infant himself during the first months of life, such as head rolling, body rocking and head banging may be traumatically pathogenic to the brain and its veins." Caffey went on to suggest that cerebrovascular injuries previously attributed to prenatal infections, congenital malformations, birth injuries, and genetic metabolic diseases were "undoubtedly" caused by "undetected, depreciated and inapparent whiplash-shakings during the first weeks and months of life." He concluded that indirect acceleration–deceleration traction of whiplash shaking was the cause of bilateral SDH and frequent bilateral RH with a striking lack of signs of impact to the head and usually no bruises to the face or scalp as well as no skull fractures.

What is extraordinary about this paper is that Caffey subverted not only SDH and RH, previously recognized to occur together in nontraumatic as well as traumatic circumstances in infants, but also a number of natural and congenital disease processes, and he ascribed them to inflicted trauma.

In 1974, the transcript of a lecture given in May 1973 was published (Caffey, 1974). Caffey was 79 years old, and it was 28 years since his first paper on the subject. Caffey spoke of "whiplash shaken infant syndrome," but also introduced a new syndrome: "latent whiplash shaken infant syndrome." RHs now take on importance, not as a pointer to SDH, but as the result of whiplash, and Caffey recommended that eye examination should become routine for the detection of pathogenic whiplash shaking.

By now, the essential elements of the whiplash shaken infant syndrome, as he described it, included "bilateral subdural hematomas and bilateral intraocular hemorrhages" "in the absence of signs of external trauma to the head or fractures of the calvaria," "associated with traction lesions of the periosteums [i.e., dense fibrous membrane covering the surface of bones] of the long bones in the absence of fractures and traumatic changes in the overlying skin of the extremities." Caffey was clear that the presence of this constellation of findings in the absence of external signs of trauma presented an "extraordinary diagnostic contradiction."

Pathological evidence from eight autopsied cases and one surgical observation demonstrated subdural, subarachnoid, and subpial bleeding. Three had contusions or lacerations of the brain itself, and in four, torn bridging veins were described, sometimes at the sites of their attachment to the wall of the large dural venous channels (the sagittal sinuses), which drain the blood from the brain. Caffey did not present pathological support for his interpretation of the bone X-ray findings in this paper or in any of his previous papers.

The mechanism Caffey described was rapid, repeated acceleration–deceleration flexions of the head followed by reverse extensions of the head. In each case, he thought the movement was associated with the chin striking the chest and the occiput of the head striking the back. What Caffey did not address was the anatomic and physiological limitations on this latter movement.

To support his shaking hypothesis, Caffey cited other reports in which babies appeared to have been subjected to shaking, but it was the confession of the Newsweek Nanny that provided "by far the most extensive anecdotal proof of pathogenic manual WLS [whiplash shaking syndrome]." Then as now, over 40 years later, confessions remain the sole evidence base for the shaking hypothesis.[2]

In this last paper, Caffey developed his second syndrome, "latent whiplash shaken infant," which is manifest by "mild mental retardation" and "mild cerebral palsy" and which resulted from "habitual, moderate, casual manual whiplash shaking." He builds his hypothesis as follows (author's underlining):

The exact frequency, violence and pathogenicity of this type of infantile "mild" assault have never been studied <u>and are not known, even approximately</u>. However, in view of the high vulnerability of all normal infantile brains to whiplash stresses

---

[2] *"The consistent and repeated observation that confessed shaking results in stereotypical injuries that are so frequently encountered in AHT—and which are so extraordinarily rare following accidental/impact injuries—is the evidentiary basis for shaking"* (Dias, 2011).

and the usual repetition of these causal milder shakings over protracted periods, it seems reasonable to hypothecate that habitual whiplash shakings are pathogenic to some degree in many such cases. It follows that whiplash shaking may be responsible for repeated, small but cumulative intracranial and intraocular bleedings which slowly engender progressive, cumulative permanent disorders of the brain and eyes…." "These facts being true it is highly probable that routine, regular examinations of the ocular fundi in all, even apparently healthy babies, would detect the residues of retinal hemorrhages and make possible the early stoppage of habitual casual shaking.

This passage demonstrates that, as in his other writings, Caffey's view is speculative and not grounded in any empirical evidence. In the period of almost 30 years between Caffey's first paper and his last, the only attempt to introduce scientific evidence was the reference to animal studies by Guthkelch.

Abuse was now characterized by subdural and intraocular hemorrhages without signs of external trauma to the head or skull fractures, and it was associated with radiological changes in the long bones without fractures or bruises or swelling in the overlying skin. For the first time, trauma could be assumed without any direct evidence for it.

DEVELOPMENT OF THE SHAKING HYPOTHESIS SINCE 1972

The work of Caffey and Kempe alerted physicians and the public to the reality of child abuse. Clinicians were very much aware that babies may be abused, even by parents, and that abuse could explain the enigma of SDHs and RHs in babies with no signs of trauma.

There seemed to be no looking back; these papers, based on opinion and hypothesis and without scientific support, had a profound effect on the approach to child abuse. What was the zeitgeist of the early 1970s that led to these papers being so widely and uncritically accepted? Several explanations may be considered.

One factor was the zealous promotion of child abuse in its various forms, from satanic ritual abuse, through Munchausen syndrome by proxy and "medical child abuse" (a recently introduced term used when parents or carers seek unnecessary or potentially harmful medical treatment for children). A relatively small number of influential pediatricians, among them advisors to or directors of the National Center on Shaken Baby Syndrome, have been said to have "defined new medical terminology in medical books which they've promoted to doctors, hospitals, and law enforcers. With hundreds of doctors following their lead,… [they] helped trigger a surge of Shaken Baby Syndrome prosecutions."[3]

---

[3] http://www.laweekly.com/film/is-shaken-baby-syndrome-the-new-satanic-panic-a-new-doc-reveals-the-same-experts-behind-both-5481984.

Another significant driving factor to the exponential expansion of the acceptance of SBS was the introduction of mandatory reporting (Uscinski, 2006). While the recognition, and hopefully prevention, of abuse was clearly welcome, and there were obvious ethical, humanitarian, and clinical responsibilities to recognize and report abuse, mandatory reporting added a legal obligation, with serious consequences for failure to comply.

In the US, mandatory reporting was first drafted into laws in 1963 and currently features in child abuse laws of 50 states. "As the prevalence of the 'battered child syndrome' came to popular attention in the 1960s, every state in the country required certain classes of professionals to report their suspicions of abuse to a child protection agency (1). In 1974 Congress passed the Child Abuse Prevention and Treatment Act, which provided financial assistance to states that met federal standards" (Appelbaum 1999).

Mandatory reporting has the advantages of endorsing the unacceptability of child abuse and emphasizing the responsibilities of professionals to protect children (Goodyear-Smith, 2012), but the system has not been proved to achieve these aims; "the assumptions that guided the enactment of mandated laws were largely erroneous," and the system "has transformed public child welfare agencies into investigatory bodies with diminished involvement in the provision of social services per se" (Melton, 2005).

Goodyear-Smith (2012) has noted the lack of international evidence that mandatory reporting decreases abuse detection rates and that it runs the risk of increased numbers of false reports with unnecessary damage to affected families as well as overwhelming childcare services. In reviewing trends and policies in child maltreatment in six countries, Gilbert et al. (2012) showed no consistent evidence for either a decrease or an increase in their designated indicators of child maltreatment. More alarming were the rising rates of removal of infants from their homes, affecting large numbers of infants, despite little evidence for the effectiveness of these policies.

In Australia, there have, for many years, been concerns about the escalating number of reports of maltreatment. A study of children born in Western Australia in 1990 and 1991 showed that over 13% of all children were reported to the Child Protection Department before reaching the age of 18, although 71% of these children were not found to have been maltreated. The authors suggest that this rate may be equaled or exceeded in countries with an Anglo-American forensic child protection system (Bilson, 2013). Concerns about mandatory reporting are so great that politicians in South Australia, the first state to adopt it, have called for the policy to be overhauled or abandoned.[4]

CHALLENGES TO THE SHAKING HYPOTHESIS

As the shaking hypothesis was based largely upon anecdote and the views of a very small group of pediatricians, it seems surprising that there were no serious attempts

---

[4](Richardson, T. 2015 Parties push to scrap mandatory child protection reports, 29 June. http://indaily.com.au/news/2015/06/29/parties-push-to-scrap-mandatory-child-protection-reports/).

to provide scientific and evidential support for the syndrome, or to challenge its validity, for almost a decade and a half. The challenges to the syndrome have arisen from two main aspects of research: biomechanical (the study of the effects of mechanical or physical forces on biological systems) and anatomical and pathological studies.

BIOMECHANICAL STUDIES

Duhaime, a neurosurgeon, published her study of clinical, pathological, and biomechanical aspects of SBS in 1987 (Duhaime, 1987). She took as her starting point the clinicopathological entity characterized by RH, subdural and/or subarachnoid hemorrhages, and minimal or no signs of external trauma. Duhaime acknowledged that a history of shaking was usually absent and that shaking had been assumed on the basis of the pattern of intracranial bleeding. She also acknowledged that whiplash injury resulted in tearing of the bridging veins leading to subdural and subarachnoid bleeding. She reviewed all cases of SBS seen in the Children's Hospital of Philadelphia over 7 years and, in collaboration with the Department of Bioengineering at the University of Pennsylvania, studied the biomechanics in infant models.

The clinical study involved 48 babies with detailed clinical information. All subjects had histories suggestive of abuse or neglect; witnessed or well-documented accidental trauma was excluded. Carers were specifically asked about shaking, and only one baby had a history of shaking alone. Sixty-three percent had evidence of blunt impact to the head, thirteen percent had no evidence of head trauma but had trauma to other parts of the body, and twenty-five percent of babies had no trauma to the head or elsewhere. Thirteen babies died and had autopsy examination, and all had evidence of blunt head trauma; in seven cases, these signs of impact were not evident in life and were only discovered at autopsy.

Biomechanical studies were based on models designed to represent a 1-month-old infant. Each model was subjected to repeated violent shaking by adults, and the dummy head was impacted against either a metal bar or a padded surface. Angular accelerations and angular velocity were recorded. The mean peak acceleration achieved by impacts was 428.18 G compared with 9.29 G for shaking; the accelerations due to impact exceeded those due to shaking by a factor of nearly 50 times. Duhaime concluded that results achieved by impact fell within the calculated injury ranges for concussion, SDH, and axonal injury, while those achieved by shaking fell well below the calculated injury ranges. She stated that these results were consistent with the observation that all fatal cases of SBS in the series were associated with evidence of impact to the head, and "based on these observations, we believe that shaking alone does not produce the shaken baby syndrome."

Duhaime concluded that SBS, "at least in its most severe form, is not usually caused by shaking alone. Although shaking may be part of the process, it is more likely that such infants suffer blunt impact" and that "unless a child has predisposing factors such as subdural hygromas, brain atrophy, or collagen-vascular disease, fatal cases of the shaken baby syndrome are not likely to occur from the shaking that occurs during play, feeding, or in a swing, or even from the more vigorous shaking given by a caretaker as a means of discipline."

However, Duhaime added the speculation that "the most common scenario may be a child who is shaken, then thrown into or against a crib or other surface, striking the back of the head and thus undergoing a large, brief deceleration." It seems that it is this speculation, rather than her findings, that has been the message generally taken from this study.

In a further report in 1988, Duhaime wrote that SBS was "a misnomer," as it "implies a mechanism of injury which does not account mechanically for the radiographic or pathologic findings" (Duhaime et al., 1988). The following year, the "Shaken Impact Syndrome" (Bruce and Zimmerman, 1989) was suggested, but again, the mechanism of a shake and a throw were speculative.

Subsequent biomechanical studies confirmed that the forces generated by adult shaking are insufficient to cause subdural bleeding and are far less than the forces generated by low-level falls. Prange used a dummy modeled on a 1.5-month-old infant to study responses to minor falls, shakes, and inflicted impacts (Prange et al., 2003). He found that inflicted impacts against hard surfaces may more frequently generate the forces considered necessary to produce clinically significant brain injuries than vigorous shaking or falls from less than 1.5 m. He compared the effects of impact onto soft and hard surfaces and found the responses of the dummy head during shaking and inflicted impact against unencased foam were insufficient to cause SDH or primary damage to the white matter of the infant brain. He did not study impacts on to mattresses or padded furniture.

Using the data that he had generated and that from Duhaime's study, Prange considered the effects of shaking on the infant neck. He found that shaking generated loads on the infant neck, which would be expected to cause neck damage (Prange and Myers, 2003). Real-life support for the damaging effects of whiplash on the infant and child's neck comes from descriptive reports of injuries seen in infants who have been injured by whiplash in motor vehicle accidents. These infants have fractures and dislocations of the bones of the neck, but subdural and retinal bleeding are not described (Winter et al., 2003; Fuchs et al., 1989, Johnston, 2004). Together, these studies indicate that the loading induced by shaking or whiplash would cause injuries to the infant neck at levels well below those needed to cause retinal and subdural bleeding. Christian and Block (2009) agreed that "concomitant cervical spine injury and secondary brain injury resulting from hypoxia, ischemia can sometimes be found" in cases of AHT, and Brennan et al. (2009) found "[c]ervical SCI [spinal cord injury] is a frequent but not universal finding in young children with fatal abusive head trauma." Matshes et al. (2011) made a detailed study of the spinal cord and its associated nerves in the neck, and found bleeding around these nerves in infants he thought had been shaken. He thought that neck injury during shaking, specifically damage to the nerves supplying the diaphragm, was responsible for failure to breathe, hypoxia, and anoxic brain damage.

In 2003, Cory and Jones created models to replicate Duhaime's biomechanical study. Their models had a variety of head, neck, and body designs, and were shaken to allow impact of chin-to-chest or occiput-to-back. All of their female volunteer shakers and some males showed severe fatigue after 10 seconds of violent shaking, and the authors suggested that the shaking durations postulated to cause brain injury might be physically impossible to achieve. The authors selected the thresholds of acceleration at which concussion and SDH would be expected and found that the angular acceleration they generated by shaking in all but one test crossed two of the three thresholds for concussion. None of the tests approached the required thresholds for SDH. Like Caffey (1974), they considered chin-to-chest and occiput-to-back impacts, and felt they would have "profound implications" for the ability of pure shaking to cause fatal head injury "if it is anatomically possible." Jones has since indicated that occiput-to-back contacts are limited by the neck anatomy (Jones et al., 2015). Despite having generated data showing that shaking did not even approach the threshold for SDH, the authors expressed reservations about the models used and concluded that on the basis of Duhaime's work, it cannot be categorically stated that "pure shaking" cannot cause fatal head injuries in an infant.

In recent years, computational models have been developed to further explore the biomechanics of infant head injury. These largely depend on data generated in the studies using dummies described previously. Based on a model of the 6-month-old child head, in which each element of the structure was modeled using computers (finite element modeling), Roth et al. (2006) concluded that rupture of a bridging vein can occur in both a shaking event and an inflicted impact, leading to the formation of a subdural hematoma. In this model, a 1.5-foot fall caused more stretch to bridging veins than shaking. However, the model has not been validated or compared to real-life injuries.

The effects of AHT on the eye have also been studied by computer modeling (Rangarajan et al., 2009). There are limitations of these methods "[b]ecause model predictions of tissue deformations and stresses are influenced by the geometry, anatomy, tissue material properties, tissue–tissue interactions, and applied loads used in the model, one should be aware that inaccuracy of these inputs will yield fallacious outputs, and the results of the computer model will have little or no similarity to a real-life response." "Because the material properties and tissue–tissue interactions of pediatric ocular tissues have not been measured or published, it is currently impossible for a finite element model to mimic the response of the pediatric eye. Furthermore, it is unknown what values of retinal and ocular stresses produce injury, so these models cannot be used to predict the occurrence of retinal hemorrhages or other ocular injuries" (Margulies et al., 2009). A more recent computational model (Jones et al., 2015) of the effects of shaking on the infant head and neck showed results comparable to the previous dummy models. Again, the model was considered a platform for further injury studies, rather than a solution to the current debate. The authors wrote, "[N]o study has to date demonstrated that shaking alone, without an associated impact, exceeds the injury threshold associated with SDH."

The potential for low falls to cause severe intracranial injury or death was recognized by Caffey, and several subsequent case reports have substantiated this (Plunkett, 2001; Steinbok et al., 2007). The fatal fall of a 23-month-old toddler from a climbing frame was videotaped and has been reconstructed in a biomechanics laboratory, allowing the specific accelerations generated in this simulated fall to be measured (van Ee et al., 2009). Lantz reported a 7-month-old infant who developed RHs and SDHs and died after a stairway fall, and reviewed 19 articles dealing with serious injuries or fatalities from stairway or low-height falls involving young children (Lantz and Couture, 2011).

ANATOMICAL AND PATHOLOGICAL STUDIES

The most important pathological challenge to the shaking hypothesis was the study of Geddes et al. (2001a,b). This seminal work completely changed understanding of the brain damage in these infants and led to reconsideration of previously held beliefs concerning the nature and source of infant SDH and the potential for a lucid interval in this population.

Geddes' study involved detailed microscopical study of a large series of infants thought to have suffered inflicted brain damage. The disturbance of brain function (encephalopathy) associated with SBS, which may be manifest by irritability, lethargy, seizures, or loss of consciousness, had previously been thought to depend on mechanical shearing of the nerve fibers of the white matter of the brain (diffuse axonal injury), which was well known in adult head trauma. Instead, she found that most babies had brain swelling together with findings indicating deprivation of blood or oxygen supply (hypoxic–ischaemic injury). Only a minority of babies had axonal injury, and this was restricted to very small and specific areas of the brainstem, where the brain is attached to the upper spinal cord.

The implications of these findings were enormous: whereas shearing of nerve fibers results in their immediate loss of function, the pace at which swelling occurs varies considerably from case to case, taking as much as 48 h to reach a maximum. This allows the opportunity for a "lucid interval" to occur, when a baby may be only mildly symptomatic or even seem quite well. This means that the belief that babies who have been shaken must collapse immediately, which had become an inherent part of the definition of SBS (Duhaime et al., 1998),[5] is quite wrong. It follows that the belief that the person with the baby at the time of collapse must be responsible for the collapse is also wrong.

The matter of lucid intervals was not settled by this, and the debate rumbles on. Geddes' work showed that the neuropathology of SBS, with progressive brain swelling, allowed for the possibility of a lucid interval. In this period, a baby may show common symptoms such as vomiting, irritability, or subtle changes in alertness, which may not be recognized by parents or carers, while swelling of the brain develops.

In December 2008, the Attorney General of Canada initiated a medical/legal review of alleged shaken baby cases. The Review Committee noted under the heading "Timing of Injury":

---

[5] *"An alert, well-appearing child has not already sustained a devastating acute injury that will become clinically obvious hours to days later."*

While the child will not be completely normal following traumatic head injury, there may be a variety of symptoms, a number of which may be vague and non-specific, limiting the ability to recognize the presence of a traumatic head injury. Studies have demonstrated that the diagnosis of traumatic head injuries in children, particularly young infants when presenting with vague symptoms, has been missed as the symptoms were attributed to a variety of other causes. The potential exists therefore, for hours or potentially days to pass between the injury event and loss of consciousness/collapse. This interval, during which the baby appears 'lucid' (appears to be functioning on some level), reduces the ability to pinpoint the timing of the injury and contradicts the belief that a baby will become unconscious immediately after having been shaken vigorously, a belief relied on previously to identify the perpetrator as the person with the baby at the time of collapse."

Ebbs et al. (2011).

This change in view and acceptance of the possibility of a lucid in terval was also acknowledged by Dr. Carol Jenny in a lecture in 2013, who said, "[B]ut, you know, my take home message from this case is that we need to be extremely cautious when we evaluate histories, relating them to injury timing, and the history should be meticulous and detailed. We need to watch for subtle and not-so-subtle changes in the infant and also, you know, consider alternative hypotheses. Maybe the person who was with the baby when he collapsed didn't do it."[6]

The brainstem damage shown by Geddes was minor and survivable. In some infants, there were no objective signs (bruising, skull fracture, extracranial injuries, etc.) to suggest that violence had taken place, and Geddes suggested that violence may not be necessary to injure a young child. Geddes study also showed, as Guthkelch had noted in 1971, that the subdural bleeding in cases of alleged shaking was a diffuse thin film of blood, very different from the thick space-occupying hematomas commonly seen over one side of the brain in older patients and classically associated with trauma. Geddes questioned whether the traditional assumption that subdural and retinal bleeding in infants were caused by violent shaking and whiplash was right, and went on to investigate other possible mechanisms. Geddes' work was controversial and the subject of vitriolic comment at the time (Punt et al., 2004), although these studies are now accepted as mainstream.

In 2003, Geddes (2003) published another challenge to the SBS hypothesis, this time ruffling even more feathers. The title of this paper was in the form of a question: "Dural hemorrhage in non-traumatic infant deaths: does it explain the bleeding in 'shaken baby syndrome'?". Geddes described dural bleeding in 50 infants without trauma and proposed that in some infants, subdural bleeding may be due to a combination of severe deprivation of oxygen (hypoxia), brain swelling, and raised central venous pressure. This combination would allow blood to leak from blood vessels in

---

[6] Jenny C. Medical Aspects of Child Abuse & Neglect. Conference. Schneider Children's Medical Center of Israel. October 9, 2013.

the dura, causing SDH, and from the retinal blood vessels, causing RH. These conditions would be exacerbated by additional hemodynamic forces, such as increased pressure in the venous system, the effects of sustained increased blood pressure, and episodic surges in blood pressure. These are exactly the conditions seen in babies who suffer a period of hypoxia and subsequent cardiopulmonary resuscitation and mechanical ventilation.

Geddes suggested that in these circumstances, subdural and retinal bleeding were not the result of traumatic rupture of bridging veins, but a phenomenon of immaturity. One-hundred years earlier, Cushing had proposed very much the same hypothesis, that infant SDH "may be the direct result of undue traumatism during labor or may occur when too great strain has been put upon the vessels by the profound venous stasis of postpartum asphyxiation; just as in later months they may rupture under the passive congestion brought about by a paroxysm of whooping-cough or a severe convulsion."

Geddes' work was hugely influential as well as controversial. These papers became known colloquially as Geddes I, II, and III, and the 2003 paper also referred to as the "Geddes hypothesis," in my experience, one of the most widely misinterpreted studies, both in the child abuse literature and in the courts.

GEDDES AND THE COURT OF APPEAL 2005

The real effect of Geddes' hypothesis became clear in the Court of Appeal in 2005 when four cases of SBS were heard together. The central importance of the Geddes hypothesis was set out in the judgment, "at the heart of these appeals, as they were advanced in the notices of appeal and the appellants' skeleton arguments, was a challenge to the accepted hypothesis concerning "shaken baby syndrome" (SBS); or, as we believe it should be more properly called, non-accidental head injury (NAHI)" (Gage, 2005 Rv Harris). Although these were four separate cases, each with its own specific facts and merits, the two primary objectives of the Crown were "[t]o uphold the approach taken by the CPS [Crown Prosecution Service] in SBS cases" and "[t]o remove the unified hypothesis from the Courtroom."[7]

The Appeals became a battle of the two hypotheses, Geddes versus SBS. Geddes observed (2006), "[d]efences to apparently open-and shut cases of abuse began to be mounted on the basis of the 'Geddes hypothesis,' to the fury of a group of 'SBS' experts who have been diagnosing 'violent shaking' for years from those pathognomonic findings alone. In conjunction with the police and Crown Prosecution

---

[7] In a lecture to a Meeting convened by Nottingham Pediatric Radiology Department in 2006 Howard Cohen, First Senior Treasury Counsel (for the respondents) identified five objectives for these appeals. The first two are cited above; the other three objectives were "to give guidance to the criminal justice system in how to deal with expert witnesses; to ensure that SBS cases can be prosecuted in the future and to uphold the convictions in the four conjoined cases."

Service, who were frustrated by the effect that our hypothesis was having on prosecutions they decided to fight back, and ensure that our research was discredited."

Despite this, her substantial challenges to the SBS hypothesis have been validated by subsequent research. Kemp et al. (2003) confirmed, on the basis of imaging, that there was a high incidence of diffuse brain swelling and hypoxic ischaemic damage on brain scans in babies thought to have suffered inflicted injury. Oehmichen et al. (2008) studied the neuropathology of 18 infants and confirmed Geddes' observation that most of these babies died from failure of cerebral perfusion rather than traumatic brain damage, although they encountered great difficulty in the distinction of traumatic from hypoxic axonal damage and were unable to confirm her finding of brainstem axonal injury.

Vinchon confirmed her observation that thin-film SDH is likely to be a feature of young age and does not indicate the cause of bleeding (Vinchon et al., 2002, 2010). Since Geddes' publications, imaging studies have demonstrated that almost half of healthy, asymptomatic babies have small amounts of subdural bleeding in the same areas as those described in babies thought to have been shaken (Whitby et al., 2004; Looney et al., 2007; Rooks et al., 2008). Pathologists are well aware that intradural and subdural bleeding is extremely common in neonates, even those who lack evidence of either trauma or overt hypoxia (Gilles and Nelson, 2012). Studies of large numbers of cases have confirmed this and have shown an association between dural bleeding and hypoxia in young infants, supporting the hypothesis proposed in Geddes III and confirming Cushing's observation that SDH is seen in postpartum asphyxia (Scheimberg et al., 2013; Cohen and Scheimberg, 2009; Cohen et al., 2010). The fact that intradural bleeding always accompanies SDH in nontraumatic cases and, if extensive, can leak into the subdural compartment (Cohen and Scheimberg, 2009; Scheimberg et al., 2013) is powerful evidence that the dura, rather than torn bridging veins, is the source of mild, thin-film bleeding. Embryological and anatomic studies support this; blood vessels in the immature dura are larger and more complex at birth than at any other time (Browder et al., 1975; Mack et al., 2009) and are particularly extensive in the sites where SDHs are most commonly described both in healthy neonates and in babies diagnosed with SBS (Rooks et al., 2008; Hymel et al., 1997; Duhaime et al., 1998).

The accepted SBS hypothesis depended on rupture of bridging veins during shaking as the cause of the subdural bleeding (Guthkelch, 1971). This is anatomically most unlikely, as rupture of a single vein would produce massive space-occupying fresh blood clot, which is not what is seen in SBS. Even firm protagonists of SBS now agree that new research has changed our understanding and that subdural hematoma can occur from bleeding dural veins and not only from bridging veins (Slovis et al., 2012).

The potential for birth-related bleeding to persist and develop into a chronic collection around the brain, which may subsequently present with symptoms, has been recognized for almost a century. Infant chronic SDH was considered common and hard to diagnose. The symptoms included, in order of frequency: convulsions, vomiting, irritability, and stupor. These old bleeds were associated with trauma in over half of the babies, but only a small minority (11 of 98 babies) had skull fractures. About a quarter had RHs (Guthkelch, 1953, Ingraham and Matson, 1944). Old subdural bleeding is the most common birth-related pathology identified at routine autopsy of SIDS victims (Rogers et al., 1998; Keeling, 2009). These old bleeds form a thin membrane lining the dura (Squier, 2011) and will not be seen without specialized imaging techniques. Pathologically, they are characterized by numerous thin-walled blood vessels and foci of repeated bleeding in the absence of trauma (Friede, 1989; Squier and Mack, 2009). Spontaneous, fresh SDH can be seen in the context of chronic extracerebral collections, possibly triggered by illness and dehydration (Vinchon et al., 2010).

The presence of small amounts of fresh blood in conjunction with chronic SDH must not, therefore, be taken as evidence of trauma, either accidental or abusive. Significantly, small fresh bleeds, which are seen after collapse and resuscitation, are often assumed to be the cause of collapse. They are far more likely to be the result of collapse, the bleeding coming from the large but delicate vessels in the membrane as the result of hypoxia, and the intravascular pressure changes during resuscitation.

Like SDH, RH is common after birth, occurring in about one-third of all neonates (Baum and Bulpitt, 1970; Emerson et al., 2001; Forbes et al., 2010). In 2010, Matshes produced evidence that directly supports Geddes' hypothesis with regard to RH by demonstrating that retinal and optic nerve sheath hemorrhages were significantly related to prolonged hypoxia, reperfusion, brain swelling, and cardiopulmonary resuscitation (Matshes, 2010).

SUPPORT FOR THE SHAKING HYPOTHESIS

One of the most perplexing aspects of the history of SBS is just how the syndrome described by Kempe, Guthkelch, and Caffey became "distilled"[8] into "the triad," which has, on its own, been a foundation for a diagnosis of SBS and abuse, widely used in the literature and the basis for so many prosecutions. [9,10]

THE RISE AND FALL OF "THE TRIAD"

It is difficult to trace the precise origins of the triad, but it came into use between Caffey's (1974) paper and 1998, when a group of child abuse pediatricians,

---

[8] Greeley, 2014. "The complex features of AHT are often disparagingly distilling [sic] simply to ''The Triad''; a term devoid of any real clinical meaning and not used at all in practice."

[9] R v Harris 2005 "65.The triad of injuries becomes central to a diagnosis of NAHI when there are no other signs or symptoms of trauma such as bruises or fractures."

[10] A Local Authority v S [2009] EWHC 2115 (Fam) 40. "The Local Authority's case is that there was a single primary event, which provides a full explanation for every relevant observation. It all, they submit, fits with a traumatic infliction of a shake or a shaking/impact event which led to Z exhibiting the classic triad of injuries."''62. Each of the doctors I have enumerated are of the view that other injuries, such as grip marks, bruises or fractures, either seen externally or at post-mortem, (called during the course of the case as "external injuries"), are neither inevitable nor necessary in order to conclude that trauma is the cause of the triad in a child."

commenting on the trial of Louise Woodward, a Boston nanny convicted of shaking her charge, wrote, "[T]he shaken baby syndrome (with or without evidence of impact) is now a well-characterized clinical and pathological entity with diagnostic features in severe cases virtually unique to this type of injury—swelling of the brain (cerebral edema) secondary to severe brain injury, bleeding within the head (subdural hemorrhage), and bleeding in the interior linings of the eyes (retinal hemorrhages). Let those who would challenge the specificity of these diagnostic features first do so in the peer-reviewed literature, before speculating on other causes in court." (Chadwick et al., 1998). This represented a significant metamorphosis from Caffey and Kempe's original concept of the combination of fractures and subdural hemorrhage as essential components of a diagnosis of abuse.

In 1992 Duhaime made an attempt to draw up an algorithm to assist in diagnosing abuse (Duhaime et al., 1992). She did not formally define the triad, but said, "[R]etinal hemorrhages are highly associated with inflicted injuries in very young children and, like subdural hemorrhages and diffuse axonal injury, may result from rotational, rather than translational, forces applied to the head." She studied 100 babies under 24 months of age admitted to hospital with head trauma. Cases were determined as due to accident or abuse based upon a detailed biomechanical questionnaire concerning any accidents or falls, physical and radiological examinations. Confessions were taken as evidence for abuse. Eye examinations were undertaken, but cases were categorized independently of the findings. Social service or child maltreatment consultations were analyzed separately as additional markers for suspicion of abuse.

In this algorithm, babies were categorized as abused on: "the presence of either (1) unexplained injuries such as healing long-bone fractures; (2) injuries unequivocally caused by mechanical trauma with no history of trauma obtainable; or (3) a history of forces considered by the authors to be mechanically insufficient to cause particular injury types, when seen in association with a changing or developmentally incompatible history." However, "[f]alls clearly described as less than 3 feet in height were designated as 'trivial' trauma, and when given as an explanation for a high-force injury along with variability in the history or a developmentally incompatible scenario, non-accidental injury was presumed."

Because a history of a low fall was disregarded as "trivial" or an indication of a false history, these cases were all classified as abuse, and it is hardly surprising that the authors found that "simple falls from low heights rarely, if ever, result in significant primary brain injury," and the only accidental injuries that do are "those caused by motor vehicle accidents and falls from extreme heights." The conclusions depend on circular logic; the diagnostic criteria used in the Duhaime study depended on the authors' opinion regarding the effects of mechanical trauma and the parents' ability to explain their baby's condition. Because there is no "gold standard" or reference test for abuse, the algorithm derived from this study appears to have become the most widely used "benchmark" for diagnosis of AHT, underpinning much of the literature on the subject. It follows that any studies using the same diagnostic criteria are subject to the same circularity and logical fallacies and are unreliable in determining a diagnosis of AHT.

In 2001, a policy statement from the American Academy of Pediatrics went further, stating that physicians could presume abuse in any infant with intracranial injury.[11]

The same year, the American Academy of Pediatrics published a Technical Report, which described SBS as "a clearly definable medical condition" recognized by "a constellation of clinical findings in infants, which included retinal hemorrhages, subdural and/or subarachnoid hemorrhages, and little or no evidence of external cranial trauma." This article endorsed the triad: "Subdural hemorrhage caused by the disruption of small bridging veins that connect the dura to the pia arachnoid is a common result of shaking. Such hemorrhage may be most prominent in the interhemispheric fissure and minimal over the convexities of the hemispheres. Cerebral edema with subarachnoid hemorrhage may be the only finding. A child may have subdural hemorrhages, subarachnoid hemorrhages, or both. Intracranial or retinal hemorrhages may be unilateral or bilateral. Visible cerebral contusions are unusual, but diffuse axonal injury is common." No mention is made of the bone lesions, which were an important part of Caffey's concept, although the reader is advised that "[e]vidence of other injuries, such as bruises, rib fractures, long-bone fractures, and abdominal injuries, should be meticulously searched for and documented."

The report states that "[h]omicide is the leading cause of injury-related deaths in infants younger than 4 years. Serious injuries in infants, particularly those that result in death, are rarely accidental unless there is another clear explanation, such as trauma from a motor vehicle crash." Figures published by the Center for Disease Control in 2011 show that in babies under 1 year of age, accidental injury was the fifth most common cause of death, and homicides did not even feature in the top 10 ranking of causes of death. In babies 1–4 years old, accidental (unintentional) injuries were the commonest cause of death, followed by congenital anomalies, while homicides came third and represented less than a quarter of deaths in these babies.

In 2004, an editorial in the British Medical Journal confidently asserted the diagnostic value of the triad. It was headed "Shaken baby syndrome Pathological diagnosis rests on the combined triad, not on individual injuries." It indicated that the presence of the triad allowed "confident diagnosis and the conclusion that undue force has been applied." The article even went so far as to say that the triad allowed identification of the mechanism of injury and an assessment of the degree of force required (Harding et al., 2004).

In 2005, the triad was enshrined in law in the Court of Appeal in England: "The accepted hypothesis depends on findings of a triad of intracranial injuries consisting of encephalopathy (defined as disease of the brain affecting the brain's function); subdural hemorrhages (SDH); and retinal hemorrhages (RH)." The judges, in their conclusions, expressed caution: "We turn then to the inferences which it is proper to draw. We do so with great caution, mindful both of the gravity of the matter and that

---

[11] *"While physical abuse has in the past been a diagnosis of exclusion, data regarding the nature and frequency of head trauma consistently support a medical presumption of child abuse when a child younger than 1 year of age has intracranial injury."*

(as already underlined) the mere presence of the 'triad' does not automatically or necessarily lead to a diagnosis of NAHI and/or a conclusion of unlawful killing. All the facts of the individual case must be taken into account" (Gage, 2005). To counter any seeds of doubt in the triad that the Appeals may have sown, the experts for the respondents wrote a letter affirming their belief: "[T]he triad of encephalopathy, subdural hemorrhages and retinal hemorrhages as an indicator of head injury has stood the test of time" (Richards et al., 2006).

An important point in the history of SBS came in 2009 when a policy statement of the American Academy of Pediatrics urged a change in the terminology. The statement essentially recommended the change to keep pace with advances in understanding of the pathologic mechanisms, which included recognition that blunt impact as well as shaking was capable of causing injury and that pediatricians should "embrace a less mechanistic term, abusive head trauma, when describing an inflicted injury to the head and its contents." While the statement determined that the term SBS should be dropped, shaking as a mechanism could not be dismissed, as "[c]ase histories clearly support the conclusion that shaking occurs in some injury scenarios." These histories depended on studies in which perpetrators confessed, "the commonality of a described shaking mechanism along with the infrequency of impact evidence supports shaking as an important mechanism of AHT. In addition, blunt impact trauma or impact combined with shaking can result in infant head injuries." This article did not define a triad, but made reference to a subtly different constellation of "cerebral, spinal, and cranial injuries that result from inflicted head injury to infants and young children."

In 2011, the British Crown Prosecution Service (CPS) followed suit in their "legal guidance" on "Non Accidental Head Injury Cases (NAHI, formerly referred to as Shaken Baby Syndrome [SBS])." Diagnosis rested on the original triad: "[t]he pathological features of NAHI in children often include a triad (sometimes referred to as 'the Triad') of intracranial injuries consisting of: Retinal hemorrhages (bleeding into the linings of the eyes); Subdural hemorrhages (bleeding beneath the dural membrane); Encephalopathy (damage to the brain affecting function)" but recognized other helpful diagnostic features: "the fact that the injuries are usually inflicted by a sole carer in the absence of any other witness" and "an inadequate history or account, incompatible with the severity of the injuries."

The change from SBS to AHT remains problematic. One term may imply a mechanism that is unknown, but the other implies intent. The issue of terminology remains a matter of debate. Byard, in a forensic forum, suggested the term "lethal craniocerebral trauma," which fails to address the fact that intracranial findings in infants thought to have been abused may not be lethal and can certainly occur in the absence of trauma. Guthkelch, whose contribution helped to kick off the SBS, 40 years later has suggested the term "retinodural hemorrhagic syndrome of infancy,"[12] a term that accurately describes the objective findings without any mechanistic speculation.

While "the triad" seems to have begun life in the writings of those who support the SBS hypothesis, it has also received its death warrant from those same supporters; in

---

[12]Guthkelch, A.N., 2012. Problems of infant retino-dural hemorrhage with minimal external injury, Houston. Journal of Health Law & Policy, 201–208, ISSN:1534–7907.

2011 Carol Jenny, who was a co-author in the 1998 and 2006 letters cited previously, declared that the "triad is a myth."[13] In 2012, Greeley wrote an editorial comment citing a different "triad": "[b]oth of these reports,….. independently confirm the diagnostic precision of retinal hemorrhages, SDHs, and rib fractures for AHT," and 2 years later, vehemently rejected any use of the triad: "[t]he complex features of AHT are often disparagingly distilling[sic] simply to ''The Triad'; a term devoid of any real clinical meaning and not used at all in practice" (Greeley, 2014). Even those who previously expressed support for the shaking hypothesis now reject the diagnostic value of the triad.

In 2015, a clinical report for the American Academy of Pediatrics (Christian, 2015) did not define a triad, but wrote: "Compared with children with severe accidental trauma, children with AHT are more likely to have subdural hemorrhage, retinal hemorrhages, and associated cutaneous, skeletal, and visceral injuries." In the same year, Cowley has noted "increasing emphasis on going beyond the simple triad of injuries that is often cited when arriving at a diagnosis of AHT, namely retinal hemorrhage (RH), subdural hemorrhage, and encephalopathy" (Cowley et al., 2015).

THE METAANALYSES

No new evidence has been forthcoming from empirical research to offer scientific support for the concept that shaking is the cause of the triad and collapse in previously well infants. Courts are, however, frequently offered a series of metaanalyses of the existing literature as a basis of support for the identification of AHT. A research team from the University of Cardiff in Wales has performed a series of metaanalyses on the existing child abuse literature. While one of the stated aims of this work was to improve the accuracy of the diagnosis of abuse, the authors also directed their study toward witnesses in the courts. They considered that their work would "assist clinicians in discussion with social welfare and law enforcement or other professionals involved in the child protection process," and "those testifying in courts must be able to support their opinions with scientific evidence." These papers are important because they are so frequently used to support prosecutions.

Maguire, in 2011, developed a predictive test for child abuse (Maguire et al., 2011). A validation study, from the same Cardiff group, claimed that this predictive test performed well when tested on novel data (Cowley et al., 2015).

In developing the predictive test, Maguire and her colleagues reviewed over 8000 articles and selected the 14 best available studies on the relationship between specific findings (including apnea; RH; rib, skull, and long-bone fractures; seizures; and head and/or neck bruising) and child abuse. For the purposes of these metaanalyses, Maguire did not attempt to determine whether the categorization of cases

---

[13] Carole Jenny, Presentation, The Mechanics: Distinguishing AHT/SBS from Accidents and Other Medical Conditions, slide 11, New York City Abusive Head Trauma/Shaken Baby Syndrome Training Conference (Sept. 23, 2011) at http://www.queensda.org/SBS_Conference/SBC2011.html.

as "abusive," "accidental," or "natural" in the underlying studies was correct, but instead used the first two levels of a previously published "rank of abuse" table:[14]

> *1 Abuse confirmed at case conference or civil, family, or criminal court proceedings, or admitted by perpetrator, or independently witnessed*

> *2 Abuse confirmed by stated criteria including multi-disciplinary assessment*

These definitions raise a number of questions: what are the "stated criteria?" How are they established? What evidence did courts depend on? What constitutes a multidisciplinary assessment?

Tracking back through references cited in this study to determine the origin of these criteria leads to a review of scalds in children (Maguire et al., 2008) and then to a paper on aging of bruises, which gives no information about the identification of abuse (Maguire et al., 2005), making it impossible to identify what are the criteria, how they were determined, and how the diagnosis of abuse was reached. However, this team has published many other studies on child abuse, which do indicate diagnostic criteria. In 2003, Kemp authored a study called "Apnea and brain swelling in non-accidental head injury." Kemp used criteria for abuse derived from Geddes et al. (2001a,b).[15] Geddes was concerned about the definition of abuse that she had used and explained her caveats:

> *"One of the major problems encountered in assembling cases for NAI series is that the presenting history may not be accurate, and very few confessions are obtained."*
> *"Often child abuse is first suspected when subdural bleeding or retinal hemorrhages are detected- i.e. on the basis of pathology alone. However, if one aims to produce reliable data this approach is untenable, since it may result in cases of accidental injury being included.*

> *In an attempt to be as certain as possible that we were indeed dealing with cases of inflicted head injury we drew up diagnostic criteria for this study (see Methods). Even so, we are aware that the 12 cases in one category (where a conviction was obtained, in the absence of extracranial injuries), might conceivably include cases that were not in fact NAI, even though they had the pathology widely taken to be pathognomonic or at least "highly suggestive" of child abuse. Lack of firm objective*

---

[14] The other three are:

3 diagnosis of abuse defined by stated criteria

4 abuse stated as occurring, but no supporting detail given as to how it was determined

5 abuse stated simply as "suspected," no details on whether it was confirmed or not

[15] (1) head injury where there was a confession by the perpetrator

(2) cases where nonaccidental head injury was established as a result of criminal conviction in the criminal court where there were unexplained extracranial injuries

(3) cases where there were unexplained injuries elsewhere in the body, other than head injury, but no conviction (all diagnosed at case conference except two who died)

(4) cases where the carer was convicted of injuring the child, but in which there was no extracranial injury

(5) cases where there was major discrepancy between the explanation given by the carer and significant injury, such as a skull fracture, or if the history was developmentally incompatible

grounds for concluding that cases were NAI is another drawback of many series in the literature, including clinical and forensic series."

Geddes' caveats concerning the reliability of her definition of abuse are not quoted in the Kemp study.

In 2002, in a paper called "Investigating subdural hemorrhage in infants," Kemp, from the Cardiff group, stated that in establishing abuse, "[t]here must be an early strategy meeting with all agencies to discuss the findings and come to a joint decision about the probability of child abuse," the agencies involved being "multiagency team members: pediatrician with expertise in child protection; pediatric neurologist and/or neurosurgeon; neuroradiologist; ophthalmologist; area child protection team social worker and police." While one may assume that this is the basis for the multidisciplinary assessment on which later diagnostic criteria are based, we have no real way to be sure, as the citation trail comes to a dead end without revealing any definable criteria for diagnosing abuse.

Maguire claimed that her predictive test "confirms the association of AHT with specific combinations of clinical features," but detailed examination of the study indicates that her claims are not justified; cases were categorized as abusive or nonabusive entirely on the basis of assumptions; in the metaanalyses, these categorizations are then used to prove the assumptions. Given this circularity, the metaanalyses do not provide an evidence base for diagnosing abuse; instead, they simply predict the likelihood that specific findings will be categorized as abusive or nonabusive and, consequently, the likelihood that the carers will be accused of abuse, irrespective of the accuracy of the categorization. In 2013, Maguire accepted the problem of circularity in her studies and acknowledged the role of clinical opinion in categorizing these cases. She specifically made clear that the underlying studies relied largely on the Duhaime or similar criteria, which include the assumption that the absence of a history of trauma acceptable to the investigator is evidence of abuse (Maguire).

Independently, Piteau published another metaanalysis in 2012, entitled "Clinical and Radiographic Characteristics Associated with Abusive and Nonabusive Head Trauma: A Systematic Review." It was based on 21 studies deemed to be of high quality and used the Maguire ranking scale for diagnosis of abuse. Piteau recognized the problem of circularity[16] and noted that the underlying studies were limited by

---

[16] "This meta-analysis was made difficult by inconsistencies in the criteria used to determine the etiology for head trauma, inconsistencies in defining and reporting clinical and radiographic variables, and a moderate to high degree of statistical heterogeneity between studies. As there are no standardized criteria for the definition of abuse, most authors developed their own criteria, and many of these are fraught with circular reasoning. The diagnosis of AHT relies on historical features, clinical findings, and radiological interpretations, and it is these same criteria that are used to categorize head trauma as abusive and nonabusive. We attempted to address this limitation by using a published scale to rank the quality of the criteria used for defining abuse and examined our results for all eligible studies, as well as for those using high-quality criteria. However, for features that have been traditionally associated with abuse (such as subdural hemorrhage and retinal hemorrhage), this ranking scale does not compensate well for circularity and thus our results must be interpreted cautiously."

selection bias, informational bias, and confounding bias, with some studies additionally flawed by missing data, lack of controls, and recall bias.

The Piteau and Maguire studies were hailed as a significant step in the evolution of the child maltreatment literature: "Both of these reports, using different search protocols and analyzing different data from the same body of literature, independently confirm the diagnostic precision of retinal hemorrhages, subdural hemorrhages, and rib fractures for abusive head trauma (AHT). By independently using different strategies on the same body of literature and demonstrating similar results, we see clear support for these clinical findings, which are often used in diagnosing AHT"(Greeley, 2012).

Greeley appears to have failed to identify even the limitations noted by the authors. Further, the authors of the Cardiff studies have recently acknowledged that "the circularity of the model must be considered; in the absence of a gold standard test, we based the diagnosis of AHT not on clinical features alone but rather on a multidisciplinary assessment of all aspects of the case. However, unavoidably, this assessment will be influenced by the features included in the model" (Cowley et al., 2015).

There can be few other areas in medicine or science in which studies that rely on circular reasoning and are characterized by lack of controls and major biases can be viewed as an evolution in our understanding or are sufficiently reliable to improve diagnostic precision and make major medical decisions, let alone constitute a sufficient evidentiary basis for criminal convictions or for removing babies from their parents.

WHERE ARE WE NOW?

The triad, which was the mainstay for diagnosis of abuse, has been modified and subsequently discredited. In over 40 years, no new empirical evidence has been forthcoming to support the shaken baby hypothesis. Dias observed that "[u]nfortunately, nobody has yet marshaled a coherent and comprehensive argument in support of shaking as a causal mechanism for abusive head injury" Dias, 2011), and said that confession evidence "is the evidentiary basis for shaking" just as Caffey did in 1974. But how reliable is confession evidence? When compared to clinical evidence, up to 63% of confessions are unreliable where confessions were of "shaking only" since there was clinical evidence of impact (Dias, 2011). Adamsbaum, studying confessions in SBS, considered that "[p]erpetrator admissions are not scientific evidence" and that "[n]o statement was obtained during hospitalization. All confessions came during police custody or the judicial investigation, weeks or months after the diagnosis." Further, when imaging evidence was considered, "[n]o correlation was found between repetitive shaking and SDH densities" (Adamsbaum et al., 2010). The CPS in 2011 provided further cause to doubt confessions: "[T]here is some evidence to suggest that suspects in NAHI cases sometimes confess to 'shaking,' as this may be perceived as minimizing their criminal act, rather than admitting to hitting or striking the child."

Research since the late 1980s has discredited each of the features said to support SBS; thin-film SDH has not been demonstrated to be the result of traumatic rupture of bridging veins, but is more likely to originate in the dura as a function of immaturity. Encephalopathy is not due to traumatic shearing of the nerve fibers of the brain, but is due to a secondary cascade of events including brain swelling and lack of blood and oxygen supply, and is not specific for trauma and certainly not for abuse. RHs occur in normal births and have many other natural causes in infants, one being part of the same secondary cascade. Biomechanics have shown that shaking produces less acceleration than a low fall.

CONCLUSION

From a neuropathologist's perspective, the "triad" represents the closely interrelated pathophysiological phenomena, which form part of a secondary cascade of events in the immature brain resulting from a variety of causes, including trauma. Of key importance is that these events typically occur in the immature brain, mostly under 12 months of age. We need to shift the focus to understanding what causes these three features rather than to speculating upon mechanisms.

Not only are doctors, including the leading advocates of SBS, shifting their view, but the courts have started to recognize that the science is shifting. In a family hearing in England, Judge Baker remarked, "[L]istening to the expert evidence about subdural hematomas in this case, I have been struck by the measured way in which all of the experts expressed their opinions. Manifestly there has been considerably development in medical knowledge in this area in the last decade." He cited one expert, a well-known supporter of the shaken baby hypothesis, as saying, "[W]e have enormous gaps in our knowledge. Anything anyone says is informed speculation, not scientifically proven fact, including what I say in the reports" (Baker, 2012) (Case GF11C00125 re RH, JS, and KS). Meanwhile, convictions in the US and Sweden are being overturned based on concerns that the SBS diagnosis lacks a reliable evidence base. Sweden has taken the lead in challenging the mainstream views and has instigated an independent and exhaustive review of the scientific basis for the hypothesis. It is long overdue.

In conclusion, we must remember that parents and carers do harm babies, and abuse must be urgently detected and dealt with. But the stakes are high, and we do untold harm in wrongfully removing babies from loving parents. This is a dilemma for both practicing pediatricians and the courts. Once the suggestion of abuse is made, it may be hard to ensure a fair trial. Caffey said in 1972 that the term "battered child" "tends to provoke and inflame the hearer, and spark a premature bias against accused parents before adequate medical and legal investigations can be made. The term battered child may be crucially unjust when used before the guilt of the parents has been established legally." We should continue to heed this advice today.

REFERENCES

Adamsbaum, C., Grabar, S., Mejean, N., Rey-Salmon, C., 2010. Abusive head trauma: judicial admissions highlight violent and repetitive shaking. Pediatrics 126 (3), 546–555.

Appelbaum, P.S., February 1999. Child abuse reporting laws: time for reform? Psychiatric Services 50 (1), 27–29.

Ayoub, D.M., Hyman, C., Cohen, M., Miller, M., 2014. A critical review of the classic metaphyseal lesion: traumatic or metabolic? American Journal Roentgenology 202 (1), 185–196.

Baker, J., 2012. In the Matter of the Children Act 1989 and in the Matter of JS (A Minor) Case GF11C00125.

Baum, J.D., Bulpitt, C.J., 1970. Retinal and conjunctival haemorrhage in the newborn. Archives of Disease in Childhood 45, 344–349.

Bilson, A., Cant, R., Harries, M., Thorpe, D., 2013. A longitudinal study of children reported to the child protection department in western Australia. British Journal of Social Work 1–21. http://dx.doi.org/10.1093/bjsw/bct164.

Brennan, L.K., Rubin, D., Christian, C.W., Duhaime, A.C., Mirchandani, H.G., Rorke-Adams, L.B., 2009. Neck injuries in young pediatric homicide victims. Journal of Neurosurgery. Pediatrics 3 (3), 232–239.

Browder, J., Kaplan, H.A., Krieger, A.J., 1975. Venous lakes in the suboccipital dura mater and falx cerebelli of infants: surgical significance. Surgical Neurology 4, 53–55.

Bruce, D.A., Zimmerman, R.A., 1989. Shaken impact syndrome. Pediatric Annals 18 (8), 482–489 492.

Caffey, J., 1946. Multiple fractures in the long bones of infants suffering from chronic subdural hematoma. The American Journal of Roentgenology and Radium Therapy 56 (2), 163–173.

Caffey, J., 1965. Significance of the history in the diagnosis of traumatic injury to children. The Journal of Pediatrics 67 (5), 1008–1014.

Caffey, J., 1972a. The parent-infant traumatic stress syndrome; (Caffey-Kempe syndrome), (battered babe syndrome). The American Journal of Roentgenology, Radium Therapy, and Nuclear Medicine 114 (2), 218–229.

Caffey, J., 1972b. On the theory and practice of shaking infants. Its potential residual effects of permanent brain damage and mental retardation. American Journal of Diseases of Children 124 (2), 161–169.

Caffey, J., 1974. The whiplash shaken infant syndrome: manual shaking by the extremities with whiplash-induced intracranial and intraocular bleedings, linked with residual permanent brain damage and mental retardation. Pediatrics 54 (4), 396–403.

Chadwick, D.L., et al., 1998. Shaken baby syndrome—a forensic pediatric response. Pediatrics 101, 321–323.

Christian, C.W., Block, R., 2009. Abusive head trauma in infants and children. Pediatrics 123 (5), 1409–1411.

Christian, C.W., 2015. The evaluation of suspected child physical abuse. Pediatrics. 135 (5), e1338–e1354. www.pediatrics.org/cgi/doi/10.1542/peds.2015-0356.

Clemetson, C., Spring 2006. Caffey revisited: a commentary on the origin of "shaken baby syndrome". Journal of American Physicians and Surgeons 11 (1).

Cohen, M.C., Scheimberg, I., 2009. Evidence of occurrence of intradural and subdural hemorrhage in the perinatal and neonatal period in the context of hypoxic Ischemic encephalopathy: an observational study from two referral institutions in the United Kingdom. Pediatric and Developmental Pathology 12, 169–176.

Cohen, M.C., Sprigg, A., Whitby, E.H., 2010. Subdural hemorrhage, intradural hemorrhage and hypoxia in the pediatric and perinatal post mortem: are they related? An observational study combining the use of post mortem pathology and magnetic resonance imaging. Forensic Science International 200, 100–107.

Cory, C.Z., Jones, B.M., 2003. Can shaking alone cause fatal brain injury? A biomechanical assessment of the Duhaime shaken baby syndrome model. Medicine, Science, and the Law 43 (4), 317–333.

Cowley, L.E., et al., 2015. Validation of a prediction tool for abusive head trauma. Pediatrics 136 (2), 290–298.

Dias, M.S., 2011. The case for shaking chapter 41. In: Jenny, C. (Ed.), Child Abuse and Neglect, Diagnosis, Treatment and Evidence. Elsevier Saunders.

Duhaime, A.C., Gennarelli, T.A., Thibault, L.E., Bruce, D.A., Margulies, S.S., Wiser, R., 1987. The shaken baby syndrome. A clinical, pathological, and biomechanical study. Journal of Neurosurgery 66 (3), 409–415.

Duhaime, A.C., Gennarelli, T.A., Sutton, L.N., Schut, L., 1988. "Shaken baby syndrome": a misnomer? Journal of Pediatric Neurosciences 4 (2), 77–86.

Duhaime, A.C., Alario, A.J., Lewander, W.J., Schut, L., Sutton, L.N., Seidl, T.S., Nudelman, S., Budenz, D., Hertle, R., Tsiaras, W., 1992. Head injury in very young children: mechanisms, injury types, and ophthalmologic findings in 100 hospitalized patients younger than 2 years of age. Pediatrics 90 (2 Pt 1), 179–185.

Duhaime, A.C., Christian, C.W., Rorke, L.B., Zimmerman, R.A., 1998. Nonaccidental head injury in infants–the "shaken-baby syndrome". The New England Journal of Medicine 338 (25), 1822–1829.

Ebbs, D.A., Pollanen, M., Huyer, D., Henein, M., Nethery, M., 2011. Committee Report to the Attorney General: Shaken Baby Death Review. Toronto, Ontario.

Emerson, M.V., Pieramici, D.J., Stoessel, K.M., Berreen, J.P., Gariano, R.F., 2001. Incidence and rate of disappearance of retinal hemorrhage in newborns. Ophthalmology 108, 36–39.

Forbes, B.J., Rubin, S.E., Margolin, E., Levin, A.V., 2010. Evaluation and management of retinal hemorrhages in infants with and without abusive head trauma. Journal of AAPOS 14, 267–273.

Friede, R.L., 1989. Subdural haematomas, hygromas, and effusions. In: Friede, R.L. (Ed.), Developmental Neuropathology, vol. 2. Springer-Verlag, pp. 198–208.

Fuchs, S., Barthel, M.J., Flannery, A.M., Christoffel, K.K., 1989. Cervical spine fractures sustained by young children in forward-facing car seats. Pediatrics 84 (2), 348–354.

Gage, L.J., 2005. R-v-Harris and others. [2005] EWCA Crim 1980.

Geddes, J.F., Hackshaw, A.K., Vowles, G.H., Nickols, C.D., Whitwell, H.L., 2001a. Neuropathology of inflicted head injury in children. I. Patterns of brain damage. Brain 124 (Pt 7), 1290–1298.

Geddes, J.F., Vowles, G.H., Hackshaw, A.K., Nickols, C.D., Scott, I.S., Whitwell, H.L., 2001b. Neuropathology of inflicted head injury in children. II. Microscopic brain injury in infants. Brain 124 (Pt 7), 1299–1306.

Geddes, J.F., Tasker, R.C., Hackshaw, A.K., Nickols, C.D., Adams, G.G., Whitwell, H.L., Scheimberg, I., 2003. Dural haemorrhage in non-traumatic infant deaths: does it explain the bleeding in 'shaken baby syndrome'? Neuropathology and Applied Neurobiology 29 (1), 14–22.

Gilbert, R., et al., 2012. Child maltreatment: variation in trends and policies in six developed countries. Lancet 379, 758–772.

Gilles, F., Nelson, M., 2012. The Developing Human Brain: Growth and Adversities. Mac Keith Press.

Goodyear-Smith, F., 2012. Should New Zealand introduce mandatory reporting by general practitioners of suspected child abuse? NO. Journal of Primary Health Care 4 (1), 77–79.

Greeley, C.S., 2012. The evolution of the child maltreatment literature. Pediatrics 130 (2), 347–348.

Greeley, C.S., June 2014. "Shaken baby syndrome" and forensic pathology. Forensic Science, Medicine, and Pathology 10 (2), 253–255. http://dx.doi.org/10.1007/s12024-014-9540-0.

Guthkelch, A.N., 1953. Subdural effusions in infancy: 24 cases. British Medical Journal 1, 233–239.

Guthkelch, A.N., 1971. Infantile subdural haematoma and its relationship to whiplash injuries. British Medical Journal 2 (759), 430–431.

Harding, B., Risdon, R.A., Krous, H.F., March 27, 2004. Shaken baby syndrome Editorial. BMJ 328 (7442), 720–721.

Heins, M., 1984. "The "battered child" revisited. JAMA 251 (24), 3295–3300.

Hymel, K.P., Rumack, C.M., Hay, T.C., Strain, J.D., Jenny, C., 1997. Comparison of intracranial computed tomographic (CT) findings in pediatric abusive and accidental head trauma. Pediatric Radiology 27, 743–747.

Ingraham, F.D., Matson, D.D., 1944. Subdural hematoma in infancy. Journal of Pediatrics 24, 39.

Johnston, R.A., 2004. Paediatric spinal injuries. Injury 35 (2), 105–106.

Jones, M.D., Martin, P.S., Williams, J.M., Kemp, A.M., Theobald, P., October 2015. Development of a computational biomechanical infant model for the investigation of infant head injury by shaking. Medicine, Science, and the Law 55 (4), 291–299. http://dx.doi.org/10.1177/0025802414564495 (Epub 2014 Dec 30).

Keeling, J., 2009. Sudden unexpected death in infancy. In: Paediatric Forensic Medicine and Pathology (Edward Arnold, 2009), p. 218.

Kemp, A.M., Stoodley, N., Cobley, C., Coles, L., Kemp, K.W., 2003. Apnoea and brain swelling in non-accidental head injury. Archives of Disease in Childhood 88 (6), 472–476 (discussion 472–476).

Kempe, C.H., Silverman, F.N., Steele, B.F., Droegemueller, W., Silver, H.K., 1962. The battered-child syndrome. JAMA 181, 17–24.

Knight, B., February–March 1986. The history of child abuse. Forensic Science International 30 (2–3), 135–141.

Lantz, P.E., Couture, D.E., 2011. Fatal acute intracranial injury, subdural hematoma, and retinal hemorrhages caused by stairway fall. Journal of Forensic Sciences 56 (6), 1648–1653.

Looney, C.B., Smith, J.K., Merck, L.H., et al., 2007. Intracranial hemorrhage in asymptomatic neonates: prevalence on MR images and relationship to obstetric and neonatal risk factors. Radiology 242, 535–541.

Mack, J., Squier, W., Eastman, J.T., 2009. Anatomy and development of the meninges: implications for subdural collections and CSF circulation. Pediatric Radiology 39, 200–210.

Maguire, S., Mann, M.K., Sibert, J., Kemp, A., February 2005. Can you age bruises accurately in children? A systematic review. Archives of Disease in Childhood 90 (2), 187–189.

Maguire, S., Moynihan, S., Mann, M., Potokar, T., Kemp, A.M., December 2008. A systematic review of the features that indicate intentional scalds in children. Burns 34 (8), 1072–1081. http://dx.doi.org/10.1016/j.burns.2008.02.011 (Epub 2008 Jun 6).

Maguire, S., Kemp, A., Lumb, R., Farewel, D., 2011. Estimating the probability of abusive head trauma: a pooled analysis. Pediatrics 128, e550.

Margulies, S., Coats, B., Christian, C., Forbes, B., Duhaime, A.C., 2009. What can we learn from computational model studies of the eye? Journal of AAPOS 13 (4), 332.

Matshes, E., 2010. Retinal and optic nerve sheath haemorrhages are not pathognomonic of abusive head injury. Abstract: American Association of Forensic Sciences Conference.

Matshes, E., et al., 2011. Shaken infants die of neck trauma, not brain trauma. Academic Forensic Pathology 1 (1), b–f.

Melton, G.B., January 2005. Mandated reporting: a policy without reason. Child Abuse & Neglect 29 (1), 9–18.

Mortazavi, M.M., Denning, M., Yalcin, B., Shoja, M.M., Loukas, M., Tubbs, R.S., July 2013. The intracranial bridging veins: a comprehensive review of their history, anatomy, histology, pathology, and neurosurgical implications. Childs Nervous System 29 (7), 1073–1078. http://dx.doi.org/10.1007/s00381-013-2054-3 (Epub 2013 Mar 2).

Oehmichen, M., Schleiss, D., Pedal, I., Saternus, K.S., Gerling, I., Meissner, C., 2008. Shaken baby syndrome: re-examination of diffuse axonal injury as cause of death. Acta Neuropathologica 116 (3), 317–329.

Ommaya, A.K., Goldsmith, W., Thibault, L., 2002. Biomechanics and neuropathology of adult and paediatric head injury. British Journal of Neurosurgery 16 (3), 220–242.

Plunkett, J., 2001. Fatal pediatric head injuries caused by short-distance falls. The American Journal of Forensic Medicine and Pathology 22 (1), 1–12.

Prange, M.T., Myers, B., 2003. Pathobiology and biomechanics of inflicted childhood neurotrauma response. In: Reece, R.M., Nicholson, C.E. (Eds.), Inflicted Childhood Neurotrauma. AAP Monograph, pp. 237–243.

Prange, M.T., Coats, B., Duhaime, A.C., Margulies, S.S., 2003. Anthropomorphic simulations of falls, shakes, and inflicted impacts in infants. Journal of Neurosurgery 99 (1), 143–150.

Punt, J., Bonshek, R., Jaspan, T., Mcconachie, N., Punt, N., Ratcliffe, J., 2004. The 'unified hypothesis' of Geddes et al. is not supported by the data. Pediatric Rehabilitation 7 (3), 173–184.

Rangarajan, N., Kamalakkannan, S.B., Hasija, V., Shams, T., Jenny, C., Serbanescu, I., Ho, J., Rusinek, M., Levin, A.V., 2009. Finite element model of ocular injury in abusive head trauma. Journal of AAPOS 13 (4), 364–369.

Richards, P., et al., 2006. Shaken baby syndrome. Archives of Disease in Childhood 91, 205–206. http://dx.doi.org/10.1136/adc.2005.090761.

Rogers, C.B., Itabashi, H.H., Tomiyasu, U., Heuser, E.T., 1998. Subdural neomembranes and sudden infant death syndrome. Journal of Forensic Sciences 43, 375–376.

Rooks, V.J., Eaton, J.P., Ruess, L., et al., 2008. Prevalence and evolution of intracranial hemorrhage in asymptomatic term infants. American Journal of Neuroradiology 29, 1082–1089.

Roth, S., Raul, J.S., Ludes, B., Willinger, R., 2006. Finite element analysis of impact and shaking inflicted to a child. International Journal of Legal Medicine 121 (3), 223–228.

Scheimberg, I., Cohen, M.C., Zapata Vazquez, R.E., et al., 2013. Non-traumatic intradural and subdural hemorrhage and hypoxic ischaemic encephalopathy in fetuses, infants and children up to 3 years of age. Analysis of two audits of 636 cases from two referral centers in the UK. Pediatric and Developmental Pathology. http://dx.doi.org/10.2350/12-08-1232-OA.1.

Slovis, T.L., Strouse, P.J., et al., 2012. The creation of non-disease: an assault on the diagnosis of child abuse. Pediatric Radiology 42 (8), 903–905.

Squier, W., Mack, J., 2009. The neuropathology of infant subdural haemorrhage. Forensic Science International 187, 6–13.

Steinbok, P., Singhal, A., Poskitt, K., Cochrane, D.D., 2007. Early hypodensity on computed tomographic scan of the brain in an accidental pediatric head injury. Neurosurgery 60 (4), 689–694 (discussion 694–685).

Tardieu, A., 1860. Étude médico-légale sur les sévices et mauvais traitements exercés sur des enfants. Annales d'Hygiène Publique et de Médecine Légale 13, 361–398.

Till, K., 1968. Subdural haematoma and effusion in infancy. British Medical Journal 3, 400–402.

Uscinski, R.H., 2006. Shaken baby syndrome: an odyssey. Neurologia Medico-Chirurgica (Tokyo) 46 (2), 57–61.

Van Ee, C.A., Raymond, D., Thibault, K., Hardy, W., Plunkett, J., 2009. Child ATD reconstruction of a fatal pediatric fall. ASME International Mechanical Engineering Congress and Exposition IMECE2009–12994.

Vinchon, M., Desurmont, M., Soto-Ares, G., De Foort-Dhellemmes, S., 2010. Natural history of traumatic meningeal bleeding in infants: semiquantitative analysis of serial CT scans in corroborated cases. Childs Nervous System 26, 755–762. http://dx.doi.org/10.1007/s00381-009-1047-8.

Vinchon, M., Noizet, O., Defoort-Dhellemmes, S., Soto-Ares, S., Dhellemmes, P., 2002. Infantile subdural hematomas due to traffic accidents. Pediatric Neurosurgery 37, 245–253. http://dx.doi.org/10.1159/000066216.

Whitby, E.H., Griffiths, P.D., Rutter, S., et al., 2004. Frequency and natural history of subdural haemorrhages in babies and relation to obstetric factors. Lancet 363, 846–851.

Winter, S.C., Quaghebeur, G., Richards, P.G., 2003. Unusual cervical spine injury in a 1 year old. Injury 34 (4), 316–319.

Bite Mark Evidence

5

CHAPTER OUTLINE

Case Study: Ray Krone in His Own Words

Ray Krone[1], Wendy J. Koen[2]

[1]Co-founder, Witness to Innocence, Philadelphia, PA, United States;
[2]Child Refuge, Inc., Menifee, CA, United States

There is no crueler tyranny than that which is perpetuated under the shield of law and in the name of justice.

Charles de Montesquieu

Ray Krone. Photo courtesy of Edwin Tse and Witness to Innocence.

I was the 100th person to be exonerated from death row in the US. I was convicted of murder, kidnapping, and rape based on bite mark evidence. Bite injuries on the victim's breast and neck were matched to a cast of my teeth. The bite mark "expert" testified that marks on the body matched my teeth, my teeth were unique, and the marks were made at the time of the victim's death. That made me the murderer. That was enough. Even though an abundance of evidence, including shoe prints, fingerprints, and DNA from saliva found at the bite mark pointed to someone other than me, it was all disregarded because of the bite mark evidence. Here is the story of how I was convicted and sentenced to death.

THE MURDER

The owner of a neighborhood bar in Phoenix Arizona, the CBS Lounge, came in on a Sunday morning to open up his place. He found the front door unlocked. He checked the cash register and safe; everything appeared to be there. Although he could tell that the place had been cleaned and readied for the next day's business, his night manager had left everything unlocked and her purse on the counter. When he looked in the men's bathroom, he found his night manager, Kim Ancona, lying in a pool of blood. All she had on were her socks. She was dead, and it looked like she had been stabbed.

The police investigated Kim's murder under the assumption that the perpetrator had to be someone that had a relationship with Kim. There was no evidence of a break-in or sign of a robbery. Investigators called in the people that worked with Kim and asked them who she was dating. One of the employees mentioned my name; she said Kim liked a guy named Ray Krone. That was the beginning of my nightmare.

MY INTERROGATIONS

A few hours later, I was at my house about half a mile away from the CBS Lounge. Two men in suits came to my door. One of the men asked if I was Ray Krone and whether I knew Kim Ancona. I answered, "I'm Ray Krone, but I don't think I know anyone named Kim Ancona." The officers exchanged a glance and asked with suspicion, "you don't know Kim Ancona from the CBS Lounge?" I told them I played volleyball for the CBS Lounge. There was a girl named Kim who works there; I didn't know her last name. The officers again exchanged glances and then said, incredulously, "you don't know her last name—you're her boyfriend, aren't you?" I told them, "I'm not her boyfriend," and asked what was going on. One of the men pulled out his badge and identified himself as a homicide detective and informed me that Kim was dead. I was stunned that someone who was an acquaintance was dead and the police were there to ask me about her murder. I invited them to come into my house. They insisted they question me at the police station.

They put me in a little interrogation room, and for the next 3h they grilled me about how long Kim and I had been dating, where we'd go on dates, how many times had she been over to my house; all the time I am telling them we'd never been out on a date. I knew her from the bar. They had me take my sneakers and shirt off. They took my fingerprints, pictures of my torso, and mug shots. At one point they even got a piece of styrofoam that looked like it was two circles that came off the bottoms of disposable coffee cups and were taped together. They had me bite into it. They kept returning to the boyfriend/girlfriend questions. I cooperated through it.

After 3h, I was taken home. I thought that was the end of it. I didn't kill her. I didn't know why anyone would kill her. I was home in bed when Kim was killed, and I had a roommate who knew I was home in bed. I was sure the police would do their job and figure out I was telling the truth because that is how the justice system works.

But, that wasn't the end of it. The next day was a Monday, and when I got home from work, there was a detective waiting for me. The detective said, "Mr. Krone, I don't think you have been completely truthful. I want to eliminate you as a suspect. You want to cooperate, don't you?" The detective wanted me to come downtown to answer more questions. I cooperated. As soon as we got in the interrogation room, he slammed the door behind me and took out a search warrant for a blood sample, a hair sample, and a cast of my teeth. The warrant gave them 3 h of my time.

I got a little aggravated. I was cooperating and they were getting aggressive. I cooperated anyway. They took blood from both of my arms. They pulled out hair samples from all over my body. They took four casts of my teeth and took pictures of my teeth. They poked around in my mouth for 2.5 h. Then they sat me down for more interrogation. The officer banged his fist on the table and exploded, "It's time to come clean. It's time to tell the truth. I know you did it; why don't you just confess so we can all go home?"

That was enough for me. My honor and my integrity were always something I was proud of. Apparently my employers, the US Air Force and the US Postal Service, also had a lot of faith in my integrity and honor, but here was a man who didn't even know me, calling me a liar, a rapist, and a murderer. I came up out of my chair and told him what I thought of him, the police department, and the investigation. I said, "Why are you wasting my time? Why don't you go find the person who did this? And, by the way, your 3 h are up." I was livid. He took me home.

MY ARREST

The next day, December 31, 1991, at 4:00 in the afternoon, as I was just getting home from work, I heard the screech of brakes and saw a vanload of police officers, full riot gear, guns drawn, and they are screaming, "Don't move, you are under arrest." They threw me on the ground, handcuffed me, and arrested me for murder, kidnapping, and sexual assault. I was taken to Maricopa County Jail. It was all so unbelievable; I'd never been in jail. I never even had detention in high school.

A short time later, I was sitting in jail, but I still didn't get it. I was naïve. What I was worried about those first couple of hours was, "Did I lock my car? I have a big softball tournament this weekend; they need me to pitch. Who is going to feed my dog?" I actually believed the police were out there continuing their investigation; they were going to find out that everything I told them was the truth. They'd be coming in to tell me I could go home, any minute now, any hour now, any day now, any week now. I told my family not to worry. I didn't do it. It would all be straightened out really soon. They believed me because they knew me.

THE FIRST TRIAL

The day I met my public defender, she told me, "You've been charged with murder, kidnapping, and sexual assault. You can expect to be found guilty, but we

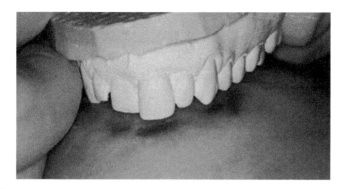

FIGURE 5.1

Krone Bite picture.

will fight it on appeal." I went crazy, she left, and that was the last I saw of her. The court appointed another attorney and granted the new attorney $5000 to represent me in a capital case. The attorney wanted me to take a plea bargain, but I refused. He didn't do any investigation. Seven months after Kim's body was found, I was sitting at the defendant's table, on trial in a capital murder case, next to an attorney who had no idea what the truth was and no way to fight the charges against me. I found out why they had me bite into the styrofoam and why they had that dentist take casts of my teeth.

They had footprints that didn't match mine, fingerprints that weren't mine, and hair they couldn't link to me, so the prosecutor hired a bite mark expert. The bite mark expert testified that marks on the body matched my teeth, that my teeth were unique, and that the marks were made at the time of Kim's death. That made me the murderer. Case closed. A single witness, the forensic expert, put me at the scene of the crime, proved that I attacked Kim, and established that I was depraved and cruel, gratified by inflicting torture on a helpless victim.

Because I had been in a car accident when I was younger and my jaw was broken and my teeth damaged, my bite was unique. The prosecutor told the jury that bite marks were like fingerprints. The cast made of my teeth was compared to a picture of the injury on Kim's body, and the expert told the jury my teeth matched perfectly (see Fig. 5.1).

A CAST OF RAY KRONE'S TEETH OVER THE BITE MARK

The prosecution's expert was deputy coroner Dr. Raymond Rawson. He was impressive. Rawson was a college professor and a Nevada state senator. He was exceptionally qualified, well spoken, and extremely convincing. As most juries are, this jury could not help but be swayed by the hard scientific proof that no one but me could have inflicted the bite mark injury on Kim.

The expert was also paid over $50,000 for his work on my case, 10 times the amount I was given to defend myself. It was slowly becoming clear just how messed up the justice system was. I was dumbfounded. I was living in some nightmare in which the country I served had come to see me as the enemy.

Rawson's most persuasive evidence was a videotape that showed an image of my teeth overlaid squarely on the photo of the bite mark on Kim's body. It looked like a perfect match. The testimony offered by the dentist hired by my attorney paled in comparison.

The trial lasted just 3.5 days. Three days were taken up by the police, the expert, and the detective. The last day, I took the stand, but I was torn apart by the prosecutor. My roommate testified on my behalf, but the prosecutor discredited him immediately by pointing out we had been in the air force together, we had known each other for over a decade, and I had always been there for him in times of need. The prosecutor ended by asking him, "You'd lie for him, wouldn't you?" It did not matter what my roommate answered. That was all it took.

The jury was out for only 3.5 h. They came back and found me guilty on murder and kidnapping. Four months later, I was back in front of the judge for sentencing. I was labeled a cold-hearted killer, an unremorseful monster, and sentenced to death.

THE APPEAL

While I was surviving on death row, my case was making its way to the Arizona Supreme Court. At trial, my attorney had objected to the admission of the videotape that showed the expert matching my teeth to the bite mark. The judge had overruled the objection, and the video evidence was allowed in. At the time of trial, my attorney argued that in light of that ruling, he would need 30 days to prepare to defend against the bite mark evidence. The judge denied his request, and the trial proceeded. The Arizona Supreme Court decided this violated the rules of discovery. As a defendant, you have the right to know what evidence is going to be used against you and time to prepare an adequate defense. They are not supposed to drop it on you the last minute. The Arizona Supreme Court determined that without this bite mark evidence, there wasn't even a case against me. The bite mark was the key evidence that convicted me. Because the trial judge had not given my attorney the time he requested to prepare to refute the bite mark video, the Arizona Supreme Court awarded me a new trial.

THE SECOND TRIAL

My folks cashed in their retirement fund, mortgaged their house, did anything they could to hire me an attorney. They realized how serious this was. It wasn't going to be like before, like those first couple of days when I was arrested and I was saying this will all just go away because I did not do anything wrong. I'd been on death row for 3 years. Every time I left my cell, they cleared the tier and marched me past the cells yelling, "Dead man walking." I knew people on that tier who they marched to their death. I was under no illusions. So we got an attorney who was familiar with my case who said he would handle it and asked us just to pay the expenses.

The second trial started in February 1996. It lasted 6.5 weeks. Almost 30 experts testified. Three bite mark experts testified for the defense. My folks sat in that court-room every day. My sister and my friends from Phoenix were there. The truth was coming out, and it was feeling good. This attorney had done his job. He found out the investigators had actually taken a swab at the area of the bite mark. It was a saliva sample. They did DNA testing on it, and that saliva was not mine. It did not match.

Of course, as always, the prosecutor had the last word with the jury. He said, "You can disregard that DNA. That DNA is meaningless and has nothing to do with this case. Don't let the defense mislead you. That is all they've been trying to do this whole trial. That DNA is easy to explain. Kim Ancona was a waitress. She handles glasses and bottles all day long. That DNA was just transferred there by accident off of somebody's glass."

The jury was out for 3.5 days. They came back and found me guilty again. I look over at the prosecution table, and they were all jumping up and down, high-fiving, like they just won the big game. But what almost killed me was when they said "guilty," I heard this most horrible scream, this incomprehensible wail from my mother and sister. I turned around and looked into their faces. I saw the horror. To me and my family, this was not a game.

Five months later, I was before the judge again for sentencing. My lawyer went over all of the evidence in the case that pointed to someone else. The shoe prints that were all over the scene that didn't match mine—they weren't my size—they were a 9.5 converse, I wore a size 11; palm prints and fingerprints found in the sink of the men's bathroom, on the paper towel dispenser, on the trash can, none of them matched me. This is where the knife was washed, dried, and hidden under the trash can. None of those prints matched mine. The DNA from hair on the body did not match mine. Neither did the DNA from the saliva found on the bite mark on Kim's breast.

When my attorney was done, the judge said that this case was going to haunt him for the rest of his life. It was hard for him to believe that someone like me had committed this crime. But it was even harder to believe that someone like me did not commit the crime and was sitting before him in judgment for a crime he did not do. In other words, he could not believe the police had gotten it wrong. Still, he had lingering residual doubt of my guilt, so, instead of giving me the death penalty, he sentenced me to 25 to life for the murder. Then he sentenced me to 21 more years for the kidnapping and made it consecutive. I was never getting out. I would die in prison because of bite mark evidence that convinced judge and jury of my guilt.

NEW DNA TESTING

In 2001, the Arizona State Legislature passed a new law allowing inmates who had untested DNA available in their case to get that DNA tested if it had direct bearing on guilt or innocence. The police had kept Kim's clothing, and we were able to get a judge to order DNA testing done on the clothes. As is often the case, the prosecution fought the testing, saying it was a wild goose chase, a waste of the court's time and money. The judge granted it anyway. The lab tested the DNA found on Kim's clothing and compared it to me. It was not mine. While this was good news and for me and my family and no surprise given the failure of the jury and the court to see the relevance of the DNA results from the saliva recovered from the bite wound, we knew it would not be enough to overturn my conviction.

However, the lab went one step further than the court order. A lab technician decided to run the DNA from Kim's clothes through the national DNA database. Results matched a man who was serving a 10-year sentence for having sexually assaulted a child just a few weeks after Kim's murder. The man was on parole at the time of the murder for another sexual assault. He lived just steps away from the bar where Kim was murdered.

He also admitted, in a taped statement, that he was in the bar the night Kim was murdered. He did not remember what happened that night because he was drunk, but when he woke up the morning after the murder, he was covered in blood.

My attorney's took the DNA results and the real perpetrator's recorded admission of guilt to the prosecutor. The prosecutor refused to accept that this new evidence mattered. He told my attorney that, "Krone is not going anywhere, we know he did it, we have the bitemark evidence." In his mind, bite mark evidence trumped DNA evidence. It looked like we had another fight on our hands.

Things changed rapidly when a local reporter heard about my case and published a front-page story. The story informed the public that I was serving a life sentence, although it was clear that someone else had raped and murdered Kim. The publicity generated by the story was not good for the prosecutor's office, and they began to feel the pressure.

On April 8, 2002, after 10 years of incarceration, my attorney called. He asked me what I was hungry for. I could eat anything I wanted, so what was it going to be? I could not understand what he was talking about. It seemed a bit cruel given the cuisine I was stuck with in prison. Then he told me he had just spoken with the prosecutor's office, and I was coming home that day. And, I did. I was the hundredth death row inmate exonerated in the US.

CONCLUSION

It is my hope that my story can act as a warning. It should *never* be forgotten that the little girl who was sexually assaulted by Kim's actual murderer would not have been if the police had simply done their job and not focused all of their efforts on nailing me. Evidence that pointed to another was ignored. Investigators focused their attention on me and did not stop until they found something substantive to convince the jury that I was the culprit. The bite mark evidence gave them what they needed. The evidence that was used to convict me was deemed to be reliable scientific proof that I had attacked Kim. It was not. It was simply wrong. Although I was unlucky enough to have dentition that could be matched to a bite injury, I was lucky enough that DNA evidence still existed and Arizona has instituted procedures for postconviction DNA testing. Others aren't so lucky. In other cases, there is no DNA evidence to test. In some states, there are no procedures for getting DNA evidence tested postconviction. Given the known miscarriages of justice caused by bite mark evidence, a moratorium on its use seems appropriate. Still, bite mark evidence is the foundation of some convictions and is used as compelling scientific evidence of guilt. Forensic dentists are still paid large sums of money to testify, though the validity of bite mark evidence is challenged and has been found inadequate by the scientific community. From where I stand, it seems courts should be quick to reject expert evidence that has been shown time and again to be both exceptionally convincing to juries and just plain wrong.

Bite Mark Evidence

C. Michael Bowers

University of Southern California, Los Angeles, CA, United States

This chapter has three sections: first, it will review how forensic science opinions have evolved and developed in criminal court systems, and where errors have occurred regarding bite mark evidence. Next, the chapter will give a brief example of how forensic science reform is influencing litigation by reviewing William Richards' wrongful conviction that was based on the erroneous pseudoscience of bite mark identification and other botched crime lab analyses (Richards, 2012). Finally, the chapter will offer a critical review of bite mark identification incorporated in a 2015 complaint filed before the Texas Forensic Science Commission (TFSC) during exoneration litigation in that state's court. The *Chaney v. State* exoneration was fueled by recanted bite mark testimony and postconviction DNA testing excluding the defendant, Steven Chaney (Chaney, 1989; The Innocence Project, 2015). The TFSC applied the scientific method to bite mark advocates' presentations and their legal history. The TFSC made the final determination that further use of bite mark evidence for human identification is not recommended in the Texas criminal justice system (Forensic Dentistry Online, 2015).

THE EVOLUTION AND DECLINE OF BITE MARK EVIDENCE

The story of the US court system's review, acceptance, or denial of what is broadly called "forensics" is the key to why bite mark evidence (from bruises, not DNA from saliva or dental tissue) used to "identify" a criminal is flawed. Bite mark evidence may be the "poster child" of the failed, unscientific approaches historically accepted in all 50 US states.

The introduction of "scientific" analyses into police criminal investigations started in Europe towards the end the 19th century. Germany, France, and Great Britain can take credit for developing the early use of trace evidence analysis, toxicology (think of Sherlock Holmes' chemical experiments), ballistics, and fingerprint interpretation. These countries can also take credit for reliance on a basic collection of human physical characteristics and recognition of suspects' "cranial characteristics of criminality."[i] Historically referenced as phrenology, psychologists created a rudimentary criminal photo/cranial line-up of known criminals whose physiognomy was thought to suggest a profile or prediction of the criminal "class" of the human population (Davies, 1955). As is always the case when scientists discover something novel, the Eugenics movement, so popular in the US during those times and into the first half of the 20th century, prompted police to expect that its use was beyond reproach (Davies, 1955; Dikötter, 1998).

Unfortunately, shared popular opinion is still a large part of the culture of forensic analysts. The process of forensic science reform, which includes debunking faulty forensic methods, requires scientists with thick skins and stubborn determination to challenge popular opinion. Sadly, it took decades for certain of these main-line "forensic methods," also known as "police sciences," to either be proven valid at some level, to be reduced in scope, to be considered invalid and totally rejected, or to be quietly ignored and simply cast off via mutual consent of its practitioners.

It is essential for the public to know that the forensic science community is unlike the much larger communities of true scientists who use empirical testing and replicating methods for confirmation. Forensic scientists in universities and industrial science applications produce a blend of opinion, generally practitioner-driven studies, and have as their audience the criminal justice system controlled by judicial "gatekeepers." This dynamic, in a practical sense, reveals that it is the court system that is the final arbiter of "approval" for the forensic concepts deemed to be important to answer or imply facts related to important questions. Also, it is apparent that vetting by judicial scientific review is significantly outdated and, in its systemic use, arbitrarily applied and self-contradictory from state to state (Frye, 1923; subsumed in Daubert, 1993).

Judges and lawyers are seldom well-versed in scientific methods and, as a substitute, rely on previously published judicial opinions on forensic subject matter. William Richards' California murder conviction is the classic example of a state court ironically being asked to overturn its own 1975 decision, *People v. Marx*, which brought a chain reaction of judicial acceptance of bite mark evidence throughout the country (Bowers, 1996). Most states ignored the fact that the bite mark in *Marx* was considered "unusual" by the prosecution's bite mark experts, who admitted that the bite mark in Marx' case was "one of the most definitive and distinct and deepest bite marks on record in human skin" (People v, 1975; p. 108; see also Vale et al., 1976).

WILLIAM RICHARDS

William Richards' case exemplifies the horrors of bite mark evidence. Here is his story, as told by the California Innocence Project (California Innocence Project).

On August 10, 1993, Pamela Richards was manually strangled, severely beaten with two fist-sized rocks, and her skull was crushed with a concrete stepping-stone. At the time of her death, Pamela lived with her husband, William "Bill" Richards, in a remote desert community in San Bernardino, California. The couple was in the process of building a home on their property. They were temporarily living in a motor home and running their power from a gasoline-powered generator.

August 10, 1993 started as a typical day for Bill Richards. Neighbors reported seeing Bill and Pamela walking and holding hands. Co-workers reported that Bill worked a normal shift and didn't seem agitated in anyway. Bill clocked out of work at his usual time and filled his ice chest with ice from a machine at work because he and Pamela did not have refrigeration at their property. Bill drove home, arriving just after midnight, and was surprised to find that there were no lights on inside the motor home or on the property. Bill went to the shed, restarted the generator, and then walked toward the motor home to find Pamela and ask her why the generator wasn't running. As he walked toward the motor home, Bill tripped over Pamela's half-naked body. When he reached down to touch her, Bill discovered that Pamela's head had been bashed in and her brain exposed. Bill immediately called 911, and when police did not arrive immediately, called two more times over the next half hour.

Finally, at 12:32 a.m., a police officer arrived, but homicide detectives did not arrive until 3:15 a.m. Because it was dark, the homicide detectives decided not to process the scene until first light, almost 3 h later.

Police failed to secure the crime scene while they waited for first light. Dogs roamed the property, obscuring footprints and blood evidence, contaminating the scene, and partially burying Pamela's body.

With the police unable to place anyone else at the crime scene, Bill was charged with his wife's murder. Bill had no defensive injuries and gave no confession. After three trials, a jury convicted Bill of Pamela's murder. Bill's conviction was based largely on the prosecution's repeated assertion, through testimony and argument, that no one other than Bill could have committed the murder because there was no evidence that anyone other than Bill and Pamela were at the crime scene. The prosecution introduced a blue thread allegedly from Bill's shirt found under Pamela's fingernail. The prosecution also argued that there appeared to be a bite mark on Pamela's body that allegedly matched Bill's teeth (see Fig. 5.2). After his conviction, Bill was sentenced to life in prison.

AUTOPSY PHOTOGRAPH OF THE BITE MARK INJURY ON PAMELA'S HAND

Had police conducted a proper and timely investigation in the early morning hours of August 11, 1993, evidence could have been gathered that would have cleared Bill. Bill presented a clear timeline of when he clocked out of work and how long it took him to

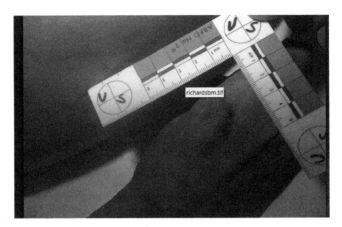

FIGURE 5.2

Autopsy photograph of the bite mark injury on Pamela's hand.

drive home. Police could have conducted simple time of death tests to determine how long Pamela had been lying dead on the ground. Fingerprinting of the couple's motor home, shed, cars, and the two fist-size rocks used to beat Pamela could have led to other suspects. Swabbing the bite mark on Pamela's body could have garnered saliva that could be used for DNA testing. Police did none of this. And while some DNA testing was done on some of the evidence at the crime scene using the technology available in the early 1990s, that testing was inconclusive and not enough to help Bill avoid life in prison.

In 2001, the California Innocence Project filed a postconviction DNA testing motion on Bill's behalf. The items that sought to be tested included the murder weapons, several items at the house that were covered in blood, and the hairs found under Pamela's fingernails. The testing revealed that the DNA on the murder weapons and the hairs under Pamela's fingernails belonged to neither Bill nor Pamela.

Judge Brian McCarville of the San Bernardino Superior Court granted Bill an evidentiary hearing to present his evidence beginning in January of 2009. The hearing took place over several days in the spring and summer months of that year. At the hearing, the California Innocence Project challenged the state's evidence presented against Bill at his 1997 trial. Two bite mark experts who had previously testified against Bill in 1997 explained to the court how current bite mark science excluded Bill as the contributor of the mark found on Pamela. The blue fiber found at autopsy under Pamela's fingernail supposedly matching the shirt Bill was wearing that night was missing from photographs of the fingers before police moved Pamela from the crime scene to the morgue, leading to the possibility that the fiber was planted there in the crime lab. And, of course, the California Innocence Project presented the DNA evidence showing a male, not Bill, wielded the murder weapon and struggled with Pam before she died.

At the conclusion of the hearing, Judge McCarville determined that the totality of the evidence presented required reversal of Bill's conviction: "Taking the evidence as to the tuft fiber. . . and the DNA and the bite mark evidence, the Court finds that the entire prosecution case has been undermined, and that [Bill] has established his burden of proof to show that the evidence before me points unerringly to innocence. Not only does the bite mark evidence appear to be questionable, it puts [Bill] as being excluded. And. . . .the DNA evidence establishes that someone other than [Bill] and the victim was at the crime scene."

Bill's celebration of the court's decision was short-lived. The district attorney appealed Judge McCarville's decision and petitioned to have the superior court grant a stay of the reversal pending its appeal. The California Court of Appeal reversed Judge McCarville's ruling (California Innocence Project).

The Supreme Court of California, too, ruled against Bill. The California Court's logic was stretched to the limit when it declared the faulty bite mark evidence used against Bill was opinion evidence, and therefore, it could not be false. After the Court's mind-boggling finding, the legislature changed the wording in the state statute to say, without ambiguity, that expert testimony can be false and thus falls under the umbrella of the false evidence standard of relief. Based on this clarification of law, the California Innocence Project filed another habeas petition before the Supreme Court of California and Bill is awaiting a decision on his case. The courtroom battle to overturn Richards' 1997 conviction has numerous levels of exoneration strategy. The following letter is in support of Bill Richards' efforts to gain freedom from flawed forensic evidence and speculative expert testimony. It alludes to the recent forensic science reform actions by the State of Texas.

RE: William Richards

Dear Sir/Madam:
I am writing regarding your upcoming review of William Richards' parole request. As an introduction, I am a practicing general dentist and a forensic dental examiner in California for many decades. My forensic activities involve assisting the Ventura County Medical Examiners Office since 1983 in cases of unidentified human remains and evidence involving dental science. In that vein, I have reviewed many cases of suspected bite mark injuries and have unfailingly observed that the forensic "specialty" of bite mark identification is a pseudo-science and is unreliable without accompanying DNA evidence. Recently the Texas Forensic Science Commission has acknowledged this failure of decades-long court approved dental testimony and two weeks ago has recommended the Texas judiciary no longer accept bitemark matching experts into criminal cases.

"An influential scientific commission in Texas called Friday for a halt in the use of bite-mark identifications in criminal trials, concluding that the validity of the technique has not been scientifically established." (http://www.nytimes. com/2016/02/13/us/texas-panel-calls-for-an-end-to-criminal-ids-via-bite-mark.html?_r=0).

The testimony of two colleagues, Drs. Sperber and Golden, at Mr. Richards' final 1997 trial confirmed to the jury that a skin injury on the hand of the murder victim, his wife Pamela, was a human bite mark (Golden) and that the bruise pattern of tooth marks was strongly characteristic of Mr. Richards' one crooked upper tooth. He testified this characteristic was present in only 2% of the human population.

Please note that in 2008, at Richards' successful but short lived habeas corpus hearing in San Bernardino, both colleagues recanted their testimony based on the current advances of science since the 1997 trial where Mr. Richards was convicted.

I have been involved in Mr. Richards' case since 1997, when I examined him outside the courtroom prior to post-conviction proceedings where I was prepared to testify that the alleged bite mark injury on Pamela's hand had no connection to Bill's teeth. My purpose for the exam was to take a wax exemplar of Bill's teeth with focus on the areas that my colleagues testified were replicated in the single autopsy photo.

The results were strikingly in favor of Bill's innocence. Upon returning to the courtroom, the finality of Bill's conviction ultimately confirmed. The judge refused Mr. Richards' request for a new trial. His motion was based on my "de novo" analysis of the evidence offered by the prosecution and the blatant miscarriage of forensic "justice" that was used to positively link him to this terrible crime.

This was 19 years ago. Bill Richards needs to see the light of freedom.

I would appreciate your proceedings to reflect this broader context of the legal proceedings which sentenced Mr. Richards to prison using evidence that the White House, the National Academy of Sciences, and the Texas Forensic Science Commission consider to be worthy of "eradication," is "unreliable," and is "not recommended" for criminal court proceedings.

Science does move on. So should the Criminal Justice system within the State of California.

With great respect,
C. Michael Bowers DDS JD
Fellow, American Academy of Forensic Sciences
Forensic dental consultant, Ventura County Medical Examiners Office
Certified Crime Scene Analyst
International Association of Identification (IAI)

CRITICAL REVIEW OF BITE MARK IDENTIFICATION

The following presentation of the *State v. Chaney*–inspired complaint to the TFSC summarizes the clear and convincing reasoning and the facts associated with the erroneous use of skin injuries (not DNA from bite marks) to identify perpetrators of serious crime. This section contains the Chaney complaint to the TFSC. This document was coauthored by Barry Scheck, Peter Neufeld, Chris Fabricant, and Dana Delgar, all from the New York Innocence Project, and Julie Lesser of the Dallas Public Defenders Office. The complaint extensively refers to material the amicus brief (described herein as "Scientists' Brief") submitted by the *Chaney* expert panel collated by ASU (Arizona State University) Law Professor Michael Saks. Its authorship was composed of 34 distinguished legal, forensics, and empirical science contributors.[ii]

July 22, 2015
Texas Forensic Science Commission
1700 North Congress Avenue, Suite 445
Austin, Texas 78701

Dear Commissioners:

Please accept this complaint, filed on behalf of our client, Steven Mark Chaney, and on behalf of the Innocence Project, Inc. We ask that the Texas Forensic Science Commission ("the Commission") exercise its statutory mandate to investigate and report on "the integrity and reliability" of bite mark evidence as used in criminal proceedings. Tex. Crim. Proc. Code Ann. § art. 38.01(4)(b-1)(1).[1]

The Innocence Project is a national litigation and public policy organization dedicated to exonerating wrongfully convicted persons through DNA testing and improving the criminal justice system to prevent future miscarriages of justice. To date, 330[iii] people in the United States, including 18 who served time on death row, have been exonerated by DNA testing. One lesson to be drawn from these exonerations is that the misapplication of forensic sciences is one of the leading causes of wrongful conviction, contributing to the original wrongful conviction in approximately half of the DNA exoneration cases. Some forensic techniques are more problematic than others, however, and of those disciplines currently in use, it is bite mark comparison evidence that poses the most acute threat to the reliability and fairness of Texas's criminal justice system. Indeed, despite the relative rarity of its application, no less than 24 people have been wrongfully convicted or indicted on the basis of bite mark evidence,[2] including *at least* two in Texas to date.[3] That this technique is responsible for so many miscarriages of justice is not surprising. As this complaint outlines, no validated and reliable science remotely supports bite mark evidence, and what science there is affirmatively disproves even the most basic assumptions which underlie it. Bite marks, moreover, "often are associated with highly sensationalized and prejudicial cases, and there can be a great deal of pressure on the examining expert to match a bite mark to a suspect" [see Appendices A, a list of exonerations (http://www.innocenceproject.org/wp-content/uploads/2016/07/Description-of-Bite-Mark-Exonerations-as-of-July-2016_final.pdf) and B, the 2009 NAS Report (https://www.ncjrs.gov/pdffiles1/nij/grants/228091.pdf)]. This, along with the fact that bite mark analysis is entirely subjective, greatly increases the risk of wrongful conviction in bite mark cases.

---

[1] Forensic odontology is not specifically enumerated as an accredited field of forensic science. *See* 37 Tex. Admin. Code § 28.145. However, it may be treated as a form of impression evidence, *see Milam v. State*, No. AP-76,379, 2012 WL 1868458, at *12-*13 (Tex. Crim. App. May 23, 2012) (unpublished opinion), which may thus be conducted out of an accredited laboratory, giving the Commission additional jurisdiction. *See* Tex. Crim. Proc. Code Ann. § art. 38.01(4)(a)(3).

[2] *See* Amanda Lee Myers, *Men Wrongly Convicted or Arrested on Bite Evidence*, Associated Press, June 16, 2013, available at http://news.yahoo.com/men-wrongly-convicted-arrested-bite-evidence-150610286.html; Amanda Lee Myers, *Bites Derided as Unreliable in Court*, Associated Press, June 16, 2013, available at http://news.yahoo.com/ap-impact-bites-derided-unreliable-court-150004412.html; *see also* Appendix A, List of Bite Mark Exonerations.

[3] For more on the exonerations of Calvin Washington and Joe Sidney Williams, and the probable wrongful convictions of Steven Mark Chaney and others in Texas, *see infra*.

Given the complete lack of science supporting bite mark analysis, and the grave risk of wrongful conviction use of the technique poses, bite marks represent an ideal and critical opportunity for this Commission to bring to bear its statutory mandate to "advance the integrity and reliability of forensic science" in Texas. See Tex. Crim. Proc. Code Ann. § art. 38.01(4)(a-1). We thus ask that this Commission undertake a thorough investigation of bite mark evidence. Our request is that this investigation includes retrospective and prospective components. Retrospectively, we ask that this Commission audit those cases in which bite mark comparison testimony was offered. Prospectively, we ask this Commission declare a moratorium on the continued use of bite mark comparison evidence in criminal prosecutions until such time as the technique has been scientifically validated and proven reliable. Doing so will not only advance this body's statutory mission, but also help ensure that no more innocent Texans are incarcerated as a result of this dangerously unreliable "science."

BITE MARK ANALYSIS HAS NEVER BEEN VALIDATED OR PROVEN RELIABLE

The use of bite mark comparison evidence in criminal trials rests on a series of unproven assumptions. First, bite mark comparison evidence assumes that the biting surfaces of teeth (i.e., the dentition) are unique. Second, it assumes that human skin is capable of accurately recording the dentition's unique features. Third, it assumes that forensic dentists can reliably associate a dentition with a bite mark. Finally, bite mark comparison assumes that, given all the foregoing, forensic dentists can provide a scientifically valid estimate as to the probative value of the association. But, as this letter will demonstrate, no science supports these assumptions, and thus no science supports the conclusion that a perpetrator can be identified from a bite mark in human skin.

The Dentition Has Never Been Scientifically Demonstrated to Be Unique

The first assumption of bite mark comparison evidence is that the human dentition (i.e., the biting surfaces of teeth) is unique. But this proposition has never been demonstrated by science to be valid or reliable. In 2009, the National Academy of Sciences (NAS), an organization made up of the nation's most accomplished scientists "charged [by an Act of Congress] with providing independent, objective advice to the nation on matters related to science and technology,"[4] undertook the first examination by an independent scientific body of bite mark evidence. After nearly 4 years of work, including thorough literature reviews and extensive testimony from a vast array of scientists, law enforcement officials, medical examiners, crime laboratory officials, investigators, attorneys, and leaders of professional and standard setting organizations, the NAS issued its groundbreaking and authoritative report. While the report criticized the scientific

---

[4] *See* National Academy of Sciences, available at http://www.nasonline.org/about-nas/mission/.

foundation for many forensic disciplines, the NAS reserved its most pointed and devastating critique for bite mark evidence, concluding that the technique lacks scientific validity and has never been proven reliable.

In particular, the NAS rejected the first assumption of bite mark analysis as baseless, finding that "[t]he uniqueness of the human dentition has not been scientifically established." Recent scientific research published largely after the NAS report suggests that not only has this uniqueness *not* been scientifically established, but that it *cannot* be. This research indicates that the limited features of the biting surfaces of teeth, which are likely to involve only one narrow surface of less than eight teeth within a bite mark (as opposed to 32 teeth with five sides for a typical adult), may not actually be unique.[5] Indeed, these studies have found there are "matches" between dentitions within certain populations.[6] An affidavit from two researchers (Bush and Bush) stated that: "Our results indicate that the biting surfaces of human anterior (front) teeth (i.e., the dentition) are not unique within measurement error. This is particularly true within a bite mark, in which only those anterior teeth may be involved."

Even If the Dentition Were Unique, Human Skin Is Not Capable of Accurately Recording Those Unique Features

Even if there were scientific support for the proposition that the dentition is unique, there is no support for the proposition that human skin is capable of accurately recording those unique features. The NAS report found that this assumption, too, was unsupported, concluding that "[t]he ability of the dentition, if unique, to transfer a unique pattern to human skin and the ability of the skin to maintain that uniqueness has not been scientifically established. . . ."

Moreover, as with the supposed uniqueness of the dentition, a new body of science, much of which emerged after publication of the NAS report, suggests that this ability will never be established. This peer-reviewed research indicates that due to its anisotropic, viscoelastic, and nonlinear properties, human skin cannot accurately record whatever uniqueness may be present in the human dentition.[7] This work

---

[5] Bush, M.A., Bush, P.J., Sheets, H.D., 2011. Statistical evidence for the similarity of the human dentition. J Forensic Sci 56 (1), 118–123 (observing significant correlations and non-uniform distributions of tooth positions as well as matches between dentitions); Sheets, H.D., Bush, P.J., Brzozowski, C., Nawrocki, L.A., Ho, P., and Bush, M.A., 2011. Dental shape match rates in selected and orthodontically treated populations in New York State: a two dimensional study. J Forensic Sci 56 (3), 621–626 (finding random dental shape matches); Bush, M.A., Bush, P.J., Sheets, H.D., 2011. Similarity and match rates of the human dentition in 3 dimensions: relevance to bitemark analysis. Int J Leg Med 125 (6), 779–784.

[6] *See supra note* 5.

[7] I Bush, M.A., Bush, P.J., Sheets, H.D. A study of multiple bitemarks inflicted in human skin by a single dentition using geometric morphometric analysis. forensic science international. 211 (2011), 1–8; Bush, M.A., Thorsrud, K., Miller, R.G., Dorion, R.B.J., Bush, P.J., 2010. The response of skin to applied stress: investigation of bitemark distortion in a cadaver model. J Forensic Sci 55 (1), 71–76; Bush, M.A., Cooper, H.I., Dorion, R.B.J., 2010. Inquiry into the scientific basis for bitemark profiling and arbitrary distortion compensation. J Forensic Sci 55 (4), 976–983; Miller, R.G., Bush, P.J., Dorion, R.B.J., Bush, M.A., 2009. Uniqueness of the dentition as impressed in human skin: a cadaver model. J Forensic Sci 54 (4), 909–914 ("Miller, Uniqueness").

demonstrates that skin's natural tension lines and tissue movement distort bite marks, often dramatically.[8] Bite marks from the same dentition may appear substantially different, depending on the angle and movement of the body and whether the mark was made parallel or perpendicular to tension or Langer lines.[9] Other studies indicate that skin is so unreliable as a medium that similarly aligned dentitions may create indistinguishable marks. Even more concerning, this research also revealed that dentitions may appear to best match marks *they did not create*.[10]

Thus, current research strongly suggests that "even if the human dentition were unique. . . human skin is not capable of faithfully recording that uniqueness with sufficient fidelity to permit bite mark comparison." See Appendix B at 174 (NAS report), "[B]ite marks on the skin will change over time and can be distorted by the elasticity of the skin, the unevenness of the surface bite, and swelling and healing. These features may severely limit the validity of forensic odontology."

Forensic Dentists Cannot Reliably Associate a Dentition With a Bite Mark

The third false assumption of bite mark analysis is that forensic dentists can reliably associate a dentition with a bite mark. But the NAS found that "[t]here is no science on the reproducibility of the different methods of analysis that lead to conclusions about the probability of a match. This includes reproducibility between experts and with the same expert over time." See Appendix B at 174 (NAS Report). Indeed, "a standard for the type, quality, and number of individual characteristics required to indicate that a bite mark has reached a threshold of evidentiary value has not been established" *Id*. at 176. This is an especially acute problem in bite mark comparison because the manner in which skin heals or decomposes over time is not predictable, and therefore, there is no methodology to account for the distortion of the injury caused by these processes. As a result, experts attempting to associate a particular dentition with a bite mark made on human skin can, at best, make educated guesses.

Moreover, while the American Board of Forensic Odontology (ABFO), forensic odontology's only board certifying body, has issued "guidelines" for a range of conclusions concerning an association between a bite mark and a suspect, its members are not required to adopt the suggested terminology, nor are they provided with any guidance on delineating between the various conclusions. More importantly, these guidelines were not arrived at scientifically but instead with nothing more than a show of hands of the members present at a meeting. See Appendix B, "The [ABFO] guidelines, however, do not indicate the criteria necessary for using each method to determine whether the bite mark can be related to a person's dentition and with what degree of probability." As the NAS found, "[e]ven when using the [ABFO] guidelines, different experts provide widely differing results. . . ." *Id*.

---

[8] Bush, M.A., Miller, R.G., Bush, P.J., Dorion, R.B., 2009. Biomechanical factors in human dermal bitemarks in a cadaver model. J Forensic Sci 54 (1), 167–176.

[9] *Id*.

[10] Miller, Uniqueness. See *infra* on the wrongful conviction of Ray Krone.

Ultimately, the NAS concluded that forensic odontologists lack "the capacity to consistently, and with a high degree of certainty, demonstrate a connection between evidence and a specific individual or source." *Id*. at seven; *see also id*. at 175 ("[T]he scientific basis is *insufficient to conclude that bite mark comparisons can result in a conclusive match*." (Emphasis added)).

Even If Bite Marks Could Be "Matched," There Is No Evidence of the Probative Value of That Association

Even if there were science to support the notion that an association could reliably be made between a dentition and a bite mark, bite mark analysis still fails in its final assumption that a scientifically valid estimate of the probative value of that association can be made. But as the NAS concluded, there is no way to determine the probability of a match because "there is no established science indicating what percentage of the population or subgroup of the population could also have produced [a] bite." *Id*. at 174; ("[S]tatistical evidence for the likelihood of a random match is, as yet, unsupportable").

This Commission recently took action regarding precisely the same type of scientifically invalid testimony in cases involving microscopic hair comparison. After the FBI acknowledged that its hair examiners had been making improper individualization claims and otherwise exaggerating the probative value of an association between a known and a suspected hair for decades, it, along with the National Association of Criminal Defense Lawyers and the Innocence Project, undertook an unprecedented review of thousands of cases to search for testimony that went beyond the bounds of science.[11]

The FBI also trained hundreds of state and local examiners to give similarly flawed testimony, and so the Commission has undertaken a case audit to "determine whether the issues identified by the FBI are also present in the testimony provided by state, county and municipal laboratories."[12] This case audit will consider whether (1) "the report or testimony contain[ed] a statement of identification"; (2) "the report or testimony assign[ed] probability or statistical weight"; and (3) "the report or testimony contain[ed] any other potentially misleading statements or inferences."[13] As the Commission has concluded,

> *A hair examiner cannot provide a scientifically valid estimate of the rareness or frequency of [an] association. The examiner's testimony should reflect the fact that hair comparison cannot be used to make a positive identification of an*

---

[11] Spencer Hsu, July 17, 2013. US reviewing 27 death penalty convictions for FBI forensic testimony errors, Washington post. Available at: http://www.washingtonpost.com/local/crime/us-reviewing-27-death-penalty-convictions-for-fbi-forensic-testimony-errors/2013/07/17/6c75a0a4-bd9b-11e2-89c9-3be8095fe767_story.html.

[12] Texas Forensic Science Commission, *Statement Regarding Texas Hair Microscopy Review Texas Forensic Science Commission*, available at: http://www.fsc.texas.gov/sites/default/files/Statement%20re%20Texas%20HM%20Review%20Final%20Draft%5B1%5D.pdf.

[13] *Id*.

individual. In other words, hair comparison can indicate, at the broad class level, that a contributor of a known sample could be included in a pool of people as a possible source of the hair evidence. However, the examiner should not give an opinion as to the probability or the likelihood of a positive association.[14]

These same limitations apply to bite mark evidence. See Appendix B at 176 (NAS Report). ("Bite mark testimony has been criticized basically on the same grounds as testimony by questioned document examiners and microscopic hair examiners"). Indeed, bite mark evidence is even more circumscribed, as the distorting properties of skin discussed previously mean that bite mark comparison experts cannot even validly make an association between a mark and a dentition.

BITE MARKS ARE PRONE TO SERIOUS ERROR

Given its lack of scientific basis, it is no surprise that bite mark comparison evidence is prone to serious error. Indeed, "error rates by forensic dentists are perhaps the highest of any forensic identification specialty still being practiced" (Scientists' Brief). Devastating new research highlighting these profound error rates, conducted in part by the Vice President of the ABFO's own Executive Committee, has recently become public. This study, entitled *Construct Validity Bitemark Assessments Using the ABFO Bitemark Decision Tree* (Construct Validity Study), demonstrates that even the ABFO's most experienced forensic odontologists cannot agree on whether an injury is a bite mark *at all*, to say nothing of whether it was caused by a particular individual.

As part of the Construct Validity Study, photographs of 100 patterned injuries were shown to 103 ABFO board-certified Diplomates. They were asked to decide three questions: first, whether there was sufficient evidence to render an opinion on whether the patterned injury was a human bite mark; second, whether, consistent with the ABFO decision tree, the injury was, indeed, a human bite mark, not a human bite mark, or suggestive of a human bite mark (the three options the ABFO's guidelines currently provide); and third, whether, if a human bite mark, it had distinct, identifiable arches and individual toothmarks.[15] Thirty-nine Diplomates, accounting for nearly 40% of practicing ABFO Diplomates, finished all 100 questions, resulting in nearly 4000 decisions. Drs. Pretty and Freeman did not examine the results for ground truth, i.e., whether the diplomates accurately determined what type of injury they were looking at, but rather, on an even more basic level, whether the diplomates agreed with one another. The results were shockingly poor. Determinations were wildly inconsistent across forensic odontologists on the vast majority of marks. As *The Washington Post* reported, on the question of whether the injury provided

---

[14] *Id.*

[15] Radley Balko, April 8, 2015. A bite mark matching advocacy group just conducted a study that discredits bite mark evidence. Washington post, Available at: http://www.washingtonpost.com/news/the-watch/wp/2015/04/08/a-bite-mark-matching-advocacy-group-just-conducted-a-study-that-discredits-bite-mark-evidence/.

sufficient information from which to make a determination as to origin,"the most basic question a bite mark specialist should answer before performing an analysis":

> *The 39 analysts came to unanimous agreement on just 4 of the 100 case studies. In only 20 of the 100 was there agreement of 90 percent or more on this question. By the time the analysts finished question two— whether the photographed mark is indeed a human bite— there remained only 16 of 100 cases in which 90 percent or more of the analysts were still in agreement. And there were only 38 cases in which at least 75 percent were still in agreement. . . By the time the analysts finished question three, they were significantly fractionalized on nearly all the cases. Of the initial 100, there remained just 8 case studies in which at least 90 percent of the analysts were still in agreement.[16]*

These failures are deeply disturbing. As a group of distinguished scientists reviewing the study's results concluded, "if dental examiners cannot agree on whether or not there is enough information in an injury to determine whether it is a bitemark, and cannot agree on whether or not a wound is a bitemark, then there is nothing more they can be relied upon to say" (Scientists' Brief).

Given the lack of a scientific basis for bite mark comparison evidence, the Construct Validity Study's results are hardly surprising, nor are they anomalous: a study published in the May 2013 Journal of Forensic Sciences largely presaged its findings.[17] As that study noted, "[w]hile most odontologists would suggest they can determine with a reasonable degree of certainty what is and what is not a bite mark, there is little evidence to support this claim."[18] Looking to close this gap, researchers asked 15 Australian forensic odontologists, who comprised the majority of those practicing forensic odontology in Australia, to examine six images of potential bite marks, five of which were of marks confirmed by living victims to have been caused by teeth.[19] The odontologists were then asked in narrative form whether the injuries were, in fact, bite marks. As with the Construct Validity Study, "conclusions between practitioners [were] highly variable."[20] Thus, "the qualitative data plainly verifie[d] the fact that there is a wide range of opinion expressed over even the most basic assumption in bite mark analysis: that of the origin of the mark itself."[21] The study further concluded that this "[i]nconsistency indicates a fundamental flaw in the methodology of bite mark analysis and should lead to concerns regarding the reliability of any conclusions reached about matching such a bite mark to a dentition."[22]

The inability of bite mark analysts to properly identify human bite marks as such in the first instance are only compounded when they are asked to make conclusions

---

[16] *Id.*

[17] Mark Page et al., May 2013. Expert interpretation of bitemark injuries—a contemporary study. J Forensic Sci 58 (3), 664.

[18] *Id.*

[19] *Id.* at 665.

[20] *Id.* at 671.

[21] *Id.* at 668.

[22] *Id.* at 670.

regarding the perpetrator. Study after study has demonstrated a "disturbingly high false-positive error rate" in bite mark comparisons."[23] For example:

- a 1975 study found that bite mark examiners made "incorrect identification[s] of. . . bites" on pig skin 24% of the time even when the bites were made "under ideal laboratory conditions" and 91% of the time when the bites were photographed 24 h after being made;
- a 1999 ABFO Bitemark Workshop in which "ABFO diplomats attempted to match four bite marks to seven dental models" resulted in 63.5% false positives; and
- a 2001 study of "bites made in pig skin" resulted in between 11.9% and 22.0% "false positive identifications. . . for various groups of forensic odontologists."[24]

These studies demonstrate that bite mark evidence simply cannot do what its practitioners purport.

BITE MARKS HAVE LED TO MANY MISCARRIAGES OF JUSTICE
Steven Mark Chaney

Simply put, there is no science that confirms biting surfaces of teeth are unique, that these unique features can be accurately recorded in human flesh, or that practitioners can objectively and systematically measure this uniqueness, which is to say there is no science whatsoever that "confirm[s] the fundamental basis for the science of bite mark comparison." See Appendix BA at 175 (NAS Report). What science there is, moreover, affirmatively disproves it. As noted bite mark researchers Mary and Peter Bush stated in their Chaney affidavit;

> *"The fundamental tenets of bitemark analysis are not supported by science. Our research, confirmed by the NAS report, suggests, moreover, that they cannot be." The practice of bite mark comparison is also prone to high rates of serious error. Yet our client, Steven Mark Chaney, and others like him, languish in prisons and jails in Texas and elsewhere, often on the basis of little more than subjective speculation masquerading as science.*

On December 14, 1987, Mr. Chaney was convicted of the murder of John Sweek and sentenced to life in prison. The primary driver of his conviction was the testimony of two forensic odontologists that Mr. Chaney's teeth matched an alleged bite mark on the body of one of the victims and that there was only a one-in-a-million chance that Mr. Chaney wasn't the source of the mark. The prosecution told the jury that it was on this evidence alone that they should convict:

> *Most of all, we have the bite mark. I wouldn't ask you to convict just based on the testimony of the tennis shoe, of the statements [Chaney] made to Investigator Westphalen, or the statements [Chaney] made to. . . [the informant]. But, by golly,*

---

[23] C. Michael Bowers, 2006. Problem-based analysis of bitemark misidentifications: the role of DNA. 159S Forensic Sci Int'l S104, S107.
[24] *Id.* at S106.

I'm going to ask you to convict on that dental testimony. . . . And [Dr. Hales] said to you that only one in a million people could have possibly made that bite mark. What more do you need?[25]

The prosecutor's exhortations had their intended effect; as one juror testified in a post-verdict colloquy, "Do you want me to tell what made my decision? [...] The bite mark."[26]

Without the link provided by forensic odontology, the case against Mr. Chaney could not have been sustained. He was arrested in June of 1987, after the bodies of a drug dealer and his wife were found murdered in the apartment they shared in East Dallas.[27] John Sweek and his wife Sally had had their throats slit, and both suffered many additional stab wounds.[28] The Sweeks had been dealing cocaine from their apartment for at least 2 years prior to their deaths, and their family members immediately informed the police that the couple's drug suppliers had threatened to kill John in the past for nonpayment.[29] The family believed these suppliers included a man named Juan Gonzalez, who they understood to be a member of the "Mexican Mafia" active in Dallas's drug trade. Gonzalez had apparently been looking for John just before the murders, and the family accordingly suspected his involvement.[30]

While this information originally led police to suspect Gonzalez, Mr. Chaney, a regular client and friend of the Sweeks, was ultimately arrested after a friend and fellow customer of the Sweeks informed police that he believed that Mr. Chaney had a motive for the murders because he owed the Sweeks approximately $500 for drugs.[31] Though Mr. Chaney had nine alibi witnesses who broadly confirmed his whereabouts the day of the murders (and no criminal history apart from two misdemeanor marijuana convictions), the state proceeded to trial against him.[32]

As the prosecutor told the jury in closing, by far the most compelling evidence of Mr. Chaney's guilt was the testimony of two forensic odontologists, Drs. Jim Hales and Homer Campbell, both of whom also played key roles in the wrongful Texas convictions of Calvin Washington and Joe Sidney Williams. Drs. Hales and Campbell each testified that the alleged bite mark on John's forearm matched Chaney's dentition. Dr. Campbell testified that Chaney made the alleged bite mark to a reasonable dental certainty. Dr. Hales also testified that there was a "[o]ne to a million" chance that someone other than Mr. Chaney could have left the bite mark.

Today, we know that the bite mark evidence offered against Mr. Chaney was not worthy of belief and should never have been proffered to a jury. Indeed the testimony proffered by Drs. Hales and Campbell is exactly the type that the NAS has recognized as unreliable and baseless and that substantial scientific evidence has

---

[25] Tr. II 801–02.

[26] Tr. II Vol. 9, p. 6.

[27] *Chaney v. State*, 775 S.W.2d 722, 723 (Tex. Ct. App. 1989).

[28] *Id.*

[29] *E.g.*, First Trial Tr. ("Tr. I") 158–61, 167; Detective Westphalen Investigative Notes, Dallas Police Department File ("W. Notes") 150.

[30] *E.g.*, W. Notes 185.

[31] *E.g.*, Second Trial Transcript ("Tr. II") 200–207; Tr. I 146-47; *Chaney* at 775 S.W.2d at 724.

[32] *E.g.*, Tr. II 530-41, 636-644, 644-58, 659-670, 711-723, 670-711, 740-46; 724-727; 727-730; *Chaney* at 775 S.W.2d at 724–25.

disproved. As an initial matter, the testimony purporting to "match" Mr. Chaney to the marks, or otherwise to identify him as the biter, is unsupportable as a matter of science. See. Appendix B at 175 (NAS Report): "[T]he scientific basis is *insufficient to conclude that bite mark comparisons can result in a conclusive match*" (emphasis added); the Chaney Scientists' Brief noted that "the uniqueness assumption [regarding the dentition] has increasingly come to be recognized as unproved and unsound. . . ." Also in the Bush Affidavit contained conclusions "that bitemark comparison evidence permitted an odontologist to determine that a particular dentition created a particular mark left in human skin (i.e., individualization). . . are not supported by science. Indeed, we know from our research that the distorting effects of skin can result in random matches of non-biting dentitions to bitemarks."

Dr. Hales' assertion that there was a "[o]ne to a million" chance that someone other than Mr. Chaney made the mark further exemplifies the foundationless conclusions characteristic of bite mark testimony. See Appendix B, 174 (NAS Report): "[T]here is no established science indicating what percentage of the population or subgroup of the population could also have produced the bite." The Scientists' Brief states, "Unfortunately, forensic dentists have very little information of the kind needed to make an informed assessment [as to the likelihood of a random match]. . . . Actual probabilities are not known because no population studies have been carried out to determine what features to consider, much less the actual degree of variation in teeth shapes, sizes, positions, etc., that exist in the population" (internal quotation marks omitted). The Bush Affidavit states that, "Dr. Hales' assertion that there was 'one to a million' chance that anyone other than Mr. Chaney created the mark has now been entirely discredited by our work and by the work of the NAS; there is simply no scientific support to offer that, or any other figure, regarding the likelihood of a random match." This proffer of statistical evidence without sufficient foundation is, moreover, exactly the same as the flawed hair microscopy testimony on which this Commission recently took action.

Mr. Chaney is currently in the process of challenging his conviction pursuant to Texas's new discredited science statute, Article 11.073. Whether or not Mr. Chaney ultimately obtains relief from the courts, it is clear that the continued incarceration of a person like Mr. Chaney on what we now know to be utterly unreliable testimony, without basis in science, is an injustice that this Commission can and should ensure that Texas avoids repeating.

Bite Mark Evidence Has Led to Many Wrongful Convictions

Bite mark evidence has also been directly responsible for the wrongful conviction or indictment of at least two dozen (see Appendix A). Ray Krone's case is the paradigmatic example of such a wrongful conviction. Mr. Krone was wrongfully convicted and sentenced to death after a bartender at a bar he frequented was kidnapped and murdered.[33] Police had a styrofoam impression made of Mr. Krone's apparently distinctive teeth for comparison to injuries found on the victim's body; he thereafter became known in the media as the "Snaggle Tooth Killer" due to his crooked teeth.[34]

---

[33] Innocence Project, *Know the Cases*: *Ray Krone*, http://www.innocenceproject.org/Content/Ray_Krone.php.

[34] Appendix A List of Bite Mark Exonerations.

Mr. Krone was convicted in two trials, both times largely on the testimony of Dr. Raymond Rawson, a board-certified ABFO Diplomate, that a bite mark found on the victim matched Mr. Krone's teeth. Mr. Krone served 10 years in prison, some of this time on death row before being exonerated by DNA testing. This testing excluded Mr. Krone but inculpated another man who had lived near the victim and who was then serving a sentence for an unrelated sexual assault.[35] A picture of the bite mark found on the victim along with Mr. Krone's dentition (see photo of Krone's teeth on page 7) is a powerful demonstration of how well-matched an innocent person's dentition may appear to be to a mark in fact made by another person.

Robert Lee Stinson, too, served more than two decades in prison for the rape and murder of an elderly woman that he did not commit. Mr. Stinson became a suspect after police officers, who had been informed by a forensic odontologist that the perpetrator was missing a tooth, told him a joke, causing him to laugh and expose his teeth.[36] Mr. Stinson's ultimate conviction rested largely on the testimony of a forensic dentist that bite marks found on the victim "had to have been made by teeth identical" to Mr. Stinson's. The dentist testified that there was "no margin for error" in his conclusion.[37] DNA later demonstrated that, despite the odontologists' certainty, Mr. Stinson was innocent.[38] Mr. Krone and Mr. Stinson's stories represent only a few of the injustices borne from the use of this so-called science.[39]

In addition to the decades stolen from innocent people, bite mark evidence has also been responsible for at least one needless death after a real perpetrator was left free to rape and kill.[40] Levon Brooks was wrongfully convicted of the rape and murder of a 3-year-old girl after bite mark comparison not only wrongly included him, but also excluded the actual perpetrator, Justin Albert Johnson. After Johnson evaded punishment for this terrible crime, he raped and murdered another 3-year-old child.[41] After this second child was killed, bite mark evidence was used *again* to inculpate another

---

[35] Innocence Project, *Know the Cases*: *Ray Krone*, http://www.innocenceproject.org/Content/Ray_Krone.php.

[36] Innocence Project, *Know the Cases*: *Robert Lee Stinson*, http://www.innocenceproject.org/Content/Robert_Lee_Stinson.php (another dentist also testified that the bite mark evidence was "high quality" and "overwhelming").

[37] *Id.*

[38] *Id.*

[39] In addition to Ex. A, the Innocence Project's list of known bite mark wrongful convictions and indictments, more about other wrongful convictions can be found in the Washington Post's exhaustive four-part series on bite mark evidence. *See, e.g.*, Radley Balko, *How The Flawed 'Science' Of Bite Mark Analysis Has Sent Innocent People To Prison*, Washington Post, February 13, 2015, *available at* http://www.washingtonpost.com/news/the-watch/wp/2015/02/13/how-the-flawed-science-of-bite-mark-analysis-has-sent-innocent-people-to-jail/. ("[T]he scientific community has declared that bite mark matching isn't reliable and has no scientific foundation for its underlying premises, and that until and unless further testing indicates otherwise, it shouldn't be used in the courtroom.").

[40] Innocence Project, *Know the Cases*: *Levon Brooks*, http://www.innocenceproject.org/Content/Levon_Brooks.php ("[I]t could be no one but Levon Brooks that bit this girl's arm."); Shaila Dewan, *New Suspect Is Arrested in 2 Mississippi Killings*, N.Y. TIMES, February 8, 2008, http://www.nytimes.com/2008/02/08/us/08dna.html?_r=0 ("Mr. Johnson had been excluded in both cases by bite-mark comparisons.").

[41] *See* Innocence Project, *Know the Cases*: *Kennedy Brewer*, http://www.innocenceproject.org/Content/Kennedy_Brewer.php.

innocent man, Kennedy Brewer. Mr. Brewer was convicted of capital murder and sexual battery and sentenced to death, based in part on testimony that the supposed bite marks found on the victim were "indeed and without a doubt" made by him.[42] DNA evidence ultimately proved Mr. Brewer's innocence and Johnson's guilt.[43]

Wrongful Convictions in Texas: Calvin Washington and Joe Sidney Williams

Texas has not escaped the scourge of wrongful bite mark convictions. Calvin Washington and his codefendant, Joe Sidney Williams, were exonerated after spending years in prison for a murder they did not commit. On March 1, 1986, the body of Juanita White[44] was discovered beaten, raped, and murdered in her home. A bite mark was found on her body.[45]

---

[42] *Id.*

[43] *Id.* In a similar story, Dane Collins was wrongfully charged with the rape and murder of his stepdaughter based largely on bite mark evidence. Though the state ultimately did not proceed against Mr. Collins, "the DA gave several public interviews stating that while there was not enough evidence to try the case, he believed Collins was guilty of the crime." See Appendix A List of Bite Mark Exonerations. Fifteen years later, DNA from a databank was found to match DNA left at the crime scene; the real perpetrator was already serving a sentence of life imprisonment for the kidnapping and rape of another woman. *See* Jeremy Pawloski, *Plea in '89 Slaying Eases Parents' Pain*, Albuquerque Journal, August 14, 2005, available at http://abqjournal.com/news/state/380765nm08-14-05.htm.

[44] Ms. White was also the mother of David Wayne Spence, another person possibly wrongfully convicted and executed in Texas on the basis of bite mark evidence. *See*.Michael Hall, *The Murders at the Lake*, Texas Monthly, April 2014, http://www.texasmonthly.com/story/investigating-the-lake-waco-murders?fullpage=1 (Hall, *Murders*). Mr. Spence, along with three co-defendants, was convicted in 1985 of the murders of three teenagers in Waco, Texas. *Id.* The prosecution's theory was that Muneer Deeb, the 23-year-old operator of a convenience store, had hired Mr. Spence and brothers Tony and Gilbert Melendez to kill an employee on whom, like all his employees, he had taken out a life insurance policy. The state theorized that Mr. Spence killed another woman by mistake, along with two other teenagers who had witnessed the crime. *See* National Registry of Exonerations, *Muneer Deeb*, https://www.law.umich.edu/special/exoneration/Pages/casedetail.aspx?caseid=3168 (Deeb Registry). The state's major evidence of guilt was the testimony of Dr. Homer Campbell that "Spence was 'the only individual' to a 'reasonable medical and dental certainty' who could have bitten the women." Hall, *Murders supra*. Mr. Deeb and Mr. Spence were both convicted at trial in 1985, with Mr. Spence sentenced to death; the Melendez brothers pleaded guilty. In 1992, Texas Criminal Court of Appeals overturned Mr. Deeb's conviction on the basis of improperly admitted informant testimony; he was then acquitted on retrial. *See* Deeb Registry *supra*. Despite substantial doubts about his guilt, Mr. Spence was executed in 1997. *See* Bob Herbert, *The Wrong Man*, N.Y. Times, July 25, 1997, available at ("Mr. Spence was almost certainly innocent. This is not a hypothesis conveniently floated by death-penalty opponents. Those who believe that David Spence did not commit the crime for which he died include the lieutenant, now retired, who supervised the police investigation of the murders; the detective who actually conducted the investigation, and a conservative Texas businessman who, almost against his will, looked into the case and became convinced that Mr. Spence was being railroaded."). Both Gilbert Melendez and Mr. Deeb have since passed away from natural causes. Tony Meldenez, who remains incarcerated, has recently sought and obtained DNA testing on, among other items, shoelaces used to tie up the victims; results of these tests have yet to be made public. *See* Cindy V. Culp, *Evidence From Lake Waco Murders Case To Be Sent To Arkansas Lab*, WacoTrib.com, April 4, 2013, available at http://www.wacotrib.com/news/courts_and_trials/evidence-from-lake-waco-murders-case-to-be-sent-to/article_fd971525-8adf-5375-b683-d0ab1b7717bf.html.

[45] Innocence Project, *Know the Cases*: *Calvin Washington*, http://www.innocenceproject.org/cases-false-imprisonment/calvin-washington.

The prosecution produced evidence that Mr. White and Mr. Williams were in possession of Ms. White's car the day after the murder and had sold some of her belongings the night she was killed.[46] Originally, forensic odontologist Jim Hales told police that Mr. Washington made the mark, but by the time of trial, another forensic odontologist, Homer Campbell, had concluded that Mr. Williams was the source of the mark.[47] Campbell testified at both trials that Mr. Washington's teeth were consistent with the mark found on Ms. White's body, thus linking both men to the crime.[48]

In 1992, the Texas Court of Criminal appeals set aside Mr. Williams's conviction, determining that alleged statements by Mr. Washington were improperly admitted at Mr. Williams's trial. The charges against Mr. Williams were ultimately dismissed, and he was released in 1993.[49] Mr. Washington, who remained imprisoned, continued to seek DNA testing. In 2001, he obtained tests, which proved that blood on a shirt found at his home was not the victim's, as the prosecution had claimed at trial. Later DNA tests excluded both Mr. Washington and Mr. Williams from semen found inside the victim; DNA in the semen was matched to an original suspect in the crime, who committed a similar crime shortly after Ms. White was killed.[50]

THE NEED FOR THIS COMMISSION'S INTERVENTION

Bite mark evidence is unscientific and unreliable, and thus grossly unfit for use in criminal proceedings. The Bush Affidavit states, "Unless and until these premises [regarding the uniqueness of the dentition and the ability of human skin to record that uniqueness] can be scientifically demonstrated, bitemark comparison evidence should not be admitted in criminal proceedings." The Scientists' Brief says, "[T]he foundations of bitemark identification are unsound." It thus presents a perfect opportunity for this Commission to exercise its statutory mandate to evaluate and report on the discipline's "integrity and reliability" [Tex. Crim. Proc. Code Ann. § art. 38.01(4)(b-1)(1)]. A thorough review of the state of bite mark science and an audit of the cases premised upon it would ameliorate some of the damage this technique has already done to the Texas criminal justice system; a moratorium on its use would prevent it from doing any further harm. See Tex. Crim. Proc. Code Ann. § art. 38.01(4)(b-1)(3) ("the investigation may include the preparation of a written report that contains:. . . other recommendations that are relevant, as determined by the commission").

Not only is such a report and audit well within this Commission's statutory authority, but action by an independent body like this one may well be necessary to ensure that bite marks are no longer used to convict innocent people in Texas.

---

[46] *Id.*

[47] Hall, *Murders, supra note* 44.

[48] *Id.*

[49] National Registry of Exonerations, *Joe Sidney Williams*, available at https://www.law.umich.edu/special/exoneration/Pages/casedetail.aspx?caseid=3748.

[50] *Id.*

A series of articles published earlier this year by *The Washington Post* (Hawkins, 2015; p. 39) revealed the ABFO's longstanding pattern and practice of suppressing dissent and punishing scrutiny. The articles reveal that most recently, the ABFO sought to silence one of its most prominent critics, Dr. C. Michael Bowers, by filing a retaliatory ethics complaint against him in front of the American Academy of Forensic Sciences. In addition to this "transparent attempt to purge someone who has been a problem for [the ABFO]," *The Washington Post* stories also reflect efforts by the ABFO to silence Dr. Mary and Peter Bush, who have conducted the most substantial (and indeed, largely the only) scientific research into the fundamental assumptions underlying bite mark analysis. *The Washington Post* reveals that the Bushes' basic research was welcomed and supported by the ABFO until they "began to come back with results that called the entire discipline into question. . . ." Once the Bushes' results made plain that there is no scientific basis for bite mark comparisons, the forensic dentistry community undertook "a nasty campaign to undermine [their] credibility." These campaigns by bite mark adherents to silence their critics and suppress science showing the invalidity of their claims are all the more reason for this Commission, as an independent body not subject to capture or intimidation, to intervene.

On behalf of Mr. Chaney and others like him, we ask that this Commission take action and reverse the damage bite mark comparison and its disciples have done to the integrity of criminal justice in Texas. By conducting an investigation and audit, and in calling for a moratorium, this Commission cannot only take a stand for reliability and integrity in forensic science in Texas, but also ensure that wrongful convictions like those of Calvin Washington and Joe Sidney Williams remain things of the past.

Very Truly Yours,

_____

Barry Scheck
M. Chris Fabricant
Dana M. Delger
Innocence Project, Inc.
40 Worth Street, Suite 701
New York, New York 10013
(212) 364-5997

_____

Julie Lesser
Exoneration Attorney
Dallas County Public Defender's Office
133 N. Riverfront Blvd., LB 2, 9th Floor
Dallas, Texas 75207
214-653-3564

REFERENCES

Bowers, C.M., 1996. A Statement Why Court Opinions on Bitemark Analysis Should Be Limited, ExpertLaw Library: Forensic Identification. Available at: http://www.expertlaw.com/library/identification/bite_marks.html.

Chaney v. State, 775 S.W.2d 722 (Tex. App. 1989).

California Innocence Project, Current Case, William Richards. https://californiainnocenceproject.org/read-their-stories/william-richards/.

Daubert v. Merrell Dow Pharmaceuticals, Inc., 509 U.S. 579, 113 S. Ct. 2786, 125 L. Ed. 2d 469 (1993).

Davies, J.D., 1955. Phrenology, Fad and Science: A 19th Century American Crusade, vol. 62. Yale University Press.

Dikötter, F., 1998. Race culture: recent perspectives on the history of eugenics. The American Historical Review 103 (2), 467–478.

Forensic Dentistry Online, 2015. Texas Will Look Back at Bitemarks. Available at: https://www.forensicdentistryonline.org/texas-will-look-back-at-bitemarks/.

Frye v. United States, 293 F. 1013 (Court of Appeals, Dist. of Columbia 1923).

Hawkins, 2015. *Va. attorney general says DNA evidence exonerates convicted murderer*. The Washington Post. Available at: https://www.washingtonpost.com/local/public-safety/va-attorney-general-says-dna-evidence-exonerates-convicted-murderer/2016/04/06/9dd277f2-fc3c-11e5-80e4-c381214de1a3_story.html?postshare=4581460048517647&tid=ss_tw-bottom%29.

The Innocence Project, 2015. Dallas District Attorney and Innocence Project Move to Reverse Conviction Based on False Bite Mark Testimony, News and Events. Available at: http://www.innocenceproject.org/news-events-exonerations/2015/dallas-district-attorney-and-innocence-project-move-to-reverse-conviction-based-on-false-bite-mark-testimony#sthash.DSPqqD5u.dpuf.

In re Richards, 289 P.3d 860, 55 Cal. 4th 948, 150 Cal. Rptr. 3d 84 (2012).

People v. Marx, 54 Cal. App. 3d 100, 126 Cal. Rptr. 350 (Ct. App. 1975).

Vale, G., Sognnaes, R., Felando, G., Noguchi, T., 1976. Unusual three-dimensional bite mark evidence in a homicide case. Journal of Forensic Sciences 21 (3), 642–652. http://dx.doi.org/10.1520/JFS10538J ISSN: 0022–1198.

ENDNOTES

i. Popular Science July 1939. http://blog.modernmechanix.com/head-measurements-help-to-identify-criminals/#more

ii. Editors' Note: Minimal edits and slight modifications are included in this document for clarity and economy purposes.

iii. At time of printing, this has increased to 338, with one more bitemark exoneration having been added. Keith Allen Harward from Virginia served 33 years in prison. Harward is the 25th exoneree who was wrongfully convicted based on erroneous bitemark evidence. See: https://www.washingtonpost.com/local/public-safety/va-attorney-general-says-dna-evidence-exonerates-convicted-murderer/2016/04/06/9dd277f2-fc3c-11e5-80e4-c381214de1a3_story.html?postshare=4581460048517647&tid=ss_tw-bottom).

Firearms Identification

6

CHAPTER OUTLINE

Forensic Science Reform. http://dx.doi.org/10.1016/B978-0-12-802719-6.00006-6
Copyright © 2017 Elsevier Inc. All rights reserved.

Case Study: Anthony Hinton

Wendy J. Koen

Child Refuge, Inc., Menifee, CA, United States

Science progresses while law builds slowly on precedent. Science assumes that humankind is determined by some combination of nature and nurture, while law assumes that humankind can transcend these influences and exercise free will. Science is a cooperative endeavor, while most legal institutions operate on an adversary model.

David L. Faigman

After spending 30 years in a 5-foot by 7-foot cell on death row in recompense for two murders he did not commit, Anthony Hinton knows the American criminal justice system intimately. Before being convicted, he was warned. A guard told him it did not matter if he committed the murders or not; he was a black man and he was "gonna pay the price for it." (Johnson, 2015). And he did. That guard was right. Hinton was given a lawyer who had no idea how to defend a death penalty case, no idea how to pay for an expert to refute the toolmark evidence that would seal Hinton's fate, and who was no match for the prosecution team and State's experts. Based on expert testimony that linked Hinton's gun to the bullets recovered from the crime scenes, Hinton was convicted and spent decades fighting to clear his name and regain his freedom. After Hinton was finally exonerated, he shared what he had learned:

> *[T]hey tell you justice is blind. I am telling you that justice can* see. *She sees what race you are, she sees where you went to college, she sees economics, she sees everything there is to see. And it all depends on what she sees…[what she sees determines] whether or not you go back home or not. And when she saw me, she knew I was going to death row.*
>
> **Johnson (2015)**

Anthony Ray Hinton was convicted of the capital murders of John Davidson and Thomas Wayne Vason and was sentenced to death by electrocution for each conviction. He was also the suspect in another robbery and attempted murder. Hinton was convicted based on expert testimony that the bullets from all three crimes came from the gun taken from his house.

The police believed that both murders occurred under similar circumstances. Each victim was a night manager at the restaurant where the robberies occurred. In each instance, the manager was leaving the restaurant after closing, was accosted by an unknown gunman, and forced to reenter the restaurant, open the safe, and give the armed robber the cash contents of the restaurant's safe. In each instance, the victim was directed into the restaurant's cooler and fatally shot twice in the head by the unknown robber.

Two 0.38 caliber bullets were recovered from each of the victims' bodies and were turned over to the Department of Forensic Sciences (DFS) to determine if they had been fired from the same weapon. Upon initial examination of the bullets from the Davidson murder, toolmark examiner David Higgins of the DFS concluded it was impossible for him to say that these bullets were fired from the same weapon [Equal Justice Initiative (EJI), 2015].

Higgins' supervisor, Lawden Yates, examined the two projectiles recovered from the Vason murder as well as the two projectiles from the Davidson murder. Yates concluded that all four had been fired from a single weapon. After conferring with Yates, Higgins changed his opinion, and both examiners reported to investigators that all four bullets had been fired from the same weapon (EJI, 2015).

As there were no fingerprints left at the scenes and the only witnesses had been killed, the investigation stalled until a third robbery and an attempted murder with the same modus operandi were committed in the Birmingham area. In the third robbery, night manager Sidney Smotherman was accosted in much the same way as Davidson and Vason. However, Smotherman remembered hearing news reports about the two previous murder–robberies, and when the gunman forced him into a storage room, Smotherman ducked and threw up his hands as the gunman fired two shots. Smotherman began to fall but managed to kick the door shut. The door locked automatically upon being closed and the gunman was locked outside of the room.

One of the bullets hit Mr. Smotherman in the finger and then grazed his head, but Smotherman was able to call 911 and was treated for his injuries. One projectile was discovered in Smotherman's pocket, and another was recovered from the storage room. Both bullets were turned over to the DFS, and Higgins and Yates determined that these two bullets were fired from the same weapon that had fired the bullets recovered from Davidson and Vason's bodies (EJI, 2015).

Although no fingerprints were recovered from the Smotherman crime scene, Smotherman gave officers a description of the gunman and then picked Hinton out of a photographic lineup. Incidentally, Smotherman also identified Leon Perry as his assailant. Leon Perry was a professional football player who came to Smotherman's rescue shortly after Smotherman was shot (EJI, 2015). It is noteworthy that Smotherman picked out Hinton's photo with "AH" printed on it immediately after he was told the suspect's name was Anthony Hinton (R. 804, 807–08).

Investigators recovered a 0.38 caliber Smith and Wesson gun from Hinton's mother. Hinton lived at his mother's home. The gun was test-fired by the Higgins and Yates. They determined that the Smith and Wesson had fired the bullets from all three robberies. Hinton was then arrested and charged with capital murder in the deaths of Davidson and Vason.

THE TRIAL

At Hinton's trial, the State linked Hinton to the Smotherman robbery by presenting eyewitness testimony from Smotherman and then by introducing forensic evidence that the bullets used to shoot Smotherman were the same as the bullets that were recovered from Davidson and Vason's bodies and that all of these bullets came from the gun recovered from Hinton's home (Hinton v. Alabama (2014) 134 S.Ct. 1081). Thus, firearm toolmark evidence was the lynchpin of Hinton's case. In toolmark analysis, examiners attempt to determine whether a bullet recovered from a crime scene was fired from a particular gun by comparing microscopic markings on the recovered bullet with the markings on a bullet known to have been fired from that gun. The theory is that minor differences, even between guns of the same model, will leave distinct traces on bullets that are unique enough to conclude whether the recovered bullet was or was not fired from a known weapon. The State theorized that because of the similarity of the three crimes and the forensic analysis of the bullets and the revolver, there was no doubt that Hinton committed the two murders.

The firearm identification evidence was crucial to the case. There was no other physical evidence, no fingerprints at any of the scenes, nothing incriminating was found in Hinton's home or car. The only evidence linking Hinton to the two murders were the forensic comparisons of the bullets and Hinton's Smith and Wesson [*Ex Parte Hinton*, No. 1051390 (Ala. Oct. 17, 2008)]. Both of the State's experts testified confidently, without caveat or reservation, that the six bullets found at the three crime scenes had been fired from the same weapon, and that weapon was the revolver that was recovered from Hinton's mother. The jury was led to believe that it had been conclusively and scientifically determined that the bullets from each murder scene could only have been fired from Hinton's gun, and defense counsel was unable to shake the jurors' confidence in that belief.

In preparation for trial, Hinton's attorney filed a motion for funding to hire a firearm toolmark expert witness. The trial judge granted $1000 for the expert and stated on the record:

> *I don't know as to what my limitations are as for how much I can grant, but I can grant up to $500.00 in each case [that is, for each of the two murder charges, which were tried together] as far as I know right now and I'm granting up to $500.00 in each of these two cases for this. So if you need additional experts I would go ahead and file on a separate form and I'll have to see if I can grant additional experts, but I am granting up to $500.00, which is the statutory maximum as far as I know on this and if it's necessary that we go beyond that then I may check to see if we can, but this one's granted.*
> **Ex Parte Hinton, No. 1051390 (Ala. Oct. 17, 2008) (quoting Tr. 10).**

Hinton's attorney was not impressed with the lone expert he found who was willing to conduct the analysis and testify at trial for $1000. Although the defense attorney believed his key witness to be incompetent, he did not pursue further funding [*Hinton v. State*, 548 So. 2d 547 (Ala. Crim. App. 1988)]. Counsel did not seek a better qualified expert because he was unaware that the Alabama statute [§ 15-12-21(d), Ala. Code 1975], which limited funding for experts to $500 per case, had been amended 2 years before Hinton's trial. The cap on funding for experts had been removed, and Hinton should have been afforded an expert commensurate with his needs. Hinton was entitled to any expenses reasonably incurred as long as they were approved in advance by the trial court. [*Ex Parte Hinton*, No. 1051390 (Ala. Oct. 17, 2008)].

Thus, the defense relied upon expert witness Andrew Payne, a consulting engineer with no expertise in firearms identification who was no match for the State's experts and who had no real authority on firearm identification. Mr. Payne testified that he examined each of the bullets recovered from the three incidents and the weapon recovered from the defendant's home. Payne concluded that no determination could be made that the bullets had been fired from the Smith and Wesson [*Hinton v. State*, 548 So.2d 547 (Ala.Crim.App.1988); *Hinton v. Alabama*, 134 S. Ct. 1081, 571 US., 188 L. Ed. 2d 1 (2014)]. It was Payne's contention that the toolmarks in the barrel of Hinton's firearm were corroded, making it impossible for any expert to determine whether any individual bullet had been fired from that gun [*Hinton v. Alabama*, 134 S. Ct. 1081, 571 US., 188 L. Ed. 2d 1 (2014)]. He also testified that it was his opinion that the bullets from all three crime scenes did not match each other. In sharp contrast, two experts who testified on behalf of the State were certain that all six bullets had been fired from Hinton's Smith and Wesson [(*Hinton v. Alabama*, 134 S. Ct. 1081, 571 US., 188 L. Ed. 2d 1 (2014)].

Payne was badly discredited by the prosecutor on cross-examination. Payne admitted to the jury that he had testified concerning bullet toolmarks only once in the 8 years before Hinton's trial. He also had to admit that he could not operate the microscope required to examine the toolmarks on the projectiles, and he had to ask the State's experts for help with the microscope during his examination. Payne admitted that he had only the use of one eye, making it difficult to see through a forensic microscope [*Hinton v. Alabama*, (2014) at p. 1086]. Further, Payne's area of expertise was military ordinance and not firearm toolmark identification. Payne was not trained in current methods and procedures, as he had graduated with a degree in civil engineering more than a half century before the trial. The State's experts had years of current training and relevant experience in firearm toolmark identification [*Hinton v. Alabama*, 134 S. Ct. 1081, 571 US., 188 L. Ed. 2d 1 (2014)].

In closing, the prosecutor brought home the stark contrast between the defense expert, Payne, and Higgins and Yates, who testified on behalf of the State:

> *I ask you to reject [Payne's] testimony and you have that option because you are the judges of the facts and whose testimony, Mr. Yates' or Mr. Payne's, you will give credence to, and I submit to you that as between these two men there is no match between them. There is no comparison. One man just doesn't have it and the other does it day in and day out, month in and month out, year in and year out, and is recognized across the state as an expert. (Hinton v. Alabama, 134 S. Ct. 1081, 571 U S., 188 L. Ed. 2d 1 (2014) (quoting Tr. 1733–1734).*

Although Hinton maintained that he was innocent and that Smotherman had misidentified him, and he presented several witnesses who testified that they were with him at work at a secure warehouse at the time of the Smotherman robbery, Hinton was convicted of two counts of murder, and the judge sentenced him to death.

It was universally accepted that it was the toolmark evidence that formed the entire foundation of the case against Hinton. The prosecution conceded at a suppression hearing that its case rested on the forensic testimony alone, stating "if the evidence of the firearms experts of the State of Alabama is not sufficient then, of course, a judgment of acquittal would lie…" (*Ex parte Hinton*, 2008 WL 4,603,723, at p. 2.) This lack of any other evidence led one Alabama state judge to remark: "In all my tenure on the bench, I have never seen the State successfully prosecute a capital-murder case when the only evidence of guilt consisted of testimony by a firearms and toolmark expert. This was an amazing prosecutorial feat…" [Hinton, 2006 WL 1,125,605, at *69 (Cobb, J., dissenting)].

POSTCONVICTION PROCEEDINGS

In 1990, Hinton filed a petition for postconviction relief in which he argued that his counsel at trial was ineffective for not hiring a qualified firearms identification expert for his defense. Three top American firearms experts examined the projectiles from the three robberies. Lannie Emanuel, Raymond Cooper, and John Dillon each concluded that there is no evidence substantiating the State's claim that the bullets recovered from the three crimes were fired from the same weapon (EJI, 2015). Although international professional standards promulgated by the Association of Firearms and Toolmark Examiners (AFTE) requires firearm examiners to confer when they reach different conclusions concerning firearm matches, Yates refused to meet with Emanuel, Cooper, and Dillon to discuss their conflicting findings (EJI, 2015). It may never be known how the State came to its wrongful conclusion linking the six bullets to Hinton's gun.

In postconviction proceedings, Cooper testified that Hinton's weapon was mechanically unable to produce bullets similar to those collected from the crime scenes. Emanuel, Cooper, and Dillon each testified that independent microscopic examinations of the six recovered bullets established that the bullets could not be linked to a single weapon. They also concluded that the revolver could not be matched with the recovered bullets. This testimony completely discredited the case against Mr. Hinton.

From 1990 until 2013, while Hinton served time on death row, Alabama courts heard evidence that Hinton's weapon could not have fired the crime scene bullets and then took turns analyzing whether Payne, the engineer hired in Hinton's defense, was qualified to give expert testimony regarding the identification of the weapon used in the robbery–murders [*Hinton v. State*, No. CR-04-0940 (Ala. Crim. App. Feb. 15, 2013)]. In 2013, the Court of Criminal Appeals of Alabama held that Payne was adequately qualified as an expert in firearms identification.

The US Supreme Court disagreed (*Hinton v. Alabama*, 2014; EJI, 2015). The Court also held that it could not determine whether counsel's ineffectiveness prejudiced the jury to the extent that it affected the outcome of the trial, so it remanded the case for further consideration. 13 years after Hinton's attorneys presented testimony from ballistics experts that determined the revolver from his mother's home could not be matched to the crimes, Hinton's conviction was finally thrown out and he was granted a new trial. The state quickly decided not to retry Hinton, as absolutely no evidence remained that could be used against him.

Hinton walked off of death row and is now free, though his attorneys maintain that years of Hinton's life were wasted on death row because of "[t]he refusal of state prosecutors to re-examine this case despite persuasive and reliable evidence of innocence" (Silva, 2015).

Here, two opinions from state experts linking Hinton's weapon to six spent bullets from three separate crime scenes was enough evidence to convict Hinton and to subject him to the death penalty. However, reliance on the experts' opinions was misguided, as there is now and has always been an "almost complete lack of factual and statistical data pertaining to the problem of establishing identity in the field of firearm identification" (Biasotti, 1959; Schwartz, 2004; Garrett, 2016). In fact, expert testimony that purports to "single out a particular firearm or other tool as the source of an evidence toolmark, to the exclusion of all other tools in the world" is not supported by empirical data and, if relied upon as such in court, will introduce error and mislead judges and juries (Schwartz, 2004).

REFERENCES

Alabama statute, 1975. (§ 15-12-21(d), Ala. Code.

Biasotti, A.A., 1959. A statistical study of the individual characteristics of fired bullets. Journal of Forensic Sciences 4, 34.

Equal Justice Initiative, Anthony Ray Hinton, March 2015.

Ex Parte Hinton, October 17, 2008. No. 1051390 Ala.

Faigman, D.L., 2000. Legal Alchemy: The Use and Misuse of Science in the Law. *Yale Journal of Law and Technology:* Vol. 2(1), Article 3. Available at: http://digitalcommons.law.yale.edu/yjolt/vol2/iss1/3.

Garrett, B.L., 2016. The constitutional regulation of forensic evidence. Washington and Lee Law Review 73.

Hinton, 2006. WL 1,125,605, at *69 (Cobb, J., dissenting).

Hinton v. State, 1988. 548 So. 2d 547 Ala. Crim. App.

Hinton v. State, Feburary 15, 2013. No. CR-04–0940 Ala. Crim. App.

Hinton v. Alabama, 2014. 134 S. Ct. 1081, 571 U.S., 188 L. Ed. 2d 1.

Johnson, C.G., 2015. 30 Years on Death Row: A Conversation with Anthony Ray Hinton. The Marshall Project. Available at: https://www.themarshallproject.org/2015/04/09/30-years-on-death-row-a-conversation-with-anthony-ray-hinton#.CRdsN1Ky9.

Schwartz, A., 2004-05. A systemic challenge to the reliability and admissibility of firearms and toolmark identification. 6 The Columbia Science and Technology Law Review 2, 32.

Silva, D., 2015. Anthony Ray Hinton, Alabama Man Who Spent 30 Years on Death Row, has Case Dismissed. NBC News. Available at: http://www.nbcnews.com/storyline/lethal-injection/anthony-ray-hinton-alabama-man-who-spent-30-years-death-n334881.

Firearms Identification Evidence: Emerging Themes From Recent Criticism, Research, and Case Law

Sarah L. Cooper

Birmingham City University, Birmingham, United Kingdom

INTRODUCTION

The use of firearms identification evidence to help solve crime in America can be traced back to the 1920s.[1] Firearms identification is premised on the notion that a weapon leaves unique toolmarks on the ammunition it fires, and those marks are reproduced each time the weapon is discharged.[2] Consequently, many firearms examiners

---

[1] *Reference Manual on Scientific Evidence* (Third Edition), Committee on the Development of the Third Edition of the Reference Manual on Scientific Evidence, Committee on Science, Technology, and Law, Policy and Global Affairs, Federal Judicial Center, National Research Council of the National Academies (hereinafter *Reference Manual on Scientific Evidence*), at 91.

[2] Donald E. Shelton, Twenty-First Century Forensic Science Challenges for Trial Judges in Criminal Cases: Where the "Polybutadiene" Meets the "Bitumen," 18 WIDNER L.J309, 335–36 (2009).

believe they can reliably conclude that a particular gun fired a particular bullet to the "exclusion of all other[s]…"[3] Such conclusions, known as individualization,[4] have long satisfied the leading legal standards for the admissibility of expert evidence in America,[5] with American courts routinely admitting firearms identification evidence for over 80 years.[6]

Throughout this period, there has been occasional criticism of the ability of crime-solving forensic disciplines to engage in accurate and reliable individualization.[7] This criticism strengthened, however, in the new millennium. In 2009, the National Academy of Sciences (NAS), in its landmark report, *Strengthening Forensic Science in the United States: A Path Forward (Strengthening)*, concluded that "no forensic method has been rigorously shown to have the capacity to consistently, and with a high degree of certainty, demonstrate a connection between evidence and a specific individual or source,"[8] except for nuclear DNA analysis. *Strengthening* cast significant doubt on the ability of forensic examiners, including firearms examiners, to engage in individualization.

Subsequently, some defendants have challenged the use of firearms identification evidence against them at trial on the basis it is not reliable.[9] Others have claimed that the criticism about firearms identification evidence contained in *Strengthening* is "newly discovered evidence (NDE)," which undermines their conviction.[10] American courts, however, routinely reject both types of claims.[11] Simultaneous to the development of this body of case law, there have been efforts on a national level to improve forensic science evidence in America.[12] This includes numerous studies targeted at improving knowledge about firearms identification evidence.[13]

---

[3] Adina Schwartz, *Challenging Firearms and Toolmark Identification—Part One*, champion, Oct. 2008, at 14.

[4] Comm. on identifying the needs of The Forensic Sci. Cmty., Nat'l Research Council of the Nat'l Academies, Strengthening forensic science in the United States: A path forward 7 (2009) [hereinafter *Strengthening*].

[5] Sarah Lucy Cooper, Judicial Responses to Challenges to Firearms Identification Evidence: A need for New Judicial Perspectives on Finality, 31 T M. Cooley L. Rev. 457, 464 (2014).

[6] *Reference Manual on Scientific Evidence*, *supra* note 1, at 91 ("The technique subsequently [after the 1920s] gained widespread judicial acceptance and was not seriously challenged until recently.").

[7] *See generally* Michael J. Saks, *Merlin and Solomon: Lessons from the Law's Encounters with Forensic Identification Science*, 49 Hastings L.J. 1069.

[8] *Strengthening*, *supra* note 4, at 7.

[9] *See generally* Cooper, *supra* note 5.

[10] *See generally* Sarah Lucy Cooper, Judicial Responses to Shifting Scientific Opinion in Forensic Identification Evidence and Newly Discovered Evidence Claims in the United States: The Influence of Finality and Legal Process Theory, four Brit. J. Am. Legal Stud. 649 (2015).

[11] *Id.*

[12] For example, the National Commission of Forensic Science was established in 2013. *See National Commission on Forensic Science*, US Dep't Just., http://www.justice.gov/ncfs (last visited Mar. 20, 2016).

[13] A summary of some of these studies in provided in Part II of this chapter.

This chapter presents current themes emerging from the American criminal justice system's use of firearms identification evidence with the aim of signposting readers to relevant case law, literature, and initiatives. Part I briefly outlines the process of firearms identification. Part II summarizes both recent criticism about the discipline and research efforts aimed at improving knowledge about its veracity. Part III examines judicial responses to challenges to firearms identification evidence between 2005 and 2015, showcasing current patterns in judicial decision-making. The cohort of cases discussed broadly fall into three categories: (1) cases showing a judicial demand for restrictions on expert testimony provided by firearms experts, (2) cases showing how the courts have marginalized *Strengthening* in the context of firearms identification evidence, and (3) cases that promote the adversarial system's function to weed out frailties in firearms identification evidence. From these categories, however, emerge a number of problems. This includes problems associated with the impact of variations in expert terminology, the overlooking of the general scientific method by the legal process, and difficulties that social actors, such as lawyers, judges, and jurors, encounter when assessing scientific evidence. Part IV concludes that this intersection of science, law, and criminal investigation will undoubtedly continue to evolve. In the light of increased awareness about how erroneous forensic science can cause wrongful conviction,[14] however, all stakeholders must sharply focus on assisting the criminal justice process to produce the most accurate results possible.

PART I: THE PROCESS OF FIREARMS IDENTIFICATION

Three types of firearms—rifles, handguns, and shotguns—are typically encountered in criminal investigations.[15] When the hard metal of an internal part of a firearm connects with the softer metal of the ammunition, it makes a toolmark on the ammunition (bullets or cartridges). To evaluate whether a suspect firearm is the source of suspect ammunition, examiners undertake a visual comparison between the toolmarks present on suspect ammunition and those present on test ammunition fired by the suspect weapon.[16] Notably, forensic examiners often have a law enforcement background.[17]

---

[14] The Innocence Project has found that 47% of the wrongful convictions identified by post-conviction DNA evidence are attributable in some way to erroneous science. *See The Causes of Wrongful Conviction,* Innocence Project, http://www.innocenceproject.org/causes-wrongful-conviction (last visited Mar. 21, 2016).

[15] *Reference Manual on Scientific Evidence, supra* note 1, at 91.

[16] *Strengthening, supra* note 4, at 152–3.

[17] See, Jennifer E. Laurin, *Criminal Law's Science Law: How Criminal Justice Meets Changed Scientific Understanding*, 93 Tex. L. Rev. 1751, 1765 (2015). This factor can mean that the relevant forensic examinations are neither typically rooted in research that has application beyond criminal investigations, nor practiced by professionals outside of law enforcement. Forensic examiners, in this environment, are inhibited by the fact that these disciplines can be fragmented, poorly regulated and lack standardised practices, as well as resources. Research into their methods can be limited, unpublished and narrowly circulated, and there is often a lack of will to pursue validation of the methods they employ.

Examiners need to understand the various types and characteristics of toolmarks in order to undertake an examination. When a gun is fired, two distinct types of toolmarks may be created: striations and impressions. Striations are similar to small scratches and are most often produced on the bullet as it passes through the gun barrel. Impressions usually resemble dimples or craters, and are typically produced on the cartridge as it comes into contact with the various internal parts of the firing chamber (e.g., the firing pin, breach face, extractor, and ejector).[18] Toolmarks can be divided into class, subclass, and individual characteristics. Class characteristics are "distinctively designed features" and will be present on every tool in that class.[19] Class characteristics result from design factors and are determined prior to manufacture.[20] Individual characteristics are unique to a particular tool and consist of purportedly random, microscopic imperfections, and irregularities present on the tool's surface.[21] Subclass characteristics straddle the line between class and individual characteristics.[22] Subclass characteristics arise when manufacturing processes create batches of tools that are similar to each other but distinct from other tools of the same class.[23]

For over 80 years, the primary equipment used by examiners to compare toolmarks is the comparison microscope.[24] The comparison microscope is made from two compound microscopes joined by a comparison bridge and allows examiners to compare two objects simultaneously under magnification.[25] Examiners tend to use the comparison microscope after it has been determined that the suspect and test ammunition share the same class characteristics.[26]

Before the comparison microscope was available, examiners used photomicrograph comparisons.[27] Nowadays, examiners can use ballistics imaging technology and national databases, such as the National Integrated Ballistic Information Network (NIBIN),[28] to support their work. Databases like NIBIN "assist examiners in finding possible candidate matches between pieces of evidence, including crime scene exhibits held in other geographic locations."[29] Moreover, enhanced technology can now "assess toolmarks using three-dimensional surface measurement data, taking into account the depth of the marks."[30] This technology supplements the work of examiners. Databases

---

[18] *See* Schwartz, *supra* note 3, at 11–12.

[19] *Id* at 12.

[20] *Reference Manual on Scientific Evidence*, *supra* note 1, at 92.

[21] Schwartz, *supra* note 3, at 12.

[22] *See Id*. (stating that subclass characteristics differ from individual characteristics because they are shared by more than one tool, but they cannot fall under class characteristics because every tool in that class does not share them).

[23] *Id*.

[24] Robert M. Thompson, *Firearms Identification in the Forensic Science Laboratory*, at 8, available at, http://ndaa.org/pdf/Firearms_identity_NDAAsm.pdf.

[25] *Id* at 32.

[26] *Strengthening*, *supra* note 4, at 155.

[27] Thompson, *supra* note 24, at 8.

[28] *Id* at 29–30 (summarizing NIBIN). *See generally.* https://www.atf.gov/firearms/national-integrated-ballistic-information-network-nibin.

[29] *Strengthening*, *supra* note 4, at 153.

[30] *Id*.

like NIBIN allow examiners to grow more familiar with the various patterns made by different firearms and act quite like a "search engine"[31] for firearms evidence. Still, "the final determination of a match is always done through direct physical comparison of the evidence...not the computer analysis of images."[32]

Many firearms examiners believe that through this physical comparison, they can conclude a particular gun fired a particular bullet to the exclusion of all others. In 1998, the AFTE, the leading professional organization in this field, developed a protocol detailing when an examiner may reach a certain conclusion (AFTE Protocol).[33] Presently, the AFTE Protocol is the industry standard by which examiners conduct their examinations. Under the AFTE Protocol, an examiner may make one of the following four conclusions: (1) identification, (2) inconclusive, (3) elimination, or (4) unsuitable for comparison.[34] Notably, these conclusions apply to the identification of a weapon as a whole, not just to the individual marks an examiner may be comparing. The AFTE protocol does not anticipate schizophrenic conclusions, such as, for example, that the firing pin toolmarks are Identifications, the breach face toolmarks are Inconclusive, and the ejector toolmarks are Eliminations. Rather, the protocol anticipates that the *combination* of the marks examined will cumulatively reveal which conclusion the examiner may reach regarding the weapon itself.[35]

To make an "identification" (i.e., a "match"), there must be "sufficient agreement" between the toolmarks subject to examination.[36] Under AFTE's Theory of Identification, which was adopted in 1992, "sufficient agreement" relates "to the significant duplication of random toolmarks"[37] as evidenced by "the correspondence of a pattern or combination of patterns of surface contours."[38] Agreement is considered significant "when the agreement in individual characteristics exceeds the best agreement demonstrated between toolmarks known to have been produced by different tools and is consistent with agreement demonstrated by toolmarks known to have been produced by the same tool."[39] A conclusion that there is "sufficient agreement" between two toolmarks "means that the agreement of individual characteristics is of a quantity and quality that the likelihood another tool could have made the mark is so remote as to be considered a practical impossibility."[40] The theory states that the interpretation of identifications is subjective, but "founded on scientific principles and based on the examiner's training and experience."[41]

---

[31] Thompson, *supra* note 24, at 30.

[32] *Strengthening*, *supra* note 4, at 153.

[33] Ass'n of Firearms & Toolmark Exam'rs, *Theory of Identification as It Relates to Toolmarks*, 30 Ass'n Firearms & Toolmark Examiners J., no. 1, 86 Winter 1998.

[34] *Id.* at 86–87.

[35] *Id.*

[36] *AFTE Theory of Identification*, available at: https://afte.org/about-us/what-is-afte/afte-theory-of-identification.

[37] *Id.*

[38] *Id.*

[39] *Id.*

[40] *Id.*

[41] *Id.*

PART II: RECENT CRITICISM AND RESEARCH ABOUT FIREARMS IDENTIFICATION

For decades, there has been criticism of the methodologies employed by "crime-solving" forensic sciences, such as those employed by firearms identification examiners, to engage in reliable and accurate individualization conclusions.[42] This criticism began to crystallize, however, in the new millennium. This section accounts for that criticism as observed in key reports, as well recent research efforts aimed at improving knowledge about forensic identification evidence.

RECENT CRITICISM

With regards to firearms identification evidence, concerns at a national level manifested in 2008. In 2008, the National Research Council of the National Academies published its *Ballistic Imaging Report*, which focused on the feasibility of a national ballistics database.[43] The Committee underscored that the report was not intended to be an overall assessment of firearms identification as a discipline. However, in assessing the feasibility of a national ballistics database, the report also considered the uniqueness of firearms-related toolmarks and found that a definitive correlation had not been fully demonstrated.[44] In particular, the report found the validity of the fundamental assumptions of uniqueness and reproducibility of firearms-related toolmarks had not yet been fully demonstrated.[45] The Committee was of the view that a significant amount of research would be needed to scientifically determine the degree to which firearms-related toolmarks are unique, or even to qualitatively characterize the probability of uniqueness.[46]

At the time the *Ballistics Imaging Report* was published, the NAS was also undertaking a wider review of forensic sciences. In 2005, Congress commissioned the NAS to report on the past, present, and future of forensic science in the US.[47] After 2 years of collaborating with legal and scientific scholars and practitioners, the NAS issued its report, *Strengthening*, in 2009.[48] The report concluded that the forensic science system had "serious problems,"[49] faced many challenges,[50] and was accountable for multiple wrongful convictions.[51] These conclusions were not necessarily "new," but for the first time, they carried the imprimatur of the NAS.

---

[42] See, generally, *Strengthening*, *supra* note 4.

[43] Comm. To assess the feasibility, accuracy, and technical capability of A Nat'l Ballistics Database, Nat'l Research Council of The Nat'l Academies, Ballistic Imaging (Daniel L. Cork Et Al. Eds., 2008) [Hereinafter Ballistic Imaging Report].

[44] *Id.* at 3. *See also* United States v. Taylor, 663 F. Supp. 2d 1170, 1176 (D.N.M. 2009) (discussing the focus and scope of the Ballistic Imaging Report).

[45] Taylor, *supra* note 44 at 1175.

[46] *Id* at 1175–76.

[47] *Strengthening*, *supra* note 4, at xix.

[48] *Id.* at xix-xx.

[49] *Id* at xx.

[50] *Id* at 4–5.

[51] *Id* at 4.

Strengthening did, however, make an unprecedented conclusion, namely that on the basis of the evidence before it, "no forensic method has been rigorously shown to have the capacity to consistently, and with a high degree of certainty, demonstrate a connection between evidence and a specific individual or source,"[52] except for nuclear DNA analysis.

The NAS made some specific observations about firearms identification evidence. In summary, it found that class characteristics can be "helpful in narrowing the pool of tools that may have left a distinctive mark,"[53] and that individual characteristics "might, in some cases, be distinctive enough to suggest one particular source."[54] However, overall, *Strengthening* concluded that "the scientific knowledge base for tool mark and firearms analysis is fairly limited."[55] *Strengthening* concluded that in order to make the process of individualization more precise and repeatable, "additional studies should be performed."[56] With regards to the AFTE Protocol, the report observed that it was not defined in a sufficiently precise way for examiners to follow, particularly in relation to when an examiner can "match" two samples. The NAS commented that "[t]his AFTE document, which is the best guidance available for the field of tool mark identification, does not even consider, let alone address, questions regarding variability, reliability, repeatability, or the number of correlations needed to achieve a given degree of confidence."[57]

Consequently, *Strengthening* cast significant doubt on the veracity of the methodologies employed by firearms examiners and the reliability and accuracy of their conclusions. Notably, the FBI lent some support to the value and reliability of firearms and toolmark evidence months after *Strengthening* was published. An article authored by FBI employees specializing in firearms and toolmarks was published in July 2009.[58] The authors conclude that the discipline is both "highly valuable and highly reliable in its traditional methods."[59] Still, they encourage further research. They note that research efforts in this field tend to fall into two categories: first, research that relates to examiner performance, and second, research that relates to the analysis of toolmarks by machines. With regards to examiner performance, they encourage the expansion of blind validity tests and black box tests, and note that the external administration of such tests would maximize objectivity, allow for testing in more laboratories, and minimize the workload of laboratory examiners. With regards to the latter, they urge research that develops machine systems and seeks to demonstrate the quality of machine outputs.[60]

---

[52] *Id* at 7.

[53] *Id* at 154.

[54] *Id*.

[55] *Id* at 155.

[56] *Id* at 154.

[57] *Id* at 155.

[58] See, Stephen G. Bunch et al., Is a Match Really a Match? A Primer on the Procedures and Validity of Firearm and Toolmark Identification, available at, https://www.fbi.gov/about-us/lab/forensic-science-communications/fsc/july2009/review/2009_07_review01.htm.

[59] *Id*.

[60] *Id*.

RECENT RESEARCH EFFORTS

Strengthening has been a catalyst for increased national initiatives towards improving the use and reliability of forensic science.[61] The Department of Justice has given millions of dollars to the cause. For example, after the release of *Strengthening*, the Department of Justice announced that its National Institute of Justice (NIJ) awarded $7.1 million in funding in fiscal year 2010 through its Fundamental Forensic Science Research program.[62] Perhaps most significantly, the National Commission on Forensic Science (NCoFS) was established in 2013.[63] The NCoFS, in partnership with the National Institute of Standards and Technology, is charged with enhancing the practice of forensic science and improving its reliability.[64] To date, it has developed a number of subcommittees to examine issues ranging from accreditation and proficiency to training in science and law, and reporting and testimony.[65]

Alongside these broader national efforts, research specifically targeting the improvement of knowledge about the veracity of firearms identification evidence has been (and continues to be) undertaken. Post-*Strengthening*, the NIJ has funded a variety of research projects aimed at improving the discipline. This includes research that considers how to improve the NIBIN program for use in criminal investigations,[66] examines specific tools and toolmarks,[67] and explores the use of infrared imaging to collect and examine toolmarks.[68]

The NIJ has also funded empirical research aiming to improve the scientific foundation of firearm and toolmark identification, i.e., the very heart of the NAS' concerns in *Strengthening*. Empirical studies have been undertaken in direct response to concerns outlined in *Strengthening,* especially those concerns about the reproducibility and uniqueness of toolmarks. These studies have established low error rates. A 2012 study established an error rate of less than 0.1%.[69] This study analyzed the

---

[61] Note that *Strengthening* also identified multiple studies aimed at developing "a statistical foundation for assessing the likelihood that more than one tool could have made specific marks by assessing consecutive matching striae…" *Strengthening*, *supra* note 4, at 154 n.63.

[62] See, *Department Of Justice Awards More Than $7.1 Million In Fiscal Year 2010 For Fundamental Forensic Science Research*, US Dep't Just., http://ojp.gov/newsroom/pressreleases/2010/NIJ10143.htm (last visited Mar. 20, 2016).

[63] *See National Commission on Forensic Science*, US Dep't Just., http://www.justice.gov/ncfs (last visited Mar. 20, 2016).

[64] *Id.*

[65] *See National Commission on Forensic Science*, US Dep't Just., https://www.justice.gov/ncfs/sub-committees (last visited Mar. 20, 2016).

[66] Nancy Ritter, *Study Identifies Ways To Improve AFT Ballistic Evidence Program* (2012), available at https://www.ncjrs.gov/pdffiles1/nij/247878.pdf.

[67] For example, the toolmarks made by screwdrivers. See, L. Scott Chumbley, *Quantification of Toolmarks, Final Technical Report* (2010), available at https://www.ncjrs.gov/pdffiles1/nij/grants/230162.pdf.

[68] Francine Prokoski Use of Infrared Imaging, a Robust Matching Engine, and Associated Algorithms to Enhance Identification of Both 2D and 3D Impressions (2009), available at https://www.ncjrs.gov/pdffiles1/nij/grants/227933.pdf.

[69] Thomas G. Fadul Jr et al., An Empirical Study to Improve the Scientific Foundation of Forensic Firearm and Tool Mark Identification Utilizing 10 Consecutively Manufactured Slides, at i, available at, https://www.ncjrs.gov/pdffiles1/nij/grants/237960.pdf.

repeatability and uniqueness of striations/impressions on fired cartridge cases fired in 10 consecutively manufactured Ruger slides by analyzing breech face striations/impressions. This was done through an evaluation of the participants' accuracy in making correct identifications.[70]

A 2013 study established a higher error rate of less than 1.2%.[71] This was where test sets had been designed to "determine an examiner's ability to correctly identify bullets fired from 10 consecutively manufactured Glock Enhanced Bullet Identification System (EBIS) barrels with the same EBIS pattern to test fired bullets fired from the same barrels."[72] The report commented that the toolmark identifications were made to a "practical certainty,"[73] but acknowledged that they could not be "absolute" because it is not feasible to examine every firearm and tool in the world, which is a prerequisite for making absolute determinations.[74] Moreover, it was not possible to express "practical impossibility" in mathematical terms.[75] However, the report concluded,

> As a result of extensive empirical research and validation studies such as this one that have been conducted in the field of firearm and tool mark identification, as well as the cumulative results of training and casework examinations that have been either performed or peer reviewed by a trained firearm and tool mark examiner, an opinion can be justifiably formed that it is a practical impossibility that another firearm will be found that exhibits as much individual microscopic agreement with test tool marks as the questioned tool marks that have been identified.[76]

Consequently, the current findings respond, to some extent to the concerns presented in *Strengthening*. This is because "the results of this research study, as well as past studies, indicate that sufficient empirical evidence exists to support the scientific foundation of firearm and tool mark identification."[77]

All told, significant work has begun to try and address concerns detailed by the NAS in *Strengthening*. Still, there is more to be done, both specifically in relation to firearms identification evidence, and more widely with regards to shifting cultural norms in forensic science practices, law enforcement practices, legal processes, and the mindsets of relevant social actors.[78] There is significant evidence to

---

[70] *Id.*

[71] Thomas G. Fadhul Jr et al., An Empirical Study to Improve the Scientific Foundation of Forensic Firearm and Tool Mark Identification Utilizing Consecutively Manufactured Glock EBIS Barrels with the Same EBIS Pattern at I, available at, https://www.ncjrs.gov/pdffiles1/nij/grants/244232.pdf.

[72] *Id* at 1–2.

[73] *Id* at 34.

[74] *Id.*

[75] *Id.*

[76] *Id.*

[77] *Id* at 37.

[78] *See generally* Cooper, S.L., 2016. Forensic science identification evidence: tensions between law and science, The Journal of Philosophy, Science & Law.

suggest the federal government[79] and states[80] are committed to improving forensic science. Moreover, such is the progressive nature of scientific inquiry (and, indeed, politics and criminal justice policy), that this research landscape should continue to evolve.

PART III: JUDICIAL RESPONSES TO CHALLENGES TO FIREARMS IDENTIFICATION EVIDENCE 2005–2015: EMERGING THEMES AND PROBLEMS

A number of legal challenges, grounded in the recent criticism about the reliability and accuracy of firearms identification evidence, have been brought to American courts overs the last decade. This section summarizes some of the types of claims made, general trends in judicial decision-making, and problems that arise from the courts' approaches.

TYPES OF LEGAL CLAIMS

Generally, petitioners have made one of two arguments. First, petitioners have argued that the relevant firearms identification evidence should not have been/should not be admitted against them, as the evidence does not satisfy the relevant admissibility standard. Currently, the admissibility framework crafted by the SCOTUS in **Daubert v. Merrell Dow Pharmaceuticals, Inc.**[81] generally governs the admissibility of scientific expert evidence in America. *Daubert* charges courts to examine the principles and methodologies behind proffered scientific evidence and not simply whether the expert's conclusions drawn from the evidence are generally accepted in the scientific community.[82] *Daubert* lists five key factors for judges to consider when analyzing the reliability of expert testimony: (1) whether a method can or has been tested, (2) the known or potential rate of error, (3) whether the method has been subjected to peer review, (4) whether there are standards controlling the method's operation, and (5) the general acceptance of the method within the relevant community.[83] Second, petitioners have used state NDE rules to argue that criticism about firearms identification evidence is a "new" fact that undermines their conviction.[84] NDE rules differ from state to state, but generally require a petitioner to show they have evidence that (1) constitutes a new fact that was not discoverable

---

[79] For example, see the comments of the Deputy Attorney General, available at https://www.justice.gov/opa/speech/deputy-attorney-general-sally-q-yates-delivers-remarks-during-68th-annual-scientific.

[80] For example, Texas has established the Texas Forensic Science Commission. See, http://www.fsc.texas.gov/

[81] Daubert v. Merrell Dow Pharmaceuticals, Inc., 509 U S. 579 (1993).

[82] *Id* at 595.

[83] *Id* at 593–4.

[84] *See generally* Cooper, *supra* note 10.

before trial, (2) they have presented the new fact to the court with reasonable diligence, (3) the new fact is not merely cumulative or impeaching, and (4) the new fact has verdict changing capacity.[85]

JUDICIAL RESPONSES TO PETITIONERS' LEGAL CLAIMS

An examination of case law between 2005 and 2015 shows that three categories of cases emerge from these claims. These categories are (1) cases showing a judicial demand for restrictions on expert terminology by firearms examiners, (2) cases showing how the courts have sidelined *Strengthening* in the context of firearms identification evidence, and (3) cases that promote the adversarial system's function to weed out frailties in firearms identification evidence. The subsections below signpost case law under each category, demonstrating current trends in judicial decision-making about firearms identification evidence and possible problems with those approaches. It is worth noting that some cases in this section overlap.

Cases Showing a Judicial Demand for Restrictions on Expert Terminology by Firearms Examiners

A number of cases show that there has been significant judicial demand for firearms examiners to not testify in terminology that reflects conclusions of individualization. These cases have related to admissibility challenges.

A few courts voiced concern about such conclusions prior to the publication of *Strengthening*. In the 2005 case of **United States v. Green**,[86] the trial court admitted expert testimony, but refused to allow the expert to conclude that the shell casings came from a specific pistol to the exclusion of every other firearm. Judge Gertner stated, "That conclusion—that there is a definitive match— stretches well beyond [the expert's] data and methodology."[87] The judge therefore only allowed the expert to describe his observations and comparisons regarding the shell casings.[88] The same court considered a similar challenge weeks later in **United States v. Monteiro**.[89] In *Monteiro*, the petitioner sought to exclude expert testimony that suspect cartridge cases matched firearms linked to him. The court rejected Monteiro's challenge, finding that the underlying scientific principle of individualization in firearm identification was valid.[90] But, on the basis that identifications are largely subjective in nature and there is no existing reliable statistical or scientific methodology that allows an expert to testify to a match to an absolute certainty, the examiner was only allowed to testify using the phrase to a "reasonable degree of ballistic certainty."[91] Notably,

---

[85] See, Keith Findley, *Defining Innocence*, 74 Alb. L. Rev. 1157, 1197 (2011).

[86] United States v. Green, 405 F. Supp. 2d 104(D. Mass. 2005).

[87] *Id.*

[88] *Id.*

[89] United States v. Monteiro, 407 F. Supp. 2d 351(D. Mass. 2006).

[90] *Id* at 366.

[91] *Id* at 372.

Monteiro was distinguished in the 2014 case of ***Arizona v. Romero***.[92] In that case, the petitioner relied on ***Monteiro*** to argue that the court should have curtailed the language used by the firearms examiner testifying against him.[93] However, the court found there was no error by the lower court because the examiner in ***Romero*** testified "that there was a match to "a reasonable degree of scientific certainty"[94], unlike the experts in ***Monteiro*** who originally "testified essentially that they could be 100 % sure of a match."[95]

In 2007, in ***United States v. Diaz***,[96] a US District Court in California found that individualization claims in the firearms identification discipline were not supported. Thus, mirroring the approach taken in *Monteiro*, the court only allowed the examiners to testify, "that a match has been made to a 'reasonable degree of certainty in the ballistics field.'"[97] This trend continued in the 2008 case of ***United States v. Glynn***,[98] but in that case, the court rejected the phraseology promoted in *Monteiro* and *Diaz*. In *Glynn*, Glynn moved to exclude the testimony, arguing the discipline was not based on sufficiently reliable methods. The court concluded that firearms identification "not only lacks the rigor of science but suffers from greater uncertainty than many other kinds of forensic evidence."[99] However, while the "subjectivity and vagueness [involved in firearms identification] might suggest that [it] involves little more than a hunch, such a characterization would be unfair."[100] This is because the court found that the methodology of firearms identification had garnered "sufficient empirical support as to warrant its admissibility."[101] The court's main concern, therefore, was how to admit the firearms identification evidence without giving the jury the impression "it has greater reliability than its imperfect methodology permits."[102] The court concluded that allowing the examiner to testify that he had matched ammunition to a particular gun "to a reasonable degree of ballistic certainty" would "seriously mislead the jury as to the nature of the expertise involved."[103] To resolve this problem, the court (1) limited the expert to testifying that a firearms match was "more likely

---

[92] State v. Romero, 236 Ariz. 451 (2014). Note this decision was vacated in part by the Arizona Supreme Court in State v Romero 365 P.3 d 358 (2016). This was on the basis that trial court erred when it excluded the expert that the defense wanted to use to challenge the firearms identification evidence against the defendant, a decision the Arizona court of appeals affirmed. ("We vacate paragraphs 19 through 32 of the opinion of the court of appeals and remand to that court to determine if the error in excluding Dr. Haber's testimony was harmless"). *Id* at 364.

[93] *Id* at 456.

[94] *Id* 456–7.

[95] *Id*.

[96] United States v. Diaz, No. 05-00,167, 2007 WL 485,967, at *1 (N.D. Cal. Feb. 12, 2007).

[97] *Id*. at *1, *14.

[98] United States v. Glynn, 578 F. Supp. 2d 567 (S.D.N.Y. 2008).

[99] *Id* at 574.

[100] *Id* at 572.

[101] *Id* at 574.

[102] *Id*.

[103] *Id*.

than not" (2) prevented the expert from testifying that he reached his conclusions to any degree of certainty, and (3) prevented the expert from testifying that ballistics was a science.[104]

After the publication of *Strengthening*, some courts have continued to curtail the terminology used by firearms examiners. For example, in ***United States v. Taylor***,[105] the defendant moved to exclude firearms identification evidence showing that his rifle could be matched to suspect ammunition in a racketeering prosecution.[106] The *Taylor* court admitted the firearms identification evidence, but in a similar fashion to ***Monteiro*** and ***Diaz***, limited the examiner to testifying that the ammunition came from the defendant's rifle within a "reasonable degree of certainty in the firearms examination field."[107]

In the 2010 case of ***United States v. Willock et al.***,[108] the defendants were charged with various RICO (Racketeer Influenced and Corrupt Organizations Act), drug, and conspiracy offences. In that case, a US District Court in Maryland adopted the recommendations of the Magistrate, Judge Grimm, who recommended that the state's firearms examiner be restricted with regards to the degree of certainty with which he expressed his opinions.[109] Judge Grimm made this recommendation in the light of the *Ballistics Imaging Report* and *Strengthening*. However, a significant factor in ***Willock*** was that the state's firearms examiner had "piggy-backed" on the conclusions of another unknown examiner.[110] Consequently, it was ordered that the examiner only be allowed to testify as to his opinions and bases "without any characterization as to the degree of certainty."[111] This approach, in the Magistrate's view, precluded the approaches taken in *Glynn*, *Taylor*, *Diaz*, and *Monteiro*.[112] He also recommended that, at a minimum, the examiner not be allowed to opine "that it is a "practical impossibility" for any other firearm to have fired the cartridges other than the common "unknown firearm" to which the examiner attributed the cartridges.[113] That said, the Magistrate's alternative, second recommendation was to follow the "more likely than not" language used in *Glynn* or, at most, follow the "to a reasonable degree of ballistic certainty" language of *Monteiro*, *Diaz*, and *Taylor*.[114]

---

[104] *Id.* at 568–9.

[105] United States v. Taylor, 663 F. Supp. 2d 1170 (D.N.M. 2009).

[106] *Id.* at 1171–2.

[107] *Id.* at 1180.

[108] United States v. Willock et al., 696 F.Supp.2d 536 (2010).

[109] *Id.*

[110] *Id* at 574.

[111] *Id* at 549.

[112] *Id* at 574.

[113] *Id.*

[114] *Id.* The U.S. District Court adopted "Recommendation (1) "[t]hat Sgt. Ensor not be allowed to opine that it is a "practical impossibility" for any other firearm to have fired the cartridges other than the common "unknown firearm" to which Sgt. Ensor attributes the cartridges"; Recommendation (2) "that Sgt. Ensor only be permitted to state his opinions and bases without any characterization as to degree of certainty.") *Id* at n.26.[fnrId15].

In ***Commonwealth v. Pytou Heang***,[115] Pytou Heang alleged that the trial court had erred in allowing the state's expert to testify that his AB-10 handgun had fired ammunition involved in the crime.[116] The court acknowledged that the accuracy, reliability, and scientific basis of firearms identification had been critiqued in the *Ballistics Imaging Report* and *Strengthening*.[117] The court, thus, found two main problems with firearms identification evidence. First, that there was "little" scientific proof to support the notion that each firearm puts "unique" toolmarks onto ammunition.[118] Second, the "matching" of individual characteristics is very subjective.[119] In an attempt to resolve these problems, the court required, inter alia, that "where a qualified expert has identified sufficient individual characteristic toolmarks reasonably to offer an opinion that a particular firearm fired a projectile or cartridge casing recovered as evidence, the expert may offer that opinion to a reasonable degree of ballistic certainty."[120]

This approach continues in more recent cases. In 2015, in ***United States v. Ashburn***,[121] an examiner was precluded from testifying that he was "certain or 100% sure" that there was a "match" and stating that he had identified the suspect weapon "to the exclusion of all other firearms in the world" or that there was a "practical impossibility" that any other gun could have fired the suspect materials.[122] In that case, the court limited the examiner to stating that his conclusions were reached "to a reasonable degree of ballistic certainty" or "a reasonable degree of certainty in the ballistics field."[123]

Emerging Problems

The cases examined in the subsection above demonstrate a trend amongst some courts to curtail the testimony of firearms examiners. In these cases, the judiciary has rejected testimony that suggests levels of absolute certainty (i.e., testimony akin to individualization). Instead, courts have required examiners to testify in, allegedly, less certain terms. This is a judicial attempt to rationalize the criticism aimed at firearms identification evidence.[124] However, it can be problematic. This is because even initial research studies have shown that both judges and jurors are comfortable converting subjective probability evidence into findings of liability.[125] Consequently, restricting firearms examiners to phrases such as those preferred in the

---

[115] Commonwealth v. Pytou Heang, 942 N E.2d 927 (Mass. 2011).

[116] *Id*. at 937–8.

[117] *Id*. at 938.

[118] *Id*. at 941.

[119] *Id*.

[120] *Id*. at 944–5.

[121] United States v Ashburn, 88 F.Supp.3d 239 (2015).

[122] *Id* at 250.

[123] *Id*.

[124] *See generally* Cooper, *supra* note, 78.

[125] Dawn McQuiston-Surrett & Michael Saks, *Communicating Opinion Evidence in the Forensic Identification Sciences: Accuracy and Impact*, 59 Hastings L.J. 1159, 1188–9 (2008).

aforementioned cases may well not have the desired effect of deterring jurors from inaccurately thinking there is an absolute "match" between suspect ammunition and a known weapon. It other words, it may not prevent the jury from being misled about the current imperfections of firearms analysis.

These alternative phrases can be confusing for jurors. For instance, in relation to firearms evidence, Bonnie Lanigan notes that "the phrase "ballistic certainty," especially when "ballistics" is not an accurate term as it encompasses all projectiles, may not sound that different to a juror from the phrase "scientific certainty."[126] Both phrases imply certainty that doesn't yet exist in this discipline.[127] This confusion is perhaps exacerbated by the courts' approach. For instance, the courts may require allegedly diluted terminology from experts, but simultaneously allow examiners to use the term "match," for instance, that the "match" was made to a "reasonable degree of certainty." In such instances, the term "match" is still heard by jurors, leaving it open for them to conclude that there was a definitive conclusion of individualization by the examiner.

Research shows that jurors undertake complex assessments when confronted with forensic science evidence. There is evidence to suggest that jurors' "perceptions of forensic science evidence are shaped by prior beliefs and expectations as well as expert testimony…"[128] There are qualitative aspects to their assessment, which can be shaped by value judgments about credibility, the risk of error, how the forensic evidence fits with other evidence presented in the case and how it is popularized and conveyed by the media and other literature.[129] The expert terminology encouraged does not take account of these complex assessments.

These diluted phrases may simply contribute to disguising current uncertainties about the empirical undermining of firearms identification evidence and how it is interpreted by relevant social actors. The National Commission on Forensic Science's Subcommittee on Reporting and Testimony has, in effect, recognized this. The subcommittee has observed that these phrases are meaningless in a scientific sense.[130] They are not used by experts outside of courtrooms, and the legal process should not insist that they are used.[131] Moreover, the committee has stated that forensic science service providers "should not endorse or promote the use of this terminology."[132]

---

[126] Bonnie Lanigan, Firearms Identification: The Need for a Critical Approach to, and Possible Guidelines for, the Admissibility of "Ballistics" Evidence, 17 Suffolk J. Trial & App. Advoc. 54, 71 (2012).

[127] Id at 72.

[128] William C. Thompson & Eryn J. Newman, Lay Understanding of Forensic Statistics: Evaluation of Random Match Probabilities, Likelihood Ratios, and Verbal Equivalents, 39 Law & Hum. Behav. 332 (2015).

[129] Id at 346.

[130] See, e.g., the sub-committee's "Views Document" concerning the phrase "reasonable scientific certainty" available at http://www.justice.gov/ncfs/file/795336/download.

[131] Id.

[132] Id.

Cases Showing How the Courts Have Sidelined Strengthening in the Context of Firearms Identification Evidence

Strengthening was a landmark publication. Unsurprisingly, therefore, numerous petitioners have supported their claims about the unreliability of firearms identification evidence by citing to *Strengthening*, whether that be as part of an admissibility-related challenge or NDE claim. This section presents a sample of cases to show how courts have reacted to the conclusions made in *Strengthening* in both instances.

Admissibility Challenges and Strengthening

An analysis of admissibility challenges shows a number of different approaches taken by the courts towards the conclusions in *Strengthening*.

A number of courts have actually used *Strengthening*'s concerns about firearms identification evidence to rationalize decisions to curtail examiners' testimony. This includes the aforementioned cases of ***Taylor, Pytou Heang, Willock,*** *and **Ashburn.*** For example, the ***Pytou Heang*** court cited to *Strengthening*, noting that "the accuracy and reliability of forensic ballistics evidence have recently been the focus of significant legal and scientific scrutiny."[133] In ***Willock***, the appellate court adopted the Magistrate's recommendation to restrict the level of certainty conveyed by the examiner's testimony. The court noted that the Magistrate's recommendation had been reached "in light" of concerns contained in *Strengthening* and the *Ballistic Imaging Report,* which "called into question toolmark identification's status as a science."[134] In ***Ashburn***, the court summarized concerns detailed in *Strengthening*, but underscored the report's findings that, in some instances, individual characteristics might be "distinctive enough to suggest one particular source."[135]

Some courts have referenced *Strengthening* when undertaking a *Daubert* analysis, i.e., an assessment of whether the relevant firearms identification evidence satisfies the *Daubert* factors. This, in some cases, has been in relation to a specific factor. For instance, in ***Taylor,*** the court considered *Strengthening* in the context of *Daubert's* controlling standards factors. The court found, "Arguably the biggest obstacle facing any firearms examiner is that there is no such thing as a "perfect match."[136] The court partially attributed this to the circular nature of the AFTE Theory of Identification, which "does not provide any uniform numerical standard examiners can use to determine whether or not there is a match."[137] Thus, much is left to the subjective eye of the examiner.[138] The court acknowledged that *Strengthening* had recognized this problem, but did not indicate whether such criticism favored admission of expert testimony.[139] Yet, the court noted that the AFTE theory met the generally accepted

---

[133] Heang, *supra* note 115, at 937–38.
[134] Willock, *supra* note 108 at 546.
[135] Ashburn, *supra* note 121 at 245.
[136] Taylor, *supra* note 105, at 1177.
[137] *Id.*
[138] *Id.*
[139] *Id* at 1177–78.

standard because it was widely accepted, although not universally followed, by trained firearms examiners.[140] By contrast, ***Ashburn*** used *Strengthening* to undertake its review of the error rates factor. The court acknowledged that the lack of objective standards prevented the production of statistics-based error rate estimations, information derived from proficiency tests suggested the discipline has a low error-rate.[141] The court found this factor weighed in favor of admissibility.[142]

In other cases, courts have given *Strengthening* a wider berth. For example, In ***United States v. Otero***,[143] *Strengthening* was cited by the defendants, who moved to exclude firearms identification testimony on the basis that individualization conclusions were "based on a theory — that is, that firearms-related toolmarks are unique and reproducible - that has not been proven scientifically."[144] The ***Otero*** court undertook a *Daubert* analysis. The court found each *Daubert* factor was satisfied, but did not mention *Strengthening* as part of its analysis. A similar approach was taken in ***Jones v. United States***.[145] In that case, as part of a *Frye* challenge,[146] the court noted the Appellant had used *Strengthening* to urge the court to find that pattern matching (in firearms identification) is no longer generally accepted.[147] The court was not persuaded, merely noting *Strengthening* in a footnote.[148] A similar, sidelining approach can be seen in ***United States v. Wrensford***.[149]

Other courts have taken a more critical approach to *Strengthening*. For example, in ***State v. Langlois***,[150] the court acknowledged that "that the scientific basis for comparative ballistics analysis has received increased critical scrutiny in recent years."[151] Citing *Strengthening*, inter alia, Langlois argued that "the reliability and accuracy of ballistics evidence falls somewhere in the space between voodoo and soft science, and nobody really knows where."[152] The court flatly rejected this argument. In so doing, the court stated,

> *Even a sympathetic reading of the 2009 report, however, indicates its primary purpose was to serve as a catalyst for reassessing the scientific premises underlying the various fields of forensic science and to summarize the current state of the research in those fields relative to the challenges raised in the report. It was not*

---

[140] *Id* at 1178.

[141] Ashburn at 246.

[142] *Id.*

[143] United States v. Otero, 849 F.Supp.2d 425 (2012).

[144] *Id* at 430.

[145] Jones v. United States, 27 A.3d 1130 (2011).

[146] The "Frye" standard was the leading admissibility framework employed in America prior to *Daubert*. To be admissible under *Frye*, expert evidence had to "generally accepted" by the relevant expert community. See, Frye v United States 293 F. 1013 (D.C. Cir. 1923).

[147] Jones, *supra* note 145 at 1136–37.

[148] *Id* at note 8.

[149] United States and the People of the Virgin Islands v Wrensford, 2014 WL 3,715,036 (2014).

[150] State v. Langlois, 2 N E.3d 936 (2013).

[151] *Id* at 944.

[152] *Id* at 945.

its purpose to opine on the long-established admissibility of tool mark and fire-arms testimony in criminal prosecutions, and indeed the NRC (National Research Council) authors made no recommendations in that regard.[153]

The court found that *Strengthening's* calls for additional research did not make "what firearms examiners do junk science, or 'voodoo.'"[154] Moreover, the court observed that *Strengthening* did not speak "to the *legal* standard for determining if what firearms examiners do is sufficiently reliable that their opinion testimony may be admitted in a criminal case."[155] In sum, *Strengthening* was "simply not dispositive of the legal issue here."[156]

These cases demonstrate that the courts have largely been unmoved by arguments that *Strengthening's* observations about firearms identification evidence renders it unreliable. Yet their approach is somewhat contradictory. On the one hand, courts are willing to sideline *Strengthening's* concerns and follow precedent that has long allowed firearms identification evidence to be admissible. However, on the other hand, the courts can be eager to accept comments in *Strengthening* that are seemingly positive about the usefulness of firearms identification evidence. Equally, the courts can be keen to sideline *Strengthening* on the basis that it lacks direct relevance to legal admissibility frameworks and legal practice, although this view has been refuted, including by the co-chair of the committee that authored *Strengthening*, Judge Harry T. Edwards.[157] As the author has concluded before, while courts may have been more critical of such forensic science evidence post-*Strengthening*, the report itself has not led to any court finding such evidence inadmissible.[158] This view has been affirmed by other scholars examining post-*Strengthening* judicial decisions that relate to firearms identification and beyond.[159] As Cole and Edmond conclude, "*Strengthening* appears to have been little more than a legal hiccup..."[160]

Newly Discovered Evidence Claims and Strengthening

Petitioners have alleged that the criticism about firearms identification evidence (in the form of standard toolmark analysis) contained in *Strengthening* is NDE. Generally, the courts have been reluctant to accept this argument.[161] A number of cases show this.

---

[153] Id at 945–46

[154] *Id* at 946.

[155] *Id.*

[156] *Id.*

[157] Harry T. Edwards, The National Academies of Sciences Report on Forensic Sciences: What it Means for the Bench and the Bar, 51 jurimetrics 1 (2010).

[158] Sarah Lucy Cooper, The Collision of Law and Science: American Court Responses to Developments in Forensic Science 33 Pace L. Rev. 234, 301 (2013).

[159] *See generally* Simon A. Cole & Gary Edmond, Science Without Precedent: The Impact of the National Research Council Report on the Admissibility and Use of Forensic Science Evidence in the United States, four Brit. J. Am. Legal Stud. 585 (2015).

[160] *Id* at 596.

[161] *See generally* Cooper, *supra* note 10.

For example, in the 2011 case of **Rues v. Denney**,[162] Denney argued that *Strengthening* constituted NDE, which would extend his limitations period. The Eighth Circuit Court of Appeals affirmed the lower court's reasoning that the criticism contained in *Strengthening* was not "new." This was because the relevant criticism had been raised previously in academic journals and was therefore discoverable prior to 2009. Therefore, *Strengthening* did not "constitute a new fact" because it did not "raise any new issues."[163]

In **Foster v. Florida**,[164] the Supreme Court of Florida rejected a similar claim, applying precedent in the form of **Johnston v. State**,[165] where they had rejected a similar claim. Johnston's claim was rejected on the basis that (1) the 2009 *Strengthening* report cited material that was published before Johnston's alleged crime was committed, and others that were published during the time he was seeking postconviction relief, and (2) the report lacked specificity "that would justify a conclusion that it provides a basis to find the forensic evidence admitted at trial to be infirm or faulty... Nothing in the report renders the forensic techniques used in this case unreliable... "[166] The Florida Supreme Court found the same reasoning applied to Foster, citing additional precedents where research studies had failed to qualify as sources of NDE.[167] They also noted that Foster had failed to identify how the relevant research "would demonstrate, in any specific way, that the testing methods or opinions in his case were deficient."[168]

A form of relief was provided the 2014 case of **Arizona v. Celaya**.[169] In that case, Celaya argued that his trial court erred when it denied him an evidentiary hearing on his claim that the conclusions in *Strengthening* "debunking the certainty of firearms comparison analysis"[170] constituted newly discovered evidence. At Celaya's trial, two state experts had testified that there was "no doubt" that a bullet found in Celaya's truck was fired by the same gun that killed the victims.[171] The appellate court determined that the trial court abused its discretion by failing to have an evidentiary hearing, but refused to comment on whether *Strengthening* constituted NDE (without such a hearing). The court remanded for an evidentiary hearing, rejecting the state's claim that one was unnecessary.[172] However, "despite signaling that the review of such issues must occur, the decision in *Celeya* fed into the conservative trend by appellate courts to...not label the findings of *Strengthening* (including the unprecedented finding that individualization was not proper in forensic disciplines such as firearms identification) as newly discovered evidence."[173]

---

[162] Rues v. Denney, 643 F.3d 618 (eighth Cir. 2011).

[163] *Id* at 622.

[164] Foster v Florida, 132 So.3d 40 (Fla. 2013).

[165] Johnston v. States, 27 So.3d 11 (Fla. 2010).

[166] Foster, *supra* note 164, at 72.

[167] *Id*.

[168] *Id*.

[169] Arizona v Celaya, Not Reported in P.3 d, 2014 WL 4,244,049 (Ariz. App. Div. 2).

[170] *Id* at *5.

[171] *Id*.

[172] *Id* at *6.

[173] Cooper, *supra* note 10, at 666.

These cases show the courts to be sidelining *Strengthening*. They do this by taking the view that the report presents no "new" facts because it cites to older research and lacks specificity to individual cases. Research suggests courts take the same approach to other types of forensic science evidence too.[174] Courts have an intense focus on specificity, and this has made it difficult for petitioners to apply general concerns detailed in *Strengthening* to specific issues is individual cases.[175] Presently, petitioners are failing to connect the dots between *Strengthening*'s concerns and the impact those concerns have on an individual case.[176]

Notably, judicial intervention has been triggered in comparative bullet lead analysis (CBLA) evidence NDE cases.

Historically, CBLA evidence had been used to show that "bullets came from the same box, the same manufacturer, were related in time or geography, or generally linked the defendant to the crime in some unspecified manner."[177] The reliability of this method, however, has been significantly criticized. Consequently, some petitioners have argued that the criticism represents a shift in scientific opinion that qualifies as NDE. These claims have generally triggered judicial intervention in favor of the petitioner.[178] Concerns about the "newness" of the criticism aimed at CBLA evidence and how probative that criticism is to a particular case (given it comes from sources unrelated to specific cases) have seemingly been sidelined by the judiciary. This is in stark contrast to how the judiciary has approached NDE claims about firearms identification evidence in the form of toolmark comparison, as discussed previously. One explanation for the unusual judicial approach towards CBLA evidence may well be that there was a wider multiinstitutional response across the criminal justice system to concerns about the use of CBLA evidence.[179] This included the FBI discontinued CBLA evidence in 2004 after a report questioning its validity was published by the NAS.[180] By comparison, although very significant, *Strengthening* was a stand-alone publication with no such agencies using its findings to support arguments for the inadmissibility of forensic science evidence. This all suggests that multiagency collaboration is a useful way to encourage the legal process to acknowledge scientific progress and adapt judicial decision-making accordingly. Given numerous initiatives post-*Strengthening* are multiagency collaborations, should the product of their work conclude certain evidence should be inadmissible, we may find that the courts take note.

---

[174] *Id* at 669–673.

[175] Cole and Edmond, *supra* note 159, at 595.

[176] Cooper, *supra* note 10, at 666.

[177] Kulbicki v. State of Maryland, 53 A.3 d 361, 377 (Md. Ct. Spec. App. 2012), *rev'd,* 99 A.3 d 730 (Md. 2014).

[178] Cooper, *supra* note 10, at 666–69.

[179] Jennifer E. Laurin, *Criminal Law's Science Law: How Criminal Justice Meets Changed Scientific Understanding*, 93 Tex. L. Rev. 1751, 1777–78 (2015).

[180] Nat'l Research Council of The Nat'l Academies, Report in Brief, Forensic Analysis: Weighing Bullet Lead Evidence, 1 (2004).

Emerging Problems

The courts are taking different approaches to the conclusions made in *Strengthening* about firearms identification evidence. This is unsurprising given the nature of the American criminal justice system;[181] however, it is also symptomatic of a general tension between the legal process and the nature of scientific inquiry.[182] This tension can have implications for the system's quest for accuracy.

The common thread throughout the admissibility and NDE cases is that courts marginalize the concerns expressed about firearms identification evidence in *Strengthening* (and other reports). In so doing, the courts avoid the need to address the scientific uncertainty about firearms identification evidence highlighted in *Strengthening*.

To rationalize their decisions to sanction the admission of scientifically dubious evidence and reject contemporary, significant criticism as NDE, the courts underscore what *Strengthening* did not do as opposed to what it did do. For example, admissibility case law suggests that judicial intervention would be triggered if *Strengthening* had declared firearms identification evidence as never reliable and therefore inadmissible (which it did not). Similarly, the NDE case law suggests intervention would be triggered if *Strengthening* was specific to individual cases (which it is not). Herein lies an example of the tension between the legal process and nature of scientific inquiry: the courts are demanding what science is not designed to provide. First, science is unlikely to provide such definite conclusions as "firearms identification evidence is always unreliable." This is because such answers go against the progressive nature of scientific inquiry. The modern scientific method can fairly be described as "a mode of investigation characterized by cycles of systematic empirical observation and hypothesis formation."[183] Products of the scientific method are widely understood to be provisional; hypotheses are routinely revised or abandoned and replaced by new dominant theories.[184] Science is skeptical of the possibility of complete knowledge and therefore tends to be unwilling to make definitive conclusions. *Strengthening* reflected this methodology. It did this by cautiously highlighting how initial research suggested certain conclusions could be made about class and individual characteristics in certain instances, but voiced stronger observations that rigorous testing had not yet developed levels of certainty in the discipline that could allow for reliable and accurate individualization conclusions. As such, the report called for further investigation and more research. In effect, all of its comments, including

---

[181] *See generally* Cole and Edmond, *supra* note 159, at 596.

[182] David L. Faigman describes the general differences between the methods of law and science as follows, "[s]science progresses while law builds slowly on precedent. Science assumes that humankind is determined by some combination of nature and nurture, while law assumes that humankind can transcend these influences and exercise free will. Science is a cooperative endeavour, while most legal institutions operate on an adversary model." David L. Faigman, Legal Alchemy: The Use and Misuse of Science in the Law (2000).

[183] Deborah M. Hussey Freeland, *Speaking Science to Law*, 25 Geo. Int'l Envtl. L. Rev. 289, 296 (2013).

[184] *Id* at 303.

its criticism, were provisional. Second, scientific discovery is unlikely to render results that are isolated in their application. Science has a general application.[185] Consequently, rejecting criticism like that contained in *Strengthening* on the basis that it does not have application to a specific case and/or legal issue lacks sense. In fact, it demands the impossible.

The case law examined provides other examples of tensions between the legal process and scientific inquiry too. For instance, as aforementioned, in ***Ashburn***, the court rationalized its assessment of error rates (i.e., its finding that the discipline had a sufficiently low error rate to be weighed in favor of admissibility) by noting *Strengthening* had observed initial information that was indicative of a low error rate. This is an example of how the legal process is willing to "inject certainty into provisional facts."[186] As Jasanoff has explained, "the law accept[s] facts that science might still deem provisional…Scientific facts needed to resolve legal disputes frequently come into being only as those disputes unfold. They are not available before the fact in some convenient storehouse of relevant, well-documented, yet case-specific facts."[187] Another example is the courts' general reluctance to find that criticism of firearms identification is "new" because *Strengthening* cites to older research that questioned the discipline. This approach arguably overlooks how "shifts in scientific opinion or the rise of controversy in a scientific discipline can take decades to crystallize."[188] The development of scientific thought tends to slow burn. As a result, a particular school of thought, for example, that firearms identification cannot engage in reliable and accurate individualization "may never objectively constitute a "scientific truth," since it is always prone to replacement as the dominant theory following a shift in scientific opinion."[189] In short, the crystallization of a "new" scientific opinion, which NDE rules demand, is arguably a fiction.[190]

The criminal justice system consumes forensic science in the form of firearms identification evidence in order to produce legitimate convictions. The tensions between science and law at this intersection are deep and complex,[191] but efforts can be (and are being) made to minimize them. As discussed in Part II, this includes wider national efforts, for example, to fund empirical testing about firearms identification, investigate the impact of expert terminology, and create national training curriculums and accreditation and proficiency programs for relevant social actors.[192] These initiatives will take time, however, and therefore, more focused lawyering strategies can be of more immediate use. For instance, lawyers should be underscoring the provisional and slow burn nature of science, identifying

---

[185] *See generally* Cooper, *supra* note 78.

[186] *Id.*

[187] Sheila Jasanoff, *Just Evidence: The Limits of Science in the Legal Process*, 34 J L. Med. & Ethics 328, 334 (2006).

[188] Cooper, *supra* note 10, at 655.

[189] *Id.*

[190] *Id.*

[191] *See generally* Cooper, *supra* note 75.

[192] See *supra* note 65.

the problems with diluted expert testimony phraseology, and identifying multia-gency concerns about forensic science evidence. Lawyers need to challenge the way courts rationalize their decision-making in order to make the products of that process more accurate.

Cases That Promote the Adversarial System's Function to Weed Out Frailties in Firearms Identification Evidence

Case law also demonstrates that when assessing challenges to the veracity of firearms identification evidence, courts rationalize their decisions by promoting the adver-sarial system's function to weed out frailties in forensic science evidence. They do this by underscoring both the role of defense counsel to cross-examine the evidence and the role of fact-finders to assess the credibility and weight of evidence.[193] This pattern likely stems from the SCOTUS' comments in *Daubert* that "[v]igorous cross-examination, presentation of contrary evidence, and careful instruction on the burden of proof are the traditional and appropriate means of attacking shaky but admissible evidence."[194] For instance, in relation to firearms toolmark evidence, the Magistrate in **Willock** summarized that,

> *The Courts that, in increasing number, have expressed concerns regarding the reliability of firearms toolmark identification evidence, have permitted its introduction in spite of their concerns, in substantial reliance on the ability of defense counsel to be able to challenge the identification at trial through effec-tive cross-examination, or by offering defense experts to challenge it. In addition to the importance of effective cross-examination or rebuttal to the Court and the Defendant, it is even more important to the jury, which is charged with deciding how much, if any, of it to accept...[195]*

Courts have rejected challenges to the veracity of firearms identification evi-dence on the basis that defense counsel's cross-examination of the expert evidence was focused. For example, in **Romero**, the court noted, "There was a spirited cross-examination"[196] of the state's expert about *Strengthening* and studies criticizing firearms identification, which allowed the jury to hear relevant criticism about the discipline. As such, the trial court's decision not to allow the defense to present a rebuttal expert was not erroneous. **State v. Turner**[197] shows similar reasoning. In that case, the court rejected Turner's challenge to the admissibility of firearms identifica-tion evidence, saying his concerns were "appropriate fodder for cross-examination at trial,"[198] and because that cross-examination was "vigorous and thorough"[199],

---

[193] See generally Cooper, *supra* note 5.

[194] *Daubert*, supra note 81, at 596.

[195] Willocksupranote 108, at 578

[196] Romero, *supra* note 92, at 460.

[197] State v. Turner, 953 N E.2d 1039 (2011).

[198] *Id* at 1053.

[199] *Id.*

the trial judge could evaluate the expert's credibility and accord his testimony whatever weight it deserved.[200]

Sometimes, however, counsel has been less effective. For example, the cases of **United States v. Perkins**[201] and **United States v. Sebbern**[202] provide examples of counsel not couching their arguments about firearms identification evidence in the most effective way. The cases of **Thomas v. State**,[203] **Jones v. United States**,[204] and **Sebbern** provide examples of counsel neglecting to do something more specific, like hire an expert or object or cross-examine in relation to the firearms identification evidence. All of these cases "show that the courts are acknowledging counsels' deficiencies but not unpicking *why* counsel may have made these inadvertent mistakes or, indeed, strategic decisions."[205] In sum, these courts have seemingly rejected challenges to firearms identification evidence on the basis that counsel had the *opportunity* to weed out frailties in the evidence, even though counsel was arguably deficient in taking that opportunity.

The courts' approach also relies on jurors to evaluate forensic science evidence accurately postcross-examination. Although some studies show that jurors can be sensitive to the relative strength of cross-examination of an expert,[206] this does not necessarily affect their perceptions of the quality of the evidence or their verdict. These studies should "give pause to anyone who believes that the traditional tools of the adversarial process will always undo the adverse effects of weak expert testimony."[207]

The courts assessment of harmless error in the context of firearms identification might well illuminate this issue. Courts sometimes conclude that admitting firearms identification evidence was nonprejudicial or harmless in light of other evidence against the defendant. For example, in **Jones v. United States**,[208] the defendant argued that the trial court should have at least precluded government experts from stating their conclusions with "absolute certainty excluding all other possible firearms."[209] The court acknowledged courts have shifted away from allowing such conclusions,[210] but noted that any such error in the instant case was harmless because counsel had thoroughly cross-examined the expert. In the court's view, "the jury's assessment of this evidence surely did not turn on the difference between a "100% certain" conclusion and a "reasonably certain" opinion."[211]

---

[200] *Id.*

[201] United States v. Perkins, 342 Fed. App'x 403 (10th Cir. 2009).

[202] United States v. Sebbern, No. 10 Cr. 87(SLT), 2012 WL 5,989,813 (E.D.N.Y. Nov. 30, 2012) (order denying motion to preclude expert testimony).

[203] Thomas v. State, No. CR-11-1243, 2013 WL 3,589,291 (Ala. Crim. App. July 12, 2013).

[204] Jones, *supra* note 145.

[205] Cooper, *supra* note 5, at 482.

[206] *See* Margaret Kovera et al., *Expert Testimony in Child Sexual Abuse Cases: Effects of Expert Evidence Type and Cross-Examination*, 18 LAW & HUM. BEHAV. 653 (1994).

[207] McQuiston-Surrett & Saks, *supra* note 125, 1188.

[208] Jones, *supra* note 145.

[209] *Id* at 1138.

[210] *Id.* at 1139.

[211] *Id.* at 1139–40.

The cases of ***Melcher v. Holland***[212] and ***United States v. Mouzone***[213] showcase similar judicial approaches. In ***Melcher***, the court found that even if the expert's testimony should have been "reigned in,"[214] no prejudice stemmed from the phrasing used by the expert, namely that the "chances of another firearm creating [the] exact same pattern are so remote to be considered practically impossible."[215] The court found the difference between the phrases "practical certainty" and "considered practically impossible" and "reasonable degree of certainty" or "more likely than not" would not tip the outcome of this case.[216] Similarly, in ***Mouzone***, the expert repeatedly testified that the casings found at two different murder scenes were "fired from the same firearm" and "there comes a point where it's a practical impossibility...That's when I'm convinced that these two [cartridge cases] were marked by the same surface."[217] The defendants appealed, arguing that this testimony was prejudicial because it presented them as killers. The Fourth Circuit disagreed, stating that the testimony only supported the notion that the same weapon fired the casings recovered at each murder scene. In other words, it potentially connected the firearm to both murders, thereby linking the murders to each other, but it did not prove that either defendant was responsible for the casings at either murder scene. As such, the court found that "to the extent that the jury concluded that the Appellants were killers and allowed that conclusion to influence their final verdict, [the expert's] testimony was not the cause."[218]

Emerging Problems

The courts' focus on the role of defense counsel to weed out frailties in forensic evidence and the role of jurors to assess that evidence accurately can be problematic. This is because it may overlook "important difficulties both lawyers and jurors have when engaging with forensic identification evidence."[219]

With regard to lawyers, "Counsel is often equipped with only blunt tools in the form of counsel's own scientific knowledge and ability to engage with scientific evidence, limited resources, and a low-impact adversarial arsenal."[220] Lawyers tend to lack significant scientific expertise and training, a point noted multiple times in *Strengthening* and by numerous scholars. This educational deficiency often places lawyers at a disadvantage when confronted with scientific evidence: "[L]awyers... often fail to ask the right questions and uncritically accept scientific assertions."[221]

---

[212] Melcher v. Holland, No. 12-0544, 2014 WL 31,359 (N.D. Cal. Jan. 3, 2014).

[213] United States v. Mouzone, 687 F.3d 207 (fourth Cir. 2012).

[214] Melcher, supra note 212, at 13.

[215] *Id* at *5.

[216] *Id*. at *13.

[217] Mouzone, *supra* note 213, at 216.

[218] *Id* at 217.

[219] Cooper, *supra* note 5, at 487.

[220] *Id*.

[221] Frederic I. Lederer, *Scientific Evidence—An Introduction*, 25 WM. & Mary L. Rev. 517, 519–20 (1984) citing Howard T. Markey, *Jurisprudence or "Juriscience"?*, 25 WM. & Mary L. Rev. 525, 529–32 (1984). With regards to the comments made by the NAS about the 'science education' of lawyers (and beyond). Also, *see generally Strengthening*, *supra* note 4, at 234–39.

Consequently, "it is unsurprising that lawyers fail to make appropriate objections, employ useful strategies, hire relevant experts, and ask potent questions on cross and direct examination or in admissibility hearings."[222] It also provides an explanation for why lawyers can overlook even the obvious information about the science at play in their cases, including legal information. In addition to this education deficit, defense counsel will likely have restricted resources to challenge forensic science evidence at trial. As the author has explained previously, "Forensic experts can be expensive to hire and time-consuming to apply for; counsel cannot 'magic up' these resources (along with an adequate scientific knowledge to engage competently with the expert)…"[223] At the same time, counsel must operate in an adversarial system, which may limit the impact of his or her efforts at challenging dubious forensic science evidence. Research shows that cross-examination and rebuttal witnesses do not automatically dilute the impact of individualization testimony given by experts. As Saks and McQuiston-Surrett explain, "[U]nfortunately, cross-examination and the use of opposing experts do not appear to effectively counter expert testimony, regardless of the logical vulnerability of the initial expert testimony."[224]

In relation to jurors, "courts are overlooking the high impact that scientific evidence has on already science-thirsty jurors who find comfort in alleged expert certainty, have inflated expectations of science, and have general difficulties engaging with scientific evidence accurately."[225] Like lawyers, most jurors are not scientists and therefore also lack significant scientific training and expertise. Therefore, "many jurors have difficulty engaging with scientific evidence accurately and, in particular, determining the appropriate weight to afford to specific testimony."[226] This is of particular concern in relation to firearms identification because of the current "controversy surrounding how limits on expert testimony should be phrased."[227] As aforementioned, these phrases can be confusing, but research has also showed jurors tend "to yield to comforting certainties of expression about the evidence being testified to,"[228] are "comfortable converting subjective probability evidence into findings of liability when the expert assert[ed] a personal interpretation of a conclusion,"[229] and have difficulties "understanding statistical, and especially probability, data, and underutilize[d] such information."[230] In addition to this, there is ample evidence that jurors consider forensic evidence "especially critical to their ultimate decision about guilt."[231] Jurors expect to see forensic science in trials, and when it is admitted,

---

[222] Cooper, *supra* note 5, at 483.

[223] *Id* at 485.

[224] McQuiston-Surrett & Saks, *supra* note 125, at 1189.

[225] Cooper, *supra* note 5, at 487.

[226] *Id* at 475.

[227] McQuiston-Surrett & Saks, *supra* note 125, at 1188.

[228] *Id*. at 1189.

[229] *Id*.

[230] *Id*.

[231] Pete Frick, *Forensic Science in Court: Challenges in the Twenty-First Century*, 27 Syracuse J. Sci. & tech. L. 145, 156 (2012); Donald E. Shelton, forensic science in court: challenges in the twenty-first century 102 (2011).

they find it highly persuasive.[232] This is especially the case when the majority of the other evidence is circumstantial. As such, judges finding "harmless error" might well be completely bypassing jurors' likely perceptions of the evidence. There is even evidence to suggest jurors can find experts who have been subject to vigorous cross-examination even more compelling.[233] In fact, the very nature of the adversarial system can hamstring jurors in making accurate evaluations of forensic science. Adversarial procedures mean that jurors "hear highly practiced alternative stories that only roughly approximate what might be termed reality."[234] With regards to expert testimony, "information that reaches the legal system [and hence the jury] does not represent the scientific field more generally."[235] Very often, jurors are presented with experts at the "margins of their disciplines [who] are chosen…because they are willing to be more extreme in the proponent's favor and thus come across as more certain of their conclusions."[236] This approach suggests the scientific field is more polarized than it actually is and blurs whatever "truth" there might be in the evidence presented.

PART IV: CONCLUSIONS

To aid the adjudication of criminal liability, firearms identification evidence has been admitted into American courtrooms for over 80 years. During this time, firearms examiners have routinely testified that they can, through analysis and comparison techniques, "match" suspect ammunition to a suspect weapon. In the new millennium, however, the methodologies employed by examiners to reach conclusions of individualization have been significantly criticized, including by the NAS.

Since then, numerous national efforts have been made (and continue to be made) to improve forensic sciences, including specific studies aimed at furthering knowledge about firearms identification evidence. Still, significant vacuums remain. Undoubtedly, given the importance of forensic science to the criminal justice system, this research landscape will continue to evolve in order to inform the methodologies used, and conclusions made by, forensic analysts, including firearms examiners.

Given the incremental nature of scientific inquiry, alongside these research initiatives, defendants will likely continue to challenge the admission of firearms identification evidence against them and argue that criticism about firearms identification evidence is a "new" fact that undermines their conviction. An examination of case law between 2005 and 2015 shows that American courts generally reject such claims. From this general approach, three themes emerge. These are a judicial trend to (1) prevent firearms examiners from testifying in terms of absolute certainty,

---

[232] Cooper, *supra* note 5, at 464.
[233] *Id* at 477.
[234] FAIGMAN, *supra* note 182, at 65.
[235] *Id.*
[236] *Id* at 54.

(2) marginalize criticism of firearms identification evidence, and (3) promote the adversarial system's function to weed out frailties in firearms identification evidence. A number of problems emerge respectively from these approaches, however. First, research shows allegedly diluted expert testimony is meaningless, ineffective for deterring jurors from "matching" defendants with suspect evidence and confusing. Second, the courts' marginalization of criticism aimed at firearms identification evidence serves to illustrate how the legal process can fail to account of the nature of scientific inquiry by demanding impossible conclusions, injecting certainty into uncertain observations, and ignoring the testing and retesting nature of the scientific process and the provisional nature of its products. Third, an overreliance on lawyers and jurors to weed out frailties in forensic science evidence overlooks the significant difficulty both groups likely have in assessing scientific evidence accurately.

This chapter has provided an overview of this cohort of case law and possible problems associated with current judicial approaches. It has also summarized the process of firearms identification evidence, recent criticism aimed at the discipline, and recent research aimed at furthering our knowledge about it. Relevant cases, literature, and ideas for informing legal strategies have been signposted along the way. Given the American criminal justice system's routine use of firearms identification evidence, this intersection of law, science, and criminal investigation will undoubtedly continue to evolve. In light of the ever-increasing tally of DNA exonerations in America and our greater understanding of how erroneous science can contribute to wrongful conviction, whatever form that evolution might take, all roads must lead towards relevant stakeholders assisting the criminal justice process to produce as substantively accurate outcomes as possible.

DNA Evidence

CHAPTER OUTLINE

Forensic Science Reform. http://dx.doi.org/10.1016/B978-0-12-802719-6.00007-8

Case Study: Amanda Knox

Wendy J. Koen

Child Refuge, Inc., Menifee, CA, United States

*Nobody denies that DNA profiling is at the very cutting edge of science, but when corners are cut, those colorful little twirls of genetic code suddenly don't look so pretty (****Langley, 2012****).*

Amannda Knox, photo courttesy of Heidi Cruz

The system most often wrongfully convicts males, and to even a greater degree, minority males (Parker et al., 2001). However, when what is believed by the jury to be hard scientific evidence is introduced, the "girl next door" who happens to be at the wrong place and time can just as easily face wrongful conviction (Ruesink and Marvin, 2007). Amanda Knox is "the girl next door," vilified in the press, subjected to lengthy grueling interrogations, and ultimately wrongfully convicted based on DNA evidence that was not actually inculpating.

On September 20, 2007, Knox, a 20-year-old student, moved into a small rental cottage in Perugia, Italy (Massei-Cristiani Report, 2010). It was then that Knox met her new flatmate, Meredith Kercher (Massei-Cristiani Report, 2010). A little over a month later, Knox met and began a relationship with Raffaele Sollecito (Massei-Cristiani Report, 2010; Injustice Anywhere).

On the morning of November 2, 2007, Knox came home to the cottage to shower and change clothes after spending the night with Sollecito (Injustice Anywhere). She noticed that the front door was not latched and assumed one of her flatmates had left it open that morning (Massei-Cristiani Report, 2010; Injustice Anywhere). Knox took a shower and noticed small drops of blood on the sink and floor mat in the first bathroom (Massei-Cristiani Report, 2010; Injustice Anywhere). Because the spots were small, Knox was not particularly concerned. However, Knox was startled upon discovering someone had defecated in the toilet in the second bathroom and had not flushed, something none of her flatmates would do. She became more concerned upon finding that Kercher's bedroom door was locked and Kercher did not answer her when she called out. Knox became fearful, walked back to Sollecito's apartment, and asked him to come back to the cottage with her.

Sollecito discovered that a window in one of the flatmates' rooms was broken (Annunziato, 2011). Knox tried to reach Kercher on her cell phone with no success. Sollecito tried to break down Kercher's door, also with no success. Knox asked Sollecito to call the police (Fisher, 2011). The police officers broke down Kercher's bedroom door and discovered Kercher's mostly naked body; Kercher had been stabbed in the throat.

For the next several days, Knox and Sollecito were subjected to several lengthy interrogations by the police (Massei-Cristiani Report, 2010; Injustice Anywhere). On November 6, 2007, after 4 days of aggressive and sometimes assaultive police questioning, Knox "confessed" that she was home when Kercher was killed and implicated her boss, Patrick Lumumba, in Kercher's murder (Massei-Cristiani Report, 2010; Injustice Anywhere). This "confession" was really only Knox's response to the detectives' repeated and angry request that Knox tell them her "vision," or what she imagined happened to Kercher (Fisher, 2011). Knox, Sollecito, and Lumumba were arrested for Kercher's murder (Massei-Cristiani Report, 2010). Although Knox renounced her confession on November 7, it was too late. 3 days after their arrest, the judge held that the three suspects were to be incarcerated while further investigations took place (Massei-Cristiani Report, 2010).

THE KNIFE

On November 15th, investigators discovered the hard scientific evidence that, on its face, would implicate Knox and Sollecito (Hampikian, 2013). A knife, belonging to Sollecito and recovered from Sollecito's kitchen, appeared to contain Knox's DNA on the handle and Kercher's DNA on the blade (Hampikian, 2013). The prosecution floated the theory that the DNA on the blade was from Kercher's blood (Pisa, 2013).

This damning DNA evidence was the smoking gun investigators were looking for. It tied both Sollecito and Knox directly to what the police said was the murder weapon. However, flaws in the interpretation of the import of the knife evidence make it plain that the knife evidence was not inculpatory (Hellmann-Zanetti Report, 2011; part 10). Often, after a careful look at the facts, the smoking gun becomes irrelevant. A subject's DNA on a piece of evidence is irrelevant if the subject had reason to come into contact with the object. Knox's DNA on the handle of Sollecito's knife meant nothing; Knox used the knife to prepare food, so experts should have expected her DNA to be on the handle of the knife. The knife only becomes relevant if it can be proven that it was the knife that was used by Knox to stab Kercher.

Thus, the finding of Kercher's blood on the blade of the knife was pivotal. Kercher had never been to Sollecito's flat, and there was no evidence that she ever had any contact with the knife. Therefore, her DNA must have been on the knife as a result of the attack.

Although the prosecution argued that the DNA found on the blade of the knife was from Kercher's blood, the sample did not test positive as blood or even as coming from a human source (Vecchiotti and Zoppis, 2013). The initial test to determine whether there is human blood on a piece of evidence is crucial; forensic experts agree that you cannot wash away every trace of blood and leave DNA (Hogenboom, 2014). Simply, by all accepted standards, whatever was on the blade and subjected to DNA testing was too small of a sample to yield any reliable or conclusive results (Vecchiotti and Zoppis, 2013).

The relevance of the DNA also rests on the analysis of the wounds and the analysis of other evidence that might shed light on the size and shape of the knife. The bloody knife used to kill Kercher was laid on a bedsheet, leaving a bloodstain in the shape of the knife. Sollecito's kitchen knife that had Knox's DNA on the handle and purportedly had Kercher's DNA on the blade was neither the size nor the shape of the bloodstain on the sheet (Vecchiotti and Zoppis, 2013). The evidence proved that 80% of the wounds on Kercher's body could not have been inflicted by the knife found in Sollecito's flat. Yet, the court relied on this specious DNA evidence to convict Knox, and these facts did not stop the press from blasting headlines such as, "Amanda Knox's DNA was found on knife prosecutors claim was used to murder British exchange student" (Pisa, 2013).

THE BRA CLASP

Forty-six days after Kercher was murdered, investigators found the fabric and metal clasp from Kercher's bra (Hogenboom, 2014). The clasp had been torn off of the bra during Kercher's struggle with the assailant (Hogenboom, 2014). Sollecito's DNA was discovered on the clasp. This evidence was relevant and had the potential to inculpate Knox because Knox and Sollecito had admitted to being together during the time of Kercher's rape and murder. If Sollecito was the assailant, Knox must have been party to the attack.

Photographic evidence shows the clasp in different areas of the room at different stages of the investigation (Fisher, 2011). After many searches were conducted by investigators and the crime scene was in total disarray, the clasp was discovered in a pile of trash in Kercher's room. Video of the investigation shows an investigator picking up the clasp with his gloved hands; the gloves were not fresh, but had been worn while the investigator looked through other items at the crime scene (Injustice Anywhere). The investigator then passed the clasp to other investigators; the other investigators did not change their gloves before handling the clasp. Finally, video shows an investigator dropping the clasp to the floor. This type of evidence handling invites contamination and renders the evidence collected suspect and the resulting DNA results meaningless (Balk, 2015).

This photographic and video evidence gives us several clues about how Sollecito's DNA could have been transferred to the clasp. Sollecito had been in the apartment; his DNA was surely on the floor, the door, door handles, and objects all over the scene. Sollecito tried to break down Kercher's door and would have left his DNA on the door. Investigators, who did not change their gloves while riffling through innumerable household objects in the flat, could easily have transferred Sollecito's DNA from any of these surfaces onto the clasp.

Scientists do not fully understand the process of DNA transfer. The director of the Forensic Institute in Glasgow, Dr. Allan Jamieson, agrees that it is well-known that DNA moves around very easily; however, he admits that "the reality is we don't know enough about DNA transfer to explain it" (Hogenboom, 2014). Especially when considering miniscule amounts of DNA, the ease of transfer, and the errors made by the investigators, it is clear that explanations for the innocent transfer of Sollecito's DNA to Kercher's bra clasp abound, rendering the DNA found on the clasp valueless.

THE PERPETRATOR

In sharp contrast to the oft exaggerated and patched together evidence used to convict Knox, much evidence pointed to an area drug dealer, known by the police, who had committed similar break-ins in Perugia in the past (Hellmann-Zanetti Report, 2011). Rudy Guede admitted he was in Kercher's room the evening of her rape and murder; his DNA, mingled with Kercher's blood, was found on Kercher's purse (DiSturco, 2014). Bloody shoeprints, matching Guede's shoes, were found in the bedroom and in the hallway of the cottage, and Guede's handprint, also in Kercher's blood, was found under Kercher's body on a pillowcase (Hellmann-Zanetti Report, 2011). The most damning evidence, however, was Guede's DNA recovered from inside Kercher's body (DiSturco, 2014; Hellmann-Zanetti Report, 2011). There was no doubt that Guede had raped Kercher and left traces of himself all over the crime scene.

Guede was convicted in a separate trial and sentenced to 30 years in prison for Kercher's murder (Boepple Jr, 2013). Instead of accepting that they had made a rush to judgment when arresting, interrogating, and prosecuting Knox and Sollecito, the authorities offered an implausible explanation for the involvement of Knox and Sollecito, claiming that Knox, Sollecito, and Guede were seeking a sexual encounter with Kercher, and when she refused, they became enraged and killed her (Dobraszczyk, 2014).

Although DNA evidence is useful in helping investigators understand what happened at a scene and who participated in the crime, DNA evidence can also be a powerful tool that can be used to convict the innocent. DNA from the rape kit conducted on Kercher's body revealed who her rapist was, but based on the officers' theory of the crime formed very early in the investigations, officers committed their focus on Knox and Sollecito, and any miniscule trace of DNA evidence that could be made to look inculpatory was seized upon, made public in damning terms, and used as the shaky foundation for a flawed conviction.

Amanda Knox's path to redemption was uncertain and tortuous. After the first trial in Perugia on December 4, 2009, where the court found Knox guilty of murder, sexual assault, and slander, and sentenced her to a prison term of 26 years, and after Knox was incarcerated for 4 years, her conviction was overturned by her first appeal and she was released.

In the Italian appellate system, the judges in a case are part of the jury that decides the outcome. These judges are required to publish a written document motivating, or justifying, the Court's verdict. In December of 2011, the presiding judge in Knox and Sollecito's appeal trial, Claudio Hellmann, and his assistant judge Massimo Zanetti, released a report explaining why they and the six ordinary jurors (known in Italy as "popular judges") were convinced that Knox and Sollecito were innocent of Kercher's murder.

The report, referred to as the Hellmann-Zanetti Report, detailed expert witness testimony concluding that the DNA on the blade of the knife was unreliable and the testing conducted did not meet international standards of reliability. In addition, the judges and jurors found reliable expert evidence signifying that the DNA on the bra clasp was contaminated and could not be the basis of a conviction.

Regardless of the reasoned opinion delivered in the Hellman-Zanetti Report, in 2013, Italy's highest court vacated the acquittal and ordered a new appeals trial (Natanson, 2013). **During the retrial, a previously untested trace of DNA found on the knife blade was tested and was attributed to Knox. Although finding Knox's DNA on the knife should have been no surprise and should have reaffirmed only Knox's contention that she had handled the knife while cooking, the appeals court decided the trace of DNA once again tied Knox to the murder weapon, and Knox's conviction was reaffirmed in January of 2014. This time, Knox was sentenced to 28.5 years in prison** (Lyman, 2014).

In 2015, after another appeal, Knox and Sollecito were eventually and finally cleared of murder when the Supreme Court of Italy agreed with the defense contention that the DNA results did not actually inculpate the accused (Hjelmgaard and Bacon, 2015). After suffering through 4 years of wrongful incarceration and 8 years of terror and uncertainty, the pair was released from their nightmare.

The injustice endured by Knox and Sollecito could easily have been avoided by a reasoned and steady approach to the investigation of Kercher's murder. Instead, the irresponsible use of dubious DNA results, coupled with a stubborn focus on suspects based on an early rush to judgment, resulted in an ugly case of international notoriety. Amanda Knox's ordeal should serve as a warning of the power of DNA evidence to convict and the very real threat that DNA evidence, used carelessly or combined with misplaced prosecutorial zeal, can lead to the conviction of the innocent.

Amanda Knox is not alone. Others have been accused of crimes and suffered incarceration because of DNA evidence that was either misinterpreted or was not actually inculpatory (Lee, 2013). Twenty-six-year-old Lukis Anderson spent 5 months in jail awaiting trial for murdering multimillionaire Raveesh Kumra (Lee, 2013). Anderson's DNA was found on Kumra's fingernails, placing Anderson with the dead man. However, Anderson had an airtight alibi; he was drunk and unconscious, lying in a hospital bed, and clearly unable to kill Mr. Kumra. There was no record of Anderson and Kumra knowing each other or coming into contact for innocent reasons. If Anderson was not the killer, how did his DNA get on Kumra's body? After an exhaustive search, the answer was found. Emergency medical technicians (EMTs) who had taken Anderson to the hospital with alcohol poisoning had also responded to Kumra's home and attended to him. Both Anderson and Kumra had been moved by the EMTs in the course of their treatment of the men. Clearly, Anderson's DNA was transferred by the EMTs. However, because of the strength of the DNA evidence, even though airtight alibi evidence should have immediately exonerated Anderson, Anderson spent 5 months in jail while the mystery of his DNA found on Kumra's body was being solved (Lee, 2013).

Anderson is not alone. Consider the case of 65-year-old David Butler in Liverpool, England (Langley, 2012). He was charged and tried for murder in the brutally beating to death a young prostitute. Although he did not appear to be healthy enough to have inflicted such great bodily harm on the young girl and nothing in his history would lead anyone to believe he would harm anyone, to the prosecution, the DNA was solid evidence sufficient to prove Butler's guilt (Langley, 2012). Professor Allan Jamieson, the defense expert, had a different theory that he posed to the jury:

> *Does anyone realize how easy it is to leave a couple of cells of your DNA somewhere? You could shake my hand and I could put that hand down hundreds of miles away and leave your cells behind. In many cases, the question is not "Is it my DNA?", but "How did it get there?".*

The jury must have determined the expert's opinion was reliable and was enough to overcome what the prosecutors believed was airtight evidence of guilt. After the jury deliberated for 11 h, Butler was cleared of all wrongdoing (Langley, 2012). The victory was sweet, but it could not erase the grueling 7 months this elderly and frail man was forced to serve while awaiting trial.

Although the two examples above ended well for the accused, we cannot be sure how many individuals have been tried and convicted based on DNA evidence that inculpated the wrong person. In the Anderson case, if his alibi had been less sound, the DNA would have sealed his fate. In the Butler case, if the defense attorney had been ignorant of the weaknesses in the armor of DNA evidence and had not challenged the DNA evidence, Butler could very well have been convicted.

DNA evidence, when left unchallenged, opens the door for wrongful convictions. Prosecuting attorneys must not rest their cases on DNA evidence alone, and when DNA evidence is the only evidence pointing to the suspect, more questions need to be asked and additional evidence must be produced. Defense attorneys must be aware of DNA's weaknesses, must be thoroughly familiar with the science, and must be willing to doggedly question DNA's reliability. What appears to be compelling DNA evidence, when challenged, can be proven to be unreliable and less than inculpatory.

REFERENCES

Annunziato, S., 2011. The Amanda Knox case: the representation of Italy in American media coverage. Historical Journal of Film, Radio and Television 31 (1), 61–78.

Balk, C., 2015. Reducing contamination in forensic science. Themis: Research Journal of Justice Studies and Forensic Science 3 (1), 12.

Boepple Jr., R.G., 2013. International extradition and the Amanda Knox case: what is a conviction anyway. Gonzaga Journal of International Law 17, 53.

DiSturco, A.J., 2014. The Trial of Amanda Knox in a Kangaroo Court: The United States' Constitutional Ban on Double Jeopardy, Bilateral Extradition Treaty Obligations, and the Vindication of the Gallina Dicta.

Dobraszczyk, C., 2014. The Prosecution of Amanda Knox: It's Not Over Yet!

Fisher, B., 2011. Injustice in Perugia: A Book detailing the wrongful conviction of Amanda Knox and Raffaele Sollecito.

Hampikian, G., 2013. Amanda Knox: How DNA Convicted and Freed an Innocent Woman.

Hellmann, P., 2011. The Hellmann-zanetti Report: On the Acquittal of Amanda Knox and Raffaele Sollecito. Available at: https://hellmannreport.wordpress.com/about/.

Hjelmgaard, K., Bacon, J., 10:39 a.m. EDT March 28, 2015. Italy's Top Court Overturns Amanda Knox Conviction, USA TODAY, available as of 04/28/15 at: http://www.usatoday.com/story/news/world/2015/03/27/italy-amanda-knox-meredith-kercher/70420700/.

Hogenboom, M., 2014. Kercher Trial: How Does DNA Contamination Occur? BBC: News, Science, and Environment. Available at: http://www.bbc.com/news/science-environment-24534110.

Injustice Anywhere, Injustice in Perugia, a website detailing the wrongful conviction of Amanda Knox and Raffaele Sollecito, available at: http://www.injusticeinperugia.org.

Langley, W., 2012. The Case Against DNA, the Telegraph. Available at: http://www.telegraph.co.uk/news/science/9115916/The-case-against-DNA.html.

Lee, H.K., 2013. How Innocent Man's DNA Was Found at Killing Scene. Chronical, San Francisco. Available at: http://www.sfgate.com/crime/article/How-innocent-man-s-DNA-was-found-at-killing-scene-4624971.php.

Lyman, E.J., 2014. Amanda Knox Found Guilty Again in Italian Murder Case. USA Today. Available at: http://www.usatoday.com/story/news/world/2014/01/30/amanda-knox-court-verdict-italy-appeal/5049041/.

Massei-Cristiani Report, 2010. On the Conviction of Amanda Knox and Raffaele Sollecito for the Murder of Meredith Kercher. Translated by Komponisto. Available at: https://masseireport.wordpress.com/contents/.

Natanson, P., 2013. Amanda Knox 'Shocked' by Court Ruling that She Will Be Tried Again for Murder. ABC News, Rome, Italy. Available at: http://abcnews.go.com/US/amanda-knox-shocked-court-ruling-murder/story?id=18809434.

Parker, K.F., Dewees, M.A., Radelet, M.L., 2001. Racial Bias and the Conviction of the Innocent. In: Wrongly Convicted: Perspectives on Failed Justice 114–131, 117.

Pisa, N., 2013. The Daily Mail Online. Available at: http://www.dailymail.co.uk/news/article-2483410/Amanda-Knoxs-DNA-knife-used-murder-Meredith-Kercher.html#ixzz3LKBSgPAc.

Ruesink, M., Marvin Jr., F.D., 2007. Wrongful convictions among women: an exploratory study of a neglected topic. Women & Criminal Justice 16 (4), 1–23.

Vecchiotti, C., Zoppis, S., 2013. DNA and the law in Italy: the experience of "the Perugia case". Frontiers in Genetics 4. Available at: http://www.ncbi.nlm.nih.gov/pmc/articles/PMC3770918/.

Essential Elements of a Critical Review of DNA Evidence

Dan E. Krane[1], Simon Ford[2]

[1]*Wright State University, Dayton, OH, United States,*
[2]*Lexigen Science and Law Consultants, San Francisco, CA, United States*

INTRODUCTION

It should be no wonder that defense attorneys get a sinking feeling when they hear that their client has been linked to a crime by DNA evidence. Promoters of forensic DNA testing have done a very good job of selling the public and even many criminal defense attorneys on the idea that DNA tests provide an infallible and indisputable identification. Amanda Knox and Raffaele Sollecito's trials for the murder of Meredith Kercher should serve as a warning of the power of DNA evidence to convict. They also illustrate the very real threat of wrongful conviction that can come from a failure to critically and objectively evaluate DNA test results, even in cases that do not turn on DNA evidence.

DNA evidence has generated investigative leads that have sent tens of thousands of people to prison. It has also played a central role in the exoneration of many hundreds of men who were falsely convicted. Even former critics of DNA testing, like Barry Scheck, are widely quoted attesting to the reliability of the DNA evidence in their cases. It is easy to assume that any problems associated with the introduction of DNA evidence to the US legal system in 1987 have been worked out and that the tests are now unassailable.

The problem with this assumption is that it ignores case-to-case variations in the nature and quality of DNA evidence. Although DNA technology has indeed improved since it was first used and the tests have the *potential* to produce powerful and convincing results, that potential is not realized in every case. Even when the reliability and admissibility of the underlying test is well established, there is no guarantee that a test will produce reliable results each time it is used. In the investigation of Meredith Kercher's murder, the testing laboratory was under significant pressure to push the limits of existing DNA tests in a way that caused case-specific issues and problems that greatly affected the quality and relevance of DNA test results. Improvements in the sensitivity of DNA testing in recent years have resulted in a new set of problems. When a DNA test is so sensitive that it can determine a DNA profile from just a few cells, it becomes very difficult to distinguish between DNA that was deposited during the commission of a crime and DNA that came to be there weeks before or after the crime was committed, or was transferred innocently during the course of the investigation itself. In such circumstances (which are surprisingly common in our experience), DNA evidence is far less probative than proponents of the tests might initially suggest.

In the initial trials associated with the murder of Meredith Kercher, the Italian criminal justice system failed to distinguish between unassailably powerful DNA evidence and weak, misleading DNA evidence, even though both were collected as part of a single investigation. The fault for this serious lapse lies partly with defense lawyers who failed to hold local DNA testing laboratories to high standards by critically evaluating the DNA evidence in earlier cases.

We consistently find that the less vigorously that DNA evidence is challenged in a jurisdiction, the more likely it is that courts will be asked to consider biased interpretations of weak DNA test results. This problem is not limited to Italian and other European courts; it is very common within the US as well. This chapter uses test results generated during the course of the investigation into Meredith Kercher's murder to describe the steps that defense lawyers should take in cases that turn on DNA evidence in order to ascertain whether and how this evidence should be challenged.

Our focus here, as was the case in the Knox and Sollecito trials, is on the identifier test. This test is currently the most widely used form of DNA testing, which examines genetic variants called short tandem repeats, or STRs. Earlier generations of STR tests are discussed in Thompson et al. (2003). Our goal is to explain: (1) what those who challenge DNA evidence need to know, (2) why they need to know it, and (3) how they get the materials and help that they need. There are alternatives to STR testing that are occasionally used (e.g., mitochondrial DNA and Y-STR testing), but they are generally associated with much weaker statistical weights and tend to be impacted by an additional set of problems on top of those associated with STR test results.

UNDERSTANDING LAB REPORTS

Lab reports, like those generated in the Kercher murder investigation, generally list the samples tested and provide a chart or table showing the *DNA profile* of each sample. The *DNA profile* is a list of the *alleles* (genetic markers) found at a number of *loci* (plural for "locus," a position) within the human genome. DNA tests do not produce a readout of the genetic code. Instead, they "type" samples by determining which alleles are present at a series of different loci (in the Kercher murder investigation a commercially available test kit, Identifiler, which examines 15 different STR loci, was used). The loci are chosen because they are sites where human DNA tends to be particularly variable between individuals in ways that are easy to measure.

Fig. 7.1 shows the DNA profiles of five samples: blood from the Kercher murder crime scene and reference samples from three suspects (Amanda Knox, Raffaele

	Evidence bloodstain	Amanda Knox	Raffaele Sollecito	Rudy Guede	Meredith Kercher
D8S1179	13, 16	11, 12	13, 15	14, 14	13, 16
D21S11	30, 33.2	29, 30	32.2, 33.2	29, 29	30, 33.2
D7S820	8, 11	9, 9	8, 11	11, 12	8, 11
CSF1PO	12, 12	11, 12	10, 12	7, 8	12, 12
D3S1358	14, 18	15, 18	16, 17	15, 16	14, 18
TH01	6, 8	6, 8	9, 9.3	7, 9	6, 8
D13S317	8, 13	11, 13	8, 12	11, 12	8, 13
D16S539	10, 14	10, 11	11, 14	9, 11	10, 14
D2S1338	20, 23	18, 20	16, 24	16, 23	20, 23
D19S433	12, 16	13, 16.2	13, 15.2	13, 14.2	12, 16
vWA	14, 16	17, 17	12, 15	18, 20	14, 16
TPOX	8, 11	8, 8	8, 9	8, 9	8, 11
D18S51	14, 15	13, 17	16, 17	14, 15	14, 15
Amelogenin	XX	XX	XY	XY	XX
D5S818	11, 12	13, 13	12, 12	12, 13	11, 12
FGA	20, 21	22, 22	20, 21	19, 23	20, 21

FIGURE 7.1

Table of alleles detected by Identifiler. Which individual is a possible source of the crime scene blood sample? Only one of the four individuals has a DNA profile that matches the DNA profile observed in the blood sample.

Sollecito, and Rudy Guede) and the victim (Meredith Kercher) as represented in a typical lab report. These samples were tested with an automated instrument called a *Genetic Analyzer*. This system (as well as the Identifiler test kit) for typing DNA was developed by a company called Applied Biosystems (ABI), a subdivision of Thermo Fisher Scientific. Other, newer test kits (such as Globalfiler) can be used with genetic analyzers to look at as many as 24 different loci, while earlier test kits (such as Profiler Plus and Cofiler) have been routinely used by crime laboratories since the late 1990s to look at a total of just 13 loci.

Identifiler simultaneously identifies and labels the STR segments that tend to vary in length from person to person due to variations in the number of times sets of four chemical units (nucleotides) are repeated. The genetic analyzer determines what alleles (types) are present by measuring the length of the labeled segments of DNA. The numbers assigned to the alleles indicate the number of repetitions in the underlying segment. For each locus, a person has two of these segments and hence two alleles, one inherited from each of their parents. In some cases, only one allele is detected, which is interpreted as meaning that by chance, the person inherited the same allele from each parent (see in Fig. 7.1, e.g., Knox's profile at locus D7S820 and Guede's profile at locus D8S1179). However, it is common to find that most of an individual's loci have two different alleles.

The Identifiler test kit gets information from one additional locus to aid in the determination of the sex of a contributor to a sample: amelogenin. Males have X and Y versions of the alleles at the amelogenin locus; females have only the X. On the basis of the results seen for the testing of the amelogenin locus alone, two of the reference profiles shown in Fig. 7.1 appear to be from males, and two appear to be from females.

Direct comparisons between the evidence and reference samples shown in Fig. 7.1 allow a determination to be made regarding who could or could not have been the source of the blood. Knox, Sollecito, and Guede are ruled out as possible sources because they have different alleles than the crime scene bloodstain at most of the tested loci. However, Kercher has exactly the same alleles at every locus; she cannot be excluded as a possible source of the blood. In a case like this, the lab report will typically say that Knox, Sollecito, and Guede are "excluded" as possible sources of the blood, and that Kercher "matches" or is "included" as a possible contributor.

Lab reports generally also contain estimates of the statistical frequency of the matching profiles in various reference populations (which are intended to represent the major racial and ethnic groups in the pool of alternative suspects). Crime labs compute these estimates by determining the frequency of each allele in a sample population and then compounding the individual frequencies by multiplying them together. For example, considering just the D3S1358 locus, if 10% (1 in 10) of Caucasian Americans are known to possess the 15 allele and 20% (1 in 5) are known to have the 16 allele, then the frequency of this pair of alleles at this locus would be estimated as $2 \times 0.10 \times 0.20 = 0.04$, or 4% among Caucasian Americans (hundreds of additional databases are available for various racial groups across the globe). The frequencies at each locus are simply multiplied together (sometimes with a minor modification meant to take into account the possibility of hidden relatedness within populations), producing frequency estimates for the overall profile that can be staggeringly small, often on the order of one in a quadrillion to one in a sextillion (1×10^{-21}) or even less. By minimizing the possibility that individuals in commonly encountered ethnic or racial groups could have been the source of a DNA sample, it becomes increasingly difficult to argue that an individual is not excluded as a possible contributor simply because of a coincidental match with another individual who is the real source of the DNA being tested. Needless to say, such evidence can be very impressive.

When the estimated frequency of a profile that an individual has in common with an evidence sample is very low, some labs will simply state that the samples *are* from the same person, assuming that person does not have an identical twin. For example, the FBI Laboratory will claim two samples *are* from the same person if the estimated frequency of the shared profile among unrelated individuals is below one in 600 billion[1]. Other labs use different cutoff values for making source attribution claims. All of the cutoff values are arbitrary; there is no scientific or statistical reason for setting the cutoff at any particular level. Moreover, these identity claims can be misleading because they imply that there could be no alternative explanation for the "match," such as laboratory error. They also ignore the fact that close relatives (other than just identical twins) are much more likely to have matching profiles than pairs of unrelated individuals (Paoletti et al. 2005) study found that on average, one out of every 154,000 pairs of siblings in

---

[1] FBI DNA Procedures Manual DNA 229, effective 12.21.12 to 05.07.15.

North America would be found to have perfectly matching DNA profiles across 13 STR loci). They also fail to convey that the DNA tests themselves are powerless to provide any insight into the timeframe or the circumstances under which the sample was deposited. For instance, the bloodstain that gave rise to the results presented in Fig. 7.1 could have been deposited by Meredith Kercher weeks prior to her murder. By the same token, the circumstances of her death also make it fairly unremarkable that some of her blood was found at the crime scene; yet, that might not be understood from a first impression of the very small chance of a coincidental match statistic.

LOOKING BEHIND THE LAB REPORT: ARE THE LABORATORY'S CONCLUSIONS FULLY SUPPORTED BY THE TEST RESULTS?

DNA analysts tell us that in 85–90% of cases in which their tests incriminate a suspect, no one outside the testing lab asks to examine the underlying laboratory notes or data. In many jurisdictions (but not all), defense lawyers simply accept the lab reports at face value without looking behind them to see whether the actual testing results fully support the laboratory's conclusions. This can be a serious mistake.

In our experience, examination of the underlying laboratory data frequently reveals limitations or problems that would not be apparent from the laboratory report, such as inconsistencies between purportedly "matching" profiles, evidence of additional unreported contributors to evidentiary samples, errors in statistical computations, opportunities for subjective/biased interpretation, indications of cross-contamination between key samples, and unreported problems with experimental controls that raise doubts about the validity of the results.

Although current DNA tests rely heavily on computer-automated equipment, the interpretation of the results often requires subjective judgment. When faced with ambiguous results where calls on individual alleles could go either way, crime lab analysts have a tendency to slant their interpretations in ways that are more consistent with prosecution than defense theories.

Part of the problem is that forensic scientists resist taking appropriate steps to "blind" themselves to the government's expected (or desired) outcome when interpreting test results. We often see indications in the laboratory notes themselves that the analysts are familiar with facts of their cases, including information that has nothing to do with genetic testing, and that they are acutely aware of which results will help or hurt the prosecution team. In the Kercher murder investigation, DNA from a rape kit used during her autopsy revealed that Rudy Guede was her rapist, but, based on the investigators' theory of the crime, officers persisted in their focus on Knox and Sollecito. Instead of accepting that they had made a rush to judgment when arresting, interrogating, and prosecuting Knox and Sollecito, Italian law enforcement worked under the assumption that Knox and Sollecito were unusually sexually active and that they became enraged and killed Kercher when she refused a sexual encounter that also involved Guede (Dobraszczyk, 2014). Unimaginably small traces of DNA evidence that could be made to look inculpatory were seized upon, made public in damning terms, and used as the shaky foundation for a flawed conviction see Case Study: Amanda Knox.

Cognitive psychologists describe extraneous details like Knox's presumed sexual motivation as "domain irrelevant information"; it makes no difference for the purposes of a DNA test if a suspect is unusually sexually active or if, as in the Kercher murder investigation, that the investigators did not feel that Knox was appropriately distressed after becoming aware of the crime.

The availability of domain irrelevant information to forensic scientists represents a significant threat to the reliability of their analyses, yet brings no balancing advantages. It is well known that people tend to see what they expect (and desire) to see when they evaluate ambiguous data (reviewed in Saks et al. 2003). This tendency can cause analysts to unintentionally slant their interpretations in a manner consistent with prosecution theories of the case. For instance, in the Kercher murder investigation, government DNA experts asserted that the results they generated gave insights into how Knox used a knife that they were told could have been the murder weapon. Prominent forensic scientist Peter Gill later questioned the reliability of the lab's interpretation: "Surprisingly the Massei report stated that the distribution of DNA on the knife handle supported the contention that it was used in an upward stabbing motion by Amanda Knox, rather than a cutting motion (e.g., to cut bread). [. . .] However, it is clear that this conclusion in the Massei motivation was pure speculation without any grounding in scientific analysis. There is not a single reported publication in the world that would support the notion that DNA analysis could reveal how a knife was used." (Gill, 2016) Backwards reasoning of this type (i.e., "we know the defendant is guilty, so the DNA evidence must be incriminating") is another factor that can cause analysts to slant their reports in a manner that supports police theories of the case. Hence, it is vital that defense counsel look behind the laboratory report to determine whether the lab's conclusions are well supported and whether there is more to the story than the report tells.

Behind each lab report's "Table of Alleles Detected" (Fig. 7.1) is a set of computer-generated graphs called *electropherograms* that display the test results. When evaluating STR evidence, a defense lawyer should always examine the electropherograms because they sometimes reveal unreported ambiguities and, fairly frequently, evidence of additional, unknown contributors. The electropherograms shown in Fig. 7.2 display the results for a bloodstain found at the scene of Meredith Kercher's murder and from Knox's, Sollecito's, Guede's and Kercher's reference samples for the same loci. The electropherograms in Fig. 7.2 show only the results obtained from four segments of DNA that the Identifiler test kit labeled with a blue fluorescent dye (similar electropherograms for segments labeled with yellow, green, and red dyes are not shown).

The "peaks" in the electropherograms indicate the presence of human DNA. The peaks on the extreme left side of the graphs represent alleles at locus D8S1179, then moving rightwards at D21S11 and D7S820, and finally CSF1PO at the extreme right. The numbers under each peak are computer-generated labels that indicate which allele each peak represents and how high the peak is relative to the baseline.

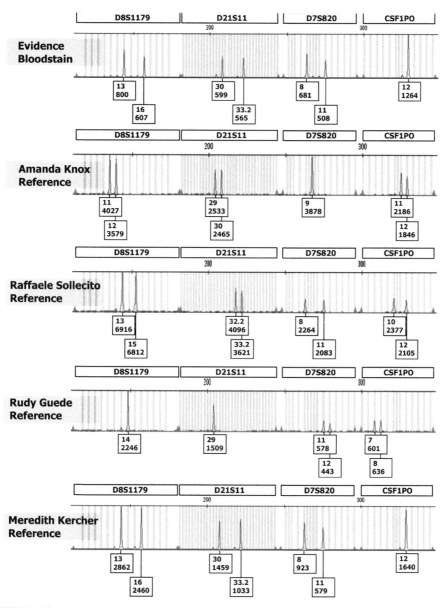

FIGURE 7.2

Electropherograms showing the results of Identifiler analysis of one evidence and four reference samples at four loci (D8S1179, D21S11, D7S820, and CSF1PO). Which individual is a possible source of the DNA in the crime scene bloodstain? *Boxes* immediately below the peaks label the name of the alleles above and their heights in relative fluorescent units (RFU) below.

By examining the electropherograms in Fig. 7.2, one can readily see that the computerized system detected two alleles in the blood from the crime scene at locus D8S1179. These are alleles 13 and 16, which are reported in the Table of Alleles (Fig. 7.1). The other alleles reported in the allele chart (Fig. 7.1) can also be seen to correspond to peaks on the electropherogram. In this example, the evidence bloodstain DNA looks to be from a single source and to be in good condition; there are no obvious problems. However, other cases are not so clear-cut.

Identifiler uses "primers" to identify the relevant STR DNA segments and then "amplifies" (replicates) these segments using a process called polymerase chain reaction (PCR). Each locus is "labeled" with one of four different colored dyes (either blue, green, yellow, or red). The genetic analyzer measures the length of the DNA segments by using an electrical current to pull them through a narrow capillary tube, wherein the shorter fragments move more quickly than the longer fragments. Under laser light, the colored dyes produce florescent light, signaling the presence of DNA. A computer-operated camera detects the light as the fragments reach the end of the capillary. The "peaks" on the electropherogram document these flashes of light. Based on the color of the light and the time it took the DNA to pass through the capillary, a computer program determines which alleles are present at each locus.

Fig. 7.2 shows the results for four loci that were labeled with blue dye. The position of the peaks on the graph (how far left or right) indicates how long it took the allele to pass through the capillary, which indicates the length of the underlying DNA fragment. From this, the computer program infers which allele is represented and generates the appropriate label.

The height of the peaks corresponds to the quantity of DNA present in the original sample. The unit of measurement for peak height is the RFU, or "relative fluorescent unit," which reflects the intensity of the fluorescent light detected by the computer-operated camera. Peaks representing alleles from a single person are expected to have roughly the same heights measured in RFUs throughout a given sample, although peak height imbalances occasionally occur.

SOURCES OF AMBIGUITY IN SHORT TANDEM REPEAT INTERPRETATION

A number of factors can complicate STR evidence, introducing ambiguities and leaving the results open to alternative interpretations. To competently represent an individual incriminated by DNA evidence, defense counsel must uncover these ambiguities, when they exist, understand their implications, and explain them to the trier-of-fact.

MIXTURES

One of the most common complications in the analysis of DNA evidence is the presence of DNA from multiple sources. A sample that contains DNA from two or more individuals is referred to as a *mixture*. A single person is expected to contribute at most two alleles for each locus. If a biological sample contains DNA from more than one person, then the DNA profiles of the individual contributors are superimposed on each other in a way that usually leads to more than two alleles at some or all loci. As a rule of thumb, if more than two peaks are visible at any locus, there is strong reason to believe that the sample is a mixture.

By their very nature, mixtures are difficult to interpret. But when a mixed sample is impacted by other factors, such as deterioration due to age or exposure to the environment, or if the mixture contains less than the optimum amount of DNA for testing for one or more of its contributors, it can be impossible to interpret the mixed DNA profile reliably. Although the presence of three or more alleles at any locus signals the presence of more than one contributor, it may still be difficult to tell whether the sample originated from two, three, or even more individuals because the various contributors may have alleles in common.

The ability for mixtures to be resolved diminishes when the ratio is either very similar (close to 1:1) or far apart (greater than 1:5). Consider a biological sample consisting of a 50:50 mixture of pristine DNA from two individuals (Fig. 7.3). In this case, armed with knowledge of the reference profiles for A and B, it seems self-evident that at the D8S1179 locus, person A contributed 11 and 12 and that person B contributed 15 and 16. However, who contributed to a mixture is often a matter of dispute, and it is necessary to determine the DNA profiles of contributors objectively and without knowledge of the DNA profiles of A and/or B. For Fig. 7.3, it is equally plausible that the mixture arose from other combinations of two DNA profiles, such as 11, 15 with 12, 16 or 11, 16 with 12, 15, and so on. There might also be three contributors. For example, X could have contributed 11 and 12, while Y contributed 15 and Z contributed 16. Many other combinations could also be consistent with the test results shown in Fig. 7.3. A study of one database of 649 individuals found over 5 million three-way combinations of individuals that would have shown four or fewer alleles across all 12 commonly tested STR loci (Paoletti et al. 2005).

Some laboratories try to determine which alleles go with which contributor based on peak heights. They assume that the taller peaks (which generally indicate larger quantities of DNA at the start of the analysis) are associated with a "major" contributor and the shorter peaks with a "minor" contributor. In the mixed profile in Fig. 7.3, there is no clear distinction between the major and minor contributors. Fig. 7.4 illustrates a mixture where there is a clear distinction. This mixture is made up of nine parts DNA from person A to one part DNA from person B. In this case it is relatively easy to deduce the DNA profile from the major contributor (D8S1179: 11, 12; D21S11: 29, 29; D7S820: 8, 11, and CSF1PO: 8, 8). However, the number of minor contributors and their DNA profiles is far less certain, particularly when the potential for artifact peaks, such as stutter (see below) is taken into account. The inferences involved in resolving mixed DNA profiles are often problematic because a variety of factors, other than the quantity of DNA present, can affect peak height. Moreover, labs are often inconsistent in the way they make such inferences.

These interpretive ambiguities make it difficult, and sometimes impossible, to estimate the statistical likelihood that a randomly chosen individual will be "included" (or, could not be "excluded") as a possible contributor to a mixed sample. Defense lawyers should look carefully at the way in which laboratories compute statistical estimates in mixture cases because these estimates often are based on debatable assumptions that may not be favorable to the defendant.

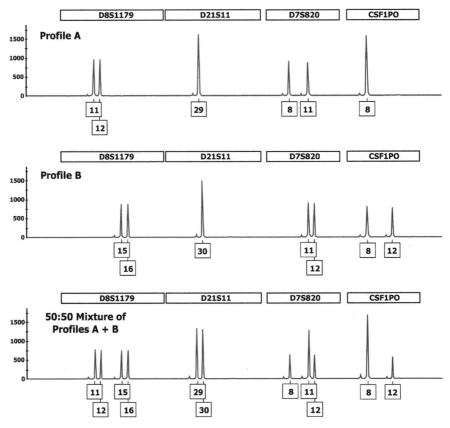

FIGURE 7.3

A mixed DNA profile. The two upper charts show the Identifiler blue loci for pristine reference samples from two people: A and B. The lower chart shows a mixture of equal amounts of DNA from these two people. In a mixture, the DNA profiles are additive; the DNA profile of person A is superimposed on top of the DNA profile of person B. Where two profiles share the same allele, the resulting peak in the mixed profile is higher because the starting material for the test contains more copies of the allele in question.

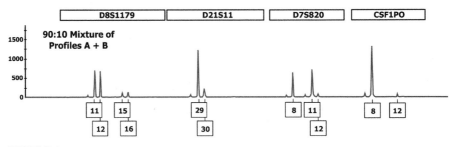

FIGURE 7.4

Electropherogram from an unequal mixture. This chart shows a mixture of nine parts DNA from person A to one part DNA from person B (see Fig. 7.3). Whereas it is easy to infer the major profile consistent with that of person A, the minor peaks from person B are similar in height to the stutter artifacts of the major profile.

SPURIOUS PEAKS

As mentioned above, the presence of more than two peaks at any one locus in a DNA profile is a strong reason to believe that the sample is a mixture. However, the interpretation of an STR profile can be complicated by the presence of spurious peaks that are not associated with the presence of human DNA in a sample. These extra peaks are referred to as "technical artifacts" and are produced by unavoidable imperfections of the DNA analysis process. The most common of these technical artifacts are *stutter*, *noise*, and *pull-up*.

Stutter peaks are small peaks that occur immediately before (and, less frequently and to a lesser degree, after) a real peak. Stutter occurs as an unavoidable and unwanted by-product of the process used to amplify DNA in both evidence and reference samples. Stutter peaks can be seen immediately to the left of many of the peaks in the bloodstain and reference samples in Fig. 7.2. In samples known to be from a single source, such as reference samples and positive controls, stutter is easily identifiable by its size and position. But this is not always the case in an evidence sample; the height of a stutter peak relative to the real peak varies from one locus to another, but is typically approximately 10%. On account of this, it is sometimes difficult to distinguish a stutter peak from a minor contributor in a sample that contains (or might contain) DNA from more than one person (see Fig. 7.4 where, for instance, at the CSF1PO locus, a possible stutter peak that precedes the major contributor's 8 allele is comparable in height to a low-level 12 allele).

The DNA profile derived from Kercher's bra fabric and metal clasp illustrates the ambiguity that can arise when the peaks attributable to a possible minor contributor in a mixed profile are similar in height to the stutter peaks from the major contributor to a sample (see Fig. 7.5). This evidence sample looks like a major–minor mixture with Kercher's alleles corresponding to those of the major contributor. It is difficult to determine with confidence how many minor contributors might be present in the mixture. Many of the lower-level peaks are consistent with those that Sollecito could have contributed, but some (such as the 11, 12, and 14 at the D8S1179 locus) are not. All of the lower-level peaks are also comparable in height to stutter artifacts associated with peaks from the sample's major contributor. It is difficult to objectively determine if peaks in stutter positions (such as the 15 at the D8S1179 locus) are entirely explained as being stutter artifacts, mostly real alleles from a minor contributor, or some combination of both. Fig. 7.5 only shows the blue loci from this evidence sample, but the other loci in the test are also difficult to interpret. Overall, there are 18 minor alleles in the full profile that could not be attributed to Sollecito, many of which are not in stutter positions, indicating that even if Sollecito's DNA is associated with this evidence sample, there could be at least two other people who left small amounts of their DNA on this item.

"*Noise*" is the term used to describe small background peaks that occur along the baseline in all samples. A wide variety of factors (including air bubbles, urea crystals, and sample contamination) can create random flashes of colored light within the genetic analyzer that occasionally may be large enough to be confused with an actual peak or to mask actual peaks.

Pull-up (sometimes referred to as bleed-through) represents a failure of the analysis software to discriminate between the different dye colors used during the

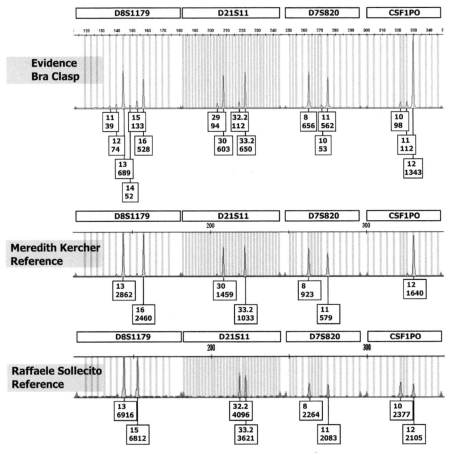

FIGURE 7.5

Electropherograms showing the results of Identifiler analysis of an evidence and two reference samples at four loci (D8S1179, D21S11, D7S820, and CSF1PO). The evidence electropherogram was generated from the fabric and metal clasp of Kercher's bra (which was only taken from the crime scene 46 days after she was murdered). The reference samples are those of Meredith Kercher (who the lab concluded was a major contributor to the evidence sample) and of Raffaele Sollecito (who the testing laboratory concluded could not be excluded as a possible minor contributor to the evidence sample).

generation of the test results. Pull-up typically arises when there is an extremely high peak in an electropherogram. For example, if there is a high peak in the green channel, artifact peaks might occur in the blue or yellow channels at the same position as the big green peak. The appearance of a small peak at precisely the same position as a high peak in another color should alert the analyst to the possibility of pull-up, but there is a danger that pull-up will go unrecognized, particularly when the result it produces is consistent with what the analyst expected or wanted to find (e.g., a peak that corresponded to an allele that a suspect could have contributed to a sample).

Although many technical artifacts are easily recognized, standards within laboratory interpretation guidelines for determining whether a peak is a true peak or a technical artifact are typically rather subjective. As such, there is often room for legitimate disagreement among experts whose opinions are based simply upon subjective criteria such as their "experience and training." Furthermore, analysts often appear inconsistent across cases in how they apply interpretive standards, accepting that a signal is a "true peak" more readily when it is consistent with the expected result than when it is not. Hence, these interpretations need to be examined carefully.

SPIKES, BLOBS, AND OTHER FALSE PEAKS

The computer-operated genetic analyzers used to type STRs are extremely sensitive devices, and a number of different technical phenomena can affect them and cause false peaks to appear in the electropherograms. Although no generally accepted objective criteria have yet been established to discriminate between these artifact peaks and real peaks, analysts will again often rely upon their professional experience as a basis for saying that their shapes "don't look right." The two most common artifact peaks are spikes and blobs, and they are of concern because they may mask the presence of a true allele or be mistakenly thought to be a real allele and lead to a false exclusion. Spikes are often attributed to fluctuation in voltage or the presence of minute air bubbles in the genetic analyzer's capillary. Spikes are typically narrower than a real peak and are usually seen in the same position in all colors. Dye blobs are thought to arise when some colored dye becomes detached from the amplified DNA and gets recorded by the detector. In contrast to spikes, blobs are usually wider than real peaks and are typically only seen in one color. Spikes and blobs are not reproducible, which means that if the sample is run through the genetic analyzer for a second time, the false peak would not be expected to appear in the same place again.

DEGRADATION

As samples age, DNA, like any chemical, begins to break down (or *degrade*). Degradation of DNA is a very unpredictable phenomenon. Under ideal circumstances, DNA molecules (e.g., in the blood meals of insects trapped in amber for hundreds of thousands of years) can persist unchanged for very long periods of time. But even brief exposure to unfavorable conditions such as warmth, moisture, and/or sunlight can (but sometimes does not) result in significant loss of the largest DNA molecules within a sample. When degradation does occur, it skews the relationship between peak heights and the quantity of DNA present. Generally, degradation produces a downward slope across the electropherograms in the height of peaks because degradation is more likely to interfere with the amplification and detection of longer sequences of repeated DNA (the alleles on the right side of the electropherogram) than shorter sequences (alleles on the left side) as shown in Fig. 7.6.

The effects of degradation upon DNA can also make it difficult to interpret DNA test results. The process of degradation can reduce the height of some peaks, making them too low to be distinguished reliably from background "noise" in the data, or

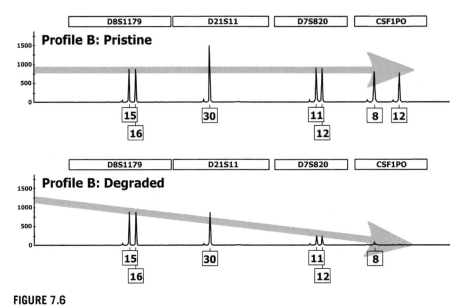

FIGURE 7.6

Degradation. The upper electropherogram shows the blue loci from a pristine sample. The lower panel shows the same profile but degraded (damaged by exposure to the elements). Note that degradation causes the peaks to become progressively lower on the right-hand side of the chart, resulting in dropout of the 12 allele at CSF1PO.

making them disappear entirely, while other peaks from the same sample can still be detected. In mixed samples, it may be impossible to determine whether the alleles of one or more contributors have become undetectable at some loci. Often analysts simply guess whether all alleles have been detected or not, which renders their conclusions speculative and leaves the results open to a variety of alternative interpretations. Further, the two or more biological samples that make up a mixture may show different levels of degradation (differential degradation), perhaps due to their having been deposited at different times or due to differences in the protection offered by different cell types. Such possibilities make the interpretation of degraded mixed samples particularly prone to subjective (unscientific) interpretation.

ALLELIC DROPOUT

In some instances, an STR test will detect only one of the two alleles from a particular contributor at a particular locus. Generally this occurs when the quantity of DNA is relatively low, either because the sample is limited or because the DNA it contains is degraded, and hence, the test is at or below the threshold where its results can be considered to be reliable (see Fig. 7.6). The potential for allelic dropout complicates the process of interpretation because analysts must decide whether a mismatch between two profiles reflects a true genetic difference or simply the failure of the test to detect all of the alleles in one of the samples. However, the occurrence of *allelic dropout* cannot be independently verified, the only evidence that this phenomenon occurred is the "inconsistency" that it purports to explain.

THRESHOLD ISSUES: SHORT PEAKS, "WEAK" ALLELES

When the quantity of DNA being analyzed is very low (as indicated by low peak heights and/or by quantitation results that suggest less than one-tenth of a nanogram of DNA is present from one or more contributors to a sample. There are one billion nanograms in a gram.), the genetic analyzer may fail to detect the entire profile of a contributor. Furthermore, it may be difficult to distinguish true low-level peaks from technical artifacts. Consequently, most forensic laboratories have established detection thresholds for "scoring" alleles. Only if the height of a peak (expressed in RFU) exceeds the detection threshold will it be considered to correspond to an allele from a possible contributor. Peaks below that threshold are considered to be "unreliable" or "indistinguishable from noise." Peaks above that threshold are typically labeled on a lab's electropherogram printouts, whereas those beneath the threshold are not.

There are no generally accepted thresholds for how high peaks must be to qualify as a "real allele." Instead, it is the responsibility of each crime laboratory to determine a detection threshold that reflects the sensitivity of its instruments and its protocols for the test kits that they use to generate DNA profiles. Laboratories that use the earliest generations of genetic analyzers such as the ABI 310 and 3130 models (used in the Kercher murder case) typically employ a detection threshold of either 50 or 75 RFU. Some laboratories with these genetic analyzers go as low as 40 or even 25 RFU in some circumstances (that can sometimes be applied inconsistently even within a single case). Hence, a defendant may be included as a possible contributor to a sample in one case based on "peaks" that would not be considered to be reliable in another case or by another lab. In some cases, there may even be unreported peaks just below the threshold that would change the interpretation of the case if considered, such as peaks indicating the presence of an unknown contributor to an evidence sample that otherwise only displays alleles that correspond to a victim.

Finding and evaluating low-level peaks can be difficult because labs can set their analytic software to ignore peaks below a specified level and can print out electropherograms in a manner that fails to draw attention to and identify low-level alleles. The best way to assess low-level alleles is to obtain copies of the electronic data files produced by the genetic analyzer and have them reanalyzed by an expert who has access to the analytic software.

THE COMPOUNDING EFFECTS OF MULTIPLE SOURCES OF AMBIGUITY
KNIFE FROM THE KERCHER MURDER INVESTIGATION

A knife collected from Sollecito's apartment was the most controversial item of DNA evidence in the Kercher murder case. The knife was found with other knives in a kitchen drawer 4 days after the murder. Prosecution experts opined that the knife could be responsible for Kercher's wounds, a conclusion that was vigorously contested by defense experts. The handling and examination of the knife was itself suspect. It was transported in makeshift packaging, and one of the officers who handled the knife at the police headquarters had been at the site of the murder earlier that day (Gill, 2016). Seven samples were taken from the knife, two of which figured prominently in the trial; sample 36-A was from the handle, and sample 36-B was from the blade. These two samples illustrate many of the issues that arise with low-level samples.

The electropherograms derived from the knife handle (Fig. 7.7) are very consistent with those that would be obtained from a low-level sample. The highest peak

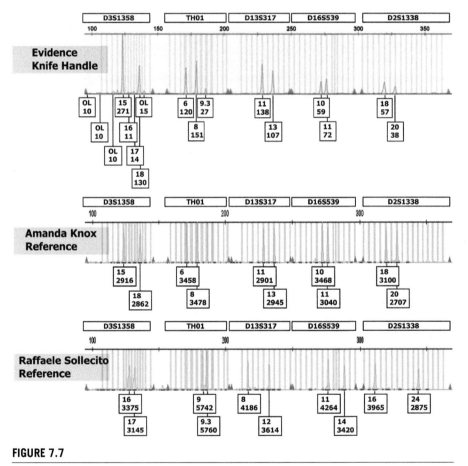

FIGURE 7.7

Knife handle. The upper panel shows the green loci of the electropherogram from the handle of the knife in the Kercher murder investigation. The middle and lower panels show the DNA profiles for the same loci for the reference samples from Knox and Sollecito. OL (Off Ladder Allele) refers to a peak that does not correspond to a frequently encountered allele.

among the green-labeled loci is just 271 RFU (15 allele at D3S1358). Although the peaks on the left side of the chart are taller than the peaks on the right, it is likely that this is due to a problem with the genetic analyzer known as "injection failure" rather than degradation. The profile appears to be a mixture of at least two contributors, and alleles that Knox could have contributed are consistently the tallest in the test result from the evidence sample. Still, the sample was analyzed at a very low level, and one of the peaks that Knox could have contributed falls below the 50 RFU reporting threshold used by the testing laboratory. Results from the amelogenin locus (not shown) indicate the possible presence of a small amount of male DNA.

Fig. 7.8 shows the green-labeled loci from two testings of the blade of the knife. It is unclear whether the two test results represent separate amplifications or are the same amplified DNA loaded twice onto the genetic analyzer. The heights of the peaks in these two sets of test results are even lower than those associated with the

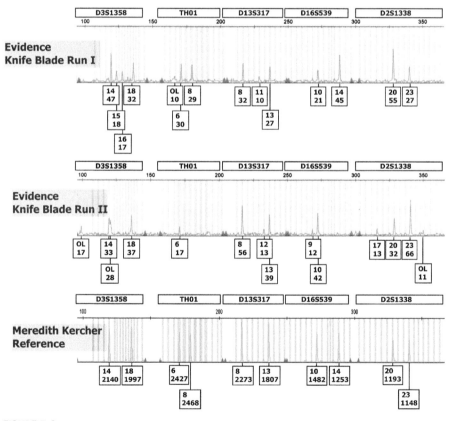

FIGURE 7.8

Knife blade. The top two panels show the green loci for two testings of the blade of the knife. The lower panel shows the same loci for the reference sample from Kercher.

knife handle (Fig. 7.7); this is a very low-level result. Only one peak in Run I and two peaks in Run II are above the laboratory's 50 RFU reporting threshold, but the electronic data was scored below the 50 RFU threshold to reveal a number of additional alleles that are consistent with those that Kercher could have contributed. There are striking and potentially important differences between the two test results from this single sample. For instance, in the first test result, low-level peaks are labeled 10 and 14 at the D16S539 locus, but in the second test result only a 9 and 10 peak are seen. The 9 peak in the second test result could be a stutter artifact associated with the 10 peak. But, either allelic dropout (of the 14 during the second analysis) or drop-in (of the 14 during the first analysis) must have occurred. It would be suspect-centric and therefore inappropriate to use information from Kercher's reference sample to determine if dropout or drop-in were more likely; the evidence sample should speak for itself.

BREAKING OPEN THE BLACK BOX: HOW TO REVIEW THE ELECTRONIC DATA

Reviewing the electronic files produced by a genetic analyzer has a number of additional benefits beyond revealing unreported low-level peaks. The software that controls these devices creates a record of all operations the device performs while typing samples in a particular case and records the results for each sample. These records can reveal a variety of problems in testing that a forensic laboratory may fail to notice or choose not to report, such as failure of experimental controls, multiple testing of samples with inconsistent results, relabeling of samples (which can flag potential sample mix-ups or uncertainty about which sample is which), and failure to follow proper procedures. We know of several cases in which review of electronic data has revealed contamination that had been expunged from the paper case file or instances in which the laboratory had manipulated electronic data in order to cover up errors such as mislabeling of samples or a failed control (a major breach of good scientific practice [Thompson, 2006]). Furthermore, the electronic files are also useful for producing trial exhibits. An expert with the right software can convert the files from their proprietary format into Adobe Acrobat files containing images that can easily be inserted into PowerPoint and Microsoft Word documents.

It is easy for crime laboratories to produce the electronic data that underlie their conclusions. The data files can readily be provided either burned to a compact disc or transferred via a commercial file hosting service, such as Dropbox. There is no legitimate excuse for refusing to turn over electronic data for defense review. In a few instances, laboratories (in Bermuda, Missouri, New York, and Ohio) have sporadically resisted producing electronic files, or have even destroyed the files, but the great majority of trial courts will not tolerate such obstructive behavior.

The electronic data produced by a genetic analyzer is in a proprietary format that is read and interpreted by software developed by ABI (though there are also third-party software programs that can do that job). When STR typing was first introduced, the standard platform was the Macintosh versions of GeneScan and Genotyper. Very few, if any, laboratories in the US are still using that platform (though it is still common to encounter Macintosh GeneScan/Genotyper electronic data in cold hit cases that are only now proceeding to trial). Most laboratories now use Windows-based GeneMapper ID or GeneMapper IDX. The electronic data files have the extension ".hid" if the testing was performed on the most recent 3500 series of genetic analyzers and ".fsa" if tested on an earlier instrument (such as what was used in the Kercher murder investigation). GeneMapper IDX is necessary to analyze data from a 3500 Genetic Analyzer. Some defense experts have access to this software and can use it to review the electronic data. The review process may take three or four hours but can take much longer in a complicated case.

ARE THERE INNOCENT EXPLANATIONS FOR THE LAB'S FINDINGS?

In many cases, careful review of the underlying laboratory notes, electropherograms, and electronic data will reveal no significant problems. Defense lawyers should never forget, however, that even clear-cut DNA test results may have innocent explanations.

SAMPLE HANDLING ERRORS

Accidental mix-up or mislabeling of samples is a possibility that always must be considered. We have encountered a number of such errors while reviewing casework. In most instances, the mix-ups readily come to light (and are caught by the testing laboratory) because they produce unexpected results; samples that are supposed to be from a man show a female DNA profile, two samples known to be from the same person show different DNA profiles, and so on. The real danger arises when sample mix-ups produce plausible results, especially if the mistaken results are consistent with a prosecution's theory of a case. In these instances, forensic analysts may overlook subtle clues that something is amiss because they expected to find the very result that was actually produced in error.

For example, after reviewing the laboratory notes in *Commonwealth v. McNeil* (a Philadelphia rape case), a defense expert noticed some clues (later confirmed by additional testing) that the Philadelphia Police Crime Laboratory had mixed up the reference samples of the defendant and the rape victim. This mix-up had falsely incriminated the defendant because the lab found what it thought was the defendant's DNA profile in a vaginal swab from the victim. In fact, it was the victim's own profile, and was mistakenly matched to the defendant due to the mix-up. Similar errors have come to light in other cases. Cellmark Diagnostics, a private testing laboratory, mistakenly mixed up the victim and defendant in a San Diego rape case, thereby mistakenly incriminating the defendant. The Las Vegas Crime Laboratory made the same error in a Las Vegas rape case that sent the wrong man to jail for over a year. In both cases, the error came to light only after a defense expert noticed inconsistencies in the laboratory records.

It is not always possible to tell from the laboratory records whether samples *actually* were mixed up or cross-contaminated. However, careful review of the laboratory records will usually provide important information about whether such errors *could have happened*. For example, evidence that a reference sample from the defendant was handled or processed in close proximity to samples from the crime scene can support the theory that a sample handling error explains incriminating results. In one Australian case, careful review of the testing results from an investigation into the murder of a toddler showed that a DNA profile matching that of a woman in a national database was likely to have arisen because the woman's database reference had been tested by the same laboratory a week before the laboratory worked with samples from the murder investigation[2]. This fact cast important new light on a seemingly incriminating result.

We suggest that defense lawyers obtain and review complete copies of all records related to evidentiary samples collected in the case (see Appendix I for a model discovery request). It should be possible to document the complete history of every sample from the time it was initially collected through its ultimate disposition.

STOCHASTIC EFFECTS AND TRANSFER OF DNA

Whereas the earliest DNA tests in the late 1980s required a fairly large amount (i.e., a bloodstain the size of a dime) of biological material to get a result, STR DNA tests are so sensitive that they can generate reliable DNA profiles from as few as 20 of an individual's cells. Our bodies are made of trillions of cells, and we shed them all the time without noticing the loss. A typical fingerprint contains on the order of 100 cells. A single human cell contains about 0.006 ng of DNA.

As long ago as 1992, Walsh et al. (1992) recognized that use of quantities of DNA below 1.0 ng (the equivalent of about 150 cells) starting amount could introduce a suite of problems for DNA profiling. "Stochastic" effects (sometimes also referred to as "preferential amplification") are at the heart of the problems associated with small quantities of template. These stochastic effects essentially arise from sampling errors that can occur when very few template DNA molecules are available for amplification (much like those that might happen when blindly drawing black and white beans from a bag, a draw that brings out a small number of beans, might suggest that all the beans in the bag are black, even though they account for only 50% of the beans in the bag) (Fig. 7.9). With starting quantities of DNA arising from fewer than 150 human cells, it is possible that one of two alleles at a locus will be amplified by the PCR process more than its counterpart (resulting in peak height imbalance or even allelic dropout). It is also possible that stray alleles originating from just a few contaminating cells could be amplified preferentially, just by chance, relative to those that actually come from an evidence

---

[2] Inquest into the death of Jaidyn Raymond Leskie; Coroners Case Number: 007/98. October 2006.

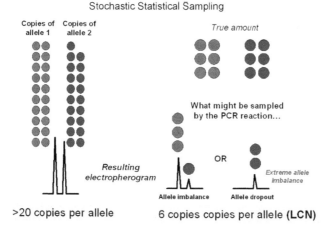

Stochastic Statistical Sampling

FIGURE 7.9

Stochastic statistical sampling during polymerase chain reaction (PCR) amplification. When more than 20 copies of an allele are being amplified at the start of a PCR amplification, it is unlikely that sampling errors will result in a large difference in the number of copies that are made of two different alleles. Sampling errors are much more likely to occur when fewer copies of the alleles are present at the start of the process.

Derived from a presentation by Dr. John Butler (US National Institute of Standards and Technology, Office of Law Enforcement Standards) at the Midwestern Academy of Forensic Sciences annual meeting in Indianapolis, Indiana on October 11, 2006.

sample (resulting in allelic drop-in). Another commonly observed stochastic effect associated with small amounts of starting DNA template is an increase in the prevalence of stutter technical artifacts. Quite simply, if there is not enough starting quantity of DNA prior to the time the PCR is started, the PCR process can produce results that are inaccurate, unreliable and very difficult to interpret.

The propensity for stochastic effects in low template analyses is well documented in the scientific literature (see Fig. 7.10). Many have pointed to the problems associated with low template testing, but Dr. Bruce Budowle, who, while serving as the Chief of the Forensic Science Research Unit and as Senior Scientist in the Biology section of the Laboratory Division of the US Federal Bureau of Investigation, summarized the issues succinctly when he said:

> *Because of the successes encountered with STR typing, it was inevitable that some individuals would endeavor to type samples containing very minute amounts of DNA. …. When few copies of DNA template are present, stochastic amplification may occur, resulting in either a substantial imbalance of two alleles at a given heterozygous locus or allelic dropout.*

> **Budowle et al., 2001. Low copy number – consideration and caution. Proc. 12th International Symposium on Human Identification.**

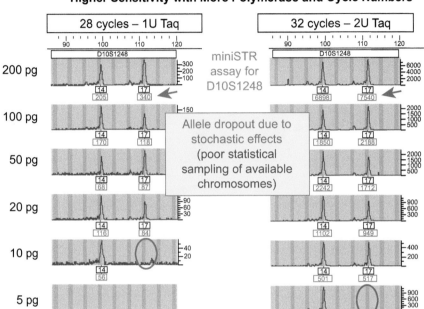

FIGURE 7.10

Higher sensitivity with more enzyme and rounds of polymerase chain reaction (PCR) amplification.

Taken from Coble and Butler, 2005. Journal of Forensic Science. 50:43–53. Derived from a presentation by Dr. John Butler (US National Institute of Standards and Technology, Office of Law Enforcement Standards) at the Midwestern Academy of Forensic Sciences annual meeting in Indianapolis, Indiana on October 11, 2006.

In the earliest days of DNA profiling, transfer and contamination were relatively minor considerations. When bloodstains the size of a dime were necessary to generate results, it was fairly easy to keep track of samples and be alert to the possibility of transfer simply through visual inspection. The dramatic increase in sensitivity that came with the advent of STR DNA tests in the late 1990s, however, made transfer and contamination much greater concerns. Vanishingly small quantities of starting material could give rise to peaks on electropherograms, even though serological tests were not sensitive enough to determine their tissue source (e.g., cells from saliva or skin could not be distinguished from blood or even semen). Making the problem worse is the fact that small amounts of DNA could persist in the environment for long periods of time (e.g., small amounts of an individual's skin cells could be deposited on an object through innocent handling months prior to their being collected as part of an investigation). In other words, the presence of a DNA profile says nothing about the time frame or the circumstances under which DNA came to be associated with an evidence sample.

Consider the specific example of the DNA that was analyzed from Meredith Kercher's bra fabric and metal clasp. The testing laboratory determined that the sample contained less than 0.1 ng of total human DNA for testing. The results (Fig. 7.5) indicate that the sample was a mixture of at least two individuals' DNA. If the major contributor (apparently Kercher herself) accounts for 75% of the sample's DNA, then less than 0.075 ng (approximately 12 cells) of her DNA was used to generate a DNA profile, and it would be reasonable to expect to see indications of stochastic effects. Of even greater concern, however, is that even if there was only one minor contributor, that minor contributor would account for less than 0.025 ng (approximately four cells) of the DNA in the sample. With such small quantities of starting material, it is not only impossible to determine how or when it came to be associated with the sample, but stochastic effects, such as allelic dropout and drop-in, may dominate the test results.

LIKELIHOOD RATIOS AND PROBABILISTIC GENOTYPING

Despite intense interest on the part of the forensic science community, there is still no generally accepted means of attaching a statistical weight to a mixed sample with an unknown number of contributors where allelic dropout may have occurred. Because a number of statistical approaches can be relied upon to attach weights to single source samples, many testing laboratories endeavor to deconvolve or separate mixed DNA samples into their component parts. Currently available deconvolution approaches are hampered by the uncertainties that are associated with low-level samples (e.g., distinguishing between signal and noise, determining the impact of stochastic effects). Much of the following discussion regarding likelihood ratios and probabilistic genotyping is explained in greater detail by Krane (2016).

Emerging probabilistic approaches may eventually provide an alternative to the deconvolution of mixed samples using rules spelled out in testing laboratory interpretation guidelines and simple mathematical formulae. These probabilistic approaches generate likelihood ratios that have the potential to capture uncertainties related to ranges of possible rates of drop-in and dropout, and can be divided into two categories: semicontinuous (relying exclusively on the alleles that are deemed to be present; peak height information is not utilized by the approach), and fully continuous (molecular biological parameters are incorporated, such as peak height ratio, hypothetical mixture ratios, and the expectation of stutter artifacts).

The computational complexity associated with fully continuous probabilistic approaches in particular is introducing an important, unprecedented set of challenges to the criminal justice system that requires careful consideration. To date, computer software (be it a word processing program or a software package that converts the raw electronic data of a DNA profiling analysis into an easily interpreted graphical format) has been used simply to assist humans during the course of activities that they could have performed less efficiently without that assistance. We may be on the cusp of a new era where computer programs take on the role of exercising judgment and arriving at conclusions that cannot be confirmed or replicated by human experts due to the sheer number and complexity of the analyses that are performed.

In conventional STR DNA profiling, where recommended amounts of template DNA for all contributors ensure that all alleles in an evidence sample have been detected and all the detected alleles are those that the prosecution would expect to see, then the probability assigned to the prosecution's theory of the case is 1 (meaning that the test results would appear as they do if the prosecution's theory of the case is, in fact, correct). The defendant's theory of the case (typically that contributions from some other, randomly chosen, unrelated individuals have together given rise to what is seen in the evidence sample) usually has a much lower probability. In these cases, the ratio of the likelihoods is simply the probability of the evidence under the prosecution's theory divided by the probability of the observed evidence under the defense's theory. If allele dropout or drop-in is a possibility (e.g., in a partial profile such as that seen in the knife blade from the Kercher murder investigation, Fig. 7.8), then there is uncertainty in whether or not an allele is present in the sample and, therefore, what genotype combinations are possible. Simply ignoring loci where it is necessary to invoke dropout to include an individual as a possible contributor to a mixed sample is a solution that brings with it a significant risk of producing apparently strong evidence against an innocent suspect (Curran and Buckleton, 2010).

In cases where it is necessary to invoke dropout (or drop-in) for the evidence sample to be consistent with the prosecution's theory of the case, the evidence is much less consistent with what would be expected if the prosecution's theory was correct. Dropout constitutes a failure of the carefully designed STR DNA test kits to generate a complete, correct result and should be expected to be a relatively rare event if the kits themselves are to be generally considered to be reliable. In some instances, the prosecution's theory of the case could be very inconsistent with the actual test results yet still be relatively more consistent than a defense hypothesis for the same case.

One helpful analogy might be to consider "who stole my biscuit?". We can accept that it is exceedingly unlikely that Father Christmas (being a person widely admired for his good character) stole my biscuit. However, it is much less likely that a unicorn (which everyone knows do not actually exist) stole my biscuit. The ratio of those two hypotheses might suggest that the prosecution's theory is a much better explanation of the loss of my biscuit unless and until we consider that alternative defense theories (e.g., that my brother stole my biscuit; who came up with the idea of a unicorn being involved in the first place?) are more consistent with the test results. When it is necessary to invoke drop-out (and/or drop-in) for test results to be consistent with a prosecution's theory of a case, it is critically important that both the numerator and the denominator be fully disclosed; yet, some probabilistic approaches currently provide only the ratio of the two likelihoods.

It is important to note that there is no correct answer to the likelihood ratios generated by probabilistic genotyping approaches for any given sample. It should not be surprising that two different approaches generate different likelihood ratios because they may be addressing different questions and they may be expressing different levels of confidence given the features they are evaluating. Proponents of probabilistic genotyping software packages should scrupulously avoid succumbing to market pressures to have their programs simply "get bigger numbers."

FINDING EXPERTS

The complexity of STR testing makes it difficult, if not impossible, for a lawyer to evaluate the evidence without expert assistance. Defense lawyers generally need expert assistance to look behind the laboratory report and evaluate whether its conclusions are fully supported by the underlying data. Defense lawyers may also need expert assistance to develop and assess alternative theories of the evidence. Experts can also be helpful and often are necessary to assess whether laboratory error or inadvertent transfer of DNA might plausibly account for the incriminating results. It is essential that defense attorneys obtain full discovery of the electronic data files and have them reanalyzed by an expert who has a license for the appropriate software to analyze the data. Failure to obtain or review the electronic data may constitute ineffective assistance of counsel. In the case of *People of the State of Michigan v. Frank Thomas Spagnola* (Berrien Circuit Court Case No. 2002-403913-FC), the defense went to trial without obtaining or reviewing the electronic data. In the postconviction hearing, the prosecution was ordered to turn over the electronic data after 8 full days of testimony from DNA experts on this issue.

CONCLUSIONS

Careful review of DNA evidence can reveal a variety of potential weaknesses, making it possible in some cases to challenge the government's conclusions and offer alternative interpretations. In order to provide effective representation to a client incriminated by DNA evidence, the defense attorney must do more than simply read the laboratory's conclusions. It is important to obtain and review the underlying scientific records, including electronic data, in order to determine whether the laboratory's conclusions are fully supported by the test results. It is also important to evaluate alternative explanations for the test results to determine whether there are plausible innocent explanations. Promoters of DNA testing have effectively used the media to convince most people, including potential jurors, that the tests are virtually infallible. As DNA testing becomes relied upon by the justice system for a growing variety of types of crime, it is vital that defense lawyers give it careful scrutiny in order to detect and expose those cases where genetic evidence deserves less weight than it is otherwise likely to receive.

APPENDIX: MODEL DISCOVERY REQUEST LANGUAGE FOR BIOLOGICAL TESTING (INCLUDING DNA)

This is a request for disclosure of scientific materials pertaining to biological testing performed in the case of _____ (case number _____). This request applies to all DNA testing, serological testing, presumptive testing, and any other biological testing that has been, is currently being, or will be performed in this case. The request is ongoing. In the event that new materials responsive to this request are produced, discovered, or otherwise come into the possession of the prosecution or its agents, said materials should be provided to the defendant without delay. For cases involving multiple agencies or testing laboratories, the prosecution is requested to direct this request to all agencies and/or laboratories that handled items or undertook DNA testing, serological testing, presumptive testing, and/or any other kind of biological testing in this case.

For a case involving a cold hit, the prosecution is requested to direct Request #10 to the laboratory responsible for maintaining the database that reported the hit.

1. Biological testing case file: Please provide a complete copy of the case file, including all records made by each laboratory in connection with biological testing in the instant case, including biological screening, serological testing, presumptive testing, microscopy, and DNA testing. Please provide documentation of any DNA profile uploaded to a Local, State, or National DNA Index System database (LDIS, SDIS, or NDIS). Please provide photographic quality copies of all photographs in the original case file (including photographs of evidence). Electronic copies of photographs are acceptable.

2. Chain of custody and current disposition of evidence: Please provide copies of all records that document the treatment and handling of biological evidence in the instant case, from the initial point of collection up to the current disposition. This information should include documentation that indicates where and how the materials were stored (temperature and type of container), the amount of evidence material that was consumed in testing, the amount of material that remains, and where and how the remaining evidence is stored. In the event that the chain of custody spans several different agencies or laboratories, please address this request to each agency and/or laboratory that handled said items.

3. Data files: Please provide copies of all computer data files created in the course of performing the DNA testing and analyzing the data in this case (i.e., both raw data and processed data). These data files should include all sample files (".fsa" and/or ".hid"), project files (".ser"), matrix files, size standard files, and analysis method files. In the event that a particular data file cannot be produced, please provide name of said file with explanation for nonproduction.

4. Laboratory protocols, frequency tables, and interpretation guidelines: Please provide a copy of the standard operating protocols (SOPs), frequency tables, and interpretation guidelines relied upon to perform the testing in the instant case. Interpretation guidelines should include those that address: (1) peak detection threshold(s); (2) stochastic threshold(s); (3) interpretation of mixed samples; (4) declaration of inclusions, exclusions, and inconclusive findings; and (5) policies for reporting results and statistics.

5. Unexpected results and corrective actions: For each laboratory that performed DNA testing in the instant case, please provide copies of the laboratory's log

of unexpected results and corrective actions. The logs should be provided for the time period beginning 6 months before the start of testing and ending 6 months after the completion of testing. Documentation should be provided for unexpected result events that arose due to mechanical, chemical, and analyst operations, including: contamination, the presence of extraneous DNA, sample handling errors, or any other reason. The logs should be provided for all laboratory personnel, not just the analyst(s) who performed the testing in the instant case. Please note: this is a request for the logs themselves, not just for entries within the logs that pertain to the instant case.

6. Accreditation: Please provide copies of the following for any laboratory that performed DNA testing in the instant case:

   6.1 All licenses or other certificates of accreditation held by the laboratory.

   6.2 Quality Assurance Audit Documents bracketing the testing in the instant case, including the last external audit before the start of testing, the first external audit after the completion of testing and all audits, both external and internal, for the time period between. This information should include the audit documents and all communications between the auditing agency and the laboratory being audited. Electronic copies preferred.

7. Laboratory personnel: Please provide background information for each person involved in conducting or reviewing the DNA testing performed in the instant case, including:

   7.1 current resume

   7.2 performance evaluation and personnel file

   7.3 a summary of proficiency test results

8. Communications: Please provide a copy of all communications between laboratory personnel and any other party with regard to the instant case, including letters, memos, emails, and records of telephone conversations [including communications with regard to any DNA profile uploaded to a Local, State, or National DNA database (LDIS, SDIS or NDIS)].

9. Cold hit: In the event that the case involves the upload of a DNA profile to either a Local, State, or National database (LDIS, SDIS, or NDIS), please provide all documentation maintained by the testing laboratory (including documentation maintained by Combined DNA Index System (CODIS) personnel within the laboratory), including:

   9.1 Documentation of all uploads, including: interpretation and/or deconvolutions of mixed profiles handwritten notes, spreadsheets, match estimator results, upload forms, and CODIS search forms.

   9.2 For each hit, please provide Match Detail Reports and long-form candidate match reports for the hit(s) including partial hits and hits that are dispositioned to be nonmatching (even if the laboratory has dispositioned a candidate as a hit).

   9.3 Any state manuals regarding the use of the SDIS and NDIS database systems.

The following language applies to cases involving a cold hit and should be addressed to the laboratory responsible for maintaining the Combined DNA Index System database:

10. Hit file: In the event that this case involves a "cold hit," please provide all records pertaining to any sample taken from the defendant for inclusion in a CODIS database, from the initial collection of said sample to its current disposition. These materials should include, but not be limited to, records of sample collection, chain of custody records, bench notes for DNA testing, printed electropherograms, electronic data, computer entry forms, Match Details Reports, and any communications pertaining to this case or searches involving samples from this case, including letters, emails, memos, and records of telephone conversations.

REFERENCES

Curran, J.M., Buckleton, J., 2010. Inclusion probabilities and dropout. Journal of Forensic Sciences 55 (5).

Dobraszczyk, C., 2014. The Prosecution of Amanda Knox: It's Not Over Yet!.

Gill, P., 2016. Analysis and implications of the miscarriages of justice of Amanda Knox and Raffaele Sollecito. Forensic Science International: Genetics 23, 9–18.

Krane, D.E., 2016. A Guide to Forensic DNA Profiling. http://www.wiley.com/WileyCDA/WileyTitle/productCd-1118751523,subjectCd-LSF0.html.

Paoletti, D., Doom, T., Krane, C., Raymer, M., Krane, D., 2005. Empirical analysis of the STR profiles resulting from conceptual mixtures. Journal of Forensic Sciences 50 (6), 1361–1366.

Saks, M.J., Risinger, D.M., Rosenthal, R., Thompson, W.C., April–June, 2003. Context effects in forensic science: a review and application of the science of science to crime laboratory practice in the United States. Science & Justice 43 (2), 77–90.

Thompson, W.C., 7 January/February 2006. Tarnish on the "gold standard:" understanding recent problems in forensic DNA testing. The Champion 30 (1), 10–16.

Thompson, W.C., Ford, S., Doom, T., Raymer, M., Krane, D.E., 2003. Evaluating forensic DNA evidence: essential elements of a competent defense review. Part 1. The Champion 27 (3), 16–25 April 2003. Part 2. The Champion 27 (4), 24–28, May 2003.

Walsh, P.S., Erlich, H.A., Hiquchi, R., 1992. Preferential PCR amplification of alleles: mechanisms and solutions. PCR Methods and Applications 1, 241–250.

Presumptive and Confirmatory Blood Testing

CHAPTER OUTLINE

Forensic Science Reform. http://dx.doi.org/10.1016/B978-0-12-802719-6.00008-X

Case Study: Lindy Chamberlain

Wendy J. Koen

Child Refuge, Inc., Menifee, CA, United States

The scientist shouldn't become too adventurous, too competitive. The trouble is, we're all so human. I've never seen a case more governed by human frailties [than the Chamberlain case].

Dr. Tony Jones, government pathologist in the Chamberlain trial

On a warm August evening in 1980, 9-week-old Azaria Chamberlain disappeared from her family's tent near Ayers Rock in the Northern Territory of Australia (Appleby, 2015). Lindy Chamberlain, Azaria's mother, always knew what happened to her baby; as Lindy was making dinner for her family, she heard Azaria cry and ran to the tent. As she approached the tent, she saw a dingo, a wild Australian dog, running from the tent, and she screamed in horror, "My God. My God. A dingo has got my baby" (*Chamberlain v. The Queen*; Brown, 2012). There was other evidence that supported Lindy's claim. There were paw prints at the door to the tent and along the side of the tent, a path in the sand that looked like something of Azaria's size was dragged and then dropped, leaving the imprint of the baby's jumper in the sand, and dragged again. Dingo hairs were found in the tent. Azaria's blood was found in the tent, and the bloodstains were consistent with a dingo attack. And there was witness testimony from fellow campers who heard Azaria cry out, sending Lindy to check on the baby, and then growling noises directly before Lindy cried out in horror.

Dingoes, wild Australian dogs, were clearly a part of the desert landscape and were seen in and around the campsites scattered near Ayers Rock. Dingoes were known to attack small children. It is not surprising that the police believed Lindy's claim and immediately began to search for Azaria in the caves and dingo lairs around Ayers Rock (Yallop, 1980). Azaria's body was never found, but her torn and bloody jumper and diaper were (Nelsson, 2012).

It did not take long for some investigators and the public to begin to doubt Lindy's explanation for her daughter's disappearance. Lindy and her husband were stoic and resigned. Their reactions to their daughter's death did not coincide with the senti- ments of other parents hearing of their ordeal. Soon, the Chamberlains were sub- jected to innuendo, speculation, and what was characterized as "the most malicious gossip ever witnessed in [Australia]" (Yallop, 1980).

It would take four inquests and three decades for the Australian court's to finally determine that what Lindy reported was true. In December 1980, the first official inquest concluded that Azaria had been killed by a dingo. Questions remained, however, because testing done on Azaria's clothing did not reveal dog saliva. The Chamberlains insisted Azaria had been wearing a matinee-style jacket over her jump- suit, and this would explain why there was no dingo saliva present (Yallop, 1980). Questions arose about tears on the jumper that looked like cuts, and it was theorized that someone had interfered with Azaria's clothes (Yallop, 1980). It appeared to the Crown's experts that Azaria's bloody clothes had been cut, removed from her body, and buried (the trial transcript in *Crown v. Lindy and Michael Chamberlain*, hereafter *Crown v. Chamberlain*, 1982).

Because questions remained, a second inquest was initiated a year later. By this time, the social discourse begun to spiral downward, and the media started to portray Lindy as "a freak of nature, a mother who had lost her natural ability to mother" (Easteal et al., 2015). Lindy did not share her grief with the public and appeared to be cool and unaffected by Azaria's death. Her emotional stoicism was characterized as unnatural and unfeminine, and it made it easy for the media to see her and portray her as a mother who would murder her infant (*Id.*). In addition to the suspicion that was percolating to the surface based on Lindy's character, testing revealed what was purported to be Azaria's blood in several areas of the Chamberlain's car.

In September 1981, more than a year after the night of Azaria's disappearance, the police took possession of the Torana hatchback car the Chamberlains had been driving and of hundreds of articles that Mr. and Mrs. Chamberlain told them had been in the tent or in the car on that evening (Chamberlain v. The Queen, 1984). The car and those items were then tested for the presence of blood. Where presumptive testing showed that blood was present, further testing was conducted to see if that blood contained fetal hemoglo- bin (HbF) and therefore came from an infant (Chamberlain v. The Queen, 1984).

ORTHO-TOLIDINE TEST: IS IT BLOOD?

The first test done was the *ortho*-tolidine test, a screening test used to detect the presence of blood. It is operated in two stages. At the first stage, a drop of *ortho*-tolidine is added to the sample. There is no reaction if blood is present. At the second stage, when a drop of hydrogen peroxide is added, a brilliant blue color is produced if blood is present. However, like other presumptive testing, the test does not react to blood alone. Other substances may produce a positive reaction, and, although an experienced technician should not be misled by the reaction produced by most other substances, some rusts may produce a reaction that appears identical as that produced by blood.

FETAL HEMOGLOBIN: IS IT FETAL BLOOD?

Infants under the age of 6 months have blood that is made up of HbF as well as adult hemoglobin (HbA). The blood of a newborn child contains roughly 75% HbF and 25% HbA. By the time an infant is 9 to 10 weeks old (Azaria's age at death), the proportion has decreased, and the infant's blood would contain 25% HbF. After the age of about 6 months, a healthy child normally has none.

The *ortho*-tolidine test indicated the presence of blood in many parts of the car, and one or other of the three tests for HbF showed that in 22 of the samples tested, the blood was fetal blood. In front of the front passenger seat of the car, investigators found what they thought to be a spray of infant blood.

Because of the blood evidence, the Supreme Court of the Northern Territory quashed the findings of the first inquest, and the coroner committed Lindy Chamberlain to stand trial for Azaria's murder. The blood evidence was damning and formed the prosecution's theory of the case: Lindy Chamberlain slit Azaria's throat in the front of their car and then hid her body (Hubert and Wainer, 2012; at p. 74). In February of 1982, Lindy was tried for murder, while Azaria's father, Michael Chamberlain, was charged as an accessory after the fact (Nelsson, 2012). In the Crown's opening statement, the case against the chamberlain's was summed up:

> *The discovery of fetal blood in the car is a critical part of the Crown case. It would be preposterous to suggest that the dingo took the child from the tent and into the car, and we will submit that the discovery of Azaria's blood in the car destroys the dingo attack explanation... Either a dingo killed Azaria, or it was homicide, because the child could hardly have inflicted injuries upon herself. If she was killed in the car, one can at once forget the dingo.... In the car is found the blood of a baby under the age of six months, and the clearest evidence that an attempt has been [made] to clean the blood up...[F]etal blood is found in a number places in the car, on a towel, on a pair of scissors, [and] on the black camera bag*
>
> ***Crown v. Chamberlain* (1982)**

In addition to the blood evidence found in the car, the jury was told that upon florescent examination, there was a human handprint, in blood, on the jumpsuit that Azaria was wearing when she disappeared, and that had been found partially buried near Ayers Rock (Morling Report, 1987). Obviously, the bloody handprint ruled out any suggestion that a dingo had killed Azaria.

The Crown alleged Lindy killed Azaria within an extremely limited timeframe and near several other people where the chances of discovery were perilous. In a period of less than 10 min, Lindy was alleged to have taken Azaria and Aiden, her 7-year-old son, from the barbecue area to the Chamberlain's tent, only 65–98 feet (20–30 m) away. She pulled tracksuit pants on over her dress, left Aiden in the tent, and took Azaria from the tent to the family car, which was parked alongside the tent. She entered the car and sat in the front passenger seat of the car with Azaria. Then, for no apparent reason, Lindy slit Azaria's throat with a sharp instrument (possibly scissors) and hid the body in a camera bag in the car. She then returned to the tent with blood on her hands, removed the tracksuit pants, and washed her hands in an ice cream container. She then had the composure to gather up Aiden, a can of beans, and a can opener, and return to the pubic barbeque area to feed Aiden, calm and composed (Chamberlain v. The Queen, 1984). The jury obviously had no problem with the Crown's version of events; based in large part on the blood evidence, on October 29, 1982, Lindy Chamberlain was found guilty and sentenced to life in prison for Azaria's murder (Nelsson, 2012).

Although Lindy began serving her life sentence for the murder of her daughter, she was not finished fighting to prove her innocence and appealed her conviction. In 1983, the Full Bench of the Federal Court heard the Chamberlain's appeal and, in a unanimous vote, rejected it. Later that year, the Chamberlains appealed their convictions to Australia's High Court, but in February of 1984 Australia's High Court, voting 3 to 2, upheld the convictions. In spite of legal setbacks, the public began to voice its support for the Chamberlains. In May of 1984, a petition with 131,000 signatures asking for Lindy's release, and a judicial inquiry into the case was presented to the Governor-General, Sir Ninian Stephen. Although that request was rejected, public support began to surge after an Australian barrister, John Bryson, wrote the book "Evil Angels," which offered an in-depth look at the Chamberlain case and revealed that the Chamberlains were wrongfully convicted. In 1985, the Northern Territory rejected an application, submitted by the Chamberlain Innocence Committee, requesting a full judicial inquiry into the case, and refused Lindy Chamberlain's application for early release from prison.

As the Chamberlains continued to fight for Lindy's exoneration, Lindy was serving her sentence, Michael was raising their children alone, and the evidence that led to Lindy's conviction began to unravel. The blood evidence was called into question when it was found that the presumptive test had likely not reacted to blood, but instead had reacted to the presence of copper oxide, a material prevalent where the Chamberlains lived in Mt. Isa, Queensland. It was also found that the analyses that confirmed the blood was that of an infant were critically flawed (Porter, 1995). What the jury did not know was that the test for HbF was highly unreliable and can give a false positive result for other substances (Hubert and Wainer, 2012; at p. 74). Some of the substances that produce false positive results are chocolate milkshakes, spray-on sound retardant, and nasal mucus, all of which were known to be present in the area of the car that tested positive for HbF (Hubert and Wainer, 2012; at p. 74). It became clear that the damning blood spatter evidence, the spray of HbF, which was key evidence that Lindy slit Azaria's throat while sitting in the front of the Torana hatchback, was actually a sound-deadening paint made from bitumen. In addition, the expert who had testified that a bloody handprint was visible on Azaria's jumpsuit conceded that he had only assumed the handprint was blood; he had never tested the stain (Brown, 2012).

In February of 1986, a tattered baby's jacket was found near Ayers Rock. After an English tourist fell to his death while climbing the rock, officers recovering his remains from an area full of dingo lairs discovered Azaria's missing matinee jacket. The small jacket offered evidence that supported the Chamberlains' claim that a dingo had killed Azaria. The absence of saliva on Azaria's jumpsuit was explained by the finding of the matinee jacket, which would have partially covered it. Two days after the discovery of the matinee jacket, on February 7, 1986, Lindy Chamberlain was released from prison.

In May of 1986, a judicial inquiry into the Chamberlain case was commenced before Justice Trevor Morling. A year later, Justice Morling issued a 379-page report that thoroughly analyzed the evidence in the Chamberlain case, including the state of the presumptive blood tests and the discovery of the matinee jacket. The Morling report concluded that the evidence against the Chamberlains was insubstantial.

On September 15, 1988, the Northern Territory Court of Criminal Appeals unanimously quashed all convictions against Lindy and Michael Chamberlain. They found that the effect of the new evidence on the Crown's case left it in "considerable disarray" (Re Conviction of Chamberlain, 1988). They held that,

> *The new scientific evidence casts serious doubt on the reliability of all the findings of blood in the car. The evidence leads me to conclude that if there were any blood in the car, it was present only in small quantities in the area of the hinge on the passenger's seat and beneath. It has not been established that any such blood was Azaria's. ... The finding most damaging to Mrs. Chamberlain was that of the alleged blood spray, such as might have come from a severed artery, on the metal plate under the dash. There is compelling evidence that the spray was made up of a sound deadening compound and contained no blood at all. The new evidence casts similar doubt on the reliability of the evidence at the trial that there was baby's blood on some of the contents of the car. At the trial, Mrs. Kuhl gave evidence that there were indications of baby's blood on the scissors found in the console of the car. It was virtually conceded before me that Mrs. Kuhl's tests did not confirm the presence of blood of any kind on the scissors. Indeed, on the evidence, it would be impossible to find that the scissors were even in the car when it was at Ayers Rock. The evidence at the trial was that there was also baby's blood on a towel, a chamois and its container found in the car and on the camera bag, which had been in the car. I am satisfied that the presence of baby's blood or of any blood on these articles has not been established.*
>
> **Re Conviction of Chamberlain (1988)**

Clearly, the blood evidence that had been so damning was simply false and was foundational to a conviction that should have never occurred for a crime that was never committed.

In 1992, Lindy Chamberlain received 1.3 million in compensation for wrongful imprisonment. However, because the second inquiry was considered incomplete, the Northern Territory Government announced there would be a third coroner's inquiry into Azaria's death. The Third Inquest was a "paper" inquiry, taking into account all of the inquiries, the appeals, and the Morling Report. The third inquest was completed in 1995 and came to the conclusion that Azaria died of unknown causes.

Given the injustice that had apparently been done to Lindy and Michael Chamberlain and the unsatisfactory absence of a conclusion published after the third inquiry, a final inquest was conducted in 2012 that took into account new evidence of the growing propensity of dingoes to attack small children. The final inquest found that the cause of Azaria's death was as the result of being attacked and taken by a dingo, and it was accepted from the findings of the inquest and from reports of other injuries and deaths since Azaria's disappearance that dingoes can and do cause harm to humans.

Thus, three decades after Azaria was taken from her parents' tent, Lindy and Michael Chamberlain were officially, decisively, and irrevocably cleared of all wrongdoing. Convictions that were built on mysterious suspicions aroused by Lindy's emotional reserve and scientific proof of fetal blood conjured by analysts hoping to find evidence to support these mysterious suspicions were quashed and revealed to be miscarriages of justice. The human frailties that governed the prosecution of the case, once revealed, should stand as a call for caution and remind us that we must demand only true, tested, and sure evidence from our expert witnesses.

REFERENCES

Appleby, R., 2015. The Death of Azaria Chamberlain. The Dingo Debate: Origins, Behaviour and Conservation, vol. 131.

Lt. Bratton, R., 1997. Hemaglow™ IAI Conference. Danvers, Massachusetts.

Brown, M., 2012. Dingo Baby Ruling Ends 32 Years of Torment for Lindy Chamberlain. The Guardian. Available at: http://www.theguardian.com/world/2012/jun/12/dingo-baby-azaria-lindy-chamberlain.

Chamberlain v. The Queen (No 2) [1984] HCA 7; (1984) 153 CLR 521. Available at: http://netk.net.au/Australia/Chamberlain.asp.

Easteal, P., Bartels, L., Nelson, N., Holland, K., August 2015. How are women who kill portrayed in newspaper media? Connections with social values and the legal system. In: Women's Studies International Forum, vol. 51. Pergamon, pp. 31–41.

Hubert, L., Wainer, H., 2012. A Statistical Guide for the Ethically Perplexed. CRC Press.

Nelsson, R., 2012. Azaria Chamberlain: Archive Coverage. The Guardian. Available at: http://www.theguardian.com/world/from the-archive-blog/2012/jun/12/azaria-chamberlain-dingo-baby-archive.

Porter, C., 1995. The evidence of experts. Australian Journal of Forensic Sciences 27 (2), 53–58.

Re Conviction of Chamberlain, September 15, 1988. Asche, C.J., Nader, Kearney, J.J. The trial transcript in Crown v. Lindy and Michael Chamberlain [1982] (Darwin court House).

Report of the Commissioner the Hon. Mr. TR Morling, 1987. Royal Commission of Inquiry into Chamberlain Convictions, Government Printer Canberra.

The Trial Transcript in Crown v Lindy and Michael Chamberlain. September 13–October 29, 1982, ("The Dingo Trial"): Selected Excerpts. Available at: http://law2.umkc.edu/faculty/projects/ftrials/chamberlain/chamberlaintranscript.html.

Yallop, R., August 19, 1980. Baby Girl Stolen by Dingo. The Guardian.

Presumptive and Confirmatory Blood Testing

Christopher Halkides[1], Kimberly Lott[2]

[1]The University of North Carolina at Wilmington, Wilmington, NC, United States
[2]Lott Law, PLLC, Durham, NC, United States; NCAST (North Carolina Attorneys for Science and Technology), Durham, NC, United States

INTRODUCTION: WHY THERE ARE BOTH PRESUMPTIVE AND CONFIRMATORY BLOOD TESTS

The purpose of this article is to discuss the interpretations of presumptive and confirmatory tests for the presence of human blood. We will use a few cases to illustrate areas of conflict between the prosecution and defense.

Having two stages of testing is common in medical and forensic disciplines. The purpose of a presumptive test for blood is to determine whether or not it is likely that this body fluid is present; in other words, a positive result indicates the *possibility* of blood. A positive result of a confirmatory test for blood allows one to conclude that blood is present. As Kobilinsky et al. (2004) noted, a forensic presumptive test should be able to identify a substance with a low probability of a false negative. By contrast, a confirmatory test is intended to have a low probability of a false positive. Castro and Coyle wrote,

> *Due to the high cost of DNA analysis and for scientific integrity, prior to sending any sample to the lab for DNA testing, it is important to determine if what appears to be blood is in fact human blood. This is achieved by performing a presumptive and then a confirmatory test on the samples in question. Presumptive tests react with the hemoglobin of all blood (human and animal) to catalyze the oxidation of a chromogenic compound, which produces a color change [25]. A positive reaction will result in the identification of the sample as possibly blood but not necessarily human blood. A presumptive test is used to describe these types of tests because they will react with substances other than blood, including certain metals and plant peroxidases [enzymes that react with molecules having oxygen–oxygen single bonds, as discussed below] resulting in false positives [5]. For this reason, anti-human hemoglobin tests (e.g. Ouchterlony, HemaTrace) to confirm species of origin are performed as a subsequent confirmatory test on any samples suspected to be blood [26]. A blood presumptive test should never be taken as a final measure, and should always be followed by confirmatory testing at the forensic science laboratory before making the statement in court that a sample is human blood.*

The final sentence in the quote above, "[a] blood presumptive test should never be taken as a final measure, and should always be followed by confirmatory testing at the forensic science laboratory before making the statement in court that a sample is human blood," must be remembered and adhered to if practitioners hope to effectively communicate their findings to courts and juries.

PART I: THE SCIENCE OF TESTING FOR BLOOD
PHYSIOLOGY OF BLOOD AND PROTEINS

Blood consists of roughly 50–64% plasma (which is basically proteins, minerals, and glucose dissolved in water) and 36–50% blood cells, almost all of which are red blood cells (RBCs). The percentages vary from one individual to the next, and the fraction of whole blood that is RBCs is slightly higher for men than women. RBCs are packed full of a protein called hemoglobin whose job it is to pick up oxygen in the lungs, carry oxygen through the blood, and then drop it off to tissues such as muscle. Hemoglobin is like a taxi that travels from lungs to muscles and back, and heme, an iron-containing prosthetic group (a molecule that helps a protein do its job) is like the seats of the car.

Proteins and the molecules that they bind are like a lock that only fits a certain key. The proteins and the molecules that they bind are complementary to each other the way that the halves of the Yin and Yang symbol are. Many important workhorse molecules in the body are proteins with various functions. Some proteins are antibodies, which bind foreign invaders (antigens). Some proteins, like hemoglobin, transport molecules from one place to another. Some proteins catalyze the conversion of (bring about the transformation of) one chemical in the body to another. Catalysts speed up chemical reactions, and biological catalysts are called enzymes. All of these proteins share a common feature in that they recognize and bind to certain chemical substances while not binding to others.

THE CHEMISTRY OF PRESUMPTIVE TESTS

The biological role of hemoglobin is to pick up oxygen and drop it off elsewhere; however, it can be converted into becoming a catalyst under the right circumstances. Presumptive tests for blood make use of the ability of hemoglobin to catalyze the same kind of reactions as the enzyme peroxidase does. The general chemical reaction that peroxidase enzymes speed up is:

$$RH_2 + H_2O_2 => R + 2H_2O$$

In this transformation, the reductant, RH_2, is an organic molecule that loses two electrons and two protons to become R. Hydrogen peroxide H_2O_2 is the oxidant, and it gains two electrons. Presumptive tests work because hemoglobin speeds up this reaction.

Some presumptive tests produce color because the product of the reaction R has a color, but the reactant, RH_2, is colorless. In the common presumptive tests used today, the identity of RH_2 is phenolphthalin (in the Kastle–Meyer test), TMB, Leucocrystal Violet, or leucomalachite green. Phenolphthalin (RH_2 in the transformation above) is the reduced form of phenolphthalein (R). The Kastle–Meyer test produces a pink color in the presence of blood, and the TMB test produces a blue–green color. Previous generations of testing were performed with benzidine or *ortho*-tolidine, which are similar to TMB.

Other presumptive tests produce light, as opposed to a change in color. The two most common luminescent tests are the luminol test and the fluorescein test. The chemiluminescent (light-producing) reagent luminol (5-Amino-2,3-dihydro-1, 4-phthalazinedione) produces blue light when it is oxidized, but the test must be performed in the dark. In contrast, when fluorescein is oxidized to fluorescein (RH_2 and R, respectively, in the transformation above), a light source producing light of wavelength 415–480 nm, which is blue light in the visible spectrum, must be used to excite fluorescein. Two common variations of the luminol test are the Weber formulation and the older Grodsky formulation. The Grodsky formulation of luminol uses sodium perborate as the oxidant (the substance that accepts electrons from luminol), and the Weber formulation uses hydrogen peroxide. All of the different tests produce the same blue light.

There are several commercial formulations of presumptive tests. For example, Hemastix is a variation of the TMB color change test. Bluestar and Hemaglow use luminol. Hemascein detects blood when fluorescein is produced and illuminated.

FALSE POSITIVES FROM OXIDANTS

In order to understand why there are false positive reactions from presumptive tests, one has to know a little bit about their chemistry. First, every presumptive test must have at least three components: a compound that gives electrons (the reductant) and changes color or produces light in the process, a compound that takes electrons (the oxidant), and a catalyst, a compound that speeds up a reaction. Second, the protocol of some presumptive tests is that the oxidant is added last, separately from the compound that changes color or produces light. This stepwise addition is designed to minimize one type of false positive, one that occurs because an oxidant is already present in the sample. If one observes a color change before the addition of hydrogen peroxide in the Kastle–Meyer test, then the test is declared inconclusive. Some protocols specify a maximum allowable time *after* the addition of hydrogen peroxide (the most common oxidant) for the color change (Cox, 1991). A color change that occurred after this interval (typically 10–60 s) is presumably the result of oxidation of the reductant by some means other than catalysis from blood. An unscrupulous worker could produce positive-seeming reactions by waiting for longer than the recommended amount of time. The red photograph of the bathroom in the murder of Meredith Kercher (the Amanda Knox/Raffaele Sollecito case) may have been produced in this way, but the origins of this photo are uncertain.

The separate addition of the color-change reagent versus the oxidant is not part of the luminol test or the Hemastix test. Therefore, these tests may produce false positives that other presumptive tests do not. Bleach, which is an oxidant, is well known to give false positives in the luminol reaction. Because bleach decomposes quickly under certain circumstances, it may be possible to avoid its interfering with a luminol test. However, some substances produce bleach upon addition of water, and this may explain why certain cleansers give false positives with luminol.

FALSE POSITIVES FROM CATALYSTS

False positives from the presence of catalysts other than human blood are an inevitable feature of presumptive tests. Animal blood will obviously produce a positive reaction with the presumptive tests. Because presumptive testing uses the pseudoperoxidase activity of hemoglobin, any substance having a sufficient quantity of the enzyme peroxidase is very likely to produce a false positive. Certain vegetables are rich in this enzyme; among them are horseradish and turnip, but wet plant matter is among the substances producing false positives (Bratton, 1997). The roots of legumes such as soybean produce a protein, leghemoglobin, which gives a false positive in the Kastle–Meyer test (Petersen and Kovics, 2014). Milk may give a false positive reaction in the *ortho*-tolidine test, probably from the presence of a peroxidase enzyme. Plant peroxidases may or may not produce false positives in the Kastle–Meyer test; there is some disagreement in the forensic literature on this question (Cox, 1991; Tobe et al., 2007).

One can make some generalizations about substances producing false positives. Some metal ions (including copper, cobalt, iron, manganese, and nickel) produce false positives in one or more of the color-change or luminescent tests; many are metal ions of the first row of transition metals in the periodic table. However, a thorough chemical understanding of false positives is challenging for a number of reasons. First, some mixtures (soil, certain varnishes) give false positives with luminol at least. One would have to test each ingredient in the mixture to be absolutely certain of the substance catalyzing the oxidation of luminol. Second, substances such as $KMnO_4$ may produce false positives by acting both as an oxidant and as a catalyst. Third, some anomalous results are almost inevitable when many substances are screened, especially when the studies are performed by different workers. For example, it has been reported that HemaGlow does not produce false positives with certain cleaning agents that luminol does, yet Hemaglow is merely a kit of one luminol formulation (Bratton, 1997). Conversely, it has been reported that manganese sulfate gives a false positive with Bluestar (another commercial luminol product), but not luminol itself. Paradoxical findings with respect to plant peroxidases and the Kastle–Meyer test were mentioned above. Therefore, it remains extremely challenging to produce a definitive list of substances that will or will not cause a false positive reaction.

Iron is an abundant element, and rust gives false positives with a number of presumptive tests. Robert Grispino wrote, "A metal staple or carpet tack in a rug or a rusted metal vehicle interior will glow after treatment with luminol, simulating a positive blood reaction" (Grispino, 1991).

PRESUMPTIVE TESTING WITH A LUMINESCENT CHEMICAL AND A COLOR-PRODUCING CHEMICAL

It is common practice to follow up a positive result from a luminescent test (a test that produces light) with a colorimetric test (a chromogenic or color-change test). Gefrides and Welch wrote, "Luminol and fluorescein will react with the same false positives such as phenolphthalein and also with bleach and other cleaning fluids." In "Biological Evidence Collection and Forensic Blood Identification," Castro and Coyle said, "It is advised that if a positive reaction with luminol is achieved, the stained area should be checked again with another reagent such as TMB, phenol-phthalein, or *ortho*-tolidine and always confirmed with a human-specific confirmatory test for blood [23]." Kobilinsky et al. (2004) wrote, "The major benefits of performing a luminol test rather than one of the colorimetric tests is that one can search large areas very rapidly, and the chemical used does not interfere with any of the other presumptive tests that may be performed following luminol testing. If the result of presumptive testing is negative, the analysis is terminated. However, if the result is positive, then a more definitive confirmatory test is performed. The reason for this is that there are a number of substances that can produce false-positive observations including bleach, plant peroxidases, chemical oxidants such as potassium permanganate ($KMnO_4$), copper, brass, lead, zinc, bronze, iron, or cobalt." Some of the compounds in the list above would probably give a false positive reaction with a color-change test. Drano has also been reported to give a false positive result for luminol (Bratton, 1997).

CAN FALSE VERSUS TRUE POSITIVES BE DISTINGUISHED IN LUMINESCENT OR COLORIMETRIC TESTS?

It is sometimes claimed that the spectral characteristics of blood versus other substances in the luminol test allow an experienced investigator to distinguish true from false positives. The Lindy Chamberlain case is discussed elsewhere in this chapter with respect to the orthotolidene test. With respect to luminol, there are some small differences. In a review on luminol, Barni et al. wrote, "An experienced practitioner may distinguish the true blood-catalyzed chemiluminescence from that produced by other substances by the evaluation of parameters observable to the naked eye such as emission intensity, duration and spatial distribution. However this approach may also lead to misinterpretation, due to a subjective, information and non-quantitative evaluation…" (Barni et al., 2007) In our judgment, the subjective evaluation of the forensic police is no substitute for follow-up testing by a color-change reagent, and finally a confirmatory test.

CONFIRMATORY BLOOD TESTS

If a stain is positive for the possibility of blood by a presumptive test, it must finally be subjected to a confirmatory test, or the possibility of a false positive remains. Confirmatory tests must be able to identify a substance with the lowest possible chances of a false positive. The confirmation that a substance is blood used to be addressed via the Takayama or Teichman tests, and from which species the blood originated was determined separately. The Takayama and Teichman tests work by creating crystals from heme, a portion of hemoglobin (see above). Other proteins besides hemoglobin also utilize heme, most notably catalases and peroxidases. These enzymes could produce false positives at sufficiently high concentrations. Newer tests differ from these crystal tests in how the detection occurs and, in some cases, which protein is detected.

It is now possible to identify a substance as blood and to limit the number of species from which it came with a single test. Many forensic tests to confirm the presence of blood involve antibodies, proteins that recognize the shapes and chemical characteristics of substances often of biological origin. When an antibody and an antigen mix in the right ratio, a lattice (Fig. 8.1) called precipitin forms and comes out of solution. A stain is sometimes used to aid in visualizing precipitin, which allows a scientist to provide a clear and permanent record. An antibody that is produced in response to a substance A is called an anti-A antibody. If it also reacts with a substance B, this is called a cross-reaction. It is suggestive that substance B is similar to substance A, although this is not always true. Cross-reactivity means that an antibody binds to two or more antigens. The fewer antigens an antibody reacts with, the more selective an antibody is. For example, there is cross-reactivity between hemoglobin from humans versus ferret in the HemaTrace test discussed below. The possible cross-reactivity of antibodies, which bind to proteins found in brain or central nervous tissue, was a contentious issue in the Mark Lundy case in New Zealand.

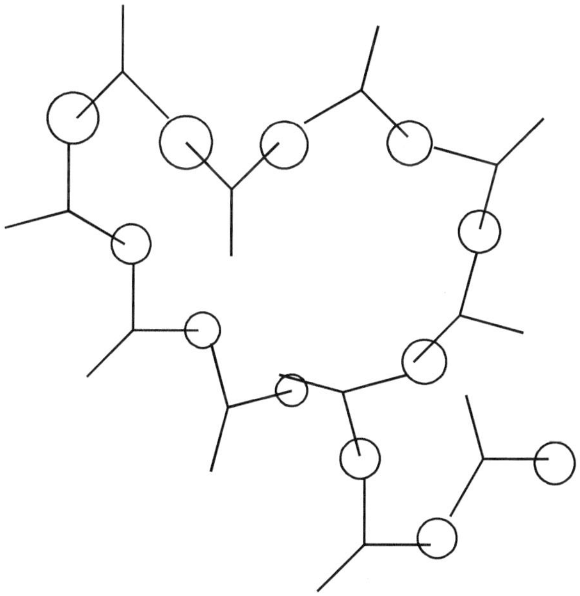

FIGURE 8.1

Formation of precipitin. When the correct ratio of antigen (*open circle*) and a complementary antibody (Y-shaped stick) are mixed, they bind and come out of solution as a lattice called precipitin. This diagram shows only a small portion of such a lattice.

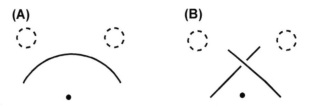

FIGURE 8.2

The Ouchterlony double diffusion method. The *solid dots* (•) represent a solution of antibodies, and the *dotted circles* represent a solution of antigens. (A) If the two antigens are identical, they form a single *curve* of precipitin. (B) If the two antigens are not identical, they react with different antibodies and form two separate precipitin *lines* that may arc slightly. More complex results are also possible.

Testing involving antibodies is performed in one of several ways. In the Ouchterlony double diffusion method, ones observes the precipitin lines as the substances diffuse through agar, a soft solid. When a solution containing antibodies is placed in a central well and two antigens are placed in side wells, one of several possible results is seen (Fig. 8.2). When the two antigens are identical, a single curved band of precipitin is observed (A). When two intersecting lines of precipitin resembling the letter X are observed (B), the two antigens are not identical. A third result, cross-reaction, is not shown. Another family of techniques, immunoelectrophoresis, involves the combination of diffusion and electrophoresis (motion of charged species in an electric field). The HemaTrace and rapid stain identification (RSID)-Blood tests are immunochromatographic methods. Liquid chromatography is the separation of molecules based upon how quickly or how far their travel through a liquid; different molecules spend different amounts of time bound to a solid support that is also present. When the solid phase uses antibodies, this subclass of methods is called immunochromatography.

Different confirmatory tests recognize different biomolecules in blood. The RSID-Blood test uses an antibody that recognizes glycophorin, a protein found on the plasma membrane of erythrocytes (red blood cells). HemaTrace uses an antibody that recognizes hemoglobin. A disadvantage of the HemaTrace test is that it produces positive results for primate and ferret blood. This has apparently caused some authors to classify HemaTrace as a presumptive test or to note that it is not considered a confirmatory test for human blood. In our view, the reactivity with primate and ferret blood only means that HemaTrace is not fully species-specific while still confirming that blood is present, yet the older crystal tests were not specific for species *at all*.

Future confirmatory tests for body fluids may utilize messenger RNA (Virkler and Lednev, 2009). As is also true for many proteins, certain sequences of mRNA are found in high quantity in one tissue type, but not others. In these tests, the enzyme reverse transcriptase makes a DNA copy of RNA in the stain. Then the DNA is itself amplified (copied many times) using the polymerase chain reaction in a manner similar to modern DNA profiling. However, extreme care is needed to be certain that one is in fact detecting RNA and not DNA. This danger was illustrated clearly by erroneous results that falsely suggested a link between the MMR vaccine and autism (Murphy and Bustin, 2009). If forensic workers failed to run (or fail to heed the results of) no-reverse transcription controls, they might detect DNA, which is virtually identical, irrespective of cell type. A false positive result of this kind could potentially mistakenly identify a stain as blood when it was not. The age of the sample in question is also important; RNA quality has been observed to decrease in the postmortem interval. However, RNA in postmortem tissue may degrade more quickly than RNA in dried stains. A second issue is that accurate quantitation of messenger RNA is thought to be more challenging than DNA.

SENSITIVITY AND LIMIT OF DETECTION

The uses of the terms sensitivity and specificity deserve special consideration, as forensic analysts will often testify using these words and sometimes confuse their meanings. Kobilinsky et al. (2004) wrote (p. 34), "Presumptive tests are usually sensitive but not specific, and thus small amounts of the substance can be detected… Presumptive tests that are positive should always be followed by *confirmatory* tests. The latter are less sensitive but more specific and therefore results are more reliable." In clinical chemistry, some, but by no means all, authors use the term "sensitivity" to refer to the detection limit of a test. With reference to the statistics of diagnostic (medical) tests, Altman and Bland (1994) wrote, "*Sensitivity* is the proportion of true positives that are correctly identified by the test. *Specificity* is the proportion of true negatives that are correctly identified by the test." In discussing presumptive blood tests, forensic chemists have used the term sensitivity to mean the ability of a test to detect a highly dilute (low in concentration) blood. The common usage of sensitivity in forensics is similar to its definition as the limit of detection. If one assumes that the only reason for a false negative result is that blood is too dilute to be detected, then the forensic definition and the statistical definition are also closely related. We suggest that lawyers ask expert witnesses to define these terms. This minimizes confusion relating to different understandings of the terms and the chances that an analyst will overstate the interpretative value of a test.

The sensitivities of a number of presumptive tests have been reported multiple times. All of the commonly used presumptive tests are able to detect highly diluted blood. The reasons for this are at least twofold. First, red blood cells contain a high concentration of hemoglobin. Second, the tests are catalytic; each molecule of hemoglobin can produce many molecules of colored product. It is common for the values reported for the same substance to differ by at least an order of magnitude. Some of these differences may be the result of different formulations of the same reagent or differences in substrate. Castro and Coyle wrote, "Various differences in sensitivity are reported by researchers for presumptive tests for blood and are undoubtedly caused by differences in the reagent concentration, methods of sample preparation, and the type of material containing the blood [27]."

HemaTrace couples the binding reaction of the antibody with hemoglobin to the production of red color (see above). Validation studies have addressed the sensitivity of

HemaTrace, and these have produced similar but not identical results. The Miami-Dade police obtained positive results in the range of dilutions between 100-fold and 100,000-fold. If the blood is too concentrated, it produces a false negative (the high-dose hook effect) that can be overcome by diluting the sample. The Michigan State Police found that blood diluted more than 10 million–fold produced a positive result. When cotton swatches with diluted blood were extracted and subjected to presumptive tests and HemaTrace, the latter was able to detect blood at dilutions of about 30,000-fold.

The RSID test for glycophorin is able to detect 0.25 μL of blood, probably less. This compares with the reported value of 1 μL for the Takayama test. Saferstein wrote (Criminalistics, ninth ed., p. 354), "crystal tests [Takayama and Teichmann] are far less sensitive than color tests for blood identification and are more susceptible to interference from contaminants that may be present in the stain." The precipitin test for human serum can detect blood that has been diluted up to 1 part in 256.

RELATIONSHIPS BETWEEN BLOOD TESTING AND FORENSIC DNA ANALYSIS

A positive result for the presence of forensic DNA in a stain is not a confirmation that a substance is blood; rather, it potentially individualizes the blood with the caveat mentioned below. The reason for this is that DNA is ubiquitous to virtually all cells. Furthermore, attempts to infer that a substance is or is not blood from the heights of peaks in an electropherogram is without merit. However, some courts in the US and Australia have taken the presence or absence of DNA into consideration when deciding to admit presumptive blood evidence (see below). A negative result for DNA was one of several factors that threw doubt on a positive result from a presumptive test in the Gregory Taylor case.

DNA evidence is stronger when a fluid or tissue source can be identified (Peel and Gill, 2004). DNA arising from an unknown type of fluid or tissue is called subsource DNA. The existence of DNA within a bloodstain is strong evidence that the blood was deposited by the same individual as the DNA. An exception to this occurs when the source DNA has degraded over time and a contaminating event has occurred to introduce unrelated DNA (Peel and Gill, 2004). Such a result may have occurred in the case of Gary Leiterman.

LABORATORY PRACTICE WITH RESPECT TO CONFIRMATORY TESTING

Some laboratories have discontinued confirmatory testing. Castro and Coyle wrote, "Recently, some forensic science laboratories have created a short cut in their procedures by eliminating the human blood confirmation test. In some case circumstances, this can create interpretational and legal difficulties and is not a favored approach by the authors [16–19]. Current advances in human blood identification allow for investigators and laboratories to confirm the human specificity of the blood sample within minutes [20]." We strongly agree with Castro and Coyle. Although the older crystal tests had their weaknesses, modern testing with products such as HemaTrace and RSID Hemoglobin is much better.

PART II: PRESUMPTIVE TESTS AND THE LAW

If the prosecution discloses a positive result from one presumptive test but fails to disclose a negative result from another, this may harm the defense. That was the conclusion of the Illinois State Supreme Court with respect to Lovejoy. The forensic technician had obtained a positive result using the Leucocrystal Violet test and a negative result with TMB (People v. Lovejoy, 2009).

The Illinois State Supreme Court Granted Mr. Lovejoy a new trial. "Despite the positive LCV [leucocrystal violet] test, Camp tested the swab with TMB, a more sensitive and more reliable presumptive test for the presence of blood, as her protocol dictates. The TMB test was negative, indicating that the substance swabbed was not blood." The opinion goes on to state, "The parties do not dispute the facts giving rise to the alleged discovery violation. Both sides agree that Camp did not include her finding that the TMB test produced a false negative, and did not state her reason for the negative TMB test in her report." The opinion also stated, "Further, if defendant were made aware of Camp's conclusion that the TMB test produced a false negative because the LCV used all the hemoglobin in the blood, he could have called an expert to refute this contention during his case in chief, or could have chosen to pursue a different line of defense altogether. Defendant was prejudiced when Camp's conclusions were revealed for the first time at trial." Earlier in the opinion, it was made clear that such an expert indeed existed: "In that motion, defendant stated that Dr. Karl Reich, who holds a degree in molecular biology from the University of California, Los Angeles and Harvard University, was prepared to testify that the TMB test used by Camp is the most sensitive presumptive blood test available; that a negative TMB test strongly suggests that there is no blood in the area tested; and that Camp's testimony that the LCV consumed the reactive blood components, thus confounding the TMB test, was incorrect." In other words, not knowing that there was a negative TMB test nor knowing what rationale would be offered for it being negative hampered the ability to present a robust defense. Given that hemoglobin is a catalyst in this test, the notion that it was used up is extremely dubious.

Lack of discovery also plagued Russ Faria's first trial. The prosecution presented testimony that luminol revealed the presence of shoeprints. This appeared to be damning in that blood was seen on Mr. Faria's slippers. They provided no 0documentation, claiming that a camera had malfunctioned. Despite strong alibi evidence, Mr. Faria was convicted of murdering his wife. When Mr. Faria was retried, over 100 photographs (which had been withheld) were released to the defense. The photographs suggested that the camera was working, but they did not show any evidence of foot tracks. There was a luminol-positive area near the kitchen; however, the luminol had been applied after the family had reoccupied the house following the murder. The shape of the area suggested that the luminol had reacted to juice from a pork chop that had been given to the family's dog (State v. *Faria Missouri*, 2012).

Lack of discovery of laboratory notes was one of the issues highlighted by State v. Taylor North Caroline, 1993. In February 2010, Mr. Taylor was exonerated after a hearing in front of a three-judge panel of North Carolina's newly formed Innocence Inquiry Commission. Analysts testified to positive luminol and phenolphthalein tests from Mr. Taylor's truck. The only documentation given to the defense was a lab report stating these results. As part of the Innocence Commission investigation, attorneys discovered the bench notes from an analyst who had performed the confirmatory testing on the areas of the truck thought to contain blood. The notes indicated that the Takayama test was negative. Those notes were never given to the defense. This highlights the necessity to fashion your discovery requests in such a way that asks for all lab notes and other supporting materials rather than simply relying on a final report produced by the crime lab.

Forensic technicians frequently overstate the evidentiary strength of a given positive result from a presumptive test. Sometimes this is coupled with a lack of complete disclosure about negative results. As scientists, were we called to testify, we would state that a positive presumptive test with no confirmatory test means absolutely nothing. No inferences one way or another can be drawn. Likewise, a positive presumptive test with a negative confirmatory test would lead us to testify that no blood was present on the tested item. The scientist should give a neutral explanation of what the science shows, not favoring the prosecution or the defense. Unfortunately, this is not the standard for many crime lab analysts.

A study was conducted in order to explore the forensic science testimony by prosecution experts in the trials of innocent persons (Garrett and Neufeld, 2009). In each case, the defendant had been wrongfully convicted of a serious crime and was later exonerated by postconviction DNA testing. The scholars relied on 137 trial transcripts from all exonerees identified as having trial testimony by forensic analysts. In these trials, expert testimony consisted of serological analysis, microscopic hair comparison, bite mark, shoe print, soil, fiber, and fingerprint comparisons, and DNA testing. In 82 cases (60%), forensic analysts called by the prosecution provided invalid testimony at trial. The testimony was invalid because the conclusions of the experts misstated empirical data or was wholly unsupported by empirical data. The testifying analysts in the study included 72 forensic analysts called by the prosecution who were employed by 52 laboratories, practices, or hospitals in 25 states. Most of the invalid forensic testimony involved evidence presented as inculpatory. Defense counsel rarely cross-examined analysts concerning invalid testimony or obtained their own experts. When defense attorneys did challenge the forensic science, judges seldom provided relief. As the National Academy of Sciences Report concludes, "the legal system is ill-equipped to correct the problems of the forensic science community."

Besides Scientific Working Group (forensic science standards established by The National Institute of Standards and Technology) standards that guide forensic scientists on what can and cannot be claimed in terms of identification, there are ethical codes that address these issues but are not being followed. The American Board of Criminalistics Code of Ethics instructs all analysts to ensure that opinions are rendered "only to the extent justified" by the evidence and ensure that testimony is presented "in a clear, straightforward manner" that does not "extend themselves beyond their field of competence, phrasing their testimony in such a manner so that the results are not misinterpreted." The Code also states that criminalists shall "[m] aintain an attitude of independence and impartiality in order to ensure an unbiased analysis of the evidence."

The AAFS (American Academy of Forensic Sciences) Code forbids a "material misrepresentation of data upon which an expert opinion or conclusion is based." The AAFS Guidelines also adopt "good forensic practice guidelines," which add that "[u]nlike attorneys, forensic scientists are not adversaries. They take an oath in court to tell the whole truth. They should make every effort to uphold that oath." Additionally, when presenting their opinions, "[e]very reasonable effort should be made to ensure that others (including attorneys) do not distort the forensic scientist's opinions."

The CAC (California Association of Criminalists) Code requires that "[i]n all respects, the criminalist will avoid the use of terms and opinions which will be assigned greater weight than are due them. Where an opinion requires qualification or explanation, it is not only proper but incumbent upon the witness to offer such qualification." The CAC Code stipulates that the expert indicate when an opinion "may lack the certainty of other opinions he might offer" and will "leave no false impressions in the minds of the jurors." Additionally, the CAC Code expects that an expert "will not. . . assign greater significance to an interpretation than is justified by the available data."

The Gregory Taylor case highlights the importance of how forensic findings are presented in reports and at trial. Duane Deaver was the lab analyst who performed tests on parts of Mr. Taylor's truck in order to determine if the victim's blood was present, linking Taylor to the crime. Mr. Deaver did not testify at Taylor's trial. During Mr. Taylor's trial, the blood evidence that Mr. Deaver tested was presented by Donald Pagani, an agent with the City County Bureau of Identification (CCBI). Pagani had processed the scene where the victim's body was found and where, coincidentally, Mr. Taylor's truck was found stuck in the mud approximately 50 yards away. He and other CCBI agents had performed phenolphthalein and luminol testing at the scene. He described the presumptive phenolphthalein test, stating that "Basically if you can see a suspicious stain and you can test it with the phenolphthalein and that will give you just the reaction that you have human blood but it is it not specific" (Taylor transcript). Later, he testified that "Phenolphthalein is an initial test that we use to determine the presence of human blood. It is not as sensitive as luminal [sic] but it is something that at least gives us an idea of what the possible stain we are looking at is and then we can do further testing at that point" (Taylor transcript). When asked by prosecutors why they would use phenolphthalein at all, he answered, "...[I]t is a test which when we can see a visible stain we use to determine if it is human blood and it is specifically designed for that purpose and it is a field expedient way of doing it" (Taylor transcript). Mr. Pagani's boss, William Hensely, also testified that "Phenolphthalein is a liquid chemical which is used to identify blood...Now it is, it is very specific for blood in that that's what it reacts to.... When you have a positive reaction, what we call a positive reaction, you get a purple, immediate purple reaction which indicates that the presence of blood." When asked by the prosecutor to compare this test to luminol, Hensley stated that phenolphthalein is more specific for the detection of blood (Taylor transcript).

When speaking about the testing of Greg Taylor's truck for the presence of blood with phenolphthalein, Mr. Pagani stated, "We got a positive testing on the fender well underneath the front passenger wheel and we also got a positive testing with phenolphthalein on the undercarriage…. Yes, there were several suspicious stains. They were tested again with phenolphthalein, showed they could possibly be human blood" (Taylor transcript). When testifying regarding the report that Duane Deaver had submitted, he stated it "gave chemical indications for the presence of blood" (Taylor transcript).

Mr. Hensley similarly testified that on the outside edge of the right front passenger side wheel well of the car, there was a red substance, which had all indications of possibly being blood, and that this gave them a visual contact that blood was in that area (Taylor transcript). He indicated there was a positive reaction to a red spot on the fender and went on to describe, "If you have a visual sighting and the test is positive, the phenolphthalein, you do not want to spray luminal [sic] on it because it will destroy the blood groupings and type (Taylor transcript). When asked about using luminol in the wheel well area, Hensley testified that they "had a lot of fluoresces in that rear" and that indicated that possibly a substance like blood might have come in contact or was slung off the wheel in that area" (Taylor transcript).

Mr. Taylor's defense attorney didn't ask Mr. Hensley a Single Question. His cross-examination of Mr. Pagani was very brief and contained no questions about the identification of blood on Taylor's truck. The defense attorney, in his closing argument, stated that no evidence had been presented as to what type of blood they found, whether animal or human, because no one from the lab came to testify and that luminol reacts to a lot of different types of blood (Taylor transcript). No one asked either analyst what the further testing of the blood evidence showed. In this case, the confirmatory test was negative for the presence of blood. That evidence never came out at the trial. An attorney should have had several follow-up questions as to the positive indication for blood. In addition to what the further testing showed, asking if the blood was human, what type it was (A, B, O, etc.), and whether that type matched the victim or the suspect would be appropriate. We have heard it said that the reason innocent people are in jail is because defense attorneys don't kick the tires hard enough. That statement, though incorrect as to the only reason innocent people are in jail, is true in this case and many others.

In addition to overstating the strength of a presumptive test, crime lab analysts will also testify in such a way that is ambiguous or use words that have different meanings in the scientific community. For instance, stating that a test is "inconclusive" can leave varying impressions, depending on how the analyst couches it. In the scientific community, an inconclusive test means absolutely nothing. It is not positive or negative, and no inferences can be made from it. Crime lab analysts will testify that inconclusive means that it is most likely a negative result or even a positive result, depending on how that test fits into their overall investigation. "Inconclusive" was used in the Greg Taylor case by the crime scene analyst to state that a particular blood test was inconclusive. It was used along with a string of tests that had shown that the blood on a tissue was the victim's blood. Both the analyst and the prosecutor interpreted the inconclusive result as an anomaly and relied on the other tests that were done to make their conclusions. Such a use is improper and should be thoroughly covered in cross-examination to reveal what the inconclusive result really shows.

As discussed previously, the terms "sensitive" and "specific" are used by lab analysts and are sometimes used interchangeably. In the Taylor case, Mr. Pagani used both words to show that the presumptive tests luminol and phenolphthalin are specific to blood. He also tried to differentiate the two tests by stating that one was more sensitive than the other. The testimony given made it sound like that if you use a presumptive test, it definitively shows that blood is present. This is, of course, completely inaccurate and misleading. When an analyst testifies regarding presumptive tests, an attorney should cross-examine him, asking how many other substances may give a false positive on a presumptive test. When an analyst uses the words sensitive or specific, an attorney should ask further questions until a good definition of these words is given. Better yet would be to have a different expert explain what they mean so a judge or jury can be clear as to what conclusions may or may not be drawn given the results.

The word "positive" can also be misleading in an analyst's report or testimony. Again, an attorney needs to cross-examine the witness as to what "positive" means in the present case. Does it mean that it shows definitely that human blood is present? Is it indicative of a certain pH value or range? It is indicative that a certain chemical reaction took place? How many other substances can give a similar "positive" result?

The Taylor case is an example, too, of one analyst testifying regarding the tests performed by someone else. Various jurisdictions treat this practice differently. An attorney should make every effort to ensure the analyst who performed the tests actually testifies. This way he can be cross-examined on exactly which tests were performed. He can be questioned about his bench notes and his report.

At the time of the Taylor trial, it was common practice for the crime lab to word their reports exactly the way they did in that case. The positive presumptive test was reported, and any further negative tests were not. The rationale was that the second test was simply not conclusive. This highlights the necessity to ask for not only the report, but all bench notes, pictures, interlab memoranda, and all other documentation regarding testing of blood. It is also important to know what the protocol was for the crime lab at the time the evidence was tested. Protocols change and policies change. Ask why they changed and whether the lab has gone back and addressed evidence from cases that were analyzed under an old and potentially flawed protocol.

Often, crime lab analysts do not take pictures of a result that they report. In most science labs, taking pictures are not only routine, but necessary. If a scientist wants to publish her results or use them to convince someone who was not present at the time of testing that a certain result was obtained, a picture is necessary to do so. Analysts should be questioned as to why pictures are not taken and whether a picture would assist the trier of fact in determining the outcome of the tests performed.

Duane Deaver, the analyst who did the tests in the Taylor case but reported only the presumptive results, had been questioned as to his veracity in a previous case that highlights the overstatement of the analyst's ability to determine if a substance is really blood. This was in the case of George Goode. At trial he testified that "no one during my time in the laboratory, either for myself or the people that I was responsible for, ever had a false positive based on any of the literature results" (*State v. George Goode*, trial transcript). He conceded that the scientific literature and the SBI (State Bureau of Investigation) training manual said false positives could occur, but that no one he ever trained or supervised found that to be the case. When asked if he thought, as an expert witness, he could tell a court or a jury that something is blood without a confirmatory test, he answered affirmatively (Goode transcript). Upon further questioning as to whom at the SBI authorized him to testify that he could call something blood without doing a confirmatory test, he answered, "I don't know. My supervisors I guess" (Goode transcript). Disturbingly, he also indicated that he did not routinely put the name of the test or the scientific procedure used when saying something indicated the presence of blood. Just as in the Taylor case, he said the supervisors told them to use specific wording and that they did not follow a certain manual, scientific literature, or scientific standard (Goode transcript). In the same trial, he did not correct an attorney when he called spots on boots blood when Deaver knew it was not actually blood (Goode transcript). When questioned at the Innocence Inquiry hearing of Gregory Taylor regarding how he reported his results, Duane Deaver defended the practice of writing the report that way, stating that it was "technically true" and that how reports were written were decided by his superiors, not by him; therefore, he did nothing wrong. He was merely following orders.

The revelations in Greg Taylor's case regarding the reporting and testimony practices of the NC SBI Crime Lab lead the NC Attorney General's office to commission an independent audit of the Forensic Biology (also referred to as the serology section) section of the Crime Lab. Auditors examined cases in which presumptive tests yielded "positive indications for the presence of blood" or "indications of blood" but where subsequent confirmatory tests reflecting "negative" or "inconclusive" results were omitted from the final report. Their findings were published in what became known as the Swecker Report. Out of 15,419 lab files screened and examined, this review identified 932 laboratory cases in which laboratory reports similar to the Taylor cases were present, and 230 had a positive presumptive followed by a "negative," "inconclusive," or "no result" confirmatory test, but this information was omitted from the final report (1.49% of all cases from 1987 to 2003; all death penalty cases were included regardless of timeframe). In 40 of these cases, no suspect was charged. Out of a total of 269 individuals ultimately charged in the remaining 190 cases, 80 are still serving sentences (four are on death row), 3 were executed, and 5 died in prison. In phase two of this review, the 230 cases identified in phase one were reviewed in detail and divided into four categories: (1) cases that mention that the presence of blood is not conclusive, but fail to report that a confirmatory test was conducted and with negative results ('insufficient evidence was observed to allow for the conclusive identification of blood' instead of stating that further [tests were] conducted by the Analyst that failed to confirm the presence of blood"); (2) cases with lab files that contain reports that fail to mention one or more negative or inconclusive confirmatory test(s) and are thus incomplete; (3) cases that contain misleading reports that stated that no further tests were conducted when, in fact, one or more confirmatory tests were conducted with negative or inconclusive results; and (4) cases in which the laboratory test results were overstated or lab notes contradict the reported result (there were five such cases, all handled by Duane Deaver). It was determined that during the relevant time periods, lab files were not routinely produced to an accused defendant. The report concluded that the factors that contributed to these issues ranged from poorly crafted policy, lack of objectivity, the absence of clear report writing guidance, inattention to reporting methods that left too much discretion to the individual analyst, lack of transparency, and ineffective management and oversight of the Forensic Biology Section from 1987 through 2003. The report found that some analysts, when reporting on the results of the series of serology tests conducted to detect and confirm the presence of blood, sometimes omitted the results of multiple confirmatory tests when they were negative or inconclusive. Other analysts would add a qualifying sentence stating that "additional tests failed to confirm the presence of blood." Swecker found that prior to 1997, no standard report language was prescribed by the lab. In an interview with Mark Nelson, who was Forensic Biology Section Chief from December 1, 1986 to April 1, 2002, he admitted that use of the qualifying second sentence described previously was a common practice and that omission of the confirmatory test results was a bad practice and could be confusing. He explained that report writing was discussed at section meetings, but only in the context of how to report positive results and that any policies were never intended to mislead anyone.

The SBI Training Manual in effect during the 1986 to 1997 time period correctly described the difference between a presumptive and confirmatory test and what the results of each meant. No reference was found as to the possibility an "inconclusive" result or a "no result." SBI policy issued in 1997 specifically guided serology analysts that when a presumptive test for the presence of blood or saliva was positive but confirmatory tests yield "inconclusive results or the material is of limiting quantity to do additional testing," the report should read "Examination of _____(Item(s) revealed chemical indications for the presence of _____" (blood or saliva, depending on the test conducted). According to the SBI training manual, the Takayama test was considered a positive result when "visualized microscopically by the formation of salmon colored rhomboidal or stellate crystals." No reference is made to the possibility of an "inconclusive" result or how such a result would appear under a microscope. Some analysts stated that there was no such thing as an "inconclusive" Takayama test since the crystal either formed visually under the microscope or it did not. Other analysts stated that on occasion, it appeared that the crystal was "trying to form" and turning color, but since it did not actually form, they judged the test "inconclusive" or "no result," or even went further to state that the crystal did not form because the evidence material was of such small size that the reagents applied were not able to react. The promulgation of the 1997 language seemed to have little effect on how individual analysts reported serology test results. After 2001, a written policy appeared to permit an analyst to exercise independent judgment if they thought the confirmatory test was inconclusive because there was insufficient material to test and therefore leave out the qualifying language.

The Swecker team found analysts who were trained that there was no such thing as an "inconclusive" result. Every analyst interviewed noted that they were trained that a negative or inconclusive confirmatory result did not mean that blood was not present, but instead that a negative result only meant that the analyst failed to confirm the presence of blood. This is not how the scientific community would interpret those results. Mr. Deaver clarified that says his reports were for law enforcement rather than the justice system as a whole.

Some analysts appeared to apply this recommended language to cases even when their notes reflected a negative test result. For example, in a sampling of lab files assigned to analyst Deaver from 1988 through 1993 in which a positive presumptive test was followed by a negative Takayama test, 34 reports omitted the negative confirmatory test. In five instances, the report stated that "the quantity of stain was insufficient for further testing" or "the quantity of stain was insufficient to test further" when one or sometimes multiple Takayama tests were negative. In total, there were 36 instances involving five different analysts where it was reported that no further tests were conducted due to insufficient quantity of sample when actually a confirmatory test was negative. These reports misstate the facts and leave a reader to believe that no further tests were done. Swecker and his team found anecdotal evidence that some analysts were not objective in their mindset.

Today, confirmatory tests are not always performed on blood samples. If there is a positive in a presumptive, analysts may send it to the DNA section to test for DNA, or sometimes a human species test is used (RSID or ABAcard HemaTrace). Defense attorneys should be sure to elicit testimony that a DNA test on a sample that only has a positive presumptive test does not show that any blood was present.

In the aftermath of the Taylor exoneration. "Jill Spriggs, Chief of the Bureau of Forensic Sciences for the California Department of Justice and the President-Elect of ASCLD (American Society of Crime Laboratory Directors), responded [to a question at a hearing of the North Carolina state legislature], 'That is an accurate statement. A lot of times you got no results. It didn't mean it wasn't blood; it meant you didn't have enough sample, or maybe the sample was old. …What else is red-brown that will give you a positive presumptive test for blood? There's nothing that I know'" (Jamison, 2011). The question has at least two answers, namely rust and soybean roots.

In the Taylor case, the NC SBI failed to report exculpatory testing results and claimed that the Kastle–Meyer test revealed the "presence of blood" (a positive presumptive test only indicates the possibility of blood). Using this case as a cautionary tale, Erin Murphy (Inside the Cell: The Dark Side of Forensic DNA, 2015) discussed the chummy relationship between the ASCLD/LAB (Laboratory Accreditation Board), the accrediting body for many forensic laboratories, and the laboratories that they oversee. "It [ASCLD/LAB] simply argued that that the disputed wording was used by all labs during that period. That assertion, however, was later contradicted by a survey of laboratories, at least eight of which stated that it did not report results in this potentially misleading manner." A lawyer defending a case involving blood cannot rely upon the accreditation status as a guarantee of quality, nor is the language of the reports implicitly trustworthy.

The intensive investigation of this particular lab highlights the pitfalls encountered in blood evidence evaluation. It highlights the need for discovery requests that are comprehensive, the need for analysts who do the testing to testify, the need for attorneys to have the protocols and standards in effect when the testing was done, and for conducting cross-examinations of analysts that uncover the true meaning of what boilerplate report language really means.

The status of a positive luminol result that is not buttressed by further testing (see above) varies from one state to another. There are a number of cases from the US that deal with unsupported luminol evidence. They fall into two basic categories. In one category are cases in which luminol evidence alone is excluded as evidence. Into this category is *Brenk v. State* (Arkansas, 1993) and *Palmer v. State* (Arkansas, 1994). In the *Brenk* case, the court stated, "Since we have determined that luminol tests done without follow-up procedures are unreliable to prove the presence of human blood or that the substance causing the reaction was related to the alleged crime, we find it was error for the trial court to admit the evidence of luminol testing done by Mr. Smith where there was no follow-up testing done to establish that the substance causing the luminol reaction was, in fact, human blood related to the alleged crime."

In a case before the Victorian Supreme Court, *R v. Smart* (2008) VSC 79, Justice Lasry, recognizing the dangers of luminol evidence, stated (at para. 28): "Thus, although I would admit the evidence in relation to the blood stains which are confirmed to be blood by scientific analysis and which produce relevant DNA profiles, I would not admit the evidence in relation to the luminol positive areas where there is no confirmatory testing."

A military trial, *The United States v. Hill (2007)*, is slightly different from other cases in the first category in that four luminol-positive stains were not accepted as evidence, but one stain that also was positive for DNA was accepted. A similar situation holds true in the Crider v. Oklahoma (2001) case. In our judgment, to accept luminol evidence when DNA is present was questionable because the presence of DNA is not a confirmatory test. In the Crider case, the confirmatory test was apparently negative.

The second category includes the cases in which luminol evidence is accepted, but the fact that it is a presumptive test affects its weight as evidence. In this category falls *State v. Canaan* (Kansas, 1998): "The fact that luminol also detects some other substances is irrelevant to its universal acceptance as a presumptive blood test. This fact goes to the weight, not the admissibility, of the evidence. In challenging the weight of this evidence, the defendant elicited testimony that informed the jury that luminol also reacts to other substances." We believe that such an interpretation is problematic for reasons given below.

In the Amanda Knox/Raffaele Sollecito trial for the murder of Meredith Kercher, the interpretation of several luminol-positive stains was contentious. In the bedroom of one of Ms. Knox's and Ms. Kercher's flatmates were two luminol-positive areas. One had mixed DNA from Ms. Knox and Ms. Kercher. Both were negative for blood by TMB, a result that the prosecution failed to disclose in a timely manner. In the hallway were several foot tracks that did not contain DNA and one apparent shoeprint that had mixed DNA and was negative by TMB. In Ms. Knox's room was a foot track that had her DNA but did not resemble her reference footprint. Defense expert witness Sarah Gino testified that in her experience, about half of luminol-positive areas were negative in follow-up testing. The prosecution implied that the only false positives for luminol came from fruit juice, an obviously false statement. None of the luminol-positive stains were documented to have been tested with human-specific antibodies.

A note in Southwestern Law Review discusses some of these questions. The note tackles the question of presumptive and confirmatory drug as well as blood evidence. Both areas of study have the same issues with regards to how the tests are performed, what their results mean, and how those results are or should be presented in court. Like presumptive blood tests, field tests for drugs are used because they are cheap, easy ways to determine if further evaluation of a substance is warranted to identify it as an illegal drug substance. It concludes that a presumptive test alone should never be presented as evidence and further that the presumptive test never needs to be presented at all. If only the confirmatory scientific test is presented at trial, none of the risks of the presumptive test results would exist. However, serious concerns arise if the results of both a confirmatory test and a field color test are presented at trial. He concludes that the confusion surrounding the meaning of presumptive tests cannot even be clarified through an instruction to the jury, stating, "No instruction would be powerful enough to compensate for the undue prejudice relative to their limited probative value; they are bells that would be extremely difficult to un-ring" (Harris, 2011, pp. 546–47).

In the *State of Georgia v. Stephen McDaniel*, the defense moved to exclude certain luminol evidence. Their argument had two prongs. One, there was no confirmatory testing, without which the luminol evidence fell short of being admissible. Two, the defense argued that the failure to make photographs constituted a deviation from what is an acceptable manner of documenting the results. The judge in that case granted defense attorney's motion to exclude the presumptive blood tests. This motion has a very good discussion of luminol overall and would be useful for counsel attempting to prevent a presumptive test alone from coming into evidence. The defendant in that case eventually pled guilty to the crime, as there was other substantial evidence linking him to the murder.

PART III: THE LINDY CHAMBERLAIN CASE

Lindy Chamberlain was tried, convicted, and spent 3 years in prison for the death of her baby in Australia in 1980. Eventually, she and her husband were acquitted on all charges. The handling of blood evidence was at the center of this wrongful conviction. In the Lindy Chamberlain case, the prosecution used a combination of presumptive *ortho*-tolidine test and antibody-based tests to examine items for the presence of blood. The antibody test was intended to detect hemoglobin F (HbF); therefore, it was a type of confirmatory test. The prosecution also performed tests for human plasma proteins to identify the species of blood. The forensic errors that led to the false conviction of

Lindy Chamberlain and her husband Michael in the death of their 9-week-old daughter Azaria involved both errors in the *ortho*-tolidine test and in the test for HbF.

False positives involving the *ortho*-tolidine colorimetric test were observed in the false conviction of Lindy Chamberlain in the death of her infant daughter Azaria. The area in which the Chamberlains lived had extensive copper mining, and copper oxide was present in the atmosphere. Dr. Tony Raymond (2005) wrote, "The original trial scientist, Mrs. Joy Kuhl[,] obtained positive (*ortho*-tolidine) presumptive tests for blood in a number of areas in the Torana (the Chamberlains' car) – including the carpet, bolt hole region, nearside seat hinge, console and items that were purported to have been in the car – a chamois, a towel and a pair of nail scissors. Some of these areas were incidentally inaccessible without the removal (using an appropriate screwdriver) of surface panels." In retrospect the results from inaccessible areas within the Torana should have been interpreted as substrate controls. When a substrate control is positive, it suggests that the substance is present in more than just the stain being tested but also the material to which the stain is bonded. Both Joy Kuhl and her supervisor Dr. Simon Baxter asserted that it was possible to distinguish between blood and other substances (such as peroxidases or metal ions) on the basis of experience, and Kuhl claimed that peroxidases gave a different shade of green. The basis of such a claim is extremely dubious because the colored product in the *ortho*-tolidine test is the same, regardless of the catalyst.

The prosecution claimed that many items tested were positive for HbF; these included a pair of scissors, a towel, a bag, and certain spots in the Chamberlain's car. The implication was that this could only have come from Lindy and Michael's infant daughter Azaria. The defense vigorously contested the finding of HbF. Because the Chamberlains had driven an adult who bled from a scalp injury, simply finding blood in their Torana would not have been surprising; therefore, the prosecution wished to demonstrate that only Azaria could be the source of blood that they might find. To understand this issue, some background on the various forms of hemoglobin is needed.

Fetuses produce HbF, which has a stronger affinity for oxygen than HbA does. The amount of HbF declines after birth, and within a few months, it is a very small fraction of total hemoglobin, less than 1% in most adults. Azaria was about 9 weeks old, and her blood should have contained roughly one-third HbF. HbA is made up of four polypeptide chains, two alpha chains, and two beta chains; HbF is made up of two alpha chains and two gamma chains, which are similar to, but not identical with, beta chains. Each antibody and its cognate antigen are a little bit like a cast and its negative mold; they are complementary to each other in shape and chemical properties. Yet antibodies that bind to hemoglobin (the antigen) bind only to a portion of the molecule (the epitope). In theory, antibodies that are bound only to the gamma chain would be specific for HbF, but antibodies that bound to the alpha chain would not be. The following analogy might be helpful: think of HbA as a Peterbilt 379 tractor hauling a Stoughton grain hauler, and think of HbF as a Peterbilt 379 tractor hauling a Heil liquid trailer. An antibody that recognized the alpha chain (Peterbilt tractor) would bind to both HbA and HbF, whereas an antibody that recognized the Heil trailer (the gamma chain) would be specific for HbF.

One way to decide whether two antigens are the same or different is to perform the Ouchterlony double diffusion experiment. Typically, at least three wells are formed in a plate; an antibody solution is placed in one well, and antigens are placed in the rest. The antibody and antigens diffuse toward each other, and when the conditions are right, they form precipitin (Fig. 8.1). Precipitin is a complex lattice between an antibody of a given specificity and its cognate antigen. The various shapes of the precipitin bands indicate whether or not two antigens in adjacent wells are identical or different substances (Fig. 8.2). More complex patterns are possible.

Another method for detecting precipitin is crossed electrophoresis (countercurrent electrophoresis). Electrophoresis is the movement of charged chemical species in an electric field. When performed on proteins, there is a solid matrix, such as agarose, through which the proteins move. At most values of pH (which measures acidity or alkalinity of a water solution), proteins carry a net charge, but different proteins may have different charges. In the countercurrent electrophoresis experiment, the antibody and antigen start in separate wells and then move in opposite directions to form precipitin.

In the Chamberlain case, Joy Kuhl devised a test for HbF based on countercurrent electrophoresis. There were a number of problems with her test. The first is that the great length of time elapsed between Azaria's death and the tests, and the summer heat favors denaturation of proteins, such as hemoglobin. Denaturation means that the protein has lost its biological activity and shape, and a denatured protein may react differently with antibodies versus a native or fully intact protein.

The second problem was the lack of perfect specificity of the antibodies. In other words, they did not only react with HbF, but instead also reacted with HbA. The manufacturer attempted to remove the antibodies against HbA, leaving only those that were cognate to HbF. Yet the procedure was incomplete, and the antibody preparation still cross-reacted with HbA in an Ouchterlony experiment. A 1983 letter from the manufacturer of the HbF antibodies in response to enquiries from Professor Boettcher stated, "Thirdly, nonspecific immune reactions can be observed under certain conditions due to denaturation of haemoglobin A in adult blood or due to alteration in the relative concentrations of antigen and antibody. Fourthly, the antiserum against haemoglobin F of Behringwerke, therefore, is not suitable on its own for the identification on its own of foetal/infant blood and adult blood."

A third problem is that countercurrent electrophoresis, the main technique that Joy Kuhl used, is inferior to double diffusion in certain respects. The Morling Commission's report indicated that "Prof Ouchterlony said that the cross-over test was developed for rapid clinical diagnosis and required confirmation of results. Dr. Baudner said that the application of electric current could give reactions to proteins other than the desired antibodies" (Australia, 1987). The presence of contaminating antibodies is easy to miss unless the control experiments are performed correctly (Boettcher, 1988).

A fourth problem is that Joy Kuhl's laboratory did not store the electrophoresis plates. Therefore, the defense was not afforded the opportunity to examine the results directly. This objection is made more significant by a number of questions that surrounded her recordkeeping. For example, a small number of photographs of the plates were available, and the appearance of the plates did not always exactly match Ms. Kuhl's notes. Finally, there were also questions about the adequacy of Ms. Kuhl's controls.

Ms. Kuhl claimed to find about 20 samples of HbF from the car. The most remarkable positive finding concerned a sticky spray pattern found under the dashboard and was argued to be arterial spray from Azaria. Yet there were no positive results from *ortho*-tolidine or from antihemoglobin antibody testing. This spray pattern was sound-deadening material, and some other Torana cars also had the same pattern.

Besides the technical problems discussed above, there was one additional finding that should have given the prosecution pause. Some of the reactions between the antibodies and the items of evidence were stronger than the reactions between the antibodies and cord blood, which is opposite to what should have been observed if it were actually HbF being detected. A tendency to ignore information that runs contrary to one's hypothesis was also apparent in the Knox/Sollecito and Patricia Stallings cases, although the serological question in the Stallings case involved a completely different technique.

One of the defense witnesses was Orjan Ouchterlony, the inventor of the double diffusion experiment. In a retrospective lecture on the case, he said, "Contradictory statements concerning relevant seroanalytical problems cause confusion heightened by inadequacy in the present law system for handling scientific matters. The outcome of the trial is very questionable to say the least. My own interest for the case, to begin with attracted by the serology involved, has extended to thoughts about certain flaws in the forensic system concerning the transfer of scientific information. In that precinct law and science are presently living in a marriage of inconvenience which in the Chamberlain case miscarried" (Ouchterlony, 1987). Although progress has been made since the time of the Chamberlains' exoneration, regrettably, the task remains unfinished.

SUMMARY

Several themes are apparent. The prosecution is apt to overstate the implication of a positive result from a presumptive test. The prosecution may be unwilling to disclose exculpatory information. Forensic analysts' reports and testimony in court may be full of misleading wording as well as faulty conclusions. A prudent defense attorney will make sure to ask for all underlying materials from analysts and not simply rely on a final report to disclose all pertinent information. Defense attorneys should also file appropriate motions regarding excluding presumptive test results altogether and especially if no confirmatory test or a negative or inconclusive confirmatory test is present. Lastly, defense counsel should prepare cross-examination questions for analysts or proffer expert testimony that address all of the potential trouble areas presented here.

WEB-BASED RESOURCES

http://what-when-how.com/forensic-sciences/blood-identification/
http://www.ncids.com/forensic/
http://www.aoc.state.nc.us/www/ids/Defender%20Training/2005%20
Spring%20Conference/SBI_Tests-paper.pdf
http://www.corpus-delicti.com/forensic_mis.html
https://www.ncjrs.gov/pdffiles1/nij/grants/228091.pdf
http://www.nist.gov/forensics/workgroups.cfm
http://www.criminalistics.com/ethics.html
http://www.aafs.org/wp-content/uploads/Bylaws.pdf
http://www.cacnews.org/membership/handbook.shtml
http://www.innocencecommission-nc.gov/
http://www.wral.com/asset/news/local/2009/09/16/6014105/79539-
TRANSCRP.pdf
Swecker Report, found at: http://www.ncdoj.gov/News-and-Alerts/News-
Releases-and-Advisories/Related-Information/Independent-Review-of-SBI-
Forensic-LAB.aspx
State v. McDaniel: http://legacy.13wmaz.com/story/news/local/
macon/2013/12/12/stephen-mcdaniel-court-hearing/3997269 and
http://archive.13wmaz.com/news/pdf/318MotiontoExcludeLuminol.pdf
http://www.betterconsult.com.au/blog/the-dangers-associated-with-
presumptive-testing/
http://dfs.dc.gov/sites/default/files/dc/sites/dfs/page_content/attachments/
FBS02%20KM%20Testing.pdf
http://www.amandaknoxcase.com/luminol/

ACKNOWLEDGMENTS

The authors are grateful to Professor Barry Boettcher, Professor Igor Lednev, Michael Klinkosum, and Joel Schwartz for helpful discussions.

REFERENCES

Altman, D.G., Bland, J.M., 1994. Diagnostic tests 1: sensitivity and specificity. British Medical Journal 308, 1552.
Australia Royal Commission of Inquiry into Chamberlain Convictions, 1987. Report of the Commissioner the Hon. Mr. Justice T.R. Morling/Royal Commission of Inquiry into Chamberlain Convictions, p. 379.
Barni, F., Lewis, S.W., Berti, A., Miskelley, G.M., Lago, G., 2007. Forensic application of the luminol reaction as a presumptive test for latent blood detection. Talanta 72, 896–913.
Boettcher, 1988. Contaminating antibodies may produce unexpected reactions in counter-current immunoelectrophoresis. Medicine, Science, and Law 28 (4), 336–340.

Brenk v. State, 847 S.W.2d 1, 311 Ark. 579 (1993).

Castro D.M., Coyle H.M. Biological Evidence Collection and Forensic Blood Identification, unpublished manuscript.

Cox, M., 1991. A study of the sensitivity and specificity of four presumptive tests for blood. Journal of Forensic Sciences 36 (5), 1503–1511.

Crider v. State of Oklahoma, Case No. F-99-1422, Court of Criminal Appeals OK (2001).

Garrett, B.L., Neufeld, P.J., March 2009. Invalid Forensic Science, Testimony and Wrongful Convictions. 95 Va. L. Rev. 1. Available at: http://www.virginialawreview.org/volumes/content/invalid-forensic-science-testimony-and-wrongful-convictions.

Grispino, R.R.J., 1991. Luminol and the crime scene. Prosecutor 25 (1), 28–32.

Harris, A., 2011. A test of a different color: the limited value of presumptive field drug tests and why that value demands their exclusion from trial. Southwestern Law Review 40, 531–550.

Jamieson, P., 2011. Top State Forensic Analyst under Fire for Defending Disgraced NC Crime Lab. SF Weekly January 28.

Kobilinsky, L., Liotti, T.F., Oeser-Sweat, J., 2004. DNA: Forensic and Legal Applications. Wiley-Interscience, p. 392.

Murphy, J., Bustin, S.A., 2009. Reliability of real-time reverse transcription PCR in clinical diagnostics: gold standard or substandard? Expert Review of Molecular Diagnostics 9 (2), 187–197.

Ouchterlony, O., 1987. Immunoprecipitation in court-the chamberlain case. International Archives of Allergy and Applied Immunology 82, 233–237.

Palmer v. State, 870 S.W.2d 385, 315 Ark. 696 (1994).

Peel, C., Gill, P., 2004. Attribution of DNA profiles to body fluid stains. International Congress Series 1261, 53–54.

People v. Lovejoy, 235 Ill. 2d 97, 138-9 (2009).

Petersen, D., Kovacs, F., 2014. Phenolphthalein false-positive reactions from legume root nodules. Journal of Forensic Sciences 59 (2), 481–484.

Raymond, T., 2005. Law and forensic science in the criminal trial process: the Lindy Chamberlain case. In: 10th Greek Australian Legal and Medical Conference, Mykonos, Greece, 2005.

State of Mo. v. Faria, Cause No. 12L6-CR01312.

State v. Canaan, 964 P.2d 681 (Kansas, United States, 1998).

State v. George Earl Goode, Jr., 92CRS2661-62, 92CRS2569, 2570, Johnston County, North Carolina.

State v. Russell Scott Faria, Case No. 12L6-CR01312, Lincoln County, MO (2012).

State v. Taylor, 91CRS71728, Wake County, North Carolina (1993).

Tobe, S.S., Watson, N., Nic Daeid, N., 2007. Evaluation of six presumptive tests for blood, their specificity, sensitivity, and effect on high molecular-weight DNA. Journal of Forensic Sciences 52, 102–109.

United States v. Rodney T. Hill, 473 F.3d 112 (4th Cir. 2007).

Virkler, K., Lednev, I.K., 2009. Analysis of body fluids for forensic purposes: from laboratory testing to non-destructive rapid confirmatory identification at a crime scene. Forensic Science International 188 (1–3), 1–17.

Bloodstain Pattern Analysis

CHAPTER OUTLINE

Forensic Science Reform. http://dx.doi.org/10.1016/B978-0-12-802719-6.00009-1

Case Study: David Camm

Wendy J. Koen

Child Refuge, Inc., Menifee, CA, United States

David Camm

Facts are stubborn things; and whatever may be our wishes, our inclinations, or the dictates of our passions, they cannot alter the state of facts and evidence.

John Adams

When a crime is heinous and rocks a community to its core, it is in our nature to make sure that someone pays. In our need for retribution, we often target whoever appears to be the most likely culprit and then form a case based on our initial conclusion. David Camm was a perfect target. His wife and two small children were gunned down in their garage; Camm was a serial adulterer, and he was easy to demonize. Investigators immediately honed in on him because of the way he paced and failed to make eye contact on the night of the murders. In the end, although 11 other men were playing basketball with him at the time his family was killed, as far as the State was concerned, Camm was really the only logical suspect.

The apparent smoking gun was what experts characterized as high-velocity mist or high-velocity impact spatter (HVIS). When a person is shot, in some instances, blow-back from the wound leaves a unique mist-like pattern of blood spatter on anyone or anything that is within 4 feet of the shooting (Englert and Passero, 2010). Camm had eight tiny spots of blood on his t-shirt that some thought fit that unique pattern.

Camm's nightmare began on the evening of September 28, 2000. Kim Camm and her children, 7-year-old Bradley and 5-year-old Jill, were shot to death in their garage at their home in Georgetown (*Camm v. State*, 2004). The shooting took place at around 7:30, after Kim and the two children arrived home from Bradley's swimming practice.

David Camm, a former state police officer, was playing basketball at a nearby church from 7:00 to 9:20p.m. After basketball, Camm drove home and opened his garage door. He immediately found Kim, who had been shot in the head and was obviously dead. Her body was lying on the garage floor next to her Ford Bronco. Camm then looked for his children. He found them inside the Bronco. Jill had been shot in the head, and Camm could tell immediately that she was dead. Bradley had been shot in the chest, and Camm thought Bradley might still be alive. Camm climbed into the front seat of the two-door Bronco, over the center console into the backseat area, reached for Bradley over Jill's body, removed him from the far left side of the rear seat, carried him back out of the truck, laid him on the garage floor next to Kim's body, and performed CPR. CPR could not revive Bradley, who had lost a great volume of blood from the wound to his chest. Camm called the police for help using the phone in the kitchen, ran across the street where his grandfather lived, and told his uncle of the nightmare he had walked into.

The police collected the bloodstained t-shirt, shoes, and socks Camm was wearing on the night of the murders (*Camm v. State*, 2009). Police submitted these items to a blood pattern analyst. The analyst concluded that eight tiny bloodstains found on a corner of Camm's shirt were HVIS resulting from a gunshot. Testing of some of the stains later confirmed that these bloodstains matched 5-year-old Jill's blood. Based in large part on the blood evidence, the State charged David Camm with the murders of Kim, Bradley, and Jill Camm.

Initially, phone records appeared to indicate that David Camm was at home at 7:20, making a business call from his landline. This evidence placed him at the scene at the time of the murder and led investigators to disregard statements from Camm's basketball team that placed Camm at a basketball game. This evidence also started an investigative trajectory that would cause the state to ignore pieces of evidence that seemed unimportant in their case against Camm, but would have blown the case wide open and led them immediately to the actual perpetrator. By the time investigators learned that the phone records were wrong—the business call was made at 6:30 that night—and the basketball team was right, they had decided that Camm was their man. The small problem of Camm's alibi was simply explained away; Camm must have snuck out during the basketball game, killed his family, and snuck back into the recreation center to play some more basketball. Conveniently, no one noticed him leave or return, and no one noticed the blood on his shirt or shoes.

TRIAL 1

At trial, the State used expert testimony to establish that while some of the stains on Camm's clothing were the result of transfer, some of the bloodstains on Camm's clothing, the eight tiny spots, could only be characterized as HVIS (*Camm v. State*, 2009). This evidence of HVIS was offered as proof that Camm shot his daughter Jill or was within a few feet of Jill when she was shot. Camm's defense was that none of the stains were from HVIS, but were all the result of transfer; his clothing came into contact with Kim, Bradley, and Jill's bodies when he discovered them and their blood was transferred to his clothing through the contact (*Camm v. State*, 2009).

The reliability of expert testimony regarding HVIS was the subject of a pretrial hearing. The State maintained that the reliability of BPA was well established by state and national legal precedent. The State also reminded the court that "[i]t should be unnecessary to revisit scientific techniques already deemed to have achieved sufficient general acceptance" (*Camm v. State*, 2009; citing Miller, 2007).

Camm's defense team acknowledged the general acceptance of blood pattern evidence, but contended that the expert's authority was not applicable here (*Camm v. State*, 2009). The State was hoping to establish that Camm was the shooter, not based on a bloodstain pattern or an article of clothing covered with HVIS, but based on an article of clothing with eight tiny spots that looked like HVIS. The defense contended there was simply no way for any expert to determine conclusively whether the eight tiny stains were from HVIS or from transfer due to physical contact, and allowing an expert to testify that the stains could only have come from HVIS was not scientifically sound and would unfairly prejudice the jury. The difference between what was reliable expert testimony and what was mere speculation was the difference between the examination of blood patterns and the examination of blood spots. As we will see later, BPA is a discipline; blood spot analysis is not.

The court ruled in favor of the State, and the expert testimony came in, placing Camm within 4 feet of Jill at the time of her shooting. At trial, the State presented bloodstain analysis testimony from five experts. Each witness testified that the eight tiny spots on the defendant's shirt were the result of HVIS. The defense called four bloodstain experts. Each of these experts testified that all of the bloodstains on Camm's shirt were the result of transfer.

THE GRAY SWEATSHIRT

Because Camm was their man, a gray sweatshirt, not belonging to anyone known to the Camm family and found under Bradley's body in the garage, was generally disregarded by investigators. The sweatshirt held clues that should have sent investigators scrambling. It had several bloodstains. Two of the bloodstains came from Kim and Bradley Camm. A third bloodstain contained an unknown DNA profile. The inside rear collar area, which typically contains the wearer's DNA, also contained an unknown DNA profile. The unknown profiles were not run through the DNA database before Camm's first trial, although the prosecutor assured the defense that the profile was run and no match was found. Startlingly, the sweatshirt was prison-issued clothing; whoever owned the shirt had likely spent time in state prison. Even more telling, the shirt had the name "Backbone" written on the inside of the back collar. Although Camm and his defense team always considered this evidence the real smoking gun in the case and fought to have it investigated as such, the investigator's confidence in their scientific proof, what they characterized as HVIS on Camm's t-shirt, kept them from looking any farther than David Camm.

CAMM'S CHARACTER

The State introduced a parade of witnesses to offer evidence of Camm's extramarital relationships and presented testimony from 12 different women with who Camm had engaged in varying levels of intimacy. Testimony about everything from simple flirting to full-blown affairs was offered as evidence of Camm's defective character and his motive to kill his wife and children. The State contended that Camm had a defect in his character that allowed him to engage in these extramarital relationships (*Camm v. State*, 2004).

Based on the medical examiner's testimony that 5-year-old Jill had trauma to her genital region that was consistent with molestation or a straddle fall, the State put forth the theory that Camm molested Jill and then murdered Jill and the rest of his family to escape detection. There were several reasons the State's theory was highly and unfairly prejudicial. First, the injury could have had an innocent explanation. Straddle injuries can be the result of a myriad of innocent accidents, such a fall onto a bike or a scooter or a slip getting into or out of a bathtub (Saxena et al., 2014). Second, if Jill had been the victim of sexual molestation, someone other than Camm could have molested her. Nevertheless, the State pressed the theory that Camm molested Jill. Although the jury was left to weigh whether any of the myriad of innocent explanations were adequate or whether Camm had violated his daughter, the mere allegation of child molestation is often enough to incite a jury. Based on the evidence of Camm's affairs and the spurious allegations of child abuse, combined with the HVIS evidence, Camm was convicted of three counts of murder and sentenced to 195 years in prison.

THE APPEAL

Camm appealed his conviction, arguing that the parade of witnesses to his infidelity unfairly prejudiced the jury. The court of appeal reversed Camm's conviction and found that the State's contention that Camm had a defect in his character that allowed him to engage in extramarital relationships was improper. This contention amounted to an admission that the evidence of Camm's infidelity was presented to the jury to establish Camm's poor character and that Camm was more likely to kill his wife and children because of that poor character. Evidence used for this purpose is explicitly prohibited by law. The law prohibits the State from securing the conviction of a defendant based on the defendant's defective character.

In addition, the court of appeal cautioned the trial court that evidence of Jill's genital injury was irrelevant unless it could be established that Jill was actually molested and that it was Camm who molested her.

TRIAL 2

Before Camm was tried for a second time, his defense team reasserted the necessity that the unknown DNA on the gray sweatshirt be run through the FBI's national database. The DNA came back as a match to Charles "Backbone" Boney (*Camm v. State*, 2009). Boney's DNA profile was in the FBI database before the first trial. If the prosecution had run the sweatshirt stains through the database, Boney would have been identified.

The police questioned Boney and he admitted the sweatshirt was his, but he said he had donated the shirt to the Salvation Army a month or two before the murders (*Boney v. State*, 2008). Boney denied knowing Camm, having been at the crime scene or being involved in the murders until investigators revealed they had found Boney's handprint on the Bronco. This handprint was dismissed at the first trial by the prosecution's expert as probably one of the children's, even though no comparison was possible due to the poor-quality fingerprint standards taken of the children's hands at autopsy.

Although Boney offered several iterations of the events taking place the night of the murders, he finally settled on the story that he was at Camm's house the night of the murders, but he was only there to sell Camm a gun. He told investigators that he was outside the garage when Camm killed his family.

However, Boney's presence at the crime scene should have diverted the investigator's focus away from Camm. Boney had a foot and shoe fetish (*Camm v. State*, 2009). He had four felony convictions for robbery in which he attacked women in order to steal their shoes (Boyd, 2005). The violence committed by Boney in order to complete his crimes had been escalating over time. In the 1980s, Boney was the Bloomington Shoe Bandit. He was arrested after several attacks where he tackled women to the ground and stole their shoes (Boyd, 2005). He was convicted of robbery and assault. In 1992, after he served time for these attacks and was released, he graduated to the use of firearms. In a 2-week period, he robbed an office at gunpoint and then he held three women against their will (Boyd, 2005). Boney was convicted of these crimes and served several years of a 20-year sentence. Just a few months after his release, Kim, Bradley, and Jill Camm were murdered.

All of these details about Boney should have alerted investigators that their initial investigative trajectory was simply wrong. Knowledge about Boney and his past crimes, when considered in light of the crime scene, pointed to a sexual assault and robbery gone wrong. Kim Camm was found with her pants pulled down and her feet bruised. Her shoes had been removed from her feet and were place neatly on the roof of the Bronco by someone taller than Kim Camm (*Camm v. State*, 2009). As here, Boney's previous fetish-related crimes were committed in parking garages and involved strangers. He had graduated to the use of guns, or at least the threat of guns, to subdue his victims. It is certainly not too much of a leap to consider that Boney's impulses were escalating. It has long been known that fetish-related burglary can escalate to murder (Schlesinger and Revitch, 1999).

However, investigators were so married to Camm as the perpetrator that they could not admit their initial instincts were wrong. It did not matter that Camm had a clear alibi. They welcomed Boney's explanation that Boney and Camm met accidently and Camm asked Boney to get him a gun. They accepted Boney's story that he delivered the gun to Camm the night of the murder and stood just outside the garage as Camm killed his family. They failed to see the absurdity of their new theory: a man with a foot fetish assisting a former state trooper with the murder of the trooper's family. Although Boney was charged and convicted of murdering Camm's family in a separate trial, Camm was charged and convicted in his second trial, with Boney portrayed as his partner in crime.

At his second trial, Camm was convicted in large part due to evidence that Jill had been sexually molested within 24 h of her death. The prosecution stacked speculation upon speculation and created a motive for Camm to kill his family. Jill had nonspecific injuries. Experts opined before the jury that Jill was painfully molested, she must have been molested by her father, she must have told her mother that her father molested her, Kim must have decided to leave Camm, and must have told him so that night, giving Camm motive to kill his wife and family. However, because the record is entirely void of any thread of proof that Camm molested Jill, the court of appeal, once again, overturned Camm's conviction and ordered a new trial.

TRIAL 3

During Camm's third and final trial, Boney testified, consistent with his story, that he had met Camm by chance and Camm had purchased two guns from him. Boney testified that he delivered the second gun on the night of the murders. The gun was wrapped in Boney's gray sweatshirt. According to Boney's testimony, Boney was outside the garage when Camm shot Kim, Bradley, and Jill.

In addition, the prosecutor elicited testimony about Camm's demeanor after the murders, demonstrating for the jury that Camm did not act like a grieving husband and father should and was too concerned about collecting life insurance money (Alter, 2013). In fact, the lead investigator immediately *knew* that Camm was guilty based on Camm's demeanor alone.

In addition to testimony about Camm's demeanor, there were two major differences in Camm's third trial (Alter, 2013). First, advancements in DNA testing allowed more sensitive analyses to occur. Touch DNA testing revealed that Boney had touched Kim's underwear, sweater, and shirt. This evidence was contrary to Boney's testimony that he only touched Kim's shoes and he never touched Kim Camm. The touch DNA evidence supported the theory that Boney acted alone, and the attack on Kim was motivated by Boney's sexual fetish. The second difference was an expert analysis of the blood evidence.

BLOOD PATTERN EVIDENCE

Just how eight tiny spots of Jill's blood were deposited on Camm's t-shirt was the central issue in this case (*Camm v. State*, 2004). As did the first two trials, Camm's third trial centered around the eight tiny spots of blood found on Camm's shirt (Davis, 2013). Three forensic experts testified that the stains were HVIS due to the size— each spot less than 1 mm—and ovoid shape (Alter, 2013; Boyd, 2013). The experts were certain the spots were HVIS because they were soaked into the fabric's weave and were not just on the fabric surface (Alter, 2013). The prosecutor considered the tiny spots of blood on Camm's shirt the most compelling evidence that Camm killed his wife and children (Boyd, 2013).

Camm's defense experts had a more innocent explanation. They testified that the tiny spots of blood were transfer. Blood in Jill's hair beaded up at the tips. When Camm reached past Jill's body to remove Bradley from the Bronco, the beaded blood on the tips of Jill's hair touched Camm's shirt. The tiny spots of blood soaked into the weave of the fabric and left the stains (Alter, 2013; Boyd, 2013). As discussed thoroughly by blood pattern analyst, Barie Goetz, in the following sections, using scientific methods, experimentation, and deductive reasoning, proper analysis revealed the spots of blood were caused by transfer and not blowback.

In addition, Eugene Liscio, an engineer from Toronto, Ontario, presented to the jury a 3-D reenactment based on instrument scans of the Bronco and the bullet trajectories into the children's bodies. This reenactment clearly demonstrated that the front left area of the shooter was not in the line of sight for blowback from Jill's head wound. Thus, the eight tiny spots could not have been produced by Camm shooting Jill.

There were other major differences in the interpretation of the bloodstains. The State hoped to prove that Camm shot Jill, who was strapped into her seatbelt in the back of the Bronco, at such close range that the blood blowback from Jill's head wound stained Camm's shirt. One of the experts for the defense testified that spatter stains on the roll bar of the Bronco proved that Camm was not the shooter (Boyd, 2013). The stains on the roll bar were from blowback from Jill's gunshot wound, and they each measured from 2 to 4 mm in diameter. The stains on Camm's shirt were much smaller. Basically, if the eight tiny spots on Camm's shirt came from blowback from shooting Jill, the spots on Camm's shirt would have been much larger and more similar to the spots on the roll bar (Boyd, 2013).

There were some major differences in the backgrounds of the experts who testified for the police and the defense experts. The prosecution experts had their background and experience in police work; they were not scientists. The defense experts were scientists with extensive education who had earned their stripes in the lab, and their expertise was founded in science (Alter, 2013). In the end, the jury appeared to be convinced by the defense experts, and after 10 h of deliberation, Camm was found not guilty.

Camm's legal nightmare ended with the verdict for acquittal, but the price he and society paid was enormous. Even though substantial evidence of Boney's guilt pointed away from Camm, the error that sent the police and prosecutors on the wrong trajectory—their early rush to judgment and fixation on Camm due to what they believed was HVIS—led to three costly and unnecessary trials. Camm's trials and related expenses cost the county $4.4 million (Schneider, 2013). The human toll was greater. Added to Camm's horrifying discovery of the bodies of his wife and small children was the terror of being accused of their murders and the 13-year-long struggle to prove he was not their killer. The victims' family and friends also were forced to endure the colossal legal struggle, many of them buying into the prosecution's fixation on Camm upon learning of Camm's infidelity. In the end, although Camm is not in prison, everyone lost a great deal because of a faulty interpretation of eight tiny spots of blood.

REFERENCES

Alter, M., 2013. Camm Trial in Review. Available at: http://www.wlky.com/news/local-news/david-camm/camm-trial-in-review/22429352.

Boney v. State, 2008. 880 N.E.2d 279 (Ind. Ct. App. 2008).

Boyd, J., 2005. Accused Killer was on Early Prison Release. Herald Times Online. Available at: http://ww.heraldtimesonline.com//stories/2005/03/09/news.new.1110431877.sto?code=ac9d21b4-3a05-11e5-97eb-10604b9f2f2e.

Boyd, G., 2013. Defense Analyst Says Pattern Evidence Supports Camm's Version of Events, WAVE News. Available at: http://www.wave3.com/story/23595726/camm-trial-102-defense-analyst-says-pattern-evidence-supports-camms-version-of-events.

Camm v. State, 2004. 812 N.E.2d 1127 (Ind. Ct. App. 2004).

Camm v. State, 2009. 908 N.E.2d 215 (Ind. Ct. App. 2009).

Davis, L., 2013. Former Indiana trooper David Camm found not guilty after 3rd trial in Family's Slaying. ABC News. http://abcnews.go.com/US/indiana-trooper-david-camm-found-guilty-3rd-trial/story?id=20678578.

Englert, R., Passero, K., 2010. Blood Secrets: Chronicles of a Crime Scene Reconstructionist. Macmillan.

Miller Jr., R.L., 2007. Courtroom Handbook on Indiana Evidence 236. (West 2007-08).

Saxena, A.K., Steiner, M., Höllwarth, M.E., 2014. Straddle injuries in female children and adolescents: 10-year accident and management analysis. The Indian Journal of Pediatrics 81 (8), 766–769.

Schlesinger, L.B., Revitch, E., 1999. Sexual burglaries and sexual homicide: clinical, forensic, and investigative considerations. Journal of the American Academy of Psychiatry and the Law Online 27 (2), 227–238.

Schneider, G., 2013. $1.1 million David Camm trial strapping Floyd County budget. The Courier-Journal. Available at: http://archive.courier-journal.com/article/20130929/NEWS02/309290054/-1-1-million-David-Camm-trial-strapping-Floyd-County-budget.

Bloodstain Pattern Analysis

Barie Goetz

Sangre de Cristo Forensic Services, Parker, PA, United States; Pennsylvania State University, Sharon, PA, United States

Bloodstain pattern analysis, or blood spatter analysis, as it is mistakenly called at times, is the examination of the physical aspects of the production of bloodstains during crimes of violence to potentially determine the sequence of events that occurred after blood was let. This discipline differs from the testing of blood for identification and the individualization of the source that is conducted by serologists and DNA analysts, although the procedures that identify the source of the blood give the bloodstain pattern analyst vital information and thus play an important role in bloodstain pattern analysis. The International Association of Bloodstain Pattern Analysts (IABPA) propounds that "information gained from bloodstain patterns can be used for the reconstruction of incidents and the evaluation of the statements from witnesses and the crime participants." Here, we will look at the acquisition and use of that information, starting with the history of its use and the general tenets of BPA, and then taking a detailed look at how BPA affected the trials of David Camm.

HISTORY AND EVOLUTION OF BLOODSTAIN PATTERN ANALYSIS

As long as there have been violent crimes involving the spilling of blood, there have been investigators observing and drawing conclusions from the bloodstains left behind. Scientists have been developing theories and writing treatises on bloodstain pattern interpretation since the 1800s (Laber et al., 2014). As early as 1850, scientists in Europe began to systematically study bloodstain patterns left behind at crime scenes in order to understand what had occurred (Bevel and Gardner, 2008). In 1895, Dr. Eduard Piotrowski conducted experiments using live animals to produce and study bloodstains and published the book, *Concerning Origin, Shape, Direction, and Distribution of Bloodstains Following Blow Injuries to the Head*. His work and research methods were scientifically advanced and provided a text that was unparalleled in his day (Bevel and Gardner, 2008). In the early 1900s, Hans Gross's volume on criminal investigations included a section on the use of bloodstains and became the go-to handbook for investigators of the day (Gross, 1907).

In 1955, Dr. Paul L. Kirk examined the bloodstain patterns at the scene of the murder of Marilyn Sheppard as part of the appeal process for her husband, Samuel Holmes Sheppard, M.D. (Sheppard v. Maxwell, 1966.). The Sam Sheppard case is another example of a premature determination of guilt. The police investigators were under a great deal of media pressure to solve the murder of Marilyn Sheppard. Like the David Camm case, police zeroed in on Sheppard because of his adultery and his unnaturally detached and cool manner of describing the events of that night. Sheppard was arrested for his wife's murder and then tried and convicted in what the appeal court would later label a mockery of justice. After his conviction, a handyman who worked at the Sheppard house admitted to having Marilyn's rings and to bleeding at the scene. He was later convicted of another woman's murder, but never charged with Marilyn Sheppard's.

After Sheppard's conviction, Dr. Kirk examined the preserved scene, observed the bloodstain patterns at the scene, reviewed the autopsy, and read the police reports and witness statements. He conducted experiments to prove or disprove various hypotheses. Using the physical evidence, deductive reasoning, scientific methods, and their interrelationships, Dr. Kirk learned explicit knowledge of the series of events that surrounded the commission of that crime. Based on his skill and professional habits as a scientist, he used the method that would be outlined by the members of the Association for Crime Scene Reconstruction decades later. Dr. Kirk's testimony concerning his interpretation of bloodstains and the conclusions he made were key in producing an acquittal at the 1966 retrial. Dr. Kirk and his staff continued studying bloodstain patterns after the trial, a trait of true scientists.

Dr. Kirk's work was updated and expanded in 1971 when Herbert Leon MacDonnell and Lorraine Fiske Bialousz authored a pamphlet for the National Institute of Law Enforcement and Criminal Justice, which became the National Institute of Justice, titled *Flight Characteristics and Stain Patterns of Human Blood* (MacDonell and Bialousz, 1972). Those 29 pages of text and 48 pages of charts, graphs, and photographs launched bloodstain pattern analysis into the mainstream of forensic science in the US. In the years following this publication, MacDonnell began teaching a weeklong basic course on the interpretation of bloodstains at crime scenes. Students of that course then started instructing their own 40-h basic schools. Slowly, the discipline spread across the US and the world. Today, the IABPA has resources for blood pattern analysts in the US, Australia, New Zealand, China, Denmark, Holland, Finland, France, Germany, Israel, Korea, Portugal, Spain, and Turkey (International Association of Blood Pattern Analysts). Given the handy charts available that tell you what general blood pattern characteristics indicate (Bandyopadhyay and Basu, 2015), you can even go online and analyze a case yourself (Slemko Forensic Consulting).

It would appear that the analysis of bloodstain patterns is straightforward and the skill and knowledge necessary to analyze bloodstain patterns can be quickly and easily attained. As we will see, bloodstain pattern analysis is not that simple, and the uncertainties and variabilities associated with the analysis of bloodstain patterns are vast (Attinger et al., 2013; Larkin, 2015). Still, like many forensic sciences, bloodstain pattern interpretation was introduced and deemed acceptable to courts worldwide without rigorous validation (Laber et al., 2014).

THE MACDONNELL/BIALOUSZ PAMPHLET

My first introduction to bloodstain pattern analysis was in 1976 during graduate school. As part of our Forensic Science program at the University of Pittsburgh in the US, we duplicated the patterns and lessons outlined in the MacDonnell pamphlet. Later, I would attend multiple basic and advanced courses from an assortment of instructors. A symposium first exposed me to how badly some practitioners were interpreting bloodstain patterns. Participants in the symposium presented cases that they had personally analyzed. They shared the results they obtained and the conclusions they planned to present before juries. Some of the logic in the presentations was obviously flawed, containing misinterpretations of bloodstain patterns and conclusions far beyond what the physical evidence supported. It became clear to me that the simplification of the tenets of BPA and the 1-week courses instantly making investigators into bloodstain pattern analysis experts were weakening the discipline.

THE ROLE OF LAW ENFORCEMENT INSTRUCTORS

To further understand how the discipline of bloodstain pattern interpretation has evolved, we need to look at the instructors of bloodstain pattern courses and their students. Many of the instructors that hold weeklong basic schools in bloodstain pattern interpretation are active or retired police officers. Their students are mostly police officers whose duties included crime scene investigation. Police officers instructing police officers is a desirable thing unless the training officer is not qualified or some of the material being taught is not accurate or is incomplete. When an instructing officer is inaccurate, instead of one individual officer misinterpreting bloodstain patterns, a class full of officers is trained to make the same mistakes.

Officers training officers is also questionable because the subject, when treated properly, requires a deep understanding of scientific principles, the use of experimentation, and the scientific method, and the application of biology, physics, and mathematics. For bloodstain pattern analysis to function as an objective science, and to move it from the list of subjective pseudo-sciences that have no place in the courtroom, its principles and practices cannot be simplified by the extraction of the science that would make them reliable (Larkin, 2015). One-week courses cannot hope to instill the depth of knowledge developed in an academic setting during years of tuition.

Weeklong basic bloodstain pattern classes are dangerous because, even if the instructor is well-qualified, that instructor has no control over the students or their analyses or conclusions after the week ends. Graduates of the course could be 1-week wonders who testify incorrectly on the basis of observing a few isolated stains, or they could realize that 40 h was just the beginning of their training. They could start work as an apprentice with other examiners. They could conduct experiments to verify their findings. It is the job of the attorney to only rely on the analyst who has adequate training and experience, and to refuse to rely on an analyst who has minimum training but has been vetted as an expert witness and is willing to support the attorney's theory of the case.

Arson analysis in the US parallels this phenomenon. Investigators with little or no scientific background taught other police officers how to determine if a fire was arson or not. They were not scientists and they conducted no experiments; there was no questioning of methods, and there were no reenactments. As addressed in Chapter 3, multiple individuals have been wrongfully convicted of arson because investigators did not do the experiments and did not use scientific methods. Instead, they relied on myths passed from officer to trainee. The problems that developed with arson investigation are mimicked in BPA. What one officer believes and teaches becomes folklore for an entire community of officers.

IS BLOODSTAIN PATTERN ANALYSIS SIMPLE?

In her comprehensive 513-page thesis entitled "*Bloodstain pattern analysis: scratching the surface*," British doctoral candidate Bethany Larkin examined the nature of bloodstain pattern analysis (BPA) (Larkin, 2015). In the abstract, Larkin opined:

The nature of BPA has given the illusion that its evidentiary significance is less than that of fingerprints or DNA, relying solely on the interpretation of the analyst and focusing very little on any scientific evaluation. Recent preliminary literature studies have involved a more quantitative approach, developing directly crime scene applicable equations and methodology, which have established new ways of predicting the angle of impact, impact velocity, point of origin of blood and blood pattern type

Larkin (2015)

> **IS BLOODSTAIN PATTERN ANALYSIS SIMPLE?—Cont'd**
>
> Two points can be made. First, the title of the thesis is telling: BPA is complex, and as reflected in its title, Larkins' well-researched and drafted thesis, although over 500 pages of informative, dense text, merely scratches the surface. Secondly, it is clear that contemporary jurisprudence has no place for the type of interpretation that relies solely on the analyst's intuition, and BPA today and in the future must depend on a quantitative approach. In this way, BPA will be better validated as a respected scientific field (Larkin, 2015).

THE NEED FOR TRUE SCIENTISTS

Scientists function differently than most police officers. Scientists have foundational knowledge that allows them to view evidence with a broader lens. They are trained to question and then find the truth. They have a different view of the world. Scientists want to know how things work, what makes them tick, and how their function can be improved. They study phenomena and are expected to question everything. Scientists do not take things for granted; they do not believe something until they have duplicated it on their own.

Scientists also are eager to share what they have discovered in order for their theories to be validated and expanded upon. Testing of colleagues' hypotheses proliferates and enhances the new theory. If a colleague in some way disproves or challenges a theory, the community seeks to understand how and why, increasing the general understanding of a field. A real scientist is always searching for truth. This trait should make the scientist a perfect partner for law enforcement and our systems of justice.

However, the nature of the adversarial system throws a wrench in the productive workings of the scientific method. The truth is not always the treasure being sought in court. Cooperation and a continued quest to understand another scientist's theories or results are often replaced with stubborn polarization. Scientists cease acting as scientists, dig in their heels, and the learning stops.

It is because of the nature of litigation that, in some instances, an investigator with minimal bloodstain pattern interpretation skills but with a specific suspect in mind and a theory that inculpates that suspect will be viewed as a greater asset than a pure scientist with no agenda but the truth. Obviously, this devalues the integrity of bloodstain pattern analysis and endangers innocent defendants.

It is up to attorneys and courts to seek out the services of experts who rely on scientific methods to develop theories and explanations based on a thorough understanding of the evidence. It may be that some officers, trained by other officers, with limited education in the scientific method, will have the skills necessary for this task. It is up to the hiring attorney to ensure this type of expert witness is truly capable of preforming the required analyses.

Conversely, some exquisitely trained scientists with magnificent credentials will go into court and parrot what one party hopes to hear, truth be damned. Attorneys must be vigilant and refuse to perpetuate a system based on falsehoods and exaggerations.

Although judges are the gatekeepers responsible for determining whether an expert is qualified, the judge must be given all the information necessary to fulfill that role. Attorneys on both sides of the court must be vigilant and object strenuously to experts who are not truly qualified or who testify about bloodstain pattern based on general tenets but have not reproduced that pattern with the same presumed method on the same target material, at the same relative location, and with the same position of source. Attorneys must also object strenuously and be prepared to rebut when bloodstain pattern analysts exaggerate the value of evidence or have not considered all of the evidence when drawing conclusions.

BLOODSTAIN PATTERN V. BLOODSTAIN SPOTS

This need for common sense has been reinforced over the years. The lab I worked in processed homicide scenes in 19 counties. I worked side by side with hundreds of different law enforcement officers from dozens of different local, city, county, state, and federal agencies. There were numerous times when I was confronted with blood pattern analysts who were simply unprepared to analyze a scene scientifically. I would be standing in a crime scene, looking at a myriad of bloodstain patterns associated with the violent end of a person's life. While I was observing the phenomena, a law enforcement officer who had just completed a 40-h basic bloodstain pattern course would start to tell me what they had concluded. One such officer explained he determined how far off of the floor the victim was when they received their wounds. He made this determination after he searched for and finally found a few nicely shaped bloodstains among the thousands of bloodstains in the room. He measured the length and width of each of the stains he had chosen, entered them into their calculator, and strung the stains in three dimensions. Done. However, he ignored all the other stains, patterns, and injuries, the movement of the person, and everything else, except those isolated bloodstains. These 1-week wonders could come up with the most illogical and unreasonable conclusions and remain perfectly confident in their accuracy. Forty years after first reading MacDonnell's pamphlet on blood flight characteristics, I still slowly shake my head at the conclusions that people have made by looking at a few bloodstains at a scene.

MINIMUM QUALIFICATIONS

The Scientific Working Group on Bloodstain Pattern Analysis (SWGSTAIN) is made up of bloodstain pattern analysis experts from North America, Europe, New Zealand, and Australia (Scientific Working Group on Bloodstain Pattern Analysis, 2008). SWGSTAIN provides a professional forum in which bloodstain pattern analysts can share and assess different methods and further research. SWGSTAIN's ultimate goal is to address substantive and operational issues and to build best practice guidelines. To this end, SWGSTAIN has developed minimum guidelines for bloodstain pattern analysts:

1. Minimum Pretraining Requirements for a Bloodstain Pattern Analysis Trainee
   Bachelor's degree or equivalent in a field of study related to BPA from an accredited college or university.
   -OR-
   Associate's degree or equivalent in a field of study related to BPA from an accredited college or university and two years of job-related experience.
   -OR-

1.3. High school diploma or equivalent and four years of job-related experience. (Job-related experience includes, but is not limited to, experience as a: Crime scene technician, Criminalist, or a Homicide/criminal investigator.)

2. Required Minimum Objectives Achieved Through Accepted Training Methods Specific to a Bloodstain Pattern Analysis Training Program. At the completion of training the student must be able to:
   - Demonstrate an understanding of health and safety issues associated with BPA.
   - Demonstrate an awareness of bloodborne pathogens and other related health hazards.
   - Demonstrate an awareness of biohazard safety equipment and procedures.
   - Demonstrate knowledge of the history of BPA.
   - Demonstrate an understanding of the scientific principles as they relate to BPA.
   - Demonstrate an understanding of the scientific method and its application to BPA experimentation, to include: Problem identification, Hypothesis, Experimentation/data collection, Data analysis, and Theory/conclusions.
   - Demonstrate an understanding of the principles of physics as they relate to BPA, to include: Physical laws of motion, Surface tension, Viscosity, Gravity, Air resistance, and Velocity.
   - Demonstrate an understanding of bloodstain pattern principles and their application to BPA.
   - Demonstrate an understanding of blood components and related human anatomy and physiology.
   - Demonstrate an understanding of the effects of target surface characteristics on the resulting bloodstain patterns.
   - Demonstrate an understanding of the effect of environmental factors on the formation and/or drying time of bloodstain patterns, to include: Air flow, Humidity, Temperature, Substrate characteristics, and Animal/insect activity.
   - Demonstrate an understanding of the characteristics of blood in motion, to include: Drop formation, Oscillation, Flight paths, Accompanying drop, Wave castoff, Distribution of stains, and Kinetic energy.
   - Demonstrate an understanding of the mathematical principles that relate to BPA, to include knowledge of the methods used to measure bloodstains and bloodstain patterns. These include: Methods for the measurement of individual bloodstains, Trigonometric functions as they relate to BPA, and Methods for origin determination.
   - Demonstrate an understanding of how the physical appearance of bloodstain patterns (size, shape, distribution, and location) relates to the mechanism by which they were created.
   - Demonstrate the ability to identify bloodstain patterns.
   - Demonstrate acceptable documentation methods of bloodstain pattern evidence, including: Documentation techniques specific to BPA, to include: Photography, Sketching, and Note taking.

- Demonstrate an understanding of the methodologies for the preservation and collection of bloodstain pattern evidence that allow for future examination(s).
- Demonstrate an understanding of bloodletting injuries, their locations, and their potential effects on the bloodstain pattern(s).
- Demonstrate an understanding of searching, chemical testing, and enhancement techniques as they pertain to bloodstains.
- Demonstrate an understanding of the limitations of BPA.
- Demonstrate the ability to apply BPA to assist in the reconstruction of a bloodletting event(s).
- Demonstrate the ability to communicate findings, conclusions, and opinions by written and/or verbal methods.

3. Mentorship: During the course of training, the BPA trainee and mentor must document and participate in a mentorship program. This training should include, but is not limited to, the evaluation of the required objectives, the review of completed casework, supervised BPA scene and laboratory work, and the observation of expert testimony.

4. Competency Training: A BPA trainee must participate in and successfully complete a competency test prior to performing independent analysis and rendering expert opinion. Competency testing may be administered incrementally and/or cumulatively to allow the trainee to conduct some of the analyses independently.

5. Continuing Education Requirements for a Bloodstain Pattern Analyst
A minimum of 8 h of training related to BPA should be completed annually. This may include, but is not limited to, attending professional conferences, seminars, and/or workshops.

   It is recommended that one belong to a professional organization(s) related to BPA.

As you can see, the list of issues a bloodstain pattern analyst must understand is lengthy and comprehensive, although many of these issues require demonstrable understanding that is rather subjective.

The International Association for Identification (IAI) requirements are a bit less stringent for those hoping to earn a certificate as a bloodstain pattern analyst. Although no college or trade school degree is required, the IAI does require certified bloodstain pattern analysts to have attended a 40-h course, plus 200 h of training related to the field, and at least 3 years of relevant experience (IAI at: http://www.theiai.org/certifications/bloodstain/requirements.php).

Although bloodstain pattern analysis is obviously complex and requires a broad base of scientific knowledge including principles of biology, physics, and mathematics, the guidelines for minimal qualifications do make room for practitioners with no more schooling than a high school diploma, as long as they have worked in the field of crime scene investigations for at least 4 years and attended adequate training. This training, incidentally, is often provided by law enforcement and may perpetuate some of the problems addressed earlier in this chapter. Given the complexity of bloodstain pattern analysis and the need for an overarching understanding of the science behind the practice, an attorney looking for an expert would be wise to seek out an analyst who has a more robust, science-based education. An expert should not adopt nor express an opinion concerning the method of production of a specific bloodstain pattern unless they have reproduced that pattern with the same method on the same target material, at the same relative location, and with the same position of source. If you cannot reproduce it, then it probably did not happen that way. A qualified blood pattern analyst will never assume.

The discipline is bloodstain *pattern* interpretation and not blood *spot* interpretation. If a blood pattern analyst focuses on a few spots and ignores the overall patterns, you should seriously question their findings, even if their findings support your theory of the case. Their lack of thoroughness, when compared to the work of a real expert testifying in court for your opponent, will not convince a jury. Fingerprint examiners do not make identifications by picking out a single bifurcation in the questioned and known prints. Chemists do not identify gasoline in fire debris by picking out one single peak in a gas chromatograph printout. Both the fingerprint examiner and the chemist look for patterns.

BASIC TENETS OF BLOODSTAIN PATTERN ANALYSIS

Individuals engaged in violence often receive or inflict injuries that bleed. This simple statement is a basic tenet of bloodstain pattern analysis. The volume of that blood is dependent on the type of injury, the severity of the injury, the location of the injury on the body, and how long the person bleeds while alive or drains after death. Reviewing the autopsy or medical records will often give us some of those variables. How long the person bleeds is, in turn, dependent on if and when death occurs, any medical intervention to stop the bleeding, and, of course, the coagulation of blood. The patterns produced by the blood are dependent on the type of injury, the severity of the injury, the weapon producing the injury, the movement of the person after bleeding is initiated, the location of the injury on the body, and interactions with other individuals or objects. As you can see, many variables are in play when violence produces bleeding. The analyst must keep an open mind to all these variables and deduce the source and method of deposition if possible.

Bloodstain pattern analysis can indicate the location or position of a victim at the time of bloodshed. Since most nongunshot injuries do not produce immediate death or collapse, the injured individual can often move during and after the infliction of those injuries, so there will be bloodstains produced by the impact of the weapon and the movement of the injured person at the crime scene. If medical intervention occurred, whether professional or not, bloodstains can occur, even after the death of a person. While it is true that dead people do not actively bleed, they do drain. Whenever a deceased individual is moved after having suffered bleeding wounds, drainage can be minor or at times actually produce more blood than that from the attack. It is not until an analyst has gained experience moving multiple bodies that they can appreciate the volume of blood and the patterns produced from simply moving a deceased person. Statements, reports, and interviews of emergency responders can be critical to interpreting bloodstain patterns at a scene if their actions produced some of those patterns.

There are scenes where the minimum number of blows that struck a bleeding victim can be determined. Some scenes contain sufficient distribution of blood on the walls and floor from a beating to determine the approximate location of the attacker.

BLOODSTAIN SCENE PRESERVATION

The quality of the bloodstain pattern evidence at a scene is directly correlated with how well the evidence was initially recognized, documented, photographed, and preserved (James et al., 2005; at p. 264). Other evidence can take priority over bloodstain pattern evidence and will be collected before a bloodstain pattern analyst is given access to the scene. For instance, trace evidence that can be easily lost by a light breeze or obliterated by a technician's misstep will be collected first (*Id.*). The scene is usually videotaped in order to get a good overall representation, and the video is supplemented by notes, scaled sketches, and photographs (*Id.*). Many times, bloodstain pattern analyst will not be called in to analyze a case until long after the scene has been released and cleaned up. This makes the accuracy of the documentation vital.

The following is a summary of the various basic tenets of bloodstain pattern analysis.

Direction of travel: The direction of travel of blood that struck an object can be discerned by its shape; the pointed end of a bloodstain faces its direction of travel. Satellite stains have the pointed end facing against the direction of travel.

Angle of impact: The angle of impact can be estimated by measuring the degree of circular distortion of the stain.

Impact spatter: Impact spatter occurs when an object makes forceful contact (impact) with a source of blood, projecting droplets of blood outward from the source.

Forward spatter: Forward spatter is blood that travels away from the source in the same direction as the force that caused the spatter. Forward spatter can be diminished and even prevented by sufficient hair or clothing covering the exit wound.

Back spatter: Back spatter is blood directed back towards the source of the force that caused the spatter. The presence of back spatter in gunshot wound cases depends on the location and size of the wound, the distance between wound and muzzle, any clothing, hair, or other surface covering the wound, and, of course, the energy of the fired bullet. The distance that back spatter and forward spatter will travel is limited. The energy transferred to the blood is a large factor in its production and dispersion.

Cast off: A cast-off pattern is created when a blood-covered object flings blood in an arc onto a nearby surface. The number and size of droplets and the width and pattern of the arc can all be characteristics of the bloody object being swung and/or the way a person swings the object. Objects that create cast-off patterns include fists, clubs, bricks, baseball bats, and pipes.

Arterial spray: Arterial spray or spurt is created when a victim suffers an injury to a main artery or the heart. The pressure of the continuing pumping of blood causes blood to spurt out of the injured area. Commonly, the pattern shows large spurted stains for each time the heart pumps.

Expiration: Expired blood pattern is produced by blood that is expelled from the mouth or nose. An injury to any part of the airway or lungs can produce expired blood provided that the victim continues to breath after receiving the injury. In some cases, the performance of CPR creates these patterns. A somewhat related pattern, though not technically respiratory, is blood that has been expelled from the stomach. It can have a "coffee grounds" appearance.

Flow patterns: Flow patterns are created when a large volume of blood is deposited and the surface tension along the edges of the pool ruptures. Blood flows under the force of gravity and will seek its lowest level. For example, blood flowing down the back of an individual will change direction when the person changes their orientation to the force of gravity. Blood will flow around objects in its path. If the object is then removed, the outline of its shape can remain.

Drip trail: Drip trail pattern is a series of drops that is formed by blood dripping off an object or from an injury. The amount of blood that an object can retain is limited; therefore, the path produced is limited in the number of drops. The amount of blood that a person with a wound can drip is only limited to the volume of blood in their body and their ability to continue movement.

Diluted bloodstains: Diluted bloodstain patterns occur when normal blood is diluted by a nonisotonic solution, such as water. Disruption of the red blood cells and the decrease in overall concentration produces a distinctive change in appearance. Areas around sinks, bathtubs, and showers where an injured person attempted to clean off blood will often contain these diluted bloodstains.

Transfer: Transfer of blood can occur when a bloodied object comes into contact with a surface and transfers some of the blood. When hands, footwear, weapons, and other objects transfer sufficient blood, it is possible that patterns are created that can identify the object.

Energy of impact spatter: The impact energy can be estimated by the diameter of the individual droplets. The terms low-, medium-, and high-velocity impact spatter are often associated with this energy level. Normally, the more energy transferred to the blood, the smaller the diameter of the droplets.

> **Low-velocity impact stains**: Low-velocity impact stains are caused when the source of blood is subjected to a force or energy equivalent to normal gravitational pull. This force can be up to a force or energy of 5 feet per second. The resulting stain is relatively large and is usually, although not always, 4 mm or more in diameter (Bevel and Gardner, 1997; James et al., 2005).
>
> **Medium-velocity impact spatter**: Medium-velocity impact spatter is a pattern of spatter created when the source of blood is subjected to a force with a velocity in the range of 5–25 feet per second. The stain size usually

ranges between 1 and 4 mm in diameter (Bevel and Gardner, 1997; James et al., 2005).

HVIS: HVIS is bloodstains created when the source of blood is subjected to a force with a velocity of greater than 100 feet per second. The diameters of the spatters are typically less than 1 mm, although it must be noted that smaller and larger stains are *often* observed within the bloodstain pattern created by high-velocity impact (Bevel and Gardner, 1997; James et al., 2005).

IS IT HIGH-VELOCITY IMPACT SPATTER?

The low-, medium-, and high-velocity impact classification system was initially created to act as a guide for analysts to use and not as a hard and fast rule. It is erroneous to say that if the stains are less than 1 mm in diameter that a gunshot had to be the source of the droplets. As part of the Introduction to Forensic Science course, I introduced two dozen students to the experience of taking liquid blood and projecting it around a room by various methods. The next day when I was cleaning up all the blood patterns that resulted, I noted all the very small stains that were created. I cleaned up thousands of stains less than 1 mm in diameter, numerous ones less than 0.1 mm in diameter, some almost atomized. And all those very fine bloodstains were created by college students without ever discharging a firearm.

IS IT BLOOD?

One mistake that can introduce error into a bloodstain pattern analysis occurs when an analyst assumes the stain they are analyzing is blood:

A homicide occurred where the female victim was shot 10 times with a five-shot revolver. The suspect, her spouse, probably did shoot her, but real physical evidence was lacking. As the serologist in the regional state crime lab that covered that county, I examined the clothing of the husband for bloodstains. I did not find any bloodstains, and that was not surprising because his daughter stated that the clothes were washed immediately after her father returned from their bicycle ride. The wife did not return with him and was found hours later. One of the police department investigators knew an expert in another state that could most likely "make" their case against the husband. The clothes were sent to him; he sprayed the clothes with Luminol and reported that several areas of the pants contained blood, including an oval-shaped bloodstain that was found on the rear of the crotch section. The report stated that a blood drop traveled in a parabolic arc (i.e., a symmetrical curve) and, striking the rear crotch area of the pants, created that bloodstain. The report also stated that the blood-spattered revolver created bloodstains in the front pocket of the pants. Since these conclusions differed from mine, the clothes were sent to still another expert also in another state. A defense expert, the second out-of-state expert, and I examined the clothes together. We sprayed Luminol and observed a reaction in the bottom of the front pocket and an oval area in the rear crotch area. Upon closer examination, we observed that there was a visible wear pattern in the rear crotch area that corresponds to a high friction area when riding a bicycle. Common sense should have told the initial outside expert two things. First of all, blood cannot travel in a parabolic arc from the surface of the victim, over the head of the shooter, and land in the rear crotch area of the shooter's pants. And second, when you regularly ride a bicycle with the same pair of pants, the pants develop wear patterns. The initial out of state examiner did not use common sense when interpreting the Luminal reaction.

The second area of Luminol reaction was the lower portion of the inside of the front pocket. A forensic scientist knows that Luminol reacts not only to blood, but also to metals. Common sense should tell an analyst that maybe the coins, keys, and other metallic objects that are routinely carried in the pocket caused the reaction. To test this theory, we sprayed the pockets of multiple pairs of pants worn by individuals who carry coins and keys in their pockets. They *all* reacted when sprayed with Luminol.

As you can see, there is much more to bloodstain pattern analysis than blood spatter, or to use a word the public often uses, splatter. Huge differences exist in the discipline over the source of splatter, especially what can be defined as HVIS. Expirated blood patterns, satellite stains from arterial spurting, and other very small stains often look like HVIS from gunshot wounds and have been erroneously identified as such. These errors are normally associated with analysts who examine blood spots rather than bloodstain patterns. Regardless of the tenets of BPA that are generally accepted, in a field this complex, there are few absolutes.

THE DAVID CAMM CASE

The analyses and procedures used in the David Camm case will exemplify the type of work an attorney should expect from a bloodstain pattern analyst. Specific areas of the Camm case have been presented earlier in this chapter and in Chapter 10. The lone partial bloody shoeprint experiment that was analyzed at the Camm crime scene is discussed in Chapter 10, Crime Scene Reconstruction.

Although Camm spent several years in prison for the murder of his family, he was eventually exonerated. Three areas demonstrate how reenactments and experimentation were used to discover the accurate interpretation of the evidence and led to Camm's vindication.

In 2012, as part of preparation for Camm's third trial, I was contacted by one of Camm's defense attorneys. It was requested that I examine spots of blood on a t-shirt and determine if the method of deposition was transfer or gunshot spatter. Since I cannot review just part of a case, let alone a single isolated area on one item of evidence, I requested that the entire case documentation be made available to me for review. I wanted everything and I got it.

One of the bigger reasons that I agreed to review the case was the attitude of the defense attorney who contacted me. The Camm's Ford Bronco was part of the crime scene. The defense attorney purchased a Ford Bronco similar to the Camm's Bronco for reenactment use. We used that Bronco multiple times over the next year and a half to test theories.

My late arrival in the case had its benefits. One, I had no perceived theories about the case because I had no knowledge of the case other than I was aware of a civil suit among some of the experts. And although there were multiple presentations on the case at IABPA meetings over the years, I was not present at any of them due to my schedule. Since the case had gone to court twice before my involvement, the other benefit I had over the other previous experts was transcripts of those two trials.

Upon receiving the discovery in the Camm case, I sorted and organized everything into binders with tabs. Information is great, but you have to be able to retrieve it quickly for review as you progress through the discovery. The entire list of materials that I considered in my review will not be presented here, but here is a quick summary of some of the more important ones:

- autopsy reports, photographs, and pathologists' trial testimonies
- evidence technicians' reports, notes, and trial testimonies

- crime scene reports, photographs, sketches, notes, reenactments
- reports, notes, photographs of the evidence of all laboratory analyses, including DNA, firearms, fingerprints, trace, and trial testimonies of all those analysts, including the external laboratories
- experts' reports, notes, photographs, deposition, and trial testimonies, including the eight previous bloodstain pattern experts
- reports, notes, and deposition and trial testimonies of the various investigators in the prosecuting attorneys' offices
- property receipts
- David Camm's interviews, statements, trial testimonies

As I read each page of discovery, I prepared multiple summaries. An evidence matrix was created, detailing what examinations were conducted on each item, who conducted those tests, and what were their conclusions.

I read and then summarized the testimonies of all the key witnesses in the first and second trials. This included all the expert witnesses, the investigators, and David Camm. A detailed side-by-side summary of David Camm's two interviews with the police, a letter he authored to the state police superintendent, and his testimony was created to compare the details of those four.

Witnesses to traumatic events are not always capable of remembering the details of their actions. Blanks in their memory can sometimes be filled in with inaccurate information. David Camm was criticized for providing conflicting statements of his actions at the scene. From my review and summary, those conflicts were minor and not indicators of his guilt. To the State's bloodstain pattern analysts, they were major and strong indicators of guilt. For example, Camm was not sure if he telephoned the state police before or after he moved Bradley from the Bronco. He also was not sure if he physically touched Jill or only did a visual check of her condition. To me, these conflicts are not indicators of guilt but the natural reaction to unfathomable trauma.

BLOODSTAINS ON CAMM'S SHIRT

The Two Door Ford Bronco purchased by the defense attorneys was of great interest to me after digesting the discovery. I wanted to know how David Camm could have removed Bradley from the Bronco. All the experts in the case, including those who only reviewed a small portion of the discovery, agreed that Bradley was shot while inside the Bronco and then later David Camm removed Bradley from the Bronco and laid him on the garage floor. To answer the question of how this was done, I physically attempted to remove a 50-pound bag from the location where Bradley was shot to the outside of the Bronco. It was far too difficult for me to climb over the center console, grab the bag and then maneuver back out of the truck, so I had a younger, more fit person attempt it. It was still difficult but possible if a certain route was taken both in and out. Months after that simple initial crude reenactment, we would progress to using live people of the same height and weight to reenact all of the necessary movements to accomplish the task.

This later reenactment was a major production requiring a large group of people, multiple video cameras, and a detailed visual reproduction of the various bloodstain patterns, but it was so very, very informative. Two age and gender appropriate children, same height and weight, were placed in the Bronco in locations and positions dictated by the physical evidence. An appropriate age, gender, height, weight, and fitness-level individual was told to go into the Bronco and remove the child portraying Bradley. The Bradley stand-in wore a t-shirt on which I had reproduced the various bloodstains by both pattern and DNA type. I did not tell the David Camm stand-in how to remove the Bradley stand-in and did not say where he had to go or direct his movements. I left all that up to him. The path that he took, his positions in the truck along that route, and his involuntary contact with the child portraying Jill were recorded by various video cameras positioned in the Bronco. When we reviewed the videos, it was observed that the front left bottom of the t-shirt worn by our David stand-in came into contact with the head and hair of our Jill stand-in. These observations led to a hypothesis, and then we experimented. First, the reenactment was done, then our observations turned into theories, and then we experimented. We did not start with the conclusion that the isolated spots of blood on the bottom left front of Camm's t-shirt were blowback from a gunshot wound or with the conclusion that they were transfer. We started with a real-life reenactment of Bradley's removal from the left rear seat of the Bronco. We made observations, conducted specific experiments, and then we made conclusions.

The t-shirt of David Camm was the focal point of the prosecution's physical evidence case against him. The shirt had four areas that contained the blood of Jill Camm. One of the bloodstained areas was located on the lower left front of the shirt. As discussed in the case study, this bloodstain area contained eight very small stains that the prosecution's experts concluded were blowback from the gunshot wound to Jill Camm's head. The area also contained one very small stain that was not blood. The defense's experts concluded that the bloodstains were transfers of blood.

After the reenactment of Bradley's removal from the Bronco, experiments were conducted to reproduce the movement of the bottom front left area over top of Jill's blooded head that was observed each time the David stand-in reached to retrieve the Bradley stand-in. Initial tests using human blood on an approximately 3-foot-tall doll's blooded hair produced typical hair swipe patterns on the left front bottom of the t-shirt each time. After a pause in the testing, the reaching across the blooded hair was performed again. This time, the action produced several very small isolated spots of blood on the t-shirt. Apparently, the pause allowed the bloody hair to partially dry, and the stains produced were very limited in number and very small in diameter. This action of reaching across a partially dried bloodstained head of artificial hair was repeated a total of 13 times, the last ones videotaped. A new t-shirt was used each time. Each of the t-shirts contained very small isolated bloodstains on the front left bottom of the shirts similar to the evidence stains.

On a number of the test shirts, stains were produced on the edge of the hem. This location triggered me to look at the evidence stains again where two of the evidence stains were located on the bottom of the hem along its edge. This observation raised a question. If these stains were projected onto the hem of the shirt by blowback as determined by the prosecution experts, under what conditions could these projected stains strike the very edge of the hem? Additional experiments were then conducted using new shirts and human blood. Very fine blood droplets were projected on to the bottom area of the t-shirts from various relative heights. For example, the source of the projected droplets was above the hem, at the level of the hem, and below the level of the hem.

The results of these tests demonstrated that the source of the projected droplets had to be below the level of the hem in order for any droplets to be deposited on the leading edge. Therefore, if these stains were projected and not transferred, the entrance wound to Jill Camm's head had to be below the level of David Camm's t-shirt. This relative positioning of the entrance wound and hem was a physical impossibility, considering the confines of the Bronco's interior. I concluded from this series of experiments that the eight bloodstains in the area were transfers of blood from the partially dried blood on Jill Camm's head and not blowback from her entrance wound. I testified that the transfer of blood from hair produces similar size, shape, and distribution as the stains in Area 30. I also testified about my conclusion from the results of my experiments and the reenactment:

> The bloodstains that comprise Area 30 were deposited from blood present on Jill's head coming into contact and transferring onto the t-shirt of David Camm as he reached over her body to remove Bradley from the left rear of the Bronco.

Critics of my conclusions cite the fact that I used synthetic hair instead of human hair. However, the use of synthetic hair was appropriate because the diameter of human head hair varies not only between individuals, but also on a specific person's head; the range of the diameter of Jill Camm's head hair was not determined, and the diameter of the synthetic hair on the doll fell within the range of typical Caucasian head hair. Another criticism concerns the use of a doll instead of a 5-year-old human girl. As I explained to the jury in Camm's third trial, it is not possible to use a 5-year-old girl in experiments where human blood would be deposited on her head.

Three of the other areas on David Camm's t-shirt, which contained Jill Camm's bloodstains, were located on the right hip area of the shirt. Testimony varied concerning whether one of these stains was produced by blowback from the gunshot wound to Jill Camm's head. We wanted to know what actions caused these stains. To summarize our experiments on these patterns, we determined that:

- The bloodstain patterns have the characteristics of a transfer of blood onto the t-shirt.
- The stains contain typical voids caused by bunching/folding of material as a bloody object moves across the surface.
- The stains were created by rubbing bloodstained fingers from back toward front against the t-shirt.
- The locations of the stains correspond to a height on the right hip that the right hand would naturally rub against during movement.

These findings resulted in a conclusion that the bloodstain patterns on the bottom edge of the right side of the t-shirt were created by the bloody fingers of David Camm's right hand as he rubbed his hand against the t-shirt in a back to front motion.

BLOODSTAIN ON THE DOOR

During my review of the testimonies of the bloodstain experts in the first two trials, I could not find any comparisons that were made between the areas of Jill's blood on David Camm's t-shirt and the presence of Jill's blood on the door that connects the garage and the breezeway. It seemed that Jill's blood on the door was not selected as an item of evidence that should be considered in the case. I disagreed and set about to determine what actions created the stain on the door. We conducted numerous experiments using human blood and a door, two fairly easily obtained items. Fingers, arms, elbows, gloved fingers, and blood-soaked clothing were used to create bloodstains on a door at the relative height and location as the evidence door. Our conclusion from those tests was that the bloodstain on the door had the characteristics of a transfer of blood from bloody fingers, and not those of bloody arms and elbows or blood-soaked cloth. Again, this series of experiments was not difficult, the stains were not hard to produce, and the results were clear. My testimony at trial was that the bloody fingers of David Camm's right hand created the bloodstain pattern on the door edge as he grasped and swung the door after his right hand touched a bloody surface on or near Jill Camm's body as he was removing Bradley from the rear seat.

BLOODSTAIN ON CAMM'S SHOE

There were various testimonies in the two previous trials regarding a single bloodstain on the left shoe of David Camm (see Fig. 9.1). This particular stain had an elongated appearance, leading some analysts to conclude it was projected onto the shoe and proof that Camm was present during a violent event.

DNA analysis had identified the source of the blood as Kim Camm, David Camm's wife. I found it interesting that experienced bloodstain analysts concluded that this single stain was projected onto the shoe. The reason I was surprised is the observation that all the surrounding stains were transfers of blood. Why would transfer stains surround a projected stain? And all the stains were within a fixed radius of the

FIGURE 9.1

Shoe photo (SE roll 7-18 with *circle*).

location of the knot of the tied shoelaces. Plus, there were very unusual "U"-shaped stains on David Camm's sock, and the end of the shoelace was not blood soaked, but rather a portion of the lace corresponding to where the bottom of the loop of the tied bow would be. So we had all these transfer stains in a fixed radius from the knot, some in a U shape, and the bottom of the loop of the tied laces soaked with blood.

How does one conclude from those observations that the lone single oval stain was produced by Kim's blood striking the floor and splashing onto the shoe or from being splashed by the sole of the other shoe? Experimentation that we conducted on the shoe resulted in a finding that the single oval stain was made by the same mechanism and source as the other stains on the shoe, that is, transfer from a bloodied loop of shoelace. Our experiments also showed that splashed blood produced stains totally different from the evidence stains.

Another reenactment would answer the question of how the loop of David Camm's shoelace became blood soaked with his wife's blood and how the very front of his sole became bloodstained from her bloody pants. For this real-world look at the garage floor scene, I purchased several white king-size bedsheets and colored markers. Using the crime scene photographs and notes of the processors, we laid out the bedsheet beside the stand-in Bronco and drew the body positions and bloodstain positions relative to the truck. Real live people, size and gender appropriate for Kim and Bradley Camm, were positioned on the bedsheet. Our David Camm stand-in was directed to perform CPR on Bradley. When the stand-in knelt on the floor and imitated CPR, his shoes did two things. The toe area of the right sole came into contact with the bloodstained pants of Kim Camm, and the loop of the shoelace on the left shoe came into contact with pooled blood of Kim Camm.

Other than time-consuming and tedious, the reenactments were not difficult to do. Gathering people of the appropriate size, age, and gender took some preparation time and effort. Purchasing a flat bedsheet, some markers, and the Ford Bronco was not hard. However, the information gathered from the reenactments was invaluable.

The jurors found David Camm not guilty at his third trial. It would appear that the jury agreed with our conclusions and rejected the prosecution expert's conclusions that David shot and killed his family. Both our findings and the prosecution expert's findings were based on the same evidence. I believe that our findings were accurate. My review of everything, my consideration of everything, and our following of ACSR's (Association for Crime Scene Reconstruction) guidelines resulted in the correct crime scene reconstruction and the correct bloodstain pattern interpretations.

Attorneys who need the guidance and expertise of blood pattern analysts should not settle for an analyst who does the minimum amount of work to come to a conclusion or who relies on generalizations to form an opinion. Analysts who observe the entire field of knowledge about a case, use scientific methods to prove hypotheses, and who consider the common sense realities of a scene will discover the true story told by the blood left at a scene. Prosecutors who rely on investigators without scientific backgrounds who simply find a way to corroborate the State's theory of the case fall short in their duty and risk wrongful convictions. Defense attorneys must be aware of the striking difference between a real blood pattern analyst and a minimally qualified investigator, and must work to discredit sloppy, uneducated work product. Attorneys and courts need to remember that in order to ensure just verdicts, an expert should not adopt nor express an opinion concerning the method of production of a specific bloodstain pattern unless they have reproduced that pattern with the same method on the same target material, at the same relative location, and with the same position of source. Anything less cannot be relied upon and should not be admitted in a court of law.

REFERENCES

Attinger, D., Moore, C., Donaldson, A., Jafari, A., Stone, H.A., 2013. Fluid dynamics topics in bloodstain pattern analysis: comparative review and research opportunities. Forensic Science International 231 (1), 375–396.

Bandyopadhyay, S.K., Basu, M.N., 2015. Review on common bloodstain patterns documented at a crime scene. Indian Journal of Scientific Research 10 (1), 68–71.

Bevel, T., Gardner, R.M., 1997. Bloodstain Pattern Analysis. CRC Press.

Bevel, T., Gardner, R.M., 2008. Bloodstain Pattern Analysis with an Introduction to Crime Scene Reconstruction. CRC Press.

Gross, H., 1907. Criminal Investigation. Lawyers' co-operative publishing Company [Madras printed].

International Association of Blood Pattern Analysts, International Subpages. Available at: http://www.iabpa.org/international-sub-pages.

James, S.H., Kish, P.E., Sutton, T.P., 2005. Principles of Bloodstain Pattern Analysis: Theory and Practice. CRC Press.

Laber, T., Kish, P., Taylor, M., Owens, G., Osborne, N., Curran, J., 2014. Reliability assessment of current methods in bloodstain pattern analysis. National Criminal Justice Reference Service. Available at: https://www.ncjrs.gov/pdffiles1/nij/grants/247180.pdf.

Larkin, B.A.J., 2015. Bloodstain Pattern Analysis: Scratching the Surface.

MacDonell, H.L., Bialousz, L.F., 1972. Flight characteristics and stain patterns of human blood. National Institute of Law Enforcement and Criminal Justice.

Scientific Working Group on Bloodstain Pattern Analysis (SWGSTAIN), & United States of America, 2008. Scientific Working Group on Bloodstain Pattern Analysis: Guidelines for the Minimum Educational and Training Requirements for Bloodstain Pattern Analysts.

Sheppard v. Maxwell, 1966. 384 U.S. 333, 86 S. Ct. 1507, 16 L. Ed. 2d 600.

J. Slemko Forensic Consulting, Analyze A Case; Test your Skills as a Bloodstain Pattern Analyst. Available at: http://www.bloodspatter.com/analyze-a-case.

Crime Scene Reconstruction

10

CHAPTER OUTLINE

Forensic Science Reform. http://dx.doi.org/10.1016/B978-0-12-802719-6.00010-8

299

Faulty Crime Scene Reconstruction: Glenn Ford

Wendy J. Koen

Child Refuge, Inc., Menifee, CA, United States

[I] participated in placing before the jury dubious testimony from a forensic pathologist that the shooter had to be left handed, even though there was no eye witness to the murder. And yes, Glenn Ford was left handed. All too late, I learned that the testimony was pure junk science at its evil worst.

Prosecutor Marty Stroud

In 2015, Glenn Ford sat in a wheelchair and looked into the eyes of Marty Stroud (Harris et al., 2015). Ford, an ailing elderly black man, his body ravaged by cancer, and Stroud had a long, contentious history. Because of Stroud, Ford had served 30 years on death row for a crime he did not commit. He was exonerated in 2014 when it came to light that the State had information that Ford was innocent and Jake Robinson had admitted to committing the crime, making it clear that forensic evidence used to convict Ford was flawed.

In 1984, Stroud prosecuted Ford for the murder and robbery of Isadore Rozeman. In 1984, Stroud was a cocky young prosecutor, intent on winning more than anything else. Stroud stacked the jury box with all-white jurors (Cohen, 2014; Clements and Novod, 2014). Stroud told that all-white jury they should rely upon the testimony of Dr. George McCormick, the forensic pathologist who reconstructed Rozeman's murder based on the position of the body and the trajectory of the bullet (*Glenn Ford v. Louisiana, 2014*, p. 6). McCormick told the jury that the killer was left-handed, as was Ford. Stroud told that all-white jury they should rely upon the testimony of expert Pat Wojtkiewicz, who testified that he found gunshot residue on both of Ford's hands (Cohen, 2014; Clements and Novod, 2014).

What Stroud did not tell the jury was just as vital. Stroud never told the jury or Ford's defense team about contradictions in witness testimony or that testimony given by his detectives was false (National Registry of Exonerations 2015; Harris et al., 2015). Stroud did not disclose to the defense nor did he tell the jury that two different witnesses placed Jake and Henry Robinson at the murder scene and that Ford was not involved (National Registry of Exonerations 2015). This information should have turned the entire focus of the investigation away from Ford and onto the Robinson brother. It was vital because it substantiated Ford's claim that the Robinson brothers gave him some jewelry to pawn. Ford later learned the jewelry he was given was stolen from Rozeman when he was murdered.

The case against Ford was entirely circumstantial. In November of 1983, 58-year-old Isadore Rozeman owned a jewelry and watch repair shop (*Glenn Ford v. Louisiana, 2014*). The shop was located in Rozeman's home in Shreveport, Louisiana. Rozeman was frail and had poor eyesight. He also worried about his valuable merchandise being stolen, so he required his customers to phone ahead before they came to his shop. When customers came to his shop, he always asked them to identify themselves before he would unlock the door.

At 3:00 p.m. on November 5, 1983, Dr. A.R. Ebrahim went to Rozeman's shop to look at some merchandise. When he arrived, he was surprised to find Rozeman's door open, his display cabinets empty, and his shop in chaos. Ebrahim called the police. When police arrived, they determined there were no signs of a forced entry. They found Rozeman's body between the display counter and the wall. Rozeman had been shot in the back of the head. It appeared that the bullet had passed through a duffel bag full of clothing before striking Rozeman behind his right ear and exiting through his left eye.

The first responders found that Rozeman had no pulse, his body was cool to the touch, and the blood beneath his head had started to coagulate. Investigators found a paper bag near the body that looked like it had been used as a makeshift glove.

Early in their investigation, police discovered that Rozeman had hired Glenn Ford to do his yard work. Neighbors placed Ford near Rozeman's shop on the day of the murder, and the police began to suspect that Ford had killed Rozeman. Their suspicions deepened after talking to Marvella Brown.

According to the police, Brown said she was at home with her boyfriend Jake Robinson, Jake's brother Henry, and Ford between 11:00 a.m. and noon on the day of the murder. Brown heard Ford ask Jake and Henry "if they were going," and they left her house. Ford had a brown paper grocery bag in his hands when they left. The three returned to Brown's home hours later. Ford then had a smaller paper bag with him that appeared to have something inside of it. Jake Robinson and Ford were both carrying guns. Robinson's weapon was a 0.22 caliber handgun. Jake showed her items he had acquired that day, including watches and jewelry. Although Brown's statement placed Ford in the center of the murder, Brown would later recant and testified that her entire statement was a lie and that the detectives had fabricated some of her statements (Glenn Ford v. Warden Burl Cain et al., 2015).

Ford heard that the police wanted to talk to him, and he went to the police department on the morning of November 6. He was fingerprinted and photographed, and he submitted to a gunshot residue examination. The residue test results were positive, and Ford was arrested.

Ford told investigators that he had been at Rozeman's home the day of the murder, asking for work. Rozeman did not have any work for Ford that day, so Ford left. Ford also admitted to meeting with Henry Robinson that day. Henry asked Ford to sell a 0.38 caliber revolver for him, but never gave Ford the gun. Henry did give Ford some jewelry and asked Ford to pawn it for him. Ford pawned the jewelry that evening. The police recovered several pawnshop slips from a shop near Rozeman's home and business. The slips were for several items of jewelry that had belonged to Rozeman, and they were signed by Glenn Ford. For reasons that we may never understand, the police decided neither of the Robinson brothers shot Rozeman. They built their case against Ford and theorized that Ford shot Rozeman with a 0.38 caliber weapon.

THE CORONER

The state bolstered its case with testimony from the parish coroner, Dr. George McCormick. What no one knew at the time of Ford's trial was that McCormick's work was less than reliable. McCormick generally came into the office at the end of the workday (Felder, 2008). He would then take notes from the notes his assistant, Lisa Hayes, had compiled while performing autopsies during the day. Sadly, Hayes was not a physician and had neither training nor credentials. She should never have been performing autopsies. McCormick would later take Hayes' notes and draft an autopsy report, which would sometimes be used as evidence in a trial (Felder, 2008). Hayes also forged McCormick's signature on several death certificates and forged McCormick's initials on evidence containers (Felder, 2008). In fact, for a period of 7 years, including the time of the investigation into Rozeman's murder, all autopsies conducted under McCormick's name are unreliable and suspect.

When McCormick testified against Ford, none of this was known, and the jury had no reason to doubt evidence that purportedly proved Rozeman was shot by a left-handed shooter at the time Ford was present.

THE HANDEDNESS OF THE SHOOTER

Although McCormick never actually performed the autopsy on Rozeman's body and he never actually saw Rozeman's body, McCormick testified that he could reconstruct the crime based on the trajectory of the bullet, the configuration of the room, the narrowness of the area in which the body was discovered, and the position of the body at the scene. McCormick reconstructed the murder from his examination of crime scene photographs and videotape, an autopsy report conducted by Dr. Braswell, and his own visit to Mr. Rozeman's shop, which occurred after the scene was released (State v. Ford, 1986). He testified that the killer must have forced Mr. Rozeman to lie on the floor and that the gunshot to Rozeman's head was intended to kill. The duffel bag found near Rozeman's body had been placed over Mr. Rozeman's head to muffle the gunshot and to minimize blood spatter. Because of the placement of the body in a narrow area between the display cabinet and the wall, McCormick determined that the killer must have been left-handed (State v. Ford, 1986). While testifying, McCormick showed the jury a videotape of the crime scene to help him explain how Rozeman must have been shot by a left-handed individual. McCormick testified that it was a matter of "common sense" that it was more probable than not that the victim was killed by a left-handed gunman. Because Ford is left-handed and the Robinson brothers are not, McCormick's testimony was particularly important in helping the jury decide that Ford killed Rozeman.

Since the time of Ford's trial, other experts have looked at McCormick's findings and have testified that the conclusion that the assailant was left-handed was faulty. "Dr. Riddick Leroy, a forensic pathologist and medical examiner, attacked Dr. McCormick's testimony related to handedness and time of death. [The conclusion of the] assailant being left-handed is based on several assumptions and speculation rather than on fact and scientific probability" (Clements and Novod, 2014, p. 3). Basically, McCormick guessed that the shooter was left-handed.

TIME OF DEATH

McCormick also testified as to Rozeman's time of death. According to McCormick, Rozeman had been dead longer than an hour and probably more than 2h when his body was examined by paramedics. This testimony was of importance because Ford had admitted to stopping by Rozeman's home a few hours before Rozeman's body was found to ask Rozeman if he had any work for him. This placed Ford at the scene of the crime around the time of Rozeman's death.

Experts would later conclude that McCormick's testimony about time of death was flawed (Clements and Novod, 2014). Dr. Riddick Leroy, a forensic pathologist and medical examiner, testified that Dr. McCormick's conclusions about Rozeman's time of death were unreliable because Dr. McCormick did not consider variables that are vital to the time of death determination. Also of great importance, because McCormick did not examine the victim's body himself, he could only rely on the reports of an untrained observer (Clements and Novod, 2014). He could not evaluate important indications such as body temperature and stage of rigor mortis.

GUNSHOT RESIDUE

Pat Wojtkiewicz, a ballistics expert, testified for the prosecution that after Ford had voluntarily come in to the police department for questioning, Wojtkiewicz recovered gunshot residue on Ford's hands (Clements and Novod, 2014). Wojtkiewicz testified that he recovered one particle that was unique to gunshot residue and four particles that were characteristic of gunshot residue on Ford's left hand. From Ford's right hand, he recovered three particles characteristic of gunshot residue.

Just as it later became clear that McCormick's testimony was unreliable, later examination of Ford's case would reveal that Wojtkiewicz's testimony was flawed. Firearms expert Ronald Singer analyzed the gunshot residue evidence that was used to convict Ford. Singer discounted the evidentiary value of the "characteristic particles," particles that have the same characteristics as gunshot residue, but are not uniquely gunshot residue. Singer explained that there was only one particle that was unique gunshot residue. Because the gunshot residue testing was conducted 12 to 14 h after the murder and was conducted in a police station where ambient gunshot residue is always present, the finding of one particle is of no legal relevance (Clements and Novod, 2014).

Worldwide, the importance of trace amounts of gunshot residue findings is being reconsidered, and gunshot residue evidence has been implicated in wrongful convictions (Robertson, 2014; Cole, 2014; Ireland and Beaumont, 2015; R. v. Barry George (2007) EWCA Crim 2722; Imwinkelried, 2014). Although large amounts of gunshot residue on a person's hands and clothing can indicate whether that person was within a few feet of someone who shot a gun, this evidence cannot be relied upon as evidence that a suspect was the shooter (Gardner and Anderson, 2015). Trace amounts of residue should never be used to identify a shooter.

In Ford's case, the state needed to build a foundation for Ford's conviction. Once they singled Ford out as the shooter, they compiled evidence with the help of a fraudulent parish coroner and a ballistics expert willing to stretch a single particle of residue into evidence of murder. They sat on evidence that would implicate the actual killers. The resulting conviction meant more than one wrongful conviction; it also sent ripples of injustice, murder, and mayhem through the community as the real perpetrators continued to victimize others with impunity.

FORD'S APPEALS AND EXONERATION

After a series of unsuccessful appeals, in 2000, in response to Ford's petition for a new trial that was filed by the Capital Post Conviction Project of Louisiana, the Louisiana Supreme Court ordered a hearing (State v. Ford, 1986, 1987, 1988, 2000; National Registry of Exonerations, 2015). The hearing began in 2004. A ballistics expert testified that the gunshot residue recovered from Ford's hand had no evidentiary value because it was recovered more than 12 h after the murder and it was recovered in a police station where gunshot residue is easily picked up. An expert for the defense testified that McCormick's reconstruction of the crime scene was contrary to the facts known about the scene and the case. McCormick's testimony about the shooter's handedness was mere speculation (National Registry of Exonerations, 2015).

Ford's attorneys also produced police reports that should have been disclosed to defense counsel at the time of Ford's initial trial. At trial in 1984, the prosecutor sat on documents that showed two different informants had given police information that substantiated Ford's claims that he did not participate in the robbery and murder; Jake and Henry Robinson acted alone. Reports not disclosed to the defense held conflicting statements by Marvella Brown and other witnesses who testified they saw Ford at Rozeman's around the time of the murder. These reports, had they been available to the defense, would have been used to discredit and impeach the witnesses against Ford. Other reports that had not been disclosed to the defense proved that detectives had lied on the witness stand about statements Ford had purportedly made. The false testimony was glaring, and the prosecutor knew, or should have known, that the detective's testimony was false (National Registry of Exonerations, 2015).

The motion was summarily denied (State Ex Rel. Ford v. State, 2004). It would appear that all was lost and Ford would not see freedom. In most cases, this would be the end of hope, but 9 years later, in 2013, the Caddo Parish District attorney reinvestigated Ford's case and disclosed to Ford and his attorneys that an informant had relayed to detectives that Jake Robinson admitted he shot Rozeman (National Registry of Exonerations, 2015). Based on this new evidence, in March of 2014, the state of Louisiana filed a motion to vacate Ford's conviction based on evidence that corroborated Ford's longstanding contention that he did not participate in Rozeman's robbery and murder. Based on that motion, Ford was released from Angola on March 11, 2014 (Daley, 2015). It is important to note that without the internal review by the prosecutor's office, no amount of toiling, legal drafting, investigation, and legal wrangling by postconviction defense attorneys would have led to a positive outcome for Glenn Ford. This is because the courts in the US hold so dear the presumption of guilt postconviction that it often takes an act of God or an admission of error by the prosecution to undo a conviction. In this case, the State manufactured a conviction and then fought to keep it intact for decades before one prosecutor decided it was time to admit the State had made a mistake.

THE VICTIMS

Rozeman was a victim of the two men who robbed and executed him in his home business. His death was tragic. As is almost always the case, a miscarriage of justice spawns many victims. Just how many victims this miscarriage of justice spawned is unknowable. Ford suffered every day for 29 years, 3 months, and 5 days in solitary confinement at Angola Prison (Glenn Ford v. Warden Burl Cain et al., 2015). He was restricted to a single cell for 23 h of every day (Glenn Ford v. Warden Burl Cain et al., 2015). While Ford languished on death row, his four sons grew to be men and had babies of their own (Harris et al., 2015). The suffering inflicted by solitary confinement is beyond comprehension and is a subject that would best be explored in a volume of its own. The suffering Ford endured was only furthered when Ford was diagnosed with stage 3 lung cancer months after being released from prison in 2014 (Keneally, 2015). The cancer progressed rapidly, and Ford died on June 31, 2015.

While Ford sat on death row, the Robinson brothers were free and committed as many as five other murders (Harris et al., 2015; Machi, 2014). Another suspected victim of Jake Robinson is Bruce Cotton. In February of 2004, Caddo Parish Sheriff's deputies found Bruce Cotton's body inside his car. Cotton was beaten without mercy. His flesh was slashed with a knife, and he was stabbed through the lung and sternum. Police reported that Cotton was tortured and then he bled to death (Machi, 2014).

Another likely innocent victim of the Robinson brothers is 12-year-old Charles B. Hayes (Machi, 2014). In January of 1987, the police responded to what was presumed to be a suicide. Twelve-year-old Hayes was found hanging. Investigators soon discovered Hayes' mother owed drug money to Jake Robinson, and witnesses claimed Hayes was killed as a warning to others (Machi, 2014). The police now believe Jake Robinson killed Hayes (Machi, 2015). It goes without saying that the death of 12-year-old Charles Hayes would not have happened if prosecutors had followed the evidence and the Robinson brothers were paying the price for killing Rozeman.

The story of Glenn Ford is tragic on many levels. Faulty crime scene reconstruction played a major role in this tragedy that spawned innumerable other tragedies. The only hope is that from these tragedies, all those involved in the criminal justice system can learn something about the consequences of allowing sloppy analyses, the testimony of unqualified practitioners, and unchecked and suspicious police work to abound.

REFERENCES

Clements, G., Novod, A., 2014. Louisiana's Longest-Serving Death Row Prisoner Ordered Freed after 30 Years, Glenn Ford, an Innocent Man, to Be Released Imminently, Capital Post Conviction Project of Louisiana. Available at: http://www.deathpenaltyinfo.org/documents/GFord-PR.pdf.

Cohen, A., 2014. Freedom after 30 Years on death row. The Atlantic. Available at: http://www.theatlantic.com/national/archive/2014/03/freedom-after-30-years-on-death-row/284179/.

Cole, S.A., 2014. Forensic science and miscarriages of justice. In: Encyclopedia of Criminology and Criminal Justice. Springer, New York, pp. 1763–1773.

Daley, K., 2015. Mourning Friends of Glenn Ford, Exonerated Death Row Inmate, Say 'all He Wanted Is justice'. The Times-Picayune. Available at: http://www.nola.com/crime/index.ssf/2015/06/all_he_wanted_is_justice_mourn.html.

Felder, R.D., 2008. Coroner system in crisis: the scandals and struggles plaguing Louisiana death investigation. Louisiana Law Review 69, 627.

Gardner, T., Anderson, T., 2015. Criminal Evidence: Principles and Cases. Cengage Learning.

Glenn Ford v. State of Louisiana, 2014. First Judicial District, Parrish of Caddo, Motion to Vacate Conviction and Sentence, p. 5.

Glenn Ford v. Warden Burl Cain, et al., 2015. Case 3:15-cv-00136-SDD-SCR Document 1 03/09/15, Available at: http://s3.documentcloud.org/documents/1685157/Glenn-ford-lawsuit-against-louisiana-prison.pdf.

Harris, D., Yu, K., Effron, L., 2015. Exonerated Death Row Inmate Meets the Former Prosecutor Who Put Him There. ABC News. Available at: http://abcnews.go.com/US/exonerated-death-row-inmate-meets-prosecutor-put/story?id=3039961.

Imwinkelried, E.J., 2014. Statute Overtaken by time: the need to reinterpret federal rule of evidence 803(8)(A)(iii) governing the admissibility of expert opinions in government investigative reports. St Mary's Law Journal 46, 31.

Ireland, J., Beaumont, J., 2015. Admitting scientific expert evidence in the UK: reliability challenges and the need for revised criteria–proposing an Abridged Daubert. The Journal of Forensic Practice 17 (1), 3–12.

Keneally, M., 2015. Exonerated Angola prisoner dies after nearly 30 Years in solitary confinement. USA Today. Available at: http://abcnews.go.com/US/exonerated-angola-prisoner-dies-30-years-solitary-confinement/story?id=32130542.

Machi, S., 2014. Caddo ADA: Shreveport brothers suspected in six homicides. KTBS News. Available at: http://www.ktbs.com/story/25656302/taking-a-look-at-the-robinson-cases.

Machi, S., 2015. Accused killer Jake Robinson loses judge recusal hearing. KTBS News. Available at: http://www.ktbs.com/story/27843895/accused-killer-jake-robinson-loses-judge-recusal-hearing.

National Registry of Exonerations, 2015. Glenn Ford. Available at: https://www.law.umich.edu/special/exoneration/pages/casedetail.aspx?caseid=4395.

Robertson, J., 2014. Push for Royal commission into forensic procedures. Australian Journal of Forensic Sciences 46 (4), 365–367.

R. v. Barry George, 2007. EWCA Crim 2722. Available at: http://www.bailii.org/ew/cases/EWCA/Civ/2007/2722.html.

State v. Ford, 1986. 489 So. 2d 1250 (La. 1986).

State v. Ford, 1987. 503 So. 2d 1009 (La. 1987).

State v. Ford, 1988. 533 So. 2d 368 (La. 1988).

State v. Ford, 2000. 765 So. 2d 321 (La. 2000).

State Ex Rel Ford v. State, 2004. 883 So. 2d 1029 (La. 2004).

Crime Scene Reconstruction

Barie Goetz

Sangre de Cristo Forensic Services, Parker, PA, United States;
Pennsylvania State University, Sharon, PA, United States

Crime scene reconstruction is a discipline in forensic science that examines the evidence at a crime scene to determine exactly what happened. The crime scene reconstructionist (CSR) must look at all of the evidence discovered and analyzed, such as hair, trace evidence, medical analyses and conclusions, DNA analysis, bloodstains, injury patterns, toolmarks, and fingerprints. In other words, the CSR must have a working understanding of all of the subjects covered in this book before properly analyzing a crime. Although crime scene reconstruction is a discipline and not a science, the analysts should be scientists who use scientific principles during their examinations, especially when reaching their conclusions.

Crime scene reconstruction dates back to the homicide of Abel by Cain. It is the who, what, where, when, and how of any crime. *Who* did *what* and *where* did they do it? *When* did they do it? *How* did they do it? All that seems basic enough. The *why* of a crime is certainly an important matter, but not generally a question that the CSR needs to answer; the CSR should deal with the physical and leave the philosophical aspects to the attorneys and juries.

As long as crimes have been committed, humans have been putting together what they believe to be the series of events that occurred at the scene of a crime. Police officers, detectives, prosecutors, defense attorneys, news reporters, news analysts, television audiences, witnesses, and victims have all done this. There have been television shows about crime, the police, and murder trials since we first welcomed televisions into our living rooms. The 1950 and 1960s had The Naked City, Police Story, Peter Gunn, and Dragnet. Perry Mason was a show where the defendant was always innocent and the real murderer confessed on the stand. Audiences were encouraged to figure out who really did it, and, in essence, perform a crime scene reconstruction. Depending on what methods they used, some of those reconstructions were probably spot-on, while others failed.

The goal of any reconstructionist should be the evaluation of a case in a manner that will produce a fair, balanced, unbiased, accurate, logical, and honest crime scene reconstruction that can inform a jury of what actually happened at that crime scene.

HOW IT IS SUPPOSED TO BE DONE

The members of the Association for Crime Scene Reconstruction define crime scene reconstruction:

> Crime Scene Reconstruction: *To gain explicit knowledge of the series of events that surround the commission of a crime using deductive reasoning, physical evidence, scientific methods, and their interrelationships.*

Association for Crime Scene Reconstruction, www.acsr.org.

DEDUCTIVE REASONING

To deduce is to infer by reasoning from known facts. Deduction is reasoning in which the conclusion follows necessarily from given premises. Deduction is a formal process based on rules (Goel et al., 1997). Deductive reasoning happens when a researcher works from the more general information to the more specific. Sometimes this is called the "top-down" approach because the researcher starts at the top with a very broad spectrum of information, and they work their way down to a specific conclusion.

Deductive reasoning only works if the analyst has all of the facts. Deductive reasoning leads to faulty conclusions if facts are incorrect or absent or simply not taken into consideration.

For instance, consider this scenario. A suspect told an investigator he came upon a murdered victim on a cloudy night in an unlighted area and determined the victim died by blunt force trauma from a cinderblock. The suspect determined the cause of death by observing the victim's head was in a pool of blood and a bloody cinderblock was lying on the ground at the bottom of a small hill some 6 feet from the victim (In re Richards, 2012).

The investigator used the process of deduction to determine the suspect was the killer. His premises were: on the dark night, the suspect could not have seen the bloody cinderblock at the bottom of the hill. The investigator did an impromptu experiment; on the same dark night, with no lighting, he stood where the suspect stood when the suspect spotted the cinderblock, and the investigator could not see the cinderblock at all. From the investigator's perspective, there was no way for the suspect to know by simple observance there was a cinderblock 6 feet from the body or that there was blood on the cinderblock. Therefore, since the suspect knew about the cinderblock and could not have observed it or the blood on it, the suspect must have known about the cinderblock because he used it to kill the victim and then rolled the cinderblock down the hill.

The investigator came to a logical conclusion based on the facts he had, but the conclusion was not based on all of the facts. Add these facts to the scenario: (1) the suspect had a high-powered flashlight and 30 min to observe the scene before police responded to his 911 call; (2) the suspect's DNA was not on the cinderblock; and (3) the DNA of an unknown male was on the cinderblock at the exact locations where the murderer grasped the cinderblock when bludgeoning the victim (see *In re Richards*, 2012). Obviously, these added facts should change the conclusion. Deductive reasoning is only effective if all pertinent factors are considered.

In contrast, inductive reasoning works the opposite way, moving from specific observations to broader generalizations and theories. A simple example of weak inductive reasoning is: Fred always eats strawberries; therefore, everybody always eats strawberries. In weak induction, the conclusion is not linked to the premises. Concluding that everybody eats strawberries just because one person does is not logical. Quite simply, weak induction is reasoning that is supported by faulty logic.

This is sometimes called a "bottom-up" approach. A more complex example exists among law enforcement in the US. One specific observation, the murder victim was a married female, can lead to a generalization that often determines the trajectory of murder investigations: if a wife is killed, the killer is usually the husband. Other generalizations can lead investigators to hone in on a husband as the killer: financial problems, adultery, past incidence of marital discord. So, if a wife is killed, the husband is the first suspect, and if there is evidence of general marital strife, investigators often do not look farther than the husband. Inductive reasoning has resulted in a singular suspect (see the case of David Camm later in this chapter and the Case Study in Chapter 9 and *In re Richards*, 2012).

You can see why deductive reasoning, used properly, is the correct approach when you are determining whether or not an individual committed a serious crime and should be given life in prison or even the death penalty. Start with a broad view of things, and then narrow it down using the next ingredients in our definition.

PHYSICAL EVIDENCE

Physical evidence is key when determining the reconstruction of events at a crime scene. Fingerprints, firearms and toolmarks, bullet trajectory determinations, drug chemistry, toxicology, serology, DNA analysis, hairs and fibers, chemistry of paints and metals, glass and soil, explosives, autopsy findings, bloodstain pattern interpretation, and document and handwriting analyses are all examples of physical evidence.

The CSR relies on the results of the examinations of physical evidence and bases his or her conclusions on their interactions. Therefore, should he or she have a college degree in a field of science and actual experience in analyzing physical evidence? Absolutely. Only when you have studied the principles of chemistry, physics, biology, biochemistry, genetics, and anatomy and have performed scientific analyses in a laboratory setting can you evaluate the significance of findings from autopsies, forensic laboratories, other CSRs, and your own observations and conclusions.

THE SCIENTIFIC METHOD

The scientific method is defined in many places as:

> *The principles and empirical processes of discovery and demonstration considered characteristic of or necessary for scientific investigation, generally involving the observation of phenomena, the formulation of a hypothesis concerning the phenomena, experimentation to demonstrate the truth or falseness of the hypothesis, and a conclusion that validates or modifies the hypothesis.*
>
> **See Asmis (1984).**

OBSERVATION OF PHENOMENA: SCIENTIFIC OBSERVATION

You observe everything in the crime scene. Note that we are not making conclusions at this step, just looking. And CSRs do not observe a scene with flashlights. They use high-intensity lights because they want to see everything the scene has to offer. Reliance on halogen or photoflood light to illuminate the scene is crucial. The CSR is there to observe, and you cannot properly observe when you cannot see the details of a scene, like the tiny bloodstains, the cartridge casings, the scuff marks, or the impressions left in the carpet from moved furniture.

FORMULATION OF A HYPOTHESIS

After observing everything, we start to come up with ideas of what we think happened. We are still not making conclusions, but we are *asking questions* based on our observations.

EXPERIMENTATION TO DEMONSTRATE THE TRUTH OR FALSENESS OF THE HYPOTHESIS

Performing experiments is a basic function of every scientist. It is fundamental. Scientists plan out their experiments, and they list the variables and change only one variable with each phase of the experiment. Lay people are typically not equipped to conduct proper experiments, and without the proper training, their experiments tend to be reenactments based on their conclusions. Scientists observe, see what questions are raised by their observations, and then conduct experiments that will answer those questions.

A CONCLUSION THAT VALIDATES OR MODIFIES THE HYPOTHESIS

Finally, we get to the conclusion step. Only after evaluating all the evidence and the supporting documentation do we finalize our conclusions. Unfortunately, some individuals start with this step. Bad things happen when you start out wrong and never stop to reconsider your conclusions.

THE PROCESS

Now that we have a formula "to gain explicit knowledge of the series of events that surround the commission of a crime," we need to determine what we are going to review for a successful evaluation. A scientific approach demands that the CSR consider and weigh everything that is available, everything. Start with the physical evidence, the autopsy report and photos; crime scene reports, notes, videos, and photographs; laboratory reports, notes, and photographs; and continue with witness and suspect statements, interviews, law enforcement reports, and notes from the initial responding officers to the detectives assigned to the case, search and arrest warrants and the supporting affidavits of probable cause, 911 transcripts, timelines, property sheets, everything. As attorneys, you must make sure that your CSR has actually reviewed all these things. When I conduct a crime scene reconstruction for a postconviction consultation, I review everything, and I can usually point out what materials were not reviewed and should have been in the cases of wrongful conviction I review.

<hr>

MATERIALS REVIEWED

As an example of what materials I consider, here is the list of items that I reviewed on an attempted murder case:

- a physical examination of El Paso County Sheriff Department Evidence items 1RAL, 2RAL, 3RAL, 4RAL, 5RAL, JCP2-2, JCP2-3, JCP2-4, JCP2-5, JCP2-7, JCP2-10, JCP2-11, JCP2-12, JCP2-13, JCP2-14, JCP2-16, JCP2-17, JCP2-18, JCP2-19, JCP2-20, JCP2-21, JCP2-24, DR4, and DRS;
- reports by El Paso County Sheriff Department Detective Donald Richer, El Paso County Sheriff Department Sergeant Robert Stone, El Paso County Sheriff Department Deputy Teresa Murphy, El Paso County Sheriff Department Deputy Raymond Krug, El Paso County Sheriff Department Deputy Joey Harris, El Paso County Sheriff Department Deputy Michael Waters, El Paso County Sheriff Department Deputy Kevin Tedesco, El Paso County Sheriff Department Detective Jerald Day, El Paso County Sheriff Department Detective Jon Price, El Paso County Sheriff Department Detective Ralph Losasso;
- a DVD containing the El Paso County Sheriff Department Detective Ralph Losasso's interviews of Michael Jacques and Brian Clayton;
- digital images of the crime scene at Adam Tipton's trailer located at 11890 Range View Drive, of the apartment of Megan Boyd at 1204 Potter #A, of the clothing items collected by the El Paso County Sheriff Department, of Justin Roberson's injures, of Zebulon Dyer's injures, of Brian Clayton's injuries, of the search of the white Ford Explorer operated by Brian Clayton;
- *copies of search warrants, affidavit of probable case, witness list;*
- copies of cover letters authored by Ralph Losasso to the Colorado Bureau of Investigation Forensic Laboratory;
- Colorado Bureau of Investigation Forensic Laboratory summaries titled Full Case Report, Chain of Custody Report, Request for Laboratory Examination (Submittal sheets);
- Colorado Bureau of Investigation Forensic Laboratory Biological Sciences Examination Report dated August 18, 2009, corresponding bench notes on Serology Examinations, Biological Sciences Examination Report dated August 27, 2009, corresponding bench notes on DNA Examinations and Allele Charts, Trace Examination Report dated August 19, 2009, and corresponding bench notes on bloodstain pattern interpretation, digital images taken by the laboratory examiners, correspondence records;
- *medical records of Zebulon Dyer, Justin Roberson, and Brian Clayton*; and
- interviews of Justin Roberson, Zebulon Dyer, Megan Boyd, Heather Thomas, Philip Hanna, Casey Vancil, Nick Roy, Joe Konrad, Michael Jacques, Michael Humphrey, Randy Teeters, Adam Tipton, Rochelle Renrod, Amber Ortman, and Travis Havel were utilized to review this case.

TYPICAL MATERIALS TO BE REVIEWED BY THE CRIME SCENE RECONSTRUCTIONIST

Only after examining the evidence and reviewing all of those materials should the CSR move into the next step of the scientific method phase. When observation of phenomena is completed, the next is the formulation of a hypothesis concerning the phenomena, experimentation to demonstrate the truth or falseness of the hypothesis, and a conclusion that validates or modifies the hypothesis. Experiments are performed, the hypothesis is reviewed, and more experiments are conducted. Finally, conclusions are made, and the events of the crime scene are reconstructed.

My conclusions often differ from those of the investigating officer. I am dedicated to make sure my crime scene reconstructions are accurate, impartial, logical, and practical evaluations of all aspects of the case. If the police investigator relied on a faulty premise, investigated after having decided who was guilty, or just did not want to know what actually happened between the defendant and the victim(s), the investigator's conclusions will not be the same as mine. A fear of knowing what actually happened often drives an investigation. It will determine what evidence is examined, what witnesses will be relied upon, and which ones will be discarded.

One character trait attorneys and courts should look for in a CSR is a healthy fear of being wrong and a steady understanding of the consequences of a faulty analysis. A healthy fear of error will cause a CSR to learn everything they can about a subject before making conclusions. It stands to reason that the more information you have, the more accurate your conclusions will be. Therefore, one of my requirements before I agree to review a case is that the client must give me everything on my list and not have the freedom to pick and choose. As a CSR, I need the good and the bad. Both defense and prosecution attorneys can be hesitant to give up materials. Some fear that the conclusions I come to will be different from theirs and hurt their case. Regardless of what pressure attorneys put on CSRs, their conclusions must remain fact-based. Sadly, some analysts do not abide by this philosophy and will slant their conclusions to appease one side or the other in a case. Some of these examiners have been caught manufacturing results, for example, the West Virginia serologist, Fred Zain (see Castelle, 1999), who fabricated inculpatory serology results in multiple cases, and the Florida fingerprint examiner, Donna Birks (Stutzman, 2007), who identified suspects using prints that were decidedly inconclusive and not suitable for making identifications.

AUTOPSY REPORT AND PHOTOS

When reviewing a homicide case, the starting point is the autopsy report and photographs. The report should contain:

- the manner and cause of death; these are key responsibilities of the medical examiner or forensic pathologist to determine;
- the evaluation and documentation by notes, sketches (body charts), and photography of the external and internal injuries;
- a correlation of those injuries with findings at the crime scene;
- toxicology results; and
- a list of the physical evidence that was collected.

The autopsy may reveal what weapon or weapons were used to inflict the injuries and how that weapon was utilized. The location of the injuries on the body, the severity of those injuries including whether arteries were breached, and the force needed to inflict the injuries will assist in determining the amount of blood and the possible bloodstain patterns that could have been produced at the crime scene. The presence of defensive wounds versus offensive wounds if the pathologist made that determination, the amount of blood loss, and the presence of premortem and postmortem injuries/changes are all considered by the reconstructionist to aid them in their determination of the events that occurred at the scene. The type and extent of the injuries can tell us if the deceased could have taken physical actions during the attack. If the first injury sustained was the breaching of the aorta, the deceased would have lost blood pressure immediately and most likely did not make conscious moves after this injury. That information is considered and carried over into the reconstruction.

MEDICAL RECORDS

If a victim survived their injuries, then the medical records should be reviewed. Hospital records are quite different from autopsy records. The most difficult part of reviewing hospital records is interpreting the handwritten notes made by emergency room nurses and doctors. Hopefully, those notes have been transcribed so we can determine what injuries were present upon arrival in the emergency room, the severity of those wounds, and what medical procedures were performed. Just as in autopsies, the location of the injuries on the body, the severity of those injuries, including whether arteries were breached, and the force needed to inflict the injuries will assist in determining the amount of blood and the possible bloodstain patterns that could have been produced at the crime scene. Weapon(s) used and how, amount of blood loss, prior existing injures, and current injury treatments/changes are all reviewed.

Please note that at this point, we are still in the observation phase of the process. The autopsy photographs or medical intervention photographs, if taken, are compared to the reports and the evidence at the scene. With the advent of digital photography, we should have multiple photographs of the body's condition upon arrival at the morgue. These photographs should depict the condition of the clothing and the bloodstain patterns on the body, both before and after removal of that clothing. Again, we are reviewing the autopsy report and photos so we can make comparisons with the crime scene report and photos, the laboratory examinations, the witness statements and observations, the medical intervention at the scene, any actions taken by responding personnel, and our own observations. In most cases, the pathologist who performed the autopsy will not be reviewing those items. And photographs of the external injuries are worth so much more than page after page of a pathologist describing wounds.

Interviewing the pathologist who performed the autopsy and/or the medical professionals that treated the injured person is essential. I once met with a pathologist three times during a lengthy postconviction appeal process. It was not until the third interview that he provided the defense team with the details about what he discovered at autopsy and to whom that information had been given 20 years previous (CO v. Timothy Masters). A neighboring police department then verified that information. That revelation destroyed the state's long-held certainty that the defendant was guilty. On another postconviction case, a meeting with the pathologist revealed that his findings were entirely in agreement with our conclusions, and he would have testified differently if he had only been asked the right questions (CO v. Charles Garrison).

THE CRIME SCENE

After reviewing the autopsy and/or medical information, the next step is to analyze the crime scene. A properly documented and processed crime scene is essential to reconstructing the events at that scene. Ideally, the individual responsible for the interpretation of the bloodstain patterns will have closely and carefully examined the scene and documented with notes and photographs the location of bloodstains, the patterns present, the extent of the bloodstains, and the locations where no bloodstains were present. Taking photographs where no apparent evidence is present is hard for some crime scene personnel to grasp. When we used film at scenes, cost was a factor; now the cost of taking digital photographs is very low. Scores of photographs should be taken at scenes with a quality camera.

If the deceased was still present at the scene upon arrival of crime scene personnel, the bloodstain patterns on the body should be well-documented, both those present on the visible surfaces along with photos of the surfaces not visible due to position. Bodies at crime scenes should be photographed from every angle possible with photographs that cover the entire area, as well as midrange and close-up shots. Particular attention should be paid to the hands, feet, face, obvious injuries, bloodstain patterns, and clothing position. Photograph the body in the position found. After the list of photos previously mentioned are taken, roll the body 90°, and take more photos of the body surfaces that were not visible before and the area that was underneath the body. What was under the body could be critical to determining events. Once a deceased's body is moved, the bloodstain patterns are irreversibly altered. The scene is the best opportunity to accurately document those patterns because after removal, transport, and storage, they are gone.

PHYSICAL EVIDENCE

The physical evidence at the scene should be documented by photography, notes, and sketches. Photographs should document the initial location of the item of evidence, what the underside of the item looked like, the collection, and the area after the collection. We need to know what was under the item of evidence. Although this seems like the common sense thing to do, there are homicide scenes in 2016 that go undocumented. Considering that most crime scene reconstructions are completed sometime after the scene has been released, photographs and other documentation are so very important to both the prosecution's and the defense's reconstructionist. There is only one chance to properly document a scene before it is altered. The overall layout of scene; dimensions of the various areas, the house, and all the rooms; the location of each item of evidence; the distances between the body and key items of evidence; and the position of the deceased all need to be documented.

The crime scene personnel will take notes during their processing. Those notes can contain their observations, what testing was performed, which items were discovered and collected, and those that were not collected. The crime scene report contains a small fraction of the information about the scene, the notes taken contain more, and the mind of the individual who processed the scene holds the remainder. Again, it must be stressed that sitting down with the crime scene personnel can reveal so much information that just does not appear anywhere in their reports or notes.

Physical evidence also consists of things that you cannot put in an envelope or a bag. The trajectories of projectiles, the body position, the presence of livor mortis, voids in the bloodstain patterns, areas where there was no blood, and damage to walls are all evidence. A CSR must examine that evidence.

Bullet trajectories at a scene can be critical to a reconstruction and can reveal details like whether a shooting was a suicide or homicide and where the shooter and victim stood when the bullet traveled across the room and into the wall. We assume a bullet travels in a straight line until it strikes something. Then the bullet can continue in a straight line or be deflected. Examination of the object that was struck can usually tell us what the deflection was, if any. If two surfaces are perforated, it can make it easier to determine the trajectory as long as it is understood that deflection can occur. When only one surface is penetrated, determination of trajectory can sometimes only be estimated. CSRs use trajectory data to logically narrow down the possibilities.

PROPERTY SHEETS

After collection of all the evidence at the crime scene, investigators begin the process of deciding which evidence will be submitted to the forensic laboratory and what examinations will be done. Only some of the collected evidence is submitted to the lab, and then, only some of that evidence will actually be examined. The property sheets from the law enforcement agency will list all of the evidence that was collected at the scene, everything collected at the autopsy, items taken from suspects, returns of search warrants, and other sources. The reports from the forensic laboratory will list the items submitted and the results of examinations on the items that were processed. A comparison between the property sheets, the laboratory submittal forms, and the lab results must be made. Items collected but not submitted to the lab should be of special interest to the CSR. There has to be a culling of the evidence, but the criteria for that picking and choosing needs to be carefully examined.

"BAD WRONG" PICKING AND CHOOSING

Timothy Masters of Fort Collins, Colorado, was walking to school through a field near his home on a cold and dark morning when he saw what looked like a mannequin (McLaughlin, 2010; National Registry of Exonerations). Although Tim did not know it at the time, what he thought was a mannequin was actually a woman's body. The woman had been stabbed in the back, and her genitals had been mutilated with surgical precision.

Tim left his shoeprints at the scene right where they should be if he only detoured off his path and briefly viewed the body. Multiple shoe impressions were collected from the crime scene. The scene officer determined conclusively that several of the prints were left by a Thom McAn brand casual-style dress shoe. The officer even went to the Thom McAn shoe store and photographed the tops and bottom of the particular style of shoe that had the same sole as the shoe that left an impression at the scene. However, because Tim Masters had been near the scene, investigators focused on him and on his shoeprints. Masters was 14 years old at the time of the murder. Examination of his shoe wardrobe revealed an assortment of worn-out athletic shoes, typical shoes of a 14-year-old boy. Masters did not own and would not have been caught dead wearing shoes in the style of the Thom McAns.

When the time came to decide what evidence to send to the lab, the detectives in charge of the case decided to only submit to the FBI Laboratory the shoes that the defendant was wearing the morning that the body was discovered, along with the casts and photographs of the shoe impressions from the scene. No photographs were submitted of the Thom McAn shoes found at the shoe store that matched impressions from the scene. And the submittal cover letter to the FBI Laboratory authored by the detectives never mentioned the obvious Thom McAn pattern in some of the impressions.

After their examinations of the shoes and impressions that were sent to them, the FBI Laboratory reported that the defendant's shoes did indeed match the impression that everyone admitted was the defendant's.

It gets worse. The lead detective pointed out in his voluminous and top secret, hidden written notes that the photographs taken by the FBI examiner clearly showed that the shoe impressions next to the initial body dump site and one impression with a blood transfer along the body carry trail were Thom McAns, not the shoes that Masters was wearing. This clearly indicates that the defendant could not be the one who dumped or carried the body. This bit of evidence was big. The only proper thing for the detective to do was to testify that the Thom McAns, the shoes not belonging to the defendant, but apparently belonging to whoever carried and dumped the body, were identified at the scene. But he did not. He decided to hide this fact, deny its existence, and then have all the officers who testified at trial omit all information about the existence of the Thom McAn impressions and their location and the presence of the blood transfer. Because investigators hid the truth, Masters was convicted based on evidence that it was *his* shoeprint, found in the bloody drag trail, close to the body (Masters v. People, 2002).

This was not an "oops," but is what they call "*bad* wrong." Not only was the testimony of the detective mistaken, it was purposefully so (Standard et al., 2014). Thus, Tim Masters was convicted and sentenced to death based on false shoeprint evidence (Tepfer et al., 2009). Masters spent a total of nearly 10 years incarcerated for murder before he was exonerated by DNA evidence (Vaughan, 2010). Misconduct like this is precisely why a CSR must look closely at what evidence was collected, what items made it to the lab, and, equally important, what items did not.

LABORATORY EXAMINATIONS

Continuing with the materials that have to be reviewed as part of every crime scene reconstruction, the Forensic Laboratory Examinations are next. In addition to reviewing the final report issued by the forensic laboratory examiners, it is vital to look at the examiner's bench notes, all the charts and diagrams created, and all of the photographs taken by the examiners. Photographs are often taken by laboratory examiners to document specific aspects of that item of evidence. If the examiner felt it was worth the trouble of photographing, then the CSR should be very interested in what the photograph depicts. Also of value are the cover letters to the laboratory from the submitting agency and the correspondence between examiners and investigating officers. That correspondence clarifies why some items were not examined.

From my experience working in forensic laboratories for 25 years and reviewing laboratory reports, I know that 10% of the information concerning the analysis of the items is contained in the report, 50% is in the bench notes, and 40% is in the mind of the examiner. With that in mind, to really understand what exams were conducted, what the results were, what observations were made, and what the basis was for the conclusions reported, you need to read the bench notes and then sit down and interview the examiner. Anything less than that and you are in danger of missing the significance of that evidence. Whether it is serology, DNA, firearms, toolmarks, fingerprints, footwear impressions, tire impressions, documents, chemistry, photography, toxicology, or bloodstain pattern analysis, sitting down with the examiner and going through their case folder is always informative. I have come out of some of those meetings dumbfounded by the material that was not in the report.

Forensic laboratory examiner notes contain information on evidence packaging, condition, location of evidence, amount of evidence, distribution of evidence, tests conducted, both positive and negative results, sampling strategies, observations, and conclusions. Only the conclusions make it into the report, and sometimes their notes do not support those conclusions. For example, a firearms report that was reviewed concluded that the t-shirt of the deceased did not contain gunpowder around the entrance wound; however, the bench notes clearly stated that a large amount of gunpowder was present (Weld County District Court #04 CR 1907 Colorado v. Simon Salinas). When we examined the t-shirt in the police department's property room, in direct contradiction to the report, there was so much gunpowder even the assistants who ran the property room could see it with the naked eye.

DNA allele charts (electropherograms) contain both the alleles reported and those not reported. The unreported ones can lead you to retest or perform a different DNA procedure. If you did not look at the charts, you would never know that. A competent CSR will always request the DNA allele charts and ensure that they have been properly read and interpreted and that any necessary retests have been performed.

EXAMINATION OF PHYSICAL EVIDENCE BY REVIEWER

There are few reasons why the CSR cannot personally view the physical evidence in the case after the initial laboratory examiners have completed their analysis. This is assuming that CSRs are qualified and experienced laboratory examiners with knowledge of the various disciplines. Experienced examiners are aware of the procedures to protect the evidence from alteration or contamination.

These postexamination views should take place in a clean, well-lit space. Adequate time to view the evidence is equally important. If necessary, the reviewer should provide his or her own means of magnification and measurement. While viewing, the reconstructionist can correlate the autopsy, crime scene, law enforcement reports, witness and suspect statements, 911 transcripts, and property lists to the physical evidence. After the viewing, the reconstructionist can determine if additional exams could be beneficial. Plus, this examination of the evidence will place the reviewer in a better position to apply the correct weight to the laboratory results.

Attorneys should expect the CSR to create an evidence matrix. The matrix should consist of a list of all the physical evidence, all the exams conducted, and all the results from both prosecution and defense. In this way, it is easy to view what items were examined, the results of those exams, who performed them, and other details that might become crucial to the case and might otherwise become forgotten.

LAW ENFORCEMENT FILES

The discovery, collection, analysis, and results of the physical evidence items have now been thoroughly reviewed. The next step is to look at what people said about the events at the scene. The law enforcement agency's case file consists of responding officer reports, summaries by detectives, witness lists, witness statements and interviews, copies of search and arrest warrants, and affidavits of probable cause. The questions asked in interviews and the probable cause affidavits reveal the mindset of the investigation, i.e., what do the investigators think happened.

The observations and actions of the first responding officers and emergency medical personnel upon arrival are significant. A review of their reports should answer the questions. Did they move the body? Did they move pieces of clothing, even slightly to check for vitals? Did they move the weapon and secure it? How did they enter and exit the scene? Emergency medical technicians (EMTs) can alter a scene by moving the body, moving items around the body, and leaving items behind. Then, unfortunately, they generally leave before the crime scene techs arrive. The EMTs' report will list their medical intervention, but not their scene alterations. Since we seldom have photographs of the body before medical responders intervene, we have to rely on their recollections.

WITNESSES AND SUSPECTS

Eyewitness accounts are not considered to be physical evidence; however, they can contain information that can be tested against the physical evidence and at times provide the examiner plausible ways to explain the relationships between the various areas and items of physical evidence. We must examine how the physical evidence differs from the recollections of the witnesses.

Not all witnesses are reliable, and suspects do not always tell the truth. So, if all witnesses and suspects are capable of unintentional or even purposeful inaccuracy, why spend hours becoming familiar with transcripts of their interviews? The CSR should read the witness and suspect interviews to glean as much information as possible from the witnesses' renditions and remember that sometimes they get it right and they are telling the truth. Sometimes, suspects spinning their own less damning version of events get confused and interject helpful facts that can be verified by other means.

When the interview of the person has been video and audio recorded, an efficient reconstructionist will listen to and watch the interview, and not just rely on the written transcripts. Although it may be simpler and tempting to rely on the summary reports of interviews, a CSR will have much more accurate information after watching and listening to the interview and reading the transcript word by word. I have read summaries that do not even convey the general theme of the interview or come close to documenting what the individual actually said. Typed up transcripts are great, and at times, are accurate. Other times, gaps and wishful thinking plague them. Read and listen, then compare.

Consider the time period of the interviews. The current trend in interviewing witnesses to traumatic events is delay. Let the person go through a sleep and exercise cycle before sitting down for a detailed talk about specifics. Some investigators prefer two sleep/exercise cycles before the interview. Traumatic events are just that, traumatic. Immediately after such an event, the mind is undergoing a lot of processing of images, sights, and sounds. Let the brain settle down; let it finish the processing and sorting. The details provided at the 24 and 48 h stages are thought to be more factual than those produced by an immediate drilling.

When reviewing one of these immediately-after-the-event interviews, remember that the brain will fill in gaps with guesses, introducing inaccuracy. We do not want to rely on guesses, and once the brain fills in these gaps with guesses, those substitute images become fact from that point forward.

The meticulous examination of inconsistencies between the immediately-after interview and subsequent interviews is another error that investigators make. When an interviewee states that he moved item A before moving item B at the scene in the immediately-after interview and then changes the sequence of moving those items in a following interview, some investigators will try and use that to indicate untruthfulness on the part of the person. However, research has shown that an individual will seldom accurately recall the exact sequence of events during a traumatic experience (Flor and Wessa, 2015). Their brain is just trying to make sense of things; it is filling in gaps with guesses because it just cannot or won't recall the true sequence. Even highly trained EMTs often do not remember what items they moved or what blood-stains they created during their examinations.

Consider the Timothy Masters case in Colorado, discussed earlier in this chapter (Tepfer et al., 2009; Bonpasse, 2013; Masters v. People, 2002). Investigators became convinced that subtle differences in a 14-year-old boy's recollections of glimpsing a murder victim's body in the dark were proof of his deception. This error by the investigators led them to hone in on Masters early on in the investigation and contributed to Masters' wrongful conviction and incarceration. It is ironic to note that those same investigators made and recorded their own glaring errors in observation of the body during their unhurried viewing in broad daylight.

The person who found the body should be of keen interest to both the police investigators and the crime scene processors. Like the paramedics, we need to know what did they do, did they touch the body, move the body, what objects did they move, where did they enter and exit, did they use the phone? Fig. 10.1 Collection of their clothes for bloodstain pattern examination should take place as soon as possible. We do not want to allow the discoverer to sit, stand, walk around, and undergo hours of interrogation with bloody hands while wearing bloody clothes.

911 TRANSCRIPTS

In most locations, individuals who call 911 are recorded, even when they are on hold. Like clandestine records of individuals, a transcript of the 911 call can contain valuable information. Consider the Wyoming case where a husband, upon arrival home from work, discovers his wife shot to death on a living room chair. His 911 call not only recorded his words, but also the 911 operator's instructions to him on how to perform CPR. On the tape of the call, you can hear the sounds of the husband moving the body out of the chair and onto the floor at the insistence of the operator, his spitting of blood from his mouth while performing CPR, again at the insistence of the operator, and his exclamations of the bloodstains he was producing. All those recorded things were subsequently ignored by the bloodstain pattern analyst, who concluded that the bloodstains on his clothing were from the shooting of his wife. By simply listening to the 911 recording, the origin of the blood spatter became clear, and it was obvious the man had not shot his wife.

PHYSICAL VISIT TO THE SCENE

The best 3-D reproduction of the crime scene is the actual scene, regardless of alterations made, cleanup, or other disruptions, like the destruction of artifacts. Therefore, a physical inspection of the crime scene can really bring all the physical evidence, bloodstain patterns, trajectories, laboratory results, and autopsy results to life. Just standing at the actual location and mentally replaying witness and suspect statements can bring clarity to a reconstruction. Whenever it is possible, the reconstructionist must visit the scene.

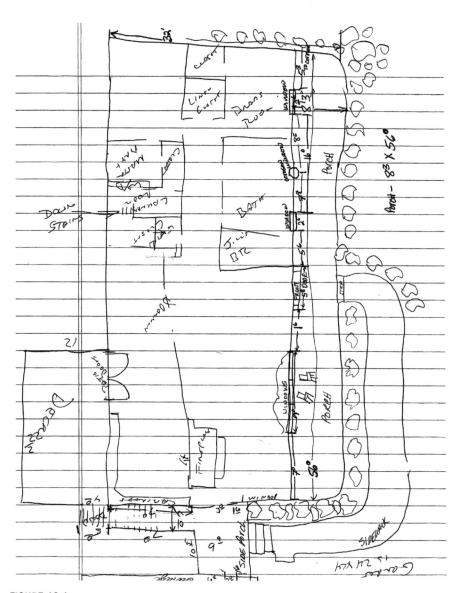

FIGURE 10.1

Map of Discoverer's Route

THE REALITY OF CRIME SCENE RECONSTRUCTION

From the beginning, most of the lay individuals who first endeavored to reconstruct the scene of a crime probably did not use deductive reasoning, physical evidence, or the scientific method when they decided who did what to whom. They did not read the police reports, the laboratory reports, or the autopsy report. They did not look at the photographs. They just figured it out. They saw who was arrested, heard that the victim was shot or stabbed or beaten, and were told by someone how it happened. This, combined with gut feelings, hunches, intuition, and their own prejudices was enough for them to decide a person's guilt. But do the modern police forces use this obviously flawed method of crime scene reconstruction when they testify about their cases in front of a judge and jury? Sometimes, yes.

I expect that most citizens of the USA assume that a science-based crime scene reconstruction conducted by a qualified, educated, and experienced examiner is done on all homicides and major crimes before those cases are presented in a courtroom. On television shows such as CSI: Crime Scene Investigation and NCIS: Naval Criminal Investigative Service, the police and prosecutors never convict the wrong man. That is how the judicial system works, right? From my experience and the number of innocence cases that have made the news over the last decades, that is definitely not the case.

It is easy to see why a science-based crime scene reconstruction conducted by a qualified, educated, and experienced examiner must be conducted on all homicides and major crimes before those cases are presented in a courtroom. Such a reconstruction may be the only logical, balanced, and honest evaluation of all the evidence in the case. A logical, balanced and systematic reviewing and weighing of the evidence is appropriate if our justice system is truly in a search for the truth.

In reality, however, picking and choosing which evidence is to be used and which evidence is to be hidden, or have its significance downplayed or its mere existence denied, happens all too frequently. This perversion of the truth is contrary to the ideals of our justice system, and it should not be permitted. I have seen how some investigators and some prosecutors approach the reconstruction of crime scenes in a manner that resulted in innocent people being convicted of homicides that they did not commit. That means innocent people spending years, even decades, in prison, some of them on death row. The following discusses two of the most common reasons for these miscarriages of justice.

PREMATURELY DECIDING GUILT

The biggest and most damaging mistake I have witnessed investigators and prosecutors make is prematurely deciding the guilt of a person. Serious consequences can arise when the police investigators decide who is responsible for the crime before any evidence is examined, before the bodies are even viewed at the scene.

This was one of the many factors that led to the wrongful conviction of David Camm. The supervisor of the crime scene investigators (CSIs), upon arrival at the scene, looked at the homeowner and *knew* that he was responsible for the crime. Before the CSI supervisor even viewed any of the bodies, he knew the *who* part of the reconstruction. On what basis was he able to determine with absolute certainty that the homeowner did it? Simple, it was the way Camm was pacing and would not make eye contact. For that crime scene investigator, all that was left to determine was the *when* and *how*.

When the *who* is decided, other evidence is neither sought nor analyzed with the same goal. Instead of working to gain explicit knowledge of the series of events that surround the commission of a crime using deductive reasoning, physical evidence, scientific methods, and their interrelationships, when the *who* is assumed, examiners tend to work to gain evidence that will support their theory. Any evidence that does not support their theory is quickly determined to be unimportant and is not analyzed. Sometimes, it is not even collected.

In David Camm's case, investigators were so married to their theory that they ignored solid physical evidence that identified the real killer and placed him at the scene of the crime at the time of the murders. As was discussed in greater detail in Chapter 9, the real killer left his sweatshirt with his prison name on it on the garage floor and left his palm print on the side of the Bronco when he leaned in to shoot the two children. That sweatshirt contained the DNA of the real killer, and his profile was in the Federal Bureau of Investigation's CODIS (Combined DNA Index System) database at the time of the murders. The sweatshirt also contained the victim's blood and the DNA of the killer's girlfriend. Bottom line: the real killer could have been quickly identified, arrested, and prosecuted if only the law enforcement personnel had not prematurely determined Camm's guilt.

We know the head of the crime scene investigation reached this conclusion prematurely because he testified under oath that he did. He was seemingly proud of his ability to determine guilt before an investigation had even begun. The result of this instantaneous jump to guilt: an innocent person spent 13 years in prison for crimes that he did not commit, the real killer was not caught for several years, and the taxpayers of the state and county paid millions of dollars for the truth to finally come out.

The big question that I asked was: under which of the principles of crime scene reconstruction do we classify the way someone who just experienced a traumatic event paces, and fails to makes eye contact. Physical Evidence? No. Scientific Methods? No. Deductive Reasoning? No, just the opposite.

Now there have been scientific studies on how people react to horrific events. And the stages of grief are known. But the great unknown is, what is normal? What is clear is that we should never build a crime scene reconstruction on the reactions of a person who just discovered the bodies of his wife and small children.

Disaster awaits investigators who decide the *who* part of the reconstruction before the investigation even begins. Once that decision is made, the remainder of the investigation and prosecution process turns into a process of molding the evidence to fit the conclusion, ignoring evidence that does not fit the conclusion and, sometimes, even hiding exculpatory evidence.

Timothy Masters spent 10 years in prison because an investigator decided his guilt and *then* investigated the homicide. Those prejudiced investigators decided what evidence would be examined, to whom it would be compared, and what results would be presented to the jury. All other persons of interest were ignored, and great lengths were taken to hide one very special alternate suspect.

FAILURE TO CONDUCT EXPERIMENTS

After formulation of a hypothesis, experiments to demonstrate the truth or falseness of the hypothesis are conducted. In the case of David Camm, the pacing homeowner who lost his entire family, a lone bloody partial shoeprint was present on the garage floor. If we use the scientific method, we would look at the bloody partial shoeprint (observation) and then think about how that shoeprint was made (hypothesis). Then we'd conduct experiments to determine how a single bloody partial shoeprint can be made.

If you already know your killer, there is no reason to try to figure out how a single footprint occurred. In Camm's case, because the shoeprint matched Camm's shoes, they had already decided Camm was guilty, and they interpreted the bloody partial footprint in light of Camm's supposed guilt; it fit within their paradigms to determine that the singular partial shoeprint meant that the scene had been cleaned up of all the other bloody shoeprints. It naturally followed that whoever left that bloody partial shoeprint was the killer. Because they had already arrived at their conclusion, they skipped over a couple of steps in the scientific method and used inductive reasoning instead of deductive.

If we refrain from supposing Camm is the killer, the approach to analyzing the footprint changes. First, we observe that the shoeprint matches only the very front portion, the tip of the sole of the athletic shoe. That means that only that part of the sole came into contact with wet blood and transferred that blood to the floor. Next, we need to ask, "How can that happen?". This is the formulation of a hypothesis. To answer this question, we experiment with shoes of the same style and type, use real blood, and a real concrete garage floor. We vary how the front portion of the sole can come into contact with blood and then vary how the wearer of the shoe could step, walk, and run after the deposition of blood.

The results of those experiments showed that when the shoe wearer kneels down on the floor, they naturally position their foot so that only the front portion or the tip of the sole comes into contact with the horizontal surface of the floor. If the floor contains wet blood, the tip of the sole comes into contact with that blood. When the shoe wearer then stands up and walks with the blood infused shoe sole tip, they do not transfer a bloody pattern on the floor, because the tip of the sole does not come into contact with the floor. Walking does not result in a transfer on the concrete floor.

However, when the wearer begins to run with the blood-infused shoe sole tip, they rise up on the front portion of the sole and transfer a blood pattern to the floor. The experiments have resulted in facts that will help us answer our hypothesis, but we are not ready to make a conclusion yet.

Additional experiments are conducted. The amount of blood on the floor is varied, and different blood-soaked objects are placed on the floor. These experiments show that when the shoe wearer kneels down and the foot is positioned so that only the very front portion of the sole rests on a bloodstained floor and then stands up and initiates a run, a blood print of the shoe tip is transferred to the floor, but the transfer of blood onto the floor is heavy and does not have the same appearance as the bloody evidence shoe print. However, when the shoe wearer kneels down on the floor and the foot is positioned so that only the very front portion of the sole rests on a blood-soaked piece of fabric similar to the blood-soaked pants observed at the scene, and then stands up and initiates a run, the transfer of blood onto the floor has the same appearance as the bloody evidence shoe print. These facts answer some of the questions about the print, but we are still not ready to come to a conclusion.

The question remains, why is there only one bloody partial shoeprint found at the scene? Additional observations are made. That lone bloody partial shoeprint is located within a few feet of the entrance to the garage. There is a grass lawn adjacent to the concrete garage floor and driveway.

Additional experiments are conducted taking the layout of the scene into account. When the shoe wearer kneels down on the floor and the foot is positioned so that only the very front portion of the sole rests on a blood-soaked piece of fabric similar to the blood-soaked pants observed at the scene, and then stands up and walks toward the driveway area of the garage floor, no bloody shoeprint is transferred to the floor. However, when the wearer initiates a run within a few feet of the grass lawn, the first step transfers blood onto the floor with the same appearance as the bloody evidence shoeprint, and the second time that shoe contacts the ground, it is on the grass.

Now, we are ready to draw some conclusion. Do we now conclude that the presence of a lone bloody partial shoeprint that matches the sole of the individual mean that that person is the killer? No. We *can* conclude that the presence of a lone bloody partial shoeprint that matches the sole of the individual means that that person could have knelt down on the floor, and the foot was positioned so that only the very front portion of the sole rested on a blood-soaked piece of fabric similar to the blood-soaked pants observed at the scene, then stood up, walked to the garage opening, and initiated a run onto the grass yard.

Although it is easier to just observe a sole bloody partial shoeprint and conclude that the other bloody shoeprints were washed up by the wearer, and therefore, the wearer is the killer, an investigator looking for the truth does not have the luxury of ease.

Conducting experiments that result in facts that can explain crime scene evidence is vital. Serious consequences arise if experiments are not done or if they are not done correctly. When a scientist testifies that the scientific evidence identifies a specific person as the killer, that testimony carries an enormous amount of weight with the court and the jury. It must be sure.

Experts should not adopt nor express an opinion concerning the method of production of a specific bloodstain pattern unless they have reproduced that pattern with the same method on the same target material, at the same relative location, and with the same position of source. If you cannot reproduce it, then it probably did not happen that way. Never assume.

The physical aspects of a crime scene must be considered in experimentation. It is lovely to theorize what probably happened at a scene. The killer probably climbed through this window, moved this object, grabbed the victims, stabbed this one and then the other, etc. But can those events really happen in the real world, the one we are currently occupying? The way to confirm or contradict theories is experiments. Reenactments are experiments dealing with real-world constraints.

In the previously mentioned series of theories, it is fairly easy to see if someone of the suspect's size and fitness level can actually climb through that window. Find a volunteer of the same size and fitness level of the suspect, tell him to climb through the window, and see if he can do it. Sounds simple, but most times, it is not done. The expert goes into court and tells the jury what they think happened at the scene. The better expert goes into court and tells the jury what can happen. Reenactments in the David Camm case were crucial for understanding what events occurred.

WHO SHOULD BE A CRIME SCENE RECONSTRUCTIONIST

The CSR relies on the results of the examinations of physical evidence and bases his conclusions on their interactions. Therefore, the CSR should have a college degree in a field of science and actual experience in analyzing physical evidence. Only when you have studied the principles of chemistry, physics, biology, biochemistry, genetics, and anatomy and have performed scientific analyses in a laboratory setting can you evaluate the significance of findings from autopsies and forensic laboratories and your own observations and conclusions. It would also be of great value if you received specific training in a number of fields, established testing protocols based on the current capabilities of forensic laboratories, and can determine what findings are possible considering the specific tests performed.

REQUIREMENTS FOR INTERNATIONAL ASSOCIATION FOR IDENTIFICATION CRIME SCENE RECONSTRUCTION CERTIFICATION

General Qualifications

An applicant for certification must be of good moral character, high integrity, and good repute, and must possess high ethical professional standing.

An applicant must be employed full-time in an occupation that includes crime scene–related activities. "Crime scene related activities" is understood to mean responding to crime scenes and having a significant role in locating, documenting, recovering, and analyzing physical evidence. Processing or enhancing physical evidence solely in a laboratory or evidence warehouse environment does not meet this description. "Crime scene–related activities" will normally be conducted by personnel employed by law enforcement agencies, but may occasionally be performed by nongovernment personnel acting in an adjunct or advisory role.

Certified Crime Scene Reconstructionist

Applicant Must:

Have a minimum of 5 years experience as a crime scene investigator involved in crime scene reconstruction.

Continued

Have completed a minimum of 120 h of Crime Scene Certification Board–approved instruction in crime scene and crime scene reconstruction related courses within the last 5 years. NOTE:

This Training Must Include the Following Courses:

The timeframe on the acceptance of bloodstain analysis courses and shooting reconstruction courses for the certified crime scene reconstructionist (CCSR) has been changed from 5 years to 10 years. Training in these two courses can take place up to 10 years prior to application for certification. This only applies to the CCSR certification, and it only applies to those specific courses of instruction:

a bloodstain pattern interpretation course that is a minimum of 40 h in length;

shooting incident reconstruction courses that total 40 h; and

additional elective courses must total a minimum of 40 h.

And One of the Following:

Applicant must have authored or coauthored an article on some phase of crime scene reconstruction published in a professional journal, made a presentation on some phase of crime scene reconstruction to a professional organization, be an active instructor in some phase of crime scene reconstruction who is currently teaching at least once a year, or submit a court transcript from an actual crime scene reconstruction case in which the applicant gave testimony on the reconstruction.

Initial In-House Training

Upon approval by the Crime Scene Certification Board, an agency's structured and specialized training program hours may be reciprocated for portions of the amount of required hours of instruction for the certification.

Testing

In addition to the listed requirements, the applicant must successfully pass a written test with a minimum score of 75%. All written tests are graded and recorded on a pass/fail basis only (numerical scores will not be provided).

The International Association for Indentification's requirements for certification as a CSR (see Sidebar 2) rest heavily on law enforcement experience and training, and do not include a bachelor's degree in science (International Association for Identification). Although two specific courses and several elective courses are required, there is no requirement for a foundational understanding of the sciences or the scientific method. This is fraught with problems and may render CSRs less equipped to do the experimentation required to truly understand what happened and who might have been involved. It may also invite the introduction of the type of folklore relied upon in arson investigation, passed from practitioner to practitioner, with no basis in science. Put simply, if a CSR's entire scientific background consists of an introductory chemistry course, then that CSR is not the person to evaluate the significance of findings from autopsies and forensic laboratories.

CONCLUSION

Crime scene reconstruction is complex and requires a thorough understanding of the entire pool of evidence relied upon to determine the who, what, when, and where of a crime. All of the information gathered in connection with a crime must be looked at through the lens of a scientist who understands and relies upon the scientific method and who uses deductive reasoning before drawing conclusions. This demands a working understanding of chemistry, physics, biology, biochemistry, genetics, and anatomy and the experienced gained by performing scientific analyses in a laboratory setting.

REFERENCES

Asmis, E., 1984. Epicurus' scientific method. Cornell Studies in Classical Philology 42, 3–385.

Bonpasse, M., 2013. Polygraphs and 200 Wrongful Conviction Exonerations.

Castelle, G., 1999. Lab fraud: lessons learned from the "fred Zain" affair. Champion 23, 12–16 See also, In the Matter of an Investigation of the West Virginia State Police Crime Laboratory, Serology Division, 190 W.Va. 321, 438 S.E.2d 501(1993).

CO v. Charles Garrison, Case Number: 01CR326, District Court, Eagle County, Colorado.

CO v. Timothy Masters, Case Number: 98CR1149, District Court, Larimer County, Colorado.

Flor, H., Wessa, M., 2015. Memory and posttraumatic stress disorder. Zeitschrift für Psychologie/Journal of Psychology.

Goel, V., Gold, B., Kapur, S., Houle, S., 1997. The seats of reason? An imaging study of deductive and inductive reasoning. NeuroReport 8 (5), 1305–1310.

In re Richards, 2012. 289 P. 3d 860, 55 Cal. 4th 948, 150 Cal. Rptr. 3d 84.

International Association for Identification, Crime Scene Certification. Available at: https://www.theiai.org/certifications/crime_scene/index.php.

Masters v. People, 58 P. 3d 979 (Colo. 2002).

McLaughlin, E.C., 2010. Murder Conviction Built on Cop's Lies, Indictment Says. CNN. Available at: http://www.cnn.com/2010/CRIME/07/29/tim.masters.police.perjury/.

National Registry of Exonerations, Timothy Masters, Available at: https://www.law.umich.edu/special/exoneration/Pages/casedetail.aspx?caseid=3412.

Standard, D., Test, F., Doyle, A.C., 2014. Ethics in Crime Scene Investigation. In: Dutelle, A.W. (Ed.), An Introduction to Crime Scene Investigation, second ed. Jones and Bartlett.

Stutzman, R., 2007. Fingerprint scandal costs analyst her job. Orlando Sentinel. Available at: http://articles.orlandosentinel.com/2007-06-07/news/PRINTPROFILE07_1_birks-eslinger-fingerprint.

Tepfer, J.A., Nirider, L.H., Tricarico, L.M., 2009. Arresting development: convictions of innocent youth. Rutgers Law Review 62, 887.

Vaughan, K., 2010. Ft. Collins officer who led charge against Tim Masters indicted for felony perjury. The Denver Post. Available at: http://www.denverpost.com/ci_15415704.

Fingerprints

Forensic Science Reform. http://dx.doi.org/10.1016/B978-0-12-802719-6.00011-X
Copyright © 2017 Elsevier Inc. All rights reserved.

Case Study: Brandon Mayfield

Wendy J. Koen

Child Refuge, Inc., Menifee, CA, United States

If attorneys train members of the defense team to conduct deep research on an expert, and if attorneys put effort into understanding the science, they will be able to stand their ground and expose bad experts. … This is a professional and ethical obligation. A client's life may depend on it.

D.C. Sims[1]

We have long trusted the assumption that makes fingerprint evidence so reliable and compelling in court: no two fingerprints are the same. This foundational assumption has led to countless convictions and is not doubted by any court. In practice, however, this foundational assumption has been built upon with other assumptions that are less than reliable and should be doubted and tested. For example, does it follow that no two partial prints are the same? In other words, if you took a partial print from a person's index finger and compared it to all the prints stored in the FBI's Integrated Automated Fingerprint Identification System (IAFIS), how many possible matches would you find? No one really knows how to answer that question, but each year, IAFIS processes over 60 million 10-print fingerprint submissions, averaging 163,145 per day (FBI). IAFIS electronically stores prints of 75.9 million subjects in the national criminal history record file and 39.6 million in the automated civil file. The Brandon Mayfield case gives a glimpse of

---

[1] Dorothy Clay Sims, Cross-Examining the Expert Witness, The Champion, January–February 2012.

the possibility for error presented by such a vast number of prints and thus is likely the most infamous fingerprint match in world history (Rozelle, 2007; Mnookin et al., 2011).

On March 11, 2004, during the morning commute, terrorists detonated bombs on four crowded commuter trains in Madrid, Spain (Spinney, 2010; Broeders, 2006). The explosions caused mass casualties: 191 people were killed, and 2000 were wounded. The Spanish National Police (SNP) were quick to find a red plastic bag containing detonator caps in a van near the commuter station from which the four trains departed. The detonator caps were similar to the ones actually used in the explosions. The plastic bag had several latent fingerprints. Spanish investigators immediately shared electronic copies of the prints with agencies worldwide, including the FBI. The FBI ran the fingerprints through its IAFIS. The software produced a dozen possible matches, and then the examiners analyzed the possible matches visually. In the end, at least three top examiners determined that latent print number 17, recovered from the bag in Madrid, was a "100 percent match" to an American, Brandon Mayfield (Fine, 2006; Kershaw et al., 2004).

Based on the FBI's analysis of the fingerprint, the Portland Division of the FBI began to investigate Brandon Mayfield. Several factors caused the FBI to begin seeing Mr. Mayfield as a possible terrorist. Mr. Mayfield was a practicing Muslim; his wife was an Egyptian immigrant and also a Muslim. When the Mayfields were under surveillance, they were seen driving to the Bilal mosque, where they worshipped regularly (Kershaw et al., 2004). In his law practice, Mayfield had represented a man linked to terrorist groups in child custody litigation (Kershaw et al., 2004). He had an interest in taking flying lessons (Thompson and Cole, 2005). Mayfield's law firm was advertised in a Muslim business directory; the directory was created by a former business associate of Osama bin Laden's former personal secretary (Fine, 2006).

Although there was no evidence that Mayfield had traveled outside of the US in the past decade, agents argued this lack of evidence was confirmation that Mayfield must be traveling under an assumed name. All of these innocent details, in conjunction with a fail-proof fingerprint "match," were enough to substantiate that Mayfield was a terrorist. The FBI came to believe they had identified one of the persons responsible for the deadly Madrid bombings. There was one problem: Mayfield was not a terrorist.

In 2004, Brandon Bieri Mayfield was a 37-year-old civil and immigration lawyer. Mayfield had a small solo practice in Portland, Oregon, where he worked alongside his wife Mona (Wax and Schatz, 2004). Strange things started happening in the Mayfield home in March of 2004 (Democracynow.org, 2006). Brandon Mayfield and his wife Mona came home from work to find someone had been in their house (Id.). Blinds they had closed had been opened (Id.). Deadbolts they did not lock had been locked (Id.). Freshly vacuumed carpets had new trails of shoeprints, which was particularly odd because the Mayfields did not wear shoes in their home (Id.). Mayfield was not sure who had been in his house, but the break-ins caused a great amount of fear and suspicion (Id.).

On the morning of May 6, 2004, it became clear who had been inside the Mayfields' home, and the Mayfield's world became nightmarish. Brandon was in his law office, preparing for a civil case, when a man and a woman knocked on his office door. The pair forced their way in, identified themselves as FBI agents, and handcuffed and arrested Brandon (Democracynow.com. 2006). Mayfield told the agents he was worried about what would happen to his law practice if it were to become known that he was being arrested in connection with the bombings. The agents assured him that "the media were close behind." (Wax and Schatz, 2004). As Brandon Mayfield was being arrested, his wife was at home watching their house being turned upside down by agents who were executing a search warrant. Agents told Mona Mayfield her husband's fingerprint was found in connection with the Madrid bombings and then tried to question her. Mona had nothing to say, other than her husband had never been to Spain. The Mayfield's were helpless to defend against the hard scientific evidence that branded Brandon a terrorist and mass murderer. Jailed and in fear for his life and well-being because of his new label, Brandon hoped that sanity and common sense would prevail. Mayfield continued to protest his innocence, requested he be released so that he could continue his work as a solo attorney, and stated continually, "That is not my print" (Wax and Schatz, 2004). The judge refused to release Mayfield, in part because he knew that a single print was enough evidence to send Mayfield away for life.

The judge ordered that an independent expert analyze the fingerprint, but on May 19, the Mayfields' hopes were dashed when the new expert agreed with the FBI's initial analysis. Directly after the expert's damning testimony, other news changed the trajectory of the case against Brandon Mayfield. The SNP had identified another man, Ouhnane Daoud, as the source of several prints left on the bag. The partial print that the FBI had matched to Mayfield was decidedly a clear match to Daoud, the SNP's suspect, finally obliterating the American's persistent belief that Mayfield was involved.

It later became clear that from the beginning, the Spanish authorities disagreed with the American expert's conclusions (Kershaw et al., 2004). The Forensic Science Division of the SNP sent the US agents a memo on April 13, 3 weeks *before* Mayfield's arrest, stating that Mayfield's fingerprint and the print on the bag did not match. The match was "conclusively negative," meaning Mayfield was ruled out and could not have left the print.

The Americans continued to hold to their theory and believe in their match long after the SNP rejected it. In the US Department of Justice (DOJ)'s subsequent investigation into the Mayfield debacle, they determined several factors that led to Mayfield's unnecessary arrest, surveillance, and incarceration. Regardless of input from the SNP, the Americans were married to the theory that Mayfield was their man and continued to argue that the print matched. The DOJ determined that they remained "absolutely confident" in their identification, in part because of their "overconfidence in the skill and superiority of its examiners" and did not take seriously the conclusions drawn by the SNP (Fine, 2006, p. 10). Because of the American examiner's overconfidence in their own skills, they rejected the idea that they had erred and did not even try to understand the reasons for the SNP's rejection of their match (Fine, 2006, p. 10).

Two frightening factors that led to the FBI's stubborn and misplaced confidence in their match were Mayfield's religion and business ties (Fine, 2006, p. 13).

Although the original match was made without any knowledge of Mayfield's ties to the Muslim faith, by the time they received the SNP's report ruling out Mayfield as a match, the Americans had taken the innocent characteristics of one of their citizens and used those characteristics to build the profile of a terrorist. One of the examiners admitted to the DOJ investigators that it was Mayfield's religious preference and business ties that caused them to hold onto their mistaken match so doggedly (Fine, 2006, p. 13).

Technical errors were also to blame for the mistaken match. Although the fingerprint database is extremely useful, it is possible for error to occur because of the massive amount of data stored. An individual's partial fingerprint may indeed be very similar to an area of another individual's print. The database allows authorities to find these "matches." The Mayfield case teaches that authorities need to use caution when dealing with huge amounts of data and should expect to find near matches, especially when looking at partial prints (Fine, 2006, p. 7).

Another common misstep of the examiners in the Mayfield case was circular reasoning. When they found 10 points of similarity between Mayfield's known print and the partial print from the bag, they began to see similarities in areas where the partial print was simply too ambiguous to rely upon (Fine, 2006, pp. 7–8). The examiners would see a feature in Mayfield's known print, look at that corresponding area on the latent print, and begin to see the characteristics of Mayfield's print in the "murky and ambiguous" area of the latent print (Fine, 2006, pp. 7–8).

In addition, fingerprint analysts at the FBI know that one discrepancy in a fingerprint analysis renders the pair of prints a nonmatch. If one point of comparison does not match, the fingerprints cannot be said to come from the same party unless there is an explanation that adequately justifies the discrepancy. Because of the 10 points of similarity the examiners originally identified, when they came upon discrepancies between the partial and Mayfield's known print, they were unwilling to declare the prints conclusively negative (Fine, 2006, p. 9). Instead, with each discrepancy they encountered, they found an explanation.

One example of a discrepancy that should have rendered the prints a mismatch was that the upper left side of the print, in its entirety, did not match Mayfield's known print (Fine, 2006, p. 9). The analysts did have an explanation, but not a reasonable one. They argued that the upper left side of the print was not a part of the latent print, but was a print from the touch of another finger. However, as the Office of the Inspector General noted, there were several clues rendering their explanation implausible. The pressures used when the left and right sides of the print were deposited on the bag were equal, making it more likely the print was from a one-touch event. Importantly, the upper left side lined up perfectly with the existing latent print. The ridges flowed from the right side to the left, making a two-touch scenario very unlikely (Fine, 2006, p. 9). The examiners should have seen these characteristics and concluded the print could not have come from Mayfield (Fine, 2006, p. 9).

Although it may not be fair to characterize Mayfield as lucky, things could have been much worse. If the Spanish police had not concluded the FBI was mistaken, if the case was not an international case and the FBI had the final word, Mayfield would likely be serving a life sentence or facing the death penalty. In most American cases in which a qualified FBI examiner concludes that the defendant's prints link him or her to the crime, there is no outside agency to come in and find the real perpetrator.

Worldwide, fingerprint identification has been the gold standard, its reliability only surpassed by DNA profiling (Lawson, 2003). Until DNA exoneration began to shake the foundations of our faith in our justice system in the 1990s, serious challenges to fingerprint evidence were rare, and where the defense dared to challenge the testimony of a qualified fingerprint expert, the challenge was usually dismissed by the jury (Lawson, 2003). For over a century, fingerprint examiners have been respected in courts worldwide, and their testimony has been taken as gospel (Cole, 1998; Haber and Haber, 2008).

But, as illustrated in the Mayfield case, fingerprint examiners can be wrong. Mayfield is not alone. Consider the cases of Steven Cowans, Lana Canen, Ricki Jackson, and Shirley McKie. Steven Cowans was convicted of shooting a police officer. Cowans' conviction was due to a fingerprint left on a coffee cup (Newman, 2007). Cowans spent 7 years in prison before he was finally exonerated by DNA testing. Further analysis of the print revealed it did not actually match Cowans'.

As will be discussed thoroughly below, Lana Canen spent 8 years in prison for murder. Although Canen denied ever having been in the victim's apartment, she was convicted based on a single fingerprint (Wieneke, 2012). Experts later discovered that the print could not have been left by Canen, and she was released from prison.

Ricki Jackson was convicted of killing his partner after an analyst testified that Jackson's prints, in blood, were on a lamp at the scene of the murder (National Registry of Exonerations, 2012). Jackson was exonerated after an investigation initiated by the International Association for Identification (IAI). The IAI is a trade association that certifies fingerprint experts, ensuring they are qualified to testify in court. The IAI determined that the fingerprints were not Jackson's and revoked the certification of the prosecution's expert who had testified against Jackson. In all, the IAI had 50 fingerprint experts examine the fingerprint evidence used against Jackson, and they all determined that the fingerprints were not Jackson's. Jackson was exonerated.

In Scotland, after the murder of Marion Ross, the investigation into the crime became muddied by fingerprint analyses that mistakenly placed an officer, Shirley McKie, inside the crime scene and another analysis that identified David Ashbury as the perpetrator. Based on fingerprint evidence, McKie was charged with perjury because she testified that she did not enter the crime scene; Ashbury was convicted of the murder (McCartney and Walker, 2014). In the end, McKie was acquitted after fingerprint experts proved the prints at the scene attributed to McKie could not have come from McKie. Ashbury's conviction was overturned because of the ambiguity introduced into the case by the erroneous fingerprint "matches."

Although in 2007, one researcher found 20 cases in the US and the UK where fingerprint evidence led directly to a wrongful conviction (Newman, 2007), we have no idea how many people have been wrongly incarcerated due to flawed fingerprint analysis. Given the overwhelming confidence judges and juries place in fingerprint evidence, its widespread use, and the natural propensity of some examiners to see matches once a suspect has been singled out by police, attorneys need be cautious when presented with such evidence (Davis and Leo, 2016). As the Scottish Parliament concluded after an extensive analysis of bungled fingerprint analyses in the Marion Ross murder case, "There is no reason to suggest that fingerprint comparison in general is an inherently unreliable form of evidence but practitioners and fact finders alike require to give due consideration to the limits of the discipline" (McCartney and Walker, 2014; see also, Jiahong, 2016). This consideration is paramount. Fingerprint examiners may be ill-equipped to adequately scrutinize their findings because of one flaw: "they are accustomed to regarding their conclusions as a matter of certainty" (McCartney and Walker, 2014). If the examiner does not know the limits of the science that become inherent when latent partial prints are examined, the trier of fact will be certain to remain uninformed. It was with this knowledge that Scottish Parliament recommended that examiners should discontinue reporting their conclusions of identification or exclusion with a claim of 100% certainty (McCartney and Walker, 2014). This knowledge should also stand as a warning to attorneys and courts to be vigilant and refuse to allow fingerprint evidence unless there has been adequate scrutiny, protection from bias, and the oversight of a well-qualified examiner who cherishes nothing but the truth.

REFERENCES

Broeders, A.P.A., 2006. Of earprints, fingerprints, scent dogs, cot deaths and cognitive contamination—a brief look at the present state of play in the forensic arena. Forensic Science International 159 (2), 148–157.

Cole, S.A., 1998. Witnessing identification latent fingerprinting evidence and expert knowledge. Social Studies of Science 28 (5–6), 687–712.

Davis, D., Leo, R.A., 2016. A damning cascade of investigative errors: flaws in homicide investigation in the USA. In: Maguire (Ed.), The Handbook on Homicide. Wiley-Blackwell.

Democracynoworg, November 30, 2006. Falsely Jailed Attorney Brandon Mayfield Discusses His Case after Feds Award $2 Million and Written Apology. Available at: http://www.democracynow.org/2006/11/30/exclusive_falsely_jailed attorney_brandon_mayfield.

FBI Integrated Automated Fingerprint Identification System: Fact Sheet. Available at: https://www.fbi.gov/about-us/cjis/fingerprints_biometrics/iafis/iafis_facts.

Fine, G.A., 2006. A Review of the FBI's Handling of the Brandon Mayfield Case. US Department of Justice Office of the Inspector General, Washington, DC.

Haber, L., Haber, R.N., 2008. Scientific validation of fingerprint evidence under Daubert. Law, Probability and Risk 7 (2), 87–109.

Jiahong, H., 2016. Miscarriage of justice and malpractice in criminal investigations in China. China Review 16 (1), 65–93.

Kershaw, S., Lichtblau, E., Fuchs, D., Bergman, L., 2004. Spain and US at odds on mistaken terror arrest. New York Times 5, A1.

Lawson, T.F., 2003. Can fingerprints lie?: re-weighing fingerprint evidence in criminal jury trials. American Journal of Criminal Law 31 (1).

McCartney, C., Walker, C., 2014. Forensic identification and miscarriages of justice in England and Wales. Advances in Forensic Human Identification 391.

Mnookin, J., Cole, S.A., Dror, I., Fisher, B.A.J., Houk, M., Inman, K., Kaye, D.H., Koehler, J.J., Langenburg, G., Risinger, D.M., Rudin, N., Siegel, J., Stoney, D.A., January 12, 2011. The Need for a Research Culture in the Forensic Sciences. Northwestern Public Law Research Paper No. 11-20; The Pennsylvania State University Legal Studies Research Paper No. 5-2011. Available at SSRN: http://ssrn.com/abstract=1755722.

National Registry of Exonerations, 2012. Ricki Jackson. Available at: http://www.law.umich.edu/special/exoneration/Pages/casedetail.aspx?caseid=3318.

Newman, D., 2007. Limitations of fingerprint identifications. The Criminal Justice 22, 36.

Rozelle, S.D., 2007. Daubert, Schmaubert: criminal defendants and the short end of the science stick. Tulsa Law Review 43, 597.

Spinney, L., 2010. Science in court: the fine print. Nature News 464 (7287), 344–346.

Thompson, W.C., Cole, S.A., 2005. Lessons from the Brandon Mayfield case. The Champion 29 (3), 42–44.

Wax, S.T., Schatz, C.J., 2004. A multitude of errors: the Brandon Mayfield case. Champion 28 (8), 6.

Wieneke, C., 2012. Fingerprint misidentification leads to wrongful conviction in Indiana: state of Indiana v. Lana Canen. Life After Exoneration. Available at: http://www.exonerated.org/index.php?option=comcontent&view=article&id=262:fingerprint-misidentification-leads-to-wrongful-conviction-in-indiana&catid=41:news-stories&Itemid=94.

The Fingerprint Expert: Do You Really Have One?

Kathleen L. Bright-Birnbaum

Desert Forensics, Tucson, AZ, United States

The case study previously mentioned illustrates how fingerprint identification can go wrong, even when the best in the field conduct the analyses. If such an egregious error can take place with those qualified to do the task, the problems and errors only multiply when someone who is not a qualified expert tackles the task. While attorneys and the courts recognize the need for experts, knowing who is or who is not an expert can be difficult if their area of expertise is not really understood. Are they exaggerating their expertise? Are they really trained in the area about which they are providing testimony? Do they really have the credentials to do what they do? What should attorneys and courts be aware of and what can they ask? The following review of the case against Lana Canen exemplifies what happens when an unqualified "expert" gives evidence, the injustice that follows, and how this injustice could have been prevented. The discussion of the Canen case is followed by a discussion about ACE-V (Analysis, Comparison, Evaluation, and Verification) methodology, absolute conclusions and error rates, the one unexplainable dissimilarity rule, Automated Fingerprint Identification System (AFIS) matches, training trends, and fingerprints' past and possible future.

LANA CANEN

It was November 28, 2002, on Thanksgiving Day; Helen Sailor spent the day surrounded by family instead of in her apartment at the Waterfall High Rise complex, known for housing the elderly, the disabled, and the handicapped in Elkhart, Indiana. Sailor was 94 years old and blind. Having the opportunity to spend time with her family was something she looked forward to. That evening her family drove her home, and all was well. The next day, two of Sailor's relatives came by the apartment, along with one of her healthcare providers. They found that the previous uplifting day was Sailor's last; they discovered that Sailor was dead, her body badly beaten. The small apartment was ransacked with dresser drawers pulled out; Sailor's bible, where she hid money and her keys, was now empty. The autopsy revealed significant injuries to Sailor's neck, face, and hands. The pathologist ruled Sailor's death was a homicide, and strangulation was the cause of death.

The detectives from Elkhart Police Department believed robbery was the motive behind the killing of Sailor. "Because there was no forced entry, Elkhart police believed the victim knew her assailant. They began interviewing residents, but they were stymied and the investigation went cold."[2]

Months passed, and the Elkhart Police Department created a cold case unit. Sailor's case was one of the unit's very first cases. Items of evidence recovered from Sailor's apartment were processed for latent prints, including a plastic tub, which contained numerous prescription medication bottles. Latent prints are "accidental" impressions (no one deliberately leaves their fingerprints on a piece of evidence) that a person may or may not leave behind when they touch something. Latents usually require chemicals or powders to make them visible. Several latent prints were developed and lifted from Sailor's plastic medication tub. Upon completion of the processing, the items were returned to their original evidence bags and resealed. The latent lifts were secured as evidence.

Investigators still believed that Sailor knew her assailant, and the search for investigative leads was expanded to all the residents of Sailor's apartment building as well as her caretakers.

In August of 2003, the police received information that a subject by the name of Andrew Royer might have been involved in the murder. When he was interviewed, he admitted that "he was responsible for Sailor's death and provided details that had not been released to the public. Royer told the police that he strangled Sailor with a rope, cleaned her apartment with towels, and that he took jewelry and money." Royer was charged with murder.[3] Sometime later, Royer revised his previous statement and implicated Lana Canen, telling police that both he and Canen broke into the apartment to get money. Canen insisted that she had nothing to do with the crime.[4]

---

[2] Maurice Possley, The National Registry of Exonerations: Lana Canen Case Detail.
[3] Hans Sherrer, *Lana Canen Exonerated of Murder Conviction After Fingerprint Testimony Exposed as False*, Nov. 7, 2012, Justice Denied, http://justicedenied.org/wordpress/archives/2306.
[4] *Id.*

The Elkhart Police Department asked Detective Dennis Chapman of the Elkhart County Sheriff's Department if he would examine the latent lifts procured earlier for a possible match to suspects in the murder. Detective Chapman was assigned to the lab full-time at the sheriff's department, and according to his own words, people would ask him "to look at prints because they knew he had fingerprint training." Chapman explained that everybody would come to him and ask for help, and based upon that, he started doing fingerprint analyses on a more regular basis. Chapman testified at Canen's trial that "in the fall of 2000, I attended an Integrated Indiana Law Enforcement Crime Scene Training School; and after that, of course, I was assigned to the lab full time."[5] The Elkhart Police Department felt comfortable with Chapman's qualifications. They submitted the latent prints and the fingerprint cards to him for comparison, including those of Sailor and an inked set of fingerprints and palm prints of Canen.

Inked prints are "deliberate" recordings of the available friction ridge detail on a person's fingers and palms. Inked fingerprints are taken under controlled conditions using black ink and a white fingerprint card, and are meant to show all of the detail available on the fingerprint. An inked set of prints would record all 10 fingers.

According to Chapman's supplementary report, he initially examined the latent prints lifted from the evidence to determine if they were identifiable and felt that, in most of the latents, there was not sufficient ridge detail to do a comparison. There was one latent lift from the plastic tub, labeled "M," that was deemed to have enough ridge detail for a comparison.

There are three basic fingerprint pattern types: (1) arch pattern, where ridges rise up gradually and flow out the opposite side of the finger; (2) loop pattern, where ridges rise up and recurve back, flowing out the same side they entered, similar in shape to a bobby pin; and (3) whorl pattern, where ridges flow in a circular pattern similar to a bull's eye in shape. Chapman determined that the latent print left on the tub of medication had a loop "with a possible ridge count of 7–17" ridges.

Using this information, he began examining the print cards for possible matches. The victim, Helen Sailor, did not leave the print; she was "eliminated right away as there was very little to no ridge detail in her prints."[6] It is not unusual to find in the elderly that the friction ridges on palms and fingers become worn down over time and may be barely discernible. After eliminating Sailor, Chapman started comparing the latent print with the various fingerprint cards that had been submitted by the police department. In addition to the prints of Lana Canen that the police submitted, Chapman also found a copy of Canen's prints in the sheriff's department files. He used this second set because "the quality was a little better, but they were both the prints of Canen."[7] At this stage, Chapman began the comparison of Canen's fingerprints:

---

[5] Trial transcript, testimony of Detective Dennis Chapman at the trial of Lana Canen, at 617.
[6] Case Supplementary Report on Offense of Murder by Detective Dennis E. Chapman, Elkhart County Sheriff's Department; case number 2002-1129-008.
[7] *Id.*

"Checking Lana Canen's print card, she did appear to have a radial loop of the right index finger. This finger was examined first, but it did not match the latent. If the print was from Lana, then it would have to be an Ulna loop from the left hand." An ulna or ulnar loop refers to a loop pattern that flows towards the little finger. It is the most common of the three basic pattern types. A radial loop is less common type loop in that it flows towards the thumb instead of the little finger.

"[Canen's] left thumb was a Whorl so it was eliminated. The left index was a possible Whorl or a Radial loop, so it was eliminated. This left the left middle, ring, and index [fingers]. The left middle had a small ridge count so this was eliminated. The left ring finger appears to be a Whorl with a possible reference to a loop so it was eliminated.".[8] Chapman advised that the left little finger remained as a possibility.

While to many, the above description given by Chapman may seem reasonable, in actuality to a trained finger print analyst, numerous red flags have been going up since we first began our review of Chapman's analyses. Many of the terms Chapman used, such as ulna and radial loop, are terms commonly used in fingerprint *classification*, which is merely a means to file a fingerprint card and involves examining inked prints for their pattern type and on which finger they occur. The terms Chapman used do not apply to the process of a latent print comparison.

After Chapman examined the left little finger on the fingerprint card of Canen and the latent print from the plastic tub labeled "M," he "found several points that matched up with each other." In his report, he stated, "[b]ased on my experience as a fingerprint examiner with the Federal Bureau of Investigation from 1976 to 1978 and my continued examination of fingerprints with the Elkhart County Sheriff's Department, the latent print from the med tub is the left little finger of Canen." Other latent prints were also compared against Canen, but the only identification that Chapman made was that of the "left little finger of Canen on the Med Tub."[9]

On March 5, 2004, Detective Chapman returned all of the latent lifts and inked fingerprint impressions to the Elkhart Police Department that had been submitted to him for his examination and comparison. Along with these returned items, Detective Chapman provided a signed supplemental report showing the results of his examination along with enlargements of the fingerprint impressions that he had made during the course of his examination. The items of evidence were returned to the evidence room, along with the enlargements and the original copy of Chapman's report. Copies of his report were provided to the Elkhart Police Department's investigating commander.

On September 2, 2004, Canen was charged with the murder of Helen Sailor. According to Canen, the lead detective on the case had for some time believed she was involved in a number of burglaries that had occurred at the apartment months before the murder. Canen had been dating the apartment building maintenance man who had a master key to all the apartments. It was Canen's belief that police felt she took the key from her boyfriend and burglarized the apartments. There was never enough evidence to prove this allegation though, and, according to Canen,

---

[8] *Id.*

[9] *Id.*

the detective allegedly said that he was going to get her for something, if not the burglaries.[10]

On August 2, 2005 the Elkhart Police Department was informed of arrangements being made for the examination and review of the latent print lifted from the plastic tub containing medications in Sailor's apartment and the inked fingerprints of Canen. The examination would be conducted by a fingerprint expert contacted by an investigator working for Canen's attorney. The items in question were retrieved from the Indiana State Police Laboratory in Fort Wayne, where they were being stored. At no time was the state lab ever asked to examine the comparison, only to retain the evidence.

Chapman was not the only unqualified fingerprint expert to analyze the prints. The fingerprint expert retained by Canen's attorney admitted during a subsequent deposition years later that he was not a full-time latent print examiner and had no formal training in latent print comparisons. He advised that he had only attended workshops about general crime scene investigations and was not familiar with many of the methodologies and protocols that competent examiners follow in their profession. He said that after examining the prints, he thought he only saw three points of comparison and that they were ones common in the population. He was unable to make an identification. He went on to say that if he had been asked, he would have told the attorney or the investigator to send the evidence to the state crime lab, but that he was never asked as to his conclusion.[11] The print was never sent to the Indiana State Crime Lab for verification.

On August 5, 2005, just days before Royer and Canen were to be jointly tried in trial, the prosecution amended the charges of murder to felony murder. Royer's statement that initially implicated Canen was excluded as evidence. The sole piece of evidence now linking Canen to the murder of Helen Sailor would be the testimony of Elkhart County Sheriff's Department Detective Dennis Chapman that there was a match between Canen's left little finger and the latent print found on the plastic tub in Sailor's apartment.

On August 8, the jury trial began, and the state's witness, Detective Dennis Chapman, took the stand. He was asked by the prosecutor about his background, training, and experience. Chapman talked about having been with Elkhart Sheriff's Department for 12 years, 6 of which were as a detective. He talked about his previous work experience, including that he had worked for the FBI for about 2 years, beginning in 1976 as a fingerprint examiner, having completed "12 weeks of training on how to classify and examine prints." When he was asked what he meant by "classify prints," he testified about how fingerprints were broken down by characteristics such as patterns, and that in each finger, there were "little lines." The prosecutor asked him about how many print cards he would need to look at in order to make a comparison. Chapman's response was that he allowed a leeway of approximately

---

[10] Correspondence with defense attorney Cara Wieneke, dated November 4, 2012.

[11] Correspondence with defense attorney Cara Wieneke, dated December 12, 2012.

five ridges in either direction.[12] What was not being revealed during this testimony, nor was Chapman questioned on, is that none of this was related to latent print comparisons, but rather, as Chapman stated earlier, fingerprint classification, a way to file fingerprints for easy retrieval at a later date and not related to the process of comparing a latent impression to an inked print. Chapman had stated he was a fingerprint examiner with the FBI. He never said he was a latent print examiner with the FBI, who often selected their latent examiners from the ranks of heavily experienced fingerprint examiners with many, many years of experience and after having shown extreme aptitude. Once chosen, training in latent prints would be vastly different and much more intensive than simply a 12-week course on how to classify and look at inked prints.

After Chapman left the FBI, he went on to explain he was employed by the Cook County Nuclear Plant in Indiana, where he "occasionally" looked at fingerprint cards being submitted for "background checks on certain individuals" to make sure the cards were "all right to be submitted."[13] While a jury might be impressed at this being a reflection of still more fingerprint experience, in actuality, this job had nothing to do with the comparison of prints, much less latent prints. The job was, in fact, to merely look to see if the prints were recorded sufficiently as to not be rejected by the FBI due to smearing or incomplete recording of the inked prints. He then explained to the court that he had made "several, maybe 100 or so" comparisons.[14] At first blush, this might seem to be a significant number, but it is far from it.

To put it in context, it is a common question to be asked, and, as an analyst, my normal answer is as follows: "I was curious about the number of prints I had examined in the beginning of my career too, so I kept a personal log until I reached 500,000 comparisons. At that point I quit keeping track and that was many, many years ago." Several prints or even 100 comparisons can easily be done in one very large case and hardly reflects the numbers expected of an experienced examiner.

At this time, the fingerprint card from Elkhart City Police Department was shown to Chapman by the prosecutor as State's Exhibit 47, and Chapman was asked, "[D] id you personally use this fingerprint card to attempt to make a classification or, I'm sorry, a comparison?". Chapman responded, "Yes, I did." Note that the terms "classification" and "comparison" were still not being distinguished, nor the difference clarified by Chapman, even though they represent completely different concepts. State's Exhibit 46 was then shown to Chapman and recognized as being the latent print received from the Elkhart City Police Department. Chapman was asked if he was able to make a comparison from State's Exhibit 47 to State's Exhibit 46, and Chapman responded: "Yes, I was."[15] Although defense counsel and the court had heard next to no testimony that Chapman was equipped to do a comparison, there were no objections as the State's Exhibit 46 and 47 were admitted.

---

[12] Trial transcript, testimony of Detective Dennis Chapman at the trial of Lana Canen, at 615-616.
[13] *Id.* at 616.
[14] *Id.* at 617.
[15] *Id.* at 621.

Questioning from the prosecution continued. "Which finger were you able to find the, at least the, characteristics that were consistent with lifter [i.e., card upon which the fingerprint was lifted] M from the medical tub?" Chapman's response was that he "knew it couldn't come from the right hand because it was gonna' have to be an ulna loop, and the ulna loop can only be from the left hand." This response, as previously stated, in fact uses terms employed in the classification of prints for filing purposes and are not applicable to latent print comparisons. Chapman was wrong on another point. Ulnar/ulna and radial loops can occur on *either* hand if loop patterns are present. The finger that they appear on and the ridge count from the core of the print to the delta are what is used as part of the method to "classify" fingerprints (the core is the center of the print, the delta is where the ridges diverge in three different directions). Prints from thousands of people can have the same "classification." As stated earlier, it is merely a means to file a fingerprint card to make for easier retrieval at a later date.

Chapman then talked about his last assignment with the FBI where he had to classify "40 prints an hour," picking through the same patterns "to find one that's a little bit different than the others...then use your magnifying glass to verify it."[16] Once again, this refers to the duties of a fingerprint examiner looking at deliberate recordings of inked prints in order to classify them for filing purposes, but is not the methodology used by latent print examiners comparing accidental latent impressions to known inked prints for purposes of making an identification or exclusion. Unfortunately, neither the prosecutor, the defense attorney, nor the court questioned this major distinction or the lack of latent print qualifications that Chapman was putting forth.

The prosecutor now brought out the charted enlargement that Chapman had made "for purposes of illustrating" the comparison of the latent print and the inked print, which he had identified as the left little finger of Canen. These charted enlargements were admitted as State's Exhibits 48 and 49, "true and accurate representations" that Chapman enlarged from the original State's Exhibits 46 and 47. When asked if the enlargements showed "the points" that he used to make his comparison, he responded simply, "[Y]es, they do."[17] The court admitted both Exhibits 48 and 49 without objection.

Chapman was questioned about the numbers and lines that he had placed on the enlargements, and he stated that these markings were to show corresponding points in each fingerprint so he could "show for the audience to look at and see, possibly show where they match up." When asked if the enlargements of the latent print and inked print were printed at exactly the same angle and exactly the same scale, he admitted that they were not. No objections were raised, and after another minor question or two, the prosecutor's line of questioning essentially ended. Cross-examination by Canen's attorney began.

During cross-examination, Canen's attorney pointed out that Chapman had numbered seven points being similar. There was no question as to why the charted enlargements were not done at the same angle or scale, as traditional charted enlargements

---

[16] *Id.* at 627.
[17] *Id.* at 631.

are done. Chapman was asked: "How do you prove that no print in mankind matches any other print in mankind?", and Chapman's simple answer of "through history" was never questioned further. There was no explanation about the biological differences, genetic aspects, or how differential growth can affect the minutia in the prints. The simple "through history" was all that was said without being expounded upon. A few more questions were asked regarding points of comparison and if the comparison had been made before they were enlarged, but nothing more. There were no further questions from Canen's attorney regarding the sole piece of evidence that could convict Canen of murder. Cross-examination then went to Royer's attorney. Royer's attorney asked Chapman about the date he received the fingerprint card and who he had received it from, but beyond that, there were no additional questions from the defense.[18]

The trial lasted for 3 days with Canen steadfastly maintaining her innocence, saying she had never been in Sailor's apartment. The fingerprint evidence was still enough to convince the jury of Canen's guilt. The jury convicted Canen and Royer of murder, each receiving a 55-year prison sentence. The overwhelming abundance of red flags and exaggerated credentials went unquestioned. Even though one single fingerprint would be the entire foundation upon which Canen's conviction was built, the attorneys went through the most basic of motions, but never recognized the blatant issues regarding fingerprints and the fingerprint testimony that was given. Years later, Elkhart County Prosecutor would go on to state that it is "reasonable to believe that the jury relied upon Detective Chapman's testimony in considering the evidence against Canen." The fingerprint testimony and the fingerprint examiner were the central parts that "placed Canen at the scene and were supporting the theory of the prosecution of the case."[19]

Years passed, and Canen steadfastly maintained her innocence in the murder of Helen Sailor. It was in 2011 that the Indiana Public Defender's Office asked defense attorney Cara Wieneke to do a routine postconviction review of Canen's case. Nothing unusual or unseemly was expected to be found, and in fact, another defense attorney had already declined to review the case. When Wieneke heard that Canen was continuing to maintain her innocence even after nearly a decade, she accepted the case and began looking into the evidence presented at trial.

One of the first discoveries that Wieneke made was that the detective hired by Canen's lawyer was not qualified to do fingerprint analysis and that Canen's lawyer had never looked into Chapman's credentials.[20] "When I reviewed the transcript, I realized the fingerprints were an important part of the trial," Wieneke said, "[a]nd so I thought maybe I'll have them tested by an independent examiner – one that was certified."[21]

---

[18] *Id.* at 636.

[19] Press Release, Curtis T. Hill, Office of the Prosecuting Attorney of Elkhart County, Ind., September 9, 2012.

[20] Maurice Possley, The National Registry of Exonerations: Lana Canen Case Detail.

[21] Sharon Hernandez, *Attorney Re-Evaluated Evidence in Elkhart Murder Case*, Elkhart Truth (Elkhart, Ind.) October 3, 2012.

I was the certified, independent examiner that Wieneke contacted. It was in June of 2011 that I received an email from Wieneke asking about my availability to review the evidence in the case. I responded that I was available and asked her to send me as much of the following as she could: high-quality photographs or scans of all the latent print evidence, copies of all fingerprints and palm prints used by the police, copies of all crime scene and laboratory exam notes and photographs, copies of all court transcripts and interviews related to the fingerprint evidence, and a set of fingerprints of Canen taken in Wieneke's presence. I essentially wanted the same information that was available during the original examination. The reason for the fingerprints of Canen taken in Wieneke's presence was to be able to compare them to the ones used by the police to be absolutely confident they were indeed those of Canen's and not just a print card "bearing the name" of Canen. While mix-ups are not necessarily common, they can and do happen. This was a way to insure that the inked prints used in the comparison were, without a doubt, those of Canen, and not simply an assumption.

A few days later, I received a package in the mail along with a letter from the Wieneke Law Office. "Pursuant to our email correspondence, enclosed find the following items: A CD containing images of my client's 10-print card and the lift card. You will notice that the cards are encased in plastic. I was not allowed to remove the cards from the plastic, even for photographing. Therefore, we were not able to get good photos of the rolled prints from the right middle or right index fingers." Wieneke included on the CD images of the latent print lift card, also photographed through the plastic evidence bag. A second CD contained (1) trial testimony from the fingerprint examiner, (2) a photo of the location of the latent prior to it being lifted from the plastic tub, (3) photographs of the enlargement charts of the inked print and the latent print; and (4) an additional "insufficient" latent print. Chapman had testified that the "insufficient" print was not of sufficient quality to do a comparison.

Upon reviewing the submitted photographs of the evidence, I found that much of it could not be used because of having been photographed through plastic, a far cry from the high-resolution images I would need to do a latent comparison with. Writing on the plastic-covered areas that I needed to see and the plastic itself distorted the images of the fingerprints. I was also disappointed that Wieneke was not able to have a new set of Canen's fingerprints taken in her presence. The only items I received that were of any useable quality were the photographs of the charted enlargements that Chapman had presented at trial. This is where I now turned my attention.

My jaw fell open and my heart leapt into my throat upon examining the charted enlargements. It was blatantly clear to me that the latent print did NOT match the charted enlargement of the inked print. The two fingerprints shown on the chart did not come from the same finger. While they were both left slant loop patterns—the ridges came in from the left side of the print on both the latent and the inked print, recurved back, and exited the same side they entered on, the left side—the similarities ended after that. I could easily see that the number of ridges between the core and the delta greatly differed between the two prints. The further I examined the details of the latent and the inked print, the more unexplainable dissimilarities I continued to find. "How could this have happened" almost became a mantra for me; I was horrified!

Turning my attention next to the transcripts Wieneke had sent me of Chapman's testimony, my answer as to how this had happened became clearer. Two things were immediately obvious to me. First, Chapman had no real latent print comparison training. There are many qualified latent print examiners who offer and teach classes, but Chapman had not indicated that he had ever taken any of these available classes. The only class that Chapman described as having taken was one dealing with general crime scenes, not one that specialized in fingerprint comparison.

The second issue was recognizing that Chapman's position with the FBI was one that dealt solely with the classification and comparison of inked fingerprint prints, not latent prints recovered from crime scenes. Latent print comparisons, like the one Chapman did in Canen's case, were done by the FBI latent print examiners and would never have been given to a fingerprint examiner to perform. These were two different job classifications with different training and qualifications. Chapman never held the position of latent print examiner with the FBI, but this was never recognized during trial, and thus, Chapman's qualifications to testify as an expert were never challenged. His qualifications were exaggerated, and his experience was limited to working with inked prints, but no one in the court realized nor questioned it.

The difference between classifying and comparing inked fingerprints and the analysis and comparison of latent fingerprints was a vital part of Chapman's testimony. Many people can have the same fingerprint classification, and comparing inked fingerprints is a relatively simple process when compared to latent fingerprints because the quality present in an inked print is usually far greater (if properly done) than that available in a typical latent print.

Due to factors such as sweat (anything such as sweat or oils on the fingers to transfer to the item), the type of surface touched (textured, porous, smooth, nonporous), how an item is touched/contacted (fingers dragged, twisted and turned, smeared, touched, and lifted), and environmental factors (did other people touch the same area, was the area cleaned afterwards), all can affect if there is a useable print left to work with. Only a portion of the fingerprint is available for comparison, and often, the quality is not very good. The training and experience needed to conduct latent print comparisons is very different than that required to work with inked fingerprints, yet like in the Canen case, there are those testifying as "experts" after having taken the merest of training.

The red flags I discovered in the testimony showed me why the erroneous identification had occurred. This was a comparison done by someone who had overstated his credentials and never clarified or corrected the misconception that he was trained and qualified to do latent print comparisons. Even the charted enlargements presented at court were not done in the proper manner, as the two fingerprints were not shown printed to the same scale nor orientated in the same direction. The reason the lines and arrows he had drawn on the enlarged fingerprints were not matching was because the two fingerprints were not from the same source. The latent print on the charted enlargement did not match the inked print on the charted enlargement.

On June 27, 2011, I called Wieneke to inform her of my findings. While she had been prepared for me to perhaps tell her that the print comparison was "inconclusive," she was not prepared for me to tell her that it was not a match. This was an unexpected turn of events. At the request of Wieneke, I completed a written scientific examination report, which included a full analysis and comparison of the fingerprints shown in the photographs of the charted enlargements. I included the results of my examination, my employment history of over 30 years in law enforcement working in forensics at that time, and my status as an IAI Certified Latent Print Examiner since January 1996. In my written report stating my conclusion that State's Exhibit 49, the photograph of the fingerprint of the left little finger of Canen did not match the fingerprint depicted in State's Exhibit 48, the latent impression from the plastic tub. I listed the reasons why the "identification" presented was erroneous. I listed the reasons with an analysis of each of the points that Chapman had used in his comparison, discussing each of the dissimilarities between the latent and the inked print.

After reviewing each of the supposedly matching points in the fingerprints, I demonstrated further reasons the two fingerprints did not match, using the same illustrations of the two fingerprints (i.e., Exhibits 48 and 49) followed by an explanation: the delta area on the latent, while not distinctly visible, has sufficient ridge flow surrounding it to determine that it is about four to five ridges from the core. The delta on the inked print is clearly visible and is 13 ridges from the core. While both the latent and the inked print are left slant loop patterns, they are clearly of a significantly different ridge count and are completely out of agreement (see illustrated photographs: delta marked as blue dot with traced surrounding ridge flow; core marked in red).[22]

At the conclusion of my report, I noted that the images submitted to me of the latent print impressions, lift cards, and inked prints of Canen were not "best evidence." Understanding that the prosecutor might balk at the conclusions of an "outsider" or "hired gun," even with all my credentials, I advised that if I was not going to be provided access to the evidence, the Indiana State Crime Lab should be requested to review the evidence, comparisons, and "identification." I was confident that the crime lab examiners would come to the same conclusion I did.

After receiving my report of the erroneous identification, Wieneke contacted the Indiana State Crime Lab to request that it review the fingerprint evidence. This request was shortly after blocked by the prosecutor's office. "The prosecutor didn't want to set a precedent by sending all of the evidence for every case there," Wieneke said in a later statement to the news.[23] I was advised by Wieneke that the prosecutor told her that even if her defense expert disagreed with the results of Chapman's comparison, it would be just the opinion of one expert against the opinion of another. This statement made me acutely aware that should I need to present my "opinion" at any subsequent hearing, I needed something very visual to

---

[22] Item 12h in the Scientific Examination Report prepared by Kathleen Bright-Birnbaum, dated July 6, 2011.

[23] Amanda Gray, *Prosecutor Curtis T. Hill Jr. Requests Conviction Vacation for Lana Canen of Elkhart*, GOSHEN NEWS (Indiana) September 29, 2012.

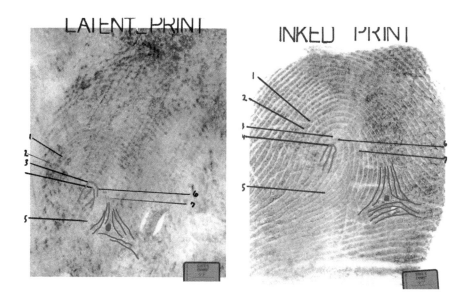

illustrate Chapman's error and not just rely on verbal discussion. I needed a "seeing is believing" presentation.

In the meantime, Wieneke prepared for a deposition with Chapman using questions that I suggested: I recommended she ask him about what methodology he used in his comparison? Is he a "point counter," i.e., someone who looks only at matching features but not everything available in a print (both quantity of features and quality of features)? Does he know what ACE-V (discussed in detail in the following) is? Does he know what SWGFAST is (Scientific Working Group on Friction Ridge Analysis, Study and Technology)? Does he follow the SWGFAST standard for latent print examinations? Is he a member of the IAI?

During the subsequent deposition, Chapman told Wieneke that "I don't look for points of dissimilarity, only points of similarity." He was not a member of any professional forensic associations, nor was he even familiar with the IAI, the primary association for the forensic community.[24] Chapman never had his "identification" verified, and while the original defense attorney had hired someone to "verify" the work, this defense expert had no formal training in fingerprint comparisons. The expert the defense hired advised Wieneke during his own deposition that he had been unable to make an identification and had recommended the prints be examined by the state crime lab.[25]

An evidentiary hearing was scheduled for August 16, 2012, and I prepared a PowerPoint presentation titled "Charting to Demonstrate a Fingerprint Identification."

---

[24] Email correspondence with Cara Wieneke regarding deposition with Chapman on September 7, 2011.

[25] Email correspondence with Cara Wieneke dated August 10, 2011.

The presentation began by showing a "traditional" charted enlargement, which presented the latent print and inked known fingerprint side by side at the same scale and orientation. As Chapman's charted enlargements did not follow "traditional" requisites, I wanted the court to visually see the differences without verbal explanation from me. The presentation then demonstrated the proper method for comparing fingerprints using all the levels of detail (Level 1: the fingerprint pattern; Level 2: the quantity of "points" and features in the fingerprints such as ending ridges, bifurcations, and dots; Level 3: details dealing with the clarity of prints, shapes, and pores found on the ridges). I explained that at Level 1, a person could be possibly eliminated, but that an identification could not be made at this level of detail. Levels 2 and 3 can both be used in making an identification if there is sufficient quantity and quality present. Once this portion of the presentation was completed, working through the levels of doing a comparison of a latent to an inked print, I felt the court had a better understanding of the comparison process. I then began the second portion of the presentation, showing Chapman's charts, with the following statement:

> *Training and experience do not allow the expert to see anything different from that which the layperson sees. Training and experience only prepare the expert to interpret that which is seen the same by both … BUT if that which is seen is clearly at odds with the interpretation put forth by the expert, then even the layperson has the right to question the interpretation. "Seeing Is Believing."*

Following the same format as just demonstrated for the proper method of comparing fingerprints, I began demonstrating the comparison of Chapman's charted enlargements by starting an analysis of the latent print and then the inked print (Level 1 detail). I marked the core of each print and showed how they compared. I marked the delta of each print and showed how they compared. One by one, I counted the ridges between the core and delta, first on the latent print and then the inked print. This time though, unlike in the previous demonstration, the ridge count on Chapman's chart between the core and delta was drastically different. The only thing that matched was that they were both left slant loops, but that was where the similarities ended (see marked images illustrated above). The ridge count between the core and the delta on the latent is approximately 6 ridges, allowing for the lack of clarity. Notably, the ridge count between the core and the delta on the inked print is approximately 12 ridges. This finding is sufficient for qualified examiners to end the comparison and conclude that the two prints were not from the same source. This finding would be considered an unexplainable dissimilarity.

I continued the comparison of Chapman's enlargements through Level 2 and 3, discussing the points and features that were similar in the two fingerprints as well as the clear and obvious unexplainable dissimilarities. I ended the presentation with a visual explanation of how this erroneous identification might have occurred. The extremely important "analysis" phase of Level 1 detail seemed to have been skipped, which would have included determining the core and delta in the pattern and then counting the ridges between the two. That the number of ridges between the core and delta of the two fingerprints did not match should have informed Chapman that the two prints were not from the same source and that they were not a match. By accepting features that "match" and ignoring "dissimilar features" as distortion, the result is an "erroneous identification" or "misattribution," as some courts prefer to call it. This misattribution lead directly to Lana's wrongful conviction and incarceration.

Upon completion of the visual PowerPoint, I then was thoroughly cross-examined by the prosecutor, who was obviously prepared with his questions. We covered everything from my background to my fees, from error rates to cognitive bias. I then was excused and went to sit behind defense council. Chapman was the next to be called to the stand, and the defense counsel wanted me to hear his testimony.

In response to Wieneke's questions, Chapman admitted he had made a mistake in his comparison of the latent print to Canen. That was basically all that defense wanted to hear. The prosecutor was next up, and it was very clear he did not like the position he had been put in by Chapman. During Chapman's subsequent testimony, I still recognized that Chapman was not clarifying the difference between latent prints and inked prints. I slipped a note to Wieneke pointing this out. Upon completion of the prosecutor's questioning of Chapman, Wieneke asked one additional question and that was in regards to Chapman's training in inked prints but complete lack of training with latent prints. Chapman agreed that his experience was with inked prints. Defense had no other questions, but the prosecution had something additional to ask:

Q: Did it ever occur to you that you weren't qualified to do this comparison?
A: Yes.
Q: Did you tell anyone?
A: No.
Q: Why did you do it?!?!

In response to this last question, Chapman answered simply that he had wanted to help.

At the conclusion of the hearing, the judge ordered the fingerprint evidence to be sent to the Indiana State Crime Lab for a complete review. The prosecutor admitted to me that he did not expect the lab's conclusion to be any different than mine. A few days later, the lab reported its results: Canen was excluded from having made the latent impression. As the lab was given access to all the evidence that I was never given, the lab subsequently matched the latent to one of Helen Sailor's caretakers, having legitimate access to the location the print was found when helping to give Sailor her medications.

After spending 8 years in prison, on November 2, 2012, the prosecutor's office requested that the homicide conviction of Canen be vacated. Canen was released. The prosecutor's office went on to state that Canen would not be retried because the fingerprint was a central part of the case against her, and without it, he could not prove she was involved. "There's just not an ability for me in good conscience to go forward and suggest that we have a sufficient amount to support a prosecution."[26] In March of 2016,

---

[26] Kelli Stopczynski, *Elkhart Murder Conviction Overturned, Woman Freed From Prison*, WSBT.com article collections, November 2, 2012.

the civil lawsuit filed by Canen's attorney asking for compensation for her wrongful incarceration was dismissed for unknown reasons. Lana will receive no compensation for the erroneous identification that convicted her and cost her 8 years of her life.

ANALYSIS, COMPARISON, EVALUATION, AND VERIFICATION METHODOLOGY

The ACE-V methodology is recognized and accepted in the field of fingerprints, especially in the US, as being the methodology employed when doing fingerprint comparisons by qualified and trained examiners. ACE-V refers to a four-step process and roughly compares to the scientific process used in other realms: first, analysis of the unknown (latent) print; second, comparison with the known (inked or live scan) print; third, evaluation of the similar and dissimilar features between the latent and the inked, to reach a conclusion of whether sufficiency exists to declare an association/identification or an exclusion, or if there is insufficiency for either conclusion. Finally, the conclusion needs to be verified by another qualified examiner before the results are reported. The verifying examiner does their own analysis, comparison, and evaluation, and should come to the same conclusion if everything is in order. In the case of Canen, ACE-V was not employed by Chapman, with disastrous results. The ACE-V methodology is a complex mental process that combines both objective and subjective components. Because of the complexity, it may not be exactly the same for two examiners looking at the same print, not even for the same examiner looking at the same print on different occasions.

It is important to recognize from the outset that "subjective" does not necessarily mean error-prone any more than "objective" means error-free. As these terms apply to ACE-V, the process itself is objective. When I demonstrated in court the process of a traditional charted enlargement and comparison between the latent print and inked print, going through the analysis of each level, comparing the features, and evaluating the results, it clearly showed defined steps followed in a consistent manner.

The ACE-V process has been thought through, described, modified, and published in discipline-specific form in peer-reviewed books and journal articles for decades. When followed correctly, ACE-V minimizes the chance of inadvertent error. The steps themselves are objective in their description and application. However, each step involves decisions in the mind of the examiner that, by very definition, are subjective in nature. A trained, experienced, tested examiner with demonstrated skills and abilities and a track record of accurate work should be able to be relied upon to make appropriate decisions that yield accurate conclusions at the end of the process if it is followed properly.

ABSOLUTE CONCLUSIONS AND ERROR RATES

In reaching a conclusion, an examiner may have developed a personal belief that two images originated from the same area of friction skin. That personal belief may be absolute. But in presenting a more objective scientific opinion in court, the examiner cannot allow personal beliefs to overstate the strength of the conclusion. In earlier years, examiners testified to their beliefs and stated them as scientific opinions in absolute terms. We recognize now that a correct application of science precludes any such absolute conclusion. No matter how strong the personal belief of an examiner that two images represent the same area of friction ridge skin, there always exists a possibility in science that they do not. It is when the examiner concludes that the possibility that they represent different areas of skin is so very, very small that the possibility can be disregarded and that an identification or association is claimed. While we do not yet have a validated model for calculating how small the possibility actually is that two similar prints came from different areas of skin, we nonetheless can reach a conclusion of identification. The difference between the ways it was stated a couple of decades ago and the way it is stated today is the fact that we, as latent print examiners, no longer disregard even the smallest possibility of two prints having the same features to render an absolute conclusion or an unjustified claim of 100% certainty. "The features observed in the unknown latent print would be what the examiner would expect to see from the person in question, but would not be expected from the random person in the general population" would be an example of how wording differs now from previously stating that "X number of points were found in both the unknown and known print; the latent impression was made by the defendant and could not have been made by anyone else."

Wording and terminology is still in the process of evolving. The US Department of the Army Crime Laboratory recently issued new guidelines firmly rejecting the use of absolute claims of identification. They no longer use the term "identification," but have instead switched to the use of "association." The term "association" though has not reached all areas and participants in the realm of fingerprints and is currently not a term that the IAI has taken an official stance on.

The IAI has struggled to keep up with the rapidly evolving practice of latent print examinations in the shift from "absolute certainty with zero error rate" to a more scientific understanding of uncertainty, probability, and likelihood statements in the rendering of conclusions. Currently, the official position of the IAI is that examiners should avoid making any statements of "absolute certainty" or "zero error rate."

It is important to define what is meant by the term "error rate," and there is often-times confusion as to its meaning. Is it referring to the "error rate" of the science of fingerprints, or is it referring to the individual examiner and asking if they personally have made errors in the process of comparing prints? There are a number of different "errors" or mistakes in judgment that can enter into the decision-making process of latent print examination. It could mean an "erroneous identification" (the print was said to be made by an incorrect source as in the Canen case), an "erroneous exclusion" (a print was said to not belong to a particular source when in fact it does), an erroneous decision of value/no value (when a print is said to be of no value when, it fact, it is identifiable or able to be used for exclusionary purposes), or a combination of all three or even more types of error or misjudgment. Generally, by "error rate," most people mean the rate of erroneous identifications with respect to incorrectly identifying a print to the wrong source.

There have been some early studies presenting "error rates" that referred to errone-ous identifications, separate from other types of error or mistake. The first of those was the statement frequently made and testified to by Stephen Meagher, then the Section Chief of Latent Prints for the FBI crime lab. Mr. Meagher frequently referred to a study done in the FBI that showed 1 "erroneous identification" for every 11 million correct identifications.[27] On the opposite end of the spectrum, a published study in the peer-reviewed Journal of Forensic Identification by Glenn Langenburg, Kasey Wertheim, and Andre Moenssen presented an "erroneous identification" rate of 1 for every 3500 correct identifications in a classroom situation in which students were comparing only "difficult" prints.[28] While those represent two extremes, the actual error rate (i.e., erroneous identifications versus correct identifications) probably lies somewhere in between. Two major factors need to be considered though in assessing the appropriate-ness of considering "error rate" when evaluating the report or testimony of an examiner is a specific case. First, the "error rate" for prints with low distortion and a high number of features (an extremely clear print) would probably be much lower than the "error rate" for prints with high distortion and fewer features (a more difficult, distorted print). Second, the "error rate" for latent print examiners probably varies greatly depending on the training, experience, visual acuity, and other factors, such as conservativeness in announcing conclusions. Therefore, it hardly seems appropriate to consider a general "error rate" calculated on the averages for a large number of examiners over a broad spectrum of distortion and apply that "error rate" to determine the reliability of a spe-cific association by one examiner and a verifier. While error rate may be applicable for other realms of science, it is one not easily able to be determined in the realm of fingerprints due to the amount of different factors involved.

THE ONE UNEXPLAINABLE DISSIMILARITY RULE

The term "dissimilarity" or "discrepancy" is another term that comes up sometimes when comparing a latent print and an inked print. The "one unexplainable dissimilarity rule" states basically that if there is a single "unexplainable" discrepancy between two images of prints of friction ridge skin, then the number of corresponding features is irrelevant and the two images must necessarily represent different areas of friction ridge skin. This "rule" was coined in context of the theory of biological uniqueness and the idea that all friction ridge skin is permanent and unique and will never be duplicated in nature. If those hypoth-eses were true, then even a single discrepancy between two representations of friction skin would imply that the two representations could not have come from the same source area of friction skin. Think of two envelopes with return addresses stamped by means of a rub-ber stamp. If you believed that no two rubber stamps had ever been made identical, and if you observed reproductions of the return address that were exact in all visible respects, you might conclude that both envelopes were stamped by the same rubber stamp. But if you

---

[27] U.S. v. Baines, 2007.
[28] Wertheim, K., Langenburg, G., Moenssens, A., January/February 2006. Report of latent print exam-iner accuracy during comparison training exercises. Journal of Forensic Identification 56.

observed even a single letter or number that was different between the two return addresses, you could conclude that they were made by different stamps, even though all the other letters and numbers match. Likewise, with fingerprints, if you observe correspondence between two images and the amount of detail is sufficient to conclude no discrepancies exist in the source area of skin producing the images, then you can conclude that both images represent the same area of friction skin. However, if you observe detail in one image that is NOT present in the other image and yet believe the same anatomical source area is represented, then, according to the "one unexplainable discrepancy rule," it would not matter if all the other detail did match. The two images could NOT represent the same source.

However, the keyword here is "unexplainable." There are at least two major considerations that enter into the examination of prints from friction ridge skin. One is distortion. Frequently, examiners are faced with two fragmentary, smeared images. It is possible then to observe dissimilar aspects of the images that, at first glance, might negate an identification. However, if the dissimilar feature is an artifact caused by distortion alone, then it does not automatically rule out an identification. The term "dissimilarity" would be used to discuss such an appearance, and it would be able to be understood and explained by a qualified, experienced examiner. Only if the examiner determined the "dissimilarity" resulted from a difference in the friction skin itself would it be determined to be an "unexplainable," having not been caused by distortion.

But a second factor comes into play, and that is the fact that scarring or damage to the skin can occur that might yield two prints from different deposition times that exhibit apparent discrepancies. Thus, the examiner must also analyze dissimilarities to determine if a difference of appearance could result from scarring or damage to the skin. Even then, cases of prints from the same area of friction skin across time have been documented with apparent unexplainable dissimilarities, but which are clearly documented as having come from the same source area of skin. In summary, then, a dissimilarity may represent a discrepancy that negates an identification, or it may not. It is an abundance of other matching detail and the skill and ability of the examiner doing the comparison, based on training and experience, which determine whether a conclusion of identification or exclusion may be reached. In the case of the erroneous identification of Canen, there was an abundance of unexplainable dissimilarities because they were, in fact, from two different sources.

AUTOMATED FINGERPRINT IDENTIFICATION SYSTEM MATCHES

In more recent times, a new realm of fingerprint comparison has come to the forefront, that of the AFIS. In both the US and abroad, there has been placed a heavier reliance on AFIS systems to find likely candidates in its matching to a fingerprint or palm print. While AFIS is a tool of excellent significance, there are those who rely on it to the point of not following the ACE-V methodology when checking the candidates proffered by the system. Some agencies and individuals have become overly dependent and confident on the AFIS results. The main difference in the comparison process between an AFIS case and one in which a named individual's known prints are provided by the requesting customer is found primarily in the evaluation phase of ACE-V. More caution is indicated in evaluating the relative similarity or dissimilarity of features in an AFIS search because of the greater likelihood of finding similarity between a very large number of candidates as opposed to a single candidate. The ACE-V methodology is the same, but the threshold for reaching a conclusion may be higher in an AFIS case than with a named person.

A number of articles and reports have alluded to the greater potential for erroneous identifications in AFIS cases versus cases involving a comparison with a limited number of known persons. The most widely read such case study is the "Stacey Report" on the erroneous identification of Brandon Mayfield in the Madrid Bombing case in 2004.[29] As a result of that case and of the Stacey Report, a greater number of latent print examiners around the US began to recognize that more caution is indicated in AFIS cases because the likelihood of an apparent correspondence of features in distorted prints is greater when a very large number of inked prints is compared to the unknown latent print. It has been proposed that a higher "threshold" for identification is indicated in AFIS cases than in cases involving a limited number of known individuals because of the increased risk of error. With the advent of AFIS, there is an increased need for fingerprint examiners to review all of the computer-generated candidate lists in both inked and latent print searches.

The following images are an actual latent that was searched through the FBI database, an extremely large database which gets larger daily. The latent impression searched is on the left, and the number 1 candidate that returned in the search is the inked print shown on the right. These prints were shown to a number of AFIS/ten-print (inked fingerprints showing all 10 fingers) examiners and asked if it was a match or not. Many stated it was a match. These same prints were also shown to a number of experienced and trained latent print examiners. Their response was significant: "Scary close, but NOT a match."

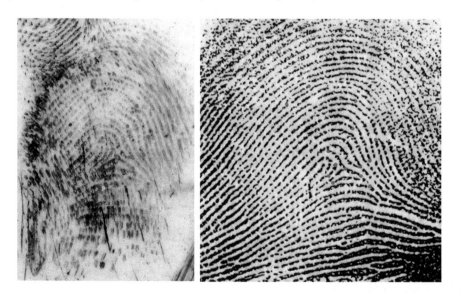

---

[29] Stacey, R.B., 2004. A report on the erroneous fingerprint individualization in the Madrid train bombing case. Journal Forensic Identification 54, 706.

In actuality, this is one of the closest nonmatches I have ever personally encountered. I can find 14 "points" (marked in the above images) that appear to correspond if I only look for similarities and ignore dissimilarities, and if I do not follow the ACE-V methodology fully.

The next images following, showing the same latent and inked print, show the tracings of the ridges of those same images shown above. I have marked the delta with a dot. The ridges marked in green are consistent with each other, but the ridges marked in red show "unexplainable" dissimilarities, not because of distortion, but because they are not from the same source. These are NOT made from the same source.

There are no shortcuts in doing print comparisons. Regardless of comparing ink prints to ink prints or latent prints to ink prints, the proper methodology of Analysis, Comparison, Evaluation, followed by Verification must be utilized. But as shown in these images, there can be images that can appear to be extremely close, and an erroneous identification can be made if shortcuts are taken, if ACE-V is not followed to its fullest, and if examiners are not attentive to the process.

Following the Stacey Report, a much broader examination of all forensic sciences was conducted by the National Academy of Sciences (NAS) in an effort to ensure valid scientific principles and practices were being applied in all crime laboratories, police departments, and the courts. The final report of this work, "Strengthening Forensic Science in the United States: A Path Forward," was published in 2009 and is referred to in forensic circles simply as the NAS Report.[30] Regarding the practice of fingerprint comparisons and identifications, the NAS Report did not explicitly state or even imply that fingerprint conclusions are unreliable. But the NAS Report was critical of the practice of fingerprint identification as rendering conclusions outside the bounds of science (i.e., "absolute"

---

[30] https://www.google.com/webhp?gws_rd=ssl#q=NAS+Report.

conclusions with a "zero error rate") and for lacking the kind of scientific validation studies that underpins the practice of DNA analysis and other sciences. As
a result of the NAS Report and the criticism of prominent academic scientists
and legal scholars, more money for research has gradually been made available
to conduct the types of studies recommended in the report. The field of friction
ridge skin impression comparisons has gradually been evolving according to the
recommendations of the NAS Report.

TRAINING TRENDS

Some police agencies recognize the necessity of extensive experience with fingerprints prior to turning a new examiner loose. In a few US police agencies, as in most
other western countries, a 5-year training program is used. More often in the US,
police agencies will balk at the expense of 5 years of training without any real pro-
ductivity. Two to three years is a more common training period. Some agencies now
give as few as 6 months of formal training. Unfortunately, in some local agencies
where an investigator does a few fingerprint comparisons on the side, attendance at
a 1- or 2-week class is deemed all that is necessary to become a fingerprint examiner
and to testify in court as an expert. New latent print examiners are now often being
trained directly into AFIS and latent print units without any lengthy foundation in
fingerprints that the old hard copy fingerprint cards had provided in the past and
where only the most skilled personnel from the fingerprint units were promoted to
the latent print identification unit, and then only after having examined and classified
many thousands of sets of fingerprints.

At the same time that AFIS computers were replacing the old fingerprint card files
and creating a need for more latent print examiners, a movement began among US
police departments to civilianize positions for which arrest powers were not essential. Budgets were tightening and local governments were paying closer attention
to the number of sworn, certified police officers per population of 1000. One strategy for police administrators to avoid excessive cuts in personnel was to civilianize as many positions as possible in the police department, keeping sworn positions
used to calculate personnel needs for only those who required arrest powers. Jailers,
dispatchers, and fingerprint officers were among the positions most affected by the
change from sworn status to civilian.

When civilianizing positions, a tact taken by many police agencies was to lower
the pay for the newly created civilian positions in a move to save money. As it affected
identification officers, a few departments saw an opportunity to hire and retain more
professional career employees. Unintended consequences in the low-pay positions
included less qualified applicants, high turnover, poorer training, lower expertise,
and personnel held in contempt by better paid sworn police officers. Departments
where the fingerprint officers were better paid attracted better educated applicants
and gave them more specialized training. There tended to be less turnover, a higher
level of expertise, and the respect of the sworn officers.

OUR PAST AND POSSIBLE FUTURE

In the view of some, there are three stages over the past century in the development of fingerprint identification as "science." These phases are not necessarily separate and distinct, but have a broad overlap in time and application: first, point standards; second, holistic; third, probabilistic.

POINT STANDARDS

The first crude model for identification was published in 1892 by Sir Francis Galton, who first derived the "12 Point Standard" for identification on the supposition that beyond that, the odds of a match were greater than the human population of planet earth. By 1914, Edmund Locard had proposed that if sufficient finer detail such as sweat pores were visible and matched along with the points, a positive identification could be made on as few as eight points. Locard also proposed that even with fewer than eight points, a probability could still be presented proportional to the number of points and amount of finer detail visible. However, that "probabilistic" part of Locard's theory was disregarded for the next century.

The idea of a "point standard" was not universally accepted in the US for most of the 20th century. Some police agencies had a strict standard, and some individuals adhered to a minimum number of points before they would claim an identification. For the most part, however, whether a latent print matched an inked print boiled down to the expert's opinion based on training, experience, skills, and abilities. The number of "points of identification" was less important in the profession than the expert's opinion.

By the 1970s, the profession as a whole subscribed to the prevailing belief that there was no valid number of points that could be used as a preset minimum. Some clusters of points were so unusual and contained so much matching detail at the microscopic level that identifications were often made on seven or fewer points.

HOLISTIC ANALYSIS

By the early 1990s, a "holistic" philosophy had been articulated under the heading "Ridgeology." This philosophy emphasized all identifications relied on a combination of "quality and quantity" of features (not only "points") to make an identification. "Sufficiency" was determined in the mind of the expert conducting the examination, and differing opinions were acceptable so long as one was "yes" and the other was "I can't tell." Still, under no circumstances was it acceptable for one expert to say "yes" and another conclude "definitely not."

PROBABILISTIC ANALYSIS

By the dawn of the 21st century, articles were beginning to appear in professional, peer-reviewed journals urging acceptance of a probabilistic approach to fingerprint identification. The early articles were written by academicians and theoretical scientists who, while not entirely unfamiliar with fingerprint comparison, were not themselves practicing examiners. While the early articles drew scorn from the practicing community of fingerprint experts, as newly graduated university trained scientists began to enter the field, the concept of probabilistic identifications began to gain momentum.

The IAI and the National Institute of Justice sponsored the Organization of Scientific Area Committees; both now support discontinuation of reporting and testifying to absolute identification to the exclusion of all other persons.

Thomas Kuhn, a historian of science, described "normal science" as a group of practitioners applying consensus dogma to solve small problems. He described a "paradigm shift" as a transition that occurred over time, beginning when new practitioners enter the group and have different ideas that are initially rejected by consensus. These new practitioners eventually overwhelm and dominate the practice as more enter the field who accept the new ideas, and the old practitioners retire. Eventually, a new "dogma" redefines the way that problems are solved. A brief review of several of the forensic sciences (i.e., arson, shaken baby syndrome, bloodstain pattern analysis, bitemark evidence) illustrate the struggle of the old guard to hold onto old dogma and the inevitable paradigm shift that occurs when the newer, recently educated practitioners begin to take over.

In the latter third of the 20th century, the condition of "falsifiability" as proposed by Karl Popper was the criteria used to define fingerprint identification as "science." If an identification was wrong, other experts would, or at least could, pronounce it wrong. A more accurate model of the practice might have been the model of science proposed by Carl Hempel. Hempel proposed that science is the application of a law of nature to provide explanations and make predictions. It was said by some that the natural law of biological uniqueness allowed the fingerprint examiner to explain why certain features were observed in an unknown print and to predict that all future prints from the same finger would produce the same features. Whether applying the philosophies of Kuhn, Popper, or Hempel, fingerprint identification as practiced during the 20th century fit the definition of science prevailing at the time.

In the 21st century, the more accepted philosophy of science in forensics is the approach of Sir Thomas Bayes formulated in Bayes' Theorem. That theorem allows for calculation of a probability or likelihood ratio based on prior probabilities, new information, and posterior probabilities. Bayes' Theorem is not universally accepted as good science because it makes calculations based frequently on subjective assessments of prior probability. But many of today's scientists do subscribe to the philosophy that nothing can be science unless it involves measurement, calculation of uncertainty, and articulation of "error rate." Without numbers expressing probability or likelihood ratios, nothing can be true "science" in the belief of many modern practitioners of forensic science.

One blogger has predicted that in the future, no formal experience looking at fingerprints will be necessary to become a fingerprint expert. A scientist with a degree in statistics will launch an unknown fingerprint into a computer program to determine "value," then search a database of known fingerprints, and finally calculate likelihood ratios for "association" and "exclusion" that can be expressed in numbers. We are not there yet, but that may be the direction in which fingerprint "identification" is heading. While the transition from "Cops in Lab Coats" to modern, professional forensic scientists independent of law enforcement is not yet complete in all agencies in the US, we have come a long way and are moving steadily forward.

REFERENCE

The most current general publication on fingerprint identification is the Fingerprint Sourcebook published in 2012 by the National Criminal Justice Reference Service. It is available free online at https://www.ncjrs.gov/pdffiles1/nij/225320.pdf. Chapters in the Sourcebook cover all areas of significance in today's practice of fingerprint examination, including history, biology, development techniques, AFIS fingerprint computers, identification philosophy, legal issues, ongoing research, vulnerabilities, and more. Although progress has been made in some areas discussed in the Sourcebook rendering a few parts outdated, it is still the best available fingerprint reference available at the time of this writing.

Index

Note: 'Page numbers followed by "f" indicate figures, "t" indicate tables and "b" indicate boxes.'